Learning C# by Programming Games

Arjan Egges · Jeroen D. Fokker ·
Mark H. Overmars

Learning C#
by Programming Games

 Springer

Arjan Egges
Dept. of Information and Computing
  Sciences
Utrecht University
Utrecht, The Netherlands

Mark H. Overmars
Dept. of Information and Computing
  Sciences
Utrecht University
Utrecht, The Netherlands

Jeroen D. Fokker
Dept. of Information and Computing
  Sciences
Utrecht University
Utrecht, The Netherlands

ISBN 978-3-642-36579-9   ISBN 978-3-642-36580-5 (eBook)
DOI 10.1007/978-3-642-36580-5
Springer Heidelberg New York Dordrecht London

Library of Congress Control Number: 2013935694

ACM Computing Classification (1998): D.1, D.3, K.8, H.5

Cover design: Cover design based on a game sprite designed by Heiny Reimes. Reused by permission.

Printed on acid-free paper

Springer is part of Springer Science+Business Media (www.springer.com)

Preface

Introduction

If you are reading this, then we assume that you are interested in learning how to develop your own computer games. If you do not yet know how to program, don't worry! Developing computer games is actually a perfect way to learn how to program in modern programming languages. This book will teach you how to program in C# without requiring any previous programming experience. It does so through the creation of computer games.

In our opinion, C# is the language of choice to learn how to program. The language is very well structured and avoids some of the problems of Java. It is also a more modern language. Moving from C# to C++, which is still the most important programming language in the game industry, is relatively easy. Also, for C# there is an excellent free programming environment available, Visual Studio C# Express Edition, which is used in this book.

Contrary to most programming books, we do not organize the book according to programming language paradigms, but instead we use the structure and elements of computer games as a framework. For instance, there are chapters on dealing with player input, game objects, game worlds, game states, levels, animation, physics, and intelligence.

While reading this book, you will create four games. We have chosen different types of games to show the various aspects of game development. We start with a simple shooting game, we move on to puzzle games consisting of multiple levels, and we conclude the book by developing a full-fledged platform game with animation, game physics, and intelligent enemies.

This book is not a cookbook. The book provides a thorough introduction to C# and object-oriented programming, organized by the structure of games. We introduce important aspects of programming in general, such as an overview of different programming paradigms, syntax diagrams, collections, exception handling, and more. We will also discuss various aspects of software architecture within a context of game development. By doing that, we propose a framework for managing levels, game states, as well as a hierarchy of self-sufficient game objects that together form an interactive game world. Furthermore, we will show a number of commonly used techniques in games, such as drawing layers of sprites, rotating, scaling and animating sprites, showing a heads-up display (HUD), dealing with physics, handling interaction between game objects, and creating nice visual effects such as snow or glitters.

Throughout the book, you will find text in gray boxes. These boxes contain tips and tricks for designing parts of your game, such as adding tutorial levels, but sometimes they also discuss a particular programming issue, such as dealing with static variables or designing game engine code.

Required Materials and Tools

Along with this book, we supply various materials. All the example programs used in this book are available as Visual Studio projects, which you can open, edit, compile, and run yourself. Furthermore, we supply a set of game assets (sprites and sounds), which are used by all the examples. Next to the example programs, we also provide detailed instruction on how to download and install the necessary tools. We have created a website where you can download all the materials. The URL of this website is http://www.csharpprogramminggames.com.

In order to develop computer games, a few tools need to be installed on your computer. The main tool that you are going to need is the XNA Game Studio software, in combination with a development environment called *Visual Studio Express 2010*, created by Microsoft. On the accompanying website, you can find detailed instructions on how to obtain and install these tools. The Visual Studio Express 2010 environment is freely available and compatible with the latest XNA Game Studio version (4.0 when this book was printed).

Using this Book as a Basis for a Programming Course

This book is geared toward being used as a basis for a game-oriented programming course. Each part in this book is concluded by exercises and challenges. Solutions to the exercises are available through the accompanying website. The challenges are generally more complex programming exercises. These challenges can serve as practical assignments for students following the programming course. On the accompanying website, a number of additional challenges are available that can be used as a basis for practical assignments as well.

By following the structure of the book throughout the course, the students will be introduced to all the main aspects of programming in an object-oriented language. Supplementary materials for organizing such a course are available on the accompanying website. A sample schedule of a course consisting of 15 sessions with three practical assignments is given as follows:

	Topic	Chapters	Exercises, deadlines
1	Introduction	1, 2	Exercises part I
2	Game loop, types, variables	3, 4	Exercises part I
3	Player input, **if**, booleans	5, 6	Exercises part I
4	Classes, methods, objects	7, 8	Exercises part II
5	**for**, **while**, randomness	8, 9	Hand in practical assignment I
6	Inheritance	10, 11	Exercises part II
7	Collections, arrays, interfaces	12	Exercises part III
8	Grids, game worlds	13, 14, 15	Exercises part III
9	Time in games, recursion	16, 17, 18	Exercises part III
10	Sprite sheets, game states	19, 20, 21	Hand in practical assignment II
11	Abstract classes, **switch**, file I/O	21, 22	Exercises part IV
12	Libraries, game structure	23, 24, 25	Exercises part IV
13	Animation, game physics	26, 27	Exercises part V
14	Enemies, exceptions	28, 29, 30	Exercises part V
15	General questions	all	Hand in practical assignment III

Utrecht, The Netherlands

Arjan Egges
Jeroen D. Fokker
Mark H. Overmars

Acknowledgements

Just as games are generally not developed by a single person but by a team, this book was a team effort as well. First of all, I would like to thank my co-authors Jeroen and Mark for their inspiring ideas and the interesting discussions we've had while writing this book.

This book is based on reading material that was handed out to the (many) students of the game programming course at Utrecht University. Their feedback and critical analysis of the material has been of great help, as well as their motivation to work with the example games. I officially apologize for any frustration that occurred due to a few ridiculously difficult levels of the Tick Tick game!

I would like to thank my colleagues for their ideas and their interest in this work. In particular, I would like to thank Cathy Ennis and Sybren Stüvel for providing corrections and for reading the text in detail. Their feedback has resulted in many improvements of the text and the sample programs.

The sprites for all the example games in this book were designed by Heiny Reimes. It was a pleasure working with him on designing the example games and improving them.

I would also like to thank Ralf Gerstner from Springer for taking the time to read the manuscript and helping to make this book a reality.

Finally, I would like to thank my wife, Sterre, for her continuing support. I dedicate this work to her.

January 2013   Arjan Egges

Contents

Part I
Getting Started

Chapter 1
Building Your First Game Application

Welcome to 'Learning C# by Programming Games'! In this book, you're going to learn how to make your own games. At the same time, you will learn the basics of one of the most popular programming paradigms ever: object-oriented programming. After you have finished reading this book, you will be able to make games for different platforms that are ready to be exploited commercially. The skills you will have acquired will help you create professional-looking games, but they will also help you build other kinds of applications. As you will see, building games can be as much (or even more!) fun than playing them. However, before you start making your own games, we need to make sure that you have all the tools available in order to get started. The main tool set that we're going to use is the XNA Game Studio by Microsoft. In this chapter, we're going to walk step-by-step through the process of transforming your computer into a game development machine.

> **Website**—Along with this book, we have created a website where you can download all the example programs used in this book, the accompanying game assets (sprites and sounds), as well as other extras. The URL of this website is http://www.csharpprogramminggames.com. Go there and follow the instructions to get the extra materials.

1.1 Structure of This Book

Each chapter in this book has its own collection of example programs. You can find all the examples on the website belonging to this book. We will explain all of the programming concepts according to these examples. The book is globally divided into five parts. The first part serves as an introduction to programming in general, and it shows how games are generally developed. We will introduce basic programming concepts such as variables, methods, and parameters. We'll also introduce the game loop and how to deal with game assets such as sprites and sounds.

A. Egges et al., *Learning C# by Programming Games*,
DOI 10.1007/978-3-642-36580-5_1, © Springer-Verlag Berlin Heidelberg 2013

In the second part of the book we will develop our first game called Painter. We will introduce the **if**-instruction, as well as loops using **for** or **while**. Furthermore we'll present the basics of object-oriented programming using the Painter game as an example. We'll also show how game objects are generally designed as a part of software, and how to create a game world consisting of interacting game objects.

In part three we will continue setting up this structure of communicating game objects by introducing arrays and collections. These programming concepts are very important for the second game, Jewel Jam, which is a pattern recognition game. We will also show how to create games that run in full screen and how to maintain and display a score.

Part four introduces the puzzle game Penguin Pairs. Here, we will show how to deal with different game states such as menus or level selection screens. We'll also discuss how to read levels from files and how to store the player's progress in a file. We will show how to deal with strips or sheets of sprites effectively. Finally we will look at organizing classes into different libraries that can be used across different game projects.

The final part revolves around the platform game Tick Tick. In this part we will deal with loading and playing animations, and we will add basic physics to the game world, such as the possibility to jump or fall, or collide with other game objects. We'll also show how to deal with exceptions.

For each part, we provide a number of programming exercises to help you get more familiar with the concepts introduced in that part. We will also give you a number of challenges. Challenges are more complicated programming exercises, and they will generally be extensions of the games we develop in this book, or sometimes even completely new games! All exercises and challenges can be found in Appendix A.

1.2 Getting and Installing the Tools

In order to develop computer games, a few tools need to be installed on your computer. The main tool that you're going to need is the XNA Game Studio software, in combination with a development environment called *Visual Studio Express 2010*, created by Microsoft. On the accompanying website, you can find detailed instructions on how to obtain and install these tools. The Visual Studio Express 2010 environment is freely available and compatible with the latest XNA Game Studio version (4.0 when this book was printed). Once you have installed the development environment, try to run it. When it has launched, you will see a screen similar to Fig. 1.1.

1.3 Creating Your First Game Application

Now that all the tools are installed, let's try and see if everything works the way it should. In order to test this, we are going to create a *project*. A project is the

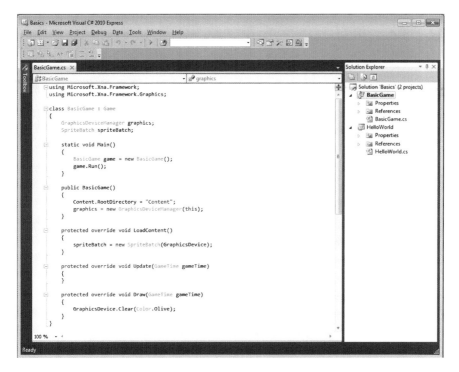

Fig. 1.1   A screenshot of the Visual Studio Express 2010 development environment

basic working environment for creating a game. We'll deal with projects in more detail later on. First, start up the Visual Studio development environment. We are now inside the development environment that we're going to use to make our own games. Now choose File → New → Project in the main menu. On the left side of the screen that pops up, choose the template folder 'XNA Game Studio 4.0'. Your pop up screen should then look something like Fig. 1.2. Now select the Windows Game 4.0 template. At the bottom of the screen, you can enter a name and a location for your project. We're not yet concerned with the other available options. After you've chosen a name and a location, click on the OK button. A new project will now be created for you.

1.4   Running the Newly Created Project

Now that we have created the project, we can run it by clicking on the green play arrow located below the main menu (see Fig. 1.3). If you click on the arrow, you should see the window shown in Fig. 1.4. This window shows the game that you've just made. Obviously, this is not really a 'game', since you cannot really do anything except look at the nice background color. So close this window, and let's look at the files in the game project we just created. On the right side of the Visual Studio editor

Fig. 1.2 Creating a new project

Fig. 1.3 The main menu of Visual Studio Express 2010

Fig. 1.4 Running the game project

Fig. 1.5   An overview of the files in the basic windows game project

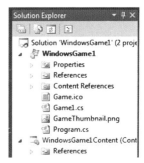

Fig. 1.6   Changing the background color of the main game window

window, you'll see a panel called 'Solution Explorer', that contains a tree structure of files (see Fig. 1.5). The project you created is written in boldface and you can see a number of files below it. Double-click on the file Game1.cs. You'll see that the file is a text file, and that we can now edit it. This file contains all the code to run the simple program that we've just executed. Try and modify this code a little bit. For example, you see the following line of code almost at the bottom of the program:

```
GraphicsDevice.Clear(Color.CornflowerBlue);
```

Now, change this line into the following line:

```
GraphicsDevice.Clear(Color.Chocolate);
```

Run the program again by pressing the green play button. The color in the window has now changed! Instead of Chocolate you can write a lot of different colors, such as AntiqueWhite, Olive, Black, and much more. Remove the .Chocolate from the line and enter a dot after the word Color, but before the closing parenthesis. You now see that the editor shows a list of all possible colors (see also Fig. 1.6). This is a very nice feature of the editor that works not only for colors, but for a lot of other aspects of creating programs.

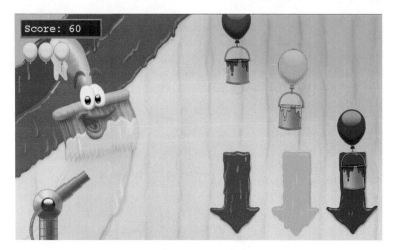

Fig. 1.7 A screenshot of the first game we're going to create

1.5 Projects and Solutions

Visual Studio organizes all the games or other programs you develop into *projects* and *solutions*. Each game or application you develop is called a *project*. Projects, in turn, are organized in *solutions*. So, one solution may contain several projects, where each project represents a game or a program that you're working on. When you create a new project, you have the possibility to indicate whether you want to create a new solution as well, or whether you want to add the new project to the current solution. Having multiple projects in one solution can be very helpful because it is easier to work on different projects at the same time, and some projects can share assets such as images and sounds. In the *solution explorer*, you can see all the projects that are currently in the solution (see Fig. 1.5).

1.6 Running the Examples in This Book

From the website, you can download all of the examples belonging to this book in a single zipped file. Once you've downloaded this file, unpack it in a folder. Because we use a lot of different examples and programs in this book, we have created a separate solution for each chapter. For example, to browse through all the samples related to Chap. 5, go to the folder 05_ReadingPlayer and double-click on the file ReadingPlayer.sln. When you look at the solution explorer, you'll see that this solution contains three different projects. The project name that is currently in boldface is the project that will be executed when you press the green play button. This project is called the *startup project*. You can select another startup project by right clicking the project name in the solution explorer and selecting 'Set as StartUp Project'. You can then press the green play button to execute that project. As a convenient shortcut, a project can also be executed by pressing F5. For example, right-click on the Balloon2 project and set it as the startup project, then press F5. You should see a window in which the mouse pointer has a balloon attached to it.

In that same solution, you can also find the Painter1 program, which is the first version of a game that we will develop in this book as an example: the Painter game. If you open the solution belonging to Chap. 11, you can see that it contains the project Painter10, which is the final version of that game. If you press F5, you can play the game. The goal of the Painter game is to make sure that the paint cans falling down from the top of the screen are in the right color (red, green, or blue) before they fall through the bottom of the screen. You can shoot at the paint cans using the paint cannon in the lower left corner of the screen, and the color to shoot with changes by pressing the R (= red), G (= green) or B (= blue) keys. Aiming and shooting is done by moving the mouse and pressing the left mouse button. Figure 1.7 shows a screenshot of this game.

1.7 What You Have Learned

In this chapter, you have learned:

- how to install the Visual Studio development environment;
- how to create a new game project, and how to compile and run it.

Chapter 2
Programming

2.1 Introduction

Generally speaking, a computer is quite stupid. It can only do exactly what you tell it to do. The only reason that modern computers and game consoles can do what they do, is that programmers have provided an extremely long list of very precise instructions that describe each task the computer should perform in detail. So, if you want to make your own game, there is no way around it: you are going to have to provide a long list of specific instructions that explains exactly what your game should do. Furthermore, the computer is even stricter than your teachers at school: one grammatical error and the game will not work. To make it even worse, you cannot even use your native language to provide these instructions! Obviously it would be nice if we could write down the following text, and the computer would simply run a game that does exactly what is written down:

Draw a castle on a screen.
Put a monster in the castle.
As soon as the player walks into the castle, the monster attacks.

Unfortunately, the computer does not understand this. The English language (or any natural language for that matter) is not very suitable to tell the computer what should be done, because natural languages often lack precision. To illustrate this, have a look again at the text we have just written. We first tell the computer to draw a castle on the screen. Where should this castle be drawn? Does it have towers, or flags, or both? Is it made of stone or some other material? Where is the entrance? The same goes for the other two lines of text. Where in the castle should we put the monster? How many heads does the monster have? How does the monster attack the player? It is clear that we need to be *very precise* when making our game, otherwise the result might not be what we expect.

But do not be discouraged! Once you have learned to deal with these issues, programming games can be even more fun than playing them. But before we get started with that, let us first have a look at how a computer or a game console works.

A. Egges et al., *Learning C# by Programming Games*,
DOI 10.1007/978-3-642-36580-5_2, © Springer-Verlag Berlin Heidelberg 2013

2.2 Computers and Programs

2.2.1 Processor and Memory

Computers consist of many different components, and discussing what each of these components does and how the components interact could fill up this entire book. Generally speaking one could say that a computer consists of a *processor* and *memory*. This is true for all modern computers, including game consoles and mobile devices. Memory comes in different varieties, mainly differing in the speed of data transfer and data access. Some memory can be read and written as many times as you want, some memory can only be read, other memory can only be written to. The main processor in the computer is called the CPU (central processing unit), but many computers and consoles have more than one processor. The most common other processor you find on a computer is a GPU (graphics processing unit). Even the CPU itself nowadays is no longer a single processor, but often consists of a number of cores.

Programs in real life—A 'program' is not something that is only written to be executed by a computer. In daily life, many programs are written and executed, if you are willing to broaden your definition of 'memory' and 'processor'. A nice example of a program is a recipe for making an apple pie. The values in the 'memory' in this case are the apples, flour, butter, cinnamon, and all the other ingredients. The cook (or: the 'processor') then executes all the instructions in the recipe which changes the values in the 'memory'. After that, we have another type of 'processor': the person who eats the pie and digests it. Other examples of daily life programs are directions for getting to a place, logistics strategies for supplying supermarkets, administrative procedures, and so on. All these things are long sequences of instructions that—when executed—have a certain effect.

Input and output equipment, such as a mouse, gamepad, keyboard, monitor, printer, and so on, seems to fall outside of the 'processor' and 'memory' categories at first glance. However, abstractly speaking, they are actually memory. A gamepad is 'read-only' memory and a printer is 'write-only' memory.

The *processor* on the other hand, is a very different beast. The main task of the processor is to execute *instructions*. The effect of executing these instructions is that the memory is changed. Especially with our very broad definition of 'memory', every instruction a processor executes changes the memory in some way. Normally, we do not want the computer to execute only one instruction. Generally, we have a very long list of instructions to be executed. "Move this part of the memory over there, clear this part of the memory, draw this sprite on the screen, check if the player is pressing a key on the gamepad, and make some coffee while you're at it." We call such a long list of instructions that is executed by the computer a *program*.

2.2.2 Programs

In summary, a *program* is a long list of instructions to change the memory. However, the program itself is also stored in memory. Before the instructions in the program are executed, they are stored on a hard disk or a DVD, or a network drive, or a USB flash disk, or any other storage medium. When they need to be executed, the program is moved to the internal memory of the machine. In principle, it is possible that a program contains instructions that change another part of the program, since the program is also stored in memory. Although this approach was in fashion for a while—mostly as a failed attempt to write artificially intelligent programs—programs like this proved to be extremely difficult to write.

For now, let us assume that a program resides in a part of the memory that is isolated from the memory that is used/changed by the program. Before the program is executed, it is placed in the memory by another specialized program, such as an *operating system.*

Programming is the activity of writing programs. Programming certainly is not an easy task, and you need a good sense of logical deduction since you need to be constantly aware of what your program will do with the memory later on, when it is executed.

2.3 Programming Languages

The instructions that, combined together, form the program need to be expressed in some way. We could try to do that with hand gestures, or by making strange sounds, however this is very hard for a computer to understand. Even typing these instructions in plain English is not something that the computer can grasp, as we have seen in the introduction. In practice, the instructions are coded as text, but we need to follow a very strict way of writing them down. There are many different ways of doing that, and each way is defined by a set of rules that determines how we should write down the instructions. We call such a set of rules a *programming language*. Many programming languages exist, because every time somebody thinks of a slightly better way of expressing a certain type of instruction, this soon becomes a new programming language. It is difficult to say how many programming languages exist, because that also depends on whether you count all the versions and dialects of a language, but suffice to say that there are thousands of them.

Fortunately, it is not necessary to learn all these different languages, because there are many similarities between them. However, in the last sixty years, a lot has happened. In the early days, the main goal of programming languages was to use the new possibilities of computers. However, more recent languages focus on bringing some order in the chaos that writing programs can cause. Programming languages that share similar properties are said to belong to the same *programming paradigm*. A paradigm refers to a set of practices that is commonly used.

2.3.1 The Early Days: Imperative Programming

A large group of programming languages belongs to the *imperative paradigm*. Therefore we call these languages *imperative languages*. Imperative languages are based on instructions to change the memory. As such, these languages are very well suited to the processor-memory model we described in the previous section.

In the early days, computers were programmed by writing the instructions directly as numbers in memory, where each number corresponded to a certain type of instruction. People soon realized that it was more convenient to use abbreviations for these instructions, instead of numbers, since these are a lot easier to remember. So, around 1950 the first (imperative) programming language was created. This language was called *Assembler*, because it could be used to 'assemble' programs easily. However, because every processor had different kinds of instructions, each of these processors had their own version of the Assembler language. This was not very practical, because every time a new processor came around, all the existing programs had to be completely rewritten for that processor. Therefore, in 1955 the language *Fortran* (an abbreviation of 'formula translator') was created. The nice thing about this language was that the instructions in the language were not made specifically for a certain processor, but they could be translated to different processors by another program.

> **Declarative programming**—The fact that we took the effort to identify the paradigm of imperative programming languages implies that there are other programming paradigms which are not based on instructions. Is this possible? What does the processor do if it does not execute instructions? Well, the processor always executes instructions, but that does not mean that the programming language contains them. For example, suppose that you build a very complicated spreadsheet with many links between different cells in the sheet. You could call this activity 'programming', and the empty spreadsheet is the 'program', ready to process actual data. In this case, the 'program' is not based on instructions, but on functional links between the cells. Next to these *functional programming languages* there are languages based on propositional logic—the *logical programming languages*—such as Prolog. These two types of programming languages together form the *declarative paradigm*.

Fortran was not an easy language to learn. Initially, this was not really a problem because computers at that time were operated only by specially trained personnel. However, as time progressed, a need started to emerge for a language that was easier to use. So, around 1965, a new language was created called *Basic* ('Beginners' All-purpose Symbolic Instruction Code'). This language became very popular in the 1970s, because it came with the early personal computers such as the Apple II in 1978 or the IBM-PC in 1979 and their descendants. Unfortunately this language was not standardized, so every computer brand used its own dialect of Basic.

2.3.2 Procedural Programming: Imperative + Procedures

As programs were getting more complex, it became clear that a better way of organizing all of these instructions was necessary. In the *procedural programming
paradigm*, related Instructions were grouped together in *procedures* (or *methods*,
which is the more common modern name). Since a procedural programming language still contains instructions, all procedural languages are also imperative.

The first real procedural language was *Algol* (a slightly strange abbreviation of
'Algorithmic Language'). This language was launched in 1960, together with an
official definition of the language, which was crucial for exchanging programs. Also
a special notation (the Backus Normal Form, or: BNF) was created that was used to
describe the structure of programs and which is still in use today. Near the end of
the 1960s, a new version of Algol came out, called Algol68 (guess in which year).
Algol68 contained a lot of new features, as opposed to the original Algol language.
In fact, it contained so many new things that it was very complicated to build good
translators for Algol68 programs. As a result, only a few of these translator programs
were built and it was game over for Algol68.

Clearly, simple programming languages were the way to go. The first simple, but
procedural language was conceived in 1971: Pascal (not an abbreviation this time,
but a reference to the French mathematician Blaise Pascal). Pascal was created by
Niklaus Wirth, a professor at the university of Zürich, with a main goal to provide
the students with an easy-to-learn programming language. Soon, this language was
also used for more serious applications.

For really big projects, Pascal was not very suitable though. An example of such a
big project was the development of the *Unix* operating system at the end of the 1970s
at Bell Labs. In any case, it was new to try to write an operating system in a procedural language, since this originally always was done in an Assembler language.
For developing Unix, a new language called *C* was defined (not an abbreviation either, but the successor of earlier prototypes called A and B). The philosophy of Unix
was that everybody could write their own extensions to the operating system, and it
made sense to write these extensions in C as well. So, C became the most important
procedural language of the 1980s, also outside the Unix world.

C is still used quite a lot, although it is slowly making way for more modern
languages, especially in the game industry. Procedural programming languages in
general are still very popular. For example, many web applications use some kind of
procedural script language such as PHP, Ruby or Python. And a lot of games have
a scripting interface for loading levels, handling events that occur in the game, and
so on.

2.3.3 Object-Oriented Programming: Procedural + Objects

Procedural languages like C allow us to group instructions in procedures (also called
methods). This already made writing programs a lot easier. However, just like the re-
alization that instructions belonged together in groups, programmers saw that some

methods belonged together as well. The *object-oriented paradigm* allows to group methods into something called a *class*. The memory that these groups of methods could change is called an *object*. The first object-oriented language ever conceived was *Simula*. It was created in 1967 by the Norwegian researchers Ole-Johan Dahl and Kristen Nygaard. They developed their own programming language Simula as an extension of Algol, because they were interested in doing simulations to analyze traffic flux or the behavior of queues of people in the post office. One of the new things in Simula was that it identified a group of variables in the memory as an *object*. This was very useful, because it allowed to describe a person in the post office or a car as an object.

Simula itself was not a very popular language, but the idea to describe a program in terms of objects and classes was picked up by researchers at Xerox in Palo Alto, who—even before Apple and Microsoft—were experimenting with windows-based systems and an actual mouse. Their language called *Smalltalk* used objects to model windows, buttons, scrollbars, and so on: all more or less independent objects. But Smalltalk was carrying things to extremes: absolutely everything was supposed to be an object, and as a result the language was not very easy to use. However, it was clear that objects were useful, and that there should be a C-like language that allowed for using objects. That language became C++, where the two plus signs indicated that it was a successor of C. The first version of C++ dates from 1978 and the official standard appeared in 1981. The C++ language was very useful for writing windows-based programs, which was becoming more and more popular in the 1980s. But the success of C++ is also due to the fact that it is a true extension of C: the old C programs still worked in C++.

Although the language C++ is standard, C++ did not contain a standard way to write windows-based programs on different types of operating systems. Writing such a program on an Apple-computer, a Windows-computer, or a Unix-computer is a completely different task, which makes running C++ programs on different operating systems a complicated issue. Initially, this was not really considered a problem, but when the Internet became more popular, the ability to run the same program on different operating systems would be very convenient.

2.3.4 Java

The time was ripe for a new programming language: one that would be standardized for usage on different operating systems. The language should be similar to C++, but it would also be a nice opportunity to remove some of that old C stuff from the language to simplify things. The language *Java* fulfilled this role (no abbreviation or mathematician this time, simply the name of the favorite coffee brand of the designers). Java was launched in 1995 by the hardware manufacturer Sun that used a revolutionary business model for that time: the software was free, and they planned to make money on the support. Also not unimportant for Sun was to compete with the growing popularity of Microsoft software, which did not run on the Unix computers produced by Sun.

One of the novelties of Java was that the language was designed so that programs could not accidentally interfere with other programs running on the same computer. In C++ this was becoming a very big problem: if such an error occurred it could crash the entire computer, or worse: evil programmers could use this to introduce viruses and spyware. With the growing popularity of the Internet, this became even a bigger problem: suddenly computers were accessible from other computers. Therefore, Java works in a fundamentally different way than C++. Instead of executing instructions directly on the processor, there is another program called a *virtual machine* that controls the instructions and that checks that memory is used only as it is indicated in the program.

2.3.5 C#

In the mean time, Microsoft was also working on their own object-oriented language, called C#, which was launched in the year 2000. C# is also an object-oriented language and it uses a virtual machine (which Microsoft calls *managed code*). The name of the language already indicates that it continues in the tradition of C and C++. Typographically, the hash sign even resembles four plus signs. In musical notation, the hash sign symbolizes a sharp note, and the language is therefore pronounced as 'C-Sharp'. A nice detail is that 'sharp' also means 'smart'. So: C# is a smarter version of C.

Both Java and C# have been under constant development. Every few years, a new version of the languages appeared with new features, sometimes inspired by the new features in the previous version of its competitor. The more recent versions of C# have even introduced features from other non-imperative programming paradigms. It is not clear where these two languages are headed. Java and C# have both been very popular the last decade and a clear 'winner' cannot really be identified. Also C++ is still being used a lot in the industry, but for how long? And what about all the script languages that are now very popular? Will these languages take over the market of the traditional compiled object-oriented languages?

In any case, C# is much easier to learn than C++, the latter being rather complicated due to its compatibility with C. Furthermore, in C# it is a bit easier to write interactive programs than in Java. C# is also an excellent language to use for developing games. This is because Microsoft has developed the XNA library, which contains all the basic tools that are needed for developing games, such as loading and displaying sprites, or playing back sound effects. Additionally, while learning C#, you are also learning the basic object-oriented programming concepts, which is a very useful skill to have. And if you ever need to write a program in C++ or Java, then you can reuse your knowledge of C# because of the many similarities between the languages.

Game programming languages—In the early days programming computer games was a very difficult task that required great skill. A game console like the very popular Atari VCS has only 128 bytes of RAM and could use cartridges with at most 4096 bytes of ROM that had to contain both the program and the game data. This limited the possibilities considerably. For example, most games had a symmetric level design because that halved the memory requirements. Also the machines were extremely slow.

Programming such games was done in an Assembler language. That was the only way in which a somewhat sophisticated game could be cramped into such a small amount of memory. Programmers were experts in squeezing out the last bits of memory and in performing extremely clever hacks to increase efficiency. The final programs, though, were unreadable and could not be understood by anyone but the programmer himself. Fortunately, that was not a problem because back then, games where typically developed by a single person.

For a long time, this focus on programming in Assembler languages continued to exist in the game community. Being an excellent Assembler language programmer was a key requirement to work in the business. But with the rapid increase in memory and processing power and the improvement of compilers this became less and less important. Elements that required top speed were still programmed in Assembler but most of the code was written in high-level languages. In particular C++ became the standard for quite a while. This was also caused by the fact that games became much larger and were created by teams rather than individuals. It became important that the game code was readable, reusable, and could more easily be debugged. Also from a financial perspective, reducing the time programmers had to work on a game became more important than the efficiency of the code. This led to the use of higher-level languages such as C#.

2.4 Translating a Program

A computer program is translated by another special program to be used on a certain computer and processor. Depending on the circumstances, this translating program is called either an assembler, a compiler or an interpreter. We will discuss the differences between these in this section.

2.4.1 Assembler

An assembler is used to translate Assembler programs to direct instructions for the processor (also called *machine code*). Because an Assembler program is different

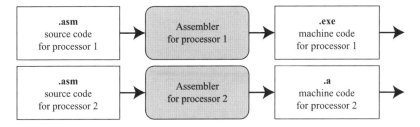

Fig. 2.1 Translating a program using an assembler

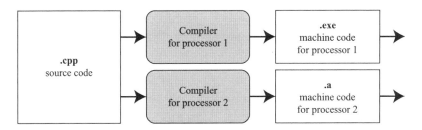

Fig. 2.2 Translating a program using a compiler

for each processor, you need different programs for different computers, each of them being translated by the corresponding assembler (see Fig. 2.1).

2.4.2 Compiler

The advantage of the majority of programming languages (except Assembler languages) is that, in principle, they can be written independently of the computer that the program will be used on. So, only one program needs to be written, one that can then be used on a variety of machines, by the use of an automatic translation program. Such a program is called a *compiler*. So, the difference between an assembler and a compiler is that whereas the assembler is specifically made to translate a processor-dependent program to machine code, a compiler can translate a program written in a processor-*independent* language to machine code. The compiler itself is machine-specific, because it targets the machine code of the computer that the program has to run on. The program written by the programmer (also called the *source code*) is machine-independent. Many procedural languages, such as C and C++, use a compiler to translate the program into machine code. Figure 2.2 shows what the translation process looks like when using a compiler.

Fig. 2.3 Translating a
program using an interpreter

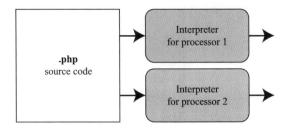

2.4.3 Interpreter

A more direct way to translate programs is to use an *interpreter*. This is a program that reads the source code and immediately executes the instructions contained
within it, without translating it to machine code first. The interpreter is specific for
a machine, but the source code is machine-independent, just like the compiler. In
a sense, the interpreter program does exactly the same as a human interpreter (or
translator). You could say that a compiler is doing something similar to translating
a written text into another written text, while an interpreter translates and speaks at
the same time.

The advantage of an interpreter over a compiler is that a translation into machine
code no longer is required. The disadvantage is that the execution of the program
is slower, because translating a program also takes time. Furthermore, any errors in
the program cannot be detected beforehand, whereas the compiler can detect such
errors. Translating using an interpreter is quite common for simpler languages, such
as script languages (see Fig. 2.3).

2.4.4 Compiler + Interpreter

The Java language chose a mixed approach. The goal of Java programs is to distribute them over the Internet. Spreading around already compiled programs is not a
very good idea: recall that compiled programs are machine-dependent, so you would
need to distribute separate versions for every possible computer. On the other hand,
spreading the source code is also not always a suitable option. The complete text
of the program is then available for everyone to modify, copy and use in their own
programs, which makes it difficult to earn money writing software. In many cases,
users are allowed to use a program, but they may not read it or modify it. Machine
code is very useful for that goal.

The approach that Java uses is a compiler that translates the source code; not into
machine code, but into another machine-independent intermediate language, called
the *bytecode* (see Fig. 2.4). The bytecode can be spread on the Internet and it is
executed on the user machine by an interpreter. The bytecode uses a very simple
language that is easy to translate into machine code, which makes it easier to incorporate it in Internet browsers. Because the main translation is already done by a

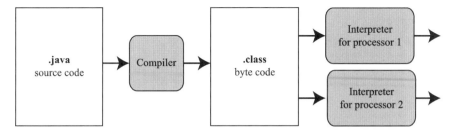

Fig. 2.4 Translating using a compiler and an interpreter

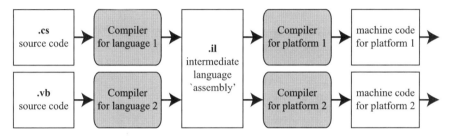

Fig. 2.5 Translating using a compiler and a compiler

compiler, interpreting the bytecode is relatively fast, although a program compiled directly to 'real' machine code will always run faster.

2.4.5 Compiler + Compiler

The C# language uses yet another variation, which relies on an *intermediate language* similar to the bytecode used in Java. What is special about this intermediate language is that it can be generated from different programming languages. This means that bigger projects can integrate programs written in different programming languages. The intermediate language is not interpreted like with Java, but it is translated again into machine code for a specific platform by another compiler. Figure 2.5 shows what this looks like. An example of such a platform is the PC, but it can also be a game console or a mobile device.

Sometimes the compilation into machine code happens at a very late stage, when the program is already running and it needs a part that is not yet compiled. In this approach, the difference between a compiler and an interpreter is not so clear anymore. Because the compiler compiles parts of the program just before the code is needed, this special type of compiler is also called a *just-in-time compiler* (or 'jitter').

> **Assembly**—Confusingly enough, the file containing the intermediate code is called an *assembly*. However, this has nothing to do with the Assembler languages we have discussed earlier in this chapter.

2.5 Programming Games

We have discussed many different programming languages in this chapter, and games can be programmed in almost any programming language. However, some languages are better suited for programming games than others. In this section, we are going to have a look what makes games so special and—very generally speaking—how we go about programming games.

2.5.1 Games Are Special Programs

Games are quite complicated programs to write. They deal with a lot of different input and output devices and the imaginary worlds that games create can be extremely complex. One of the main challenges when developing games is making sure that the game works with all the different graphics cards, sound cards, joysticks, game pads, motion trackers, network connections, and so on.

Up until the beginning of the 1990s, games were developed for specific platforms. For example, a game written for a particular console could not be used on any other console without major efforts from the programmers to adapt the game program to the differing hardware. For PC games, this effect was even worse. Nowadays, operating systems provide a *hardware abstraction layer* so that programs do not have to deal with all the different types of hardware that can be inside a computer. But at that time, each game needed to provide their own drivers for each graphics card and sound card. So when you went into the shop to buy a game, you were never sure that the game would actually run on your computer. As a result, not a lot of code written for a particular game could be reused for another game. In the 1980s, arcade games were very popular, but most of the code written for these games could never be reused because of the constant changes and improvements in computer hardware.

2.5.2 Game Engines

As games were getting more and more complex, it made sense for the game companies to start reusing code from earlier games. Why write an entirely new rendering program or collision checking program for each game? The term *game engine* was coined in the 1990s, when first-person shooters such as Doom and Quake became a very popular genre. These games were so popular that the manufacturer—iD Software—decided to license a part of the game code to other game companies as a separate piece of software. Reselling the core game code as a game engine was a very lucrative endeavor, because other companies were willing to pay a lot of money for a license to use the engine for their own games. These companies no longer needed to write their own game code from scratch anymore, but they could reuse the programs contained in the game engine and focus more on graphical models, characters, levels, and so on.

Nowadays, a lot of different game engines are available. Some game engines are built specifically for a platform such as a game console or an operating system. Other game engines can be used on different platforms without having to change the programs that use the game engine code. This is especially useful for game companies who want to publish their games on different platforms. Modern game engines provide a lot of functionality to game developers, such as a 2D and 3D rendering engine, special effects such as particles and lighting, sound, animation, artificial intelligence, scripting, and much more. Game engines are used a lot, because developing all these different tools is a lot of work and game companies prefer to put that time and effort into creating beautiful environments and challenging levels.

> **Game middleware**—Sometimes, a game engine is also called *game middleware*, because it forms a layer between the basic programming language and the actual game code.

Because of this strict separation between the core game functionalities and the game itself (levels, characters, and so on), many game companies nowadays hire more artists than programmers. However, programmers are still necessary for improving the game engine code, as well as for writing programs that deal with things that are not included in the game engine or that are specific to the game. Furthermore, game companies often develop software to support the development of games, such as level editing programs, extensions of 3D modeling software to export models and animations in the right format, prototyping tools, and so on.

2.5.3 The XNA Game Engine

This book uses the XNA game engine. XNA is developed by Microsoft and it is used together with the programming language C#. With XNA it is possible to develop games for different platforms, such as the PC, the XBox, or the Windows Phone. Although we focus on developing 2D games in this book, it is also possible to develop 3D games in XNA. XNA provides a number of tools for things like loading and displaying sprites, playing sounds, checking for collisions, and much more. In this book, we will introduce a number of these tools and we will build upon them to create our own games.

2.6 Developing Games

2.6.1 Small Scale: Edit–Compile–Run

When we want to build a game, we need to write a program that contains many lines of instructions. With Visual Studio, we can edit the source files in a project and type instructions in them. Once we are done writing down these instructions, the file containing the source code is inspected by the compiler. When all is well, the compiler will create the intermediate code, and then an *executable file*, which is our program in machine code.

However, most of the time, things will not be that easy. For one, the source code that we give to the compiler should contain valid C# code, because we cannot expect the compiler to create an executable file from random blabbering. The compiler checks whether the source code adheres to the language specifications of the C# language. If not, it will produce an error and no code is generated. Of course, programmers will make an effort to compile a real C# program, but it is easy to make a typo, and the rules for writing correct programs are very strict. So, you will most certainly encounter these errors during the compilation phase.

After a few iterations of resolving these minor errors, the compiler will have generated the intermediate code and the executable file. This means that it is time for the next phase: *executing* (also called *running*) the program. In many cases, you will then discover that the program does not exactly do what you want it to do. Of course, you made an effort to correctly express what you wanted the program to do, but conceptual mistakes are easily made.

So you go back to the editor, and you change the program. Then, you compile it (and hope you did not make new typing mistakes) and you run the program again to see if the problem is solved, only to realize that the program is indeed doing something different, but still not exactly what you want. And it is back to the editor again ... Welcome to your life as a programmer!

2.6.2 Large Scale: Design–Specify–Implement

As soon as your game starts becoming more complicated, it is not such a good idea anymore to just start typing away until you are done. Before you start *implementing* (writing and testing the game), there are two other phases.

First, you will have to *design* the game. What type of game are you building? Who is the intended audience of your game? Is it a 2D game or a 3D game? What kind of gameplay would you like to model? What kinds of character are in the game, and what are their capabilities? Especially when you are developing a game together with other people, you are going to have to write some kind of design document that contains all this information, so that everybody agrees on what game they are actually developing! Even when you are developing a game on your own, it is a good idea to write down the design of the game. The *design* phase is actually one of the most difficult tasks of game development.

Once it is clear what the game should do, the next step is to provide a global structure of the program. This is called the *specification* phase. Do you remember that the object-oriented programming paradigm organizes instructions in methods, and methods in classes? In the specification phase, an overview is made of the classes that are needed for the game, and the methods that are in these classes. At this stage, you only need to describe what a method will do, and not yet how that is done. However, keep in mind that you do not expect impossible things from the methods: they have to be implemented later on.

Once the specification of the game is finished, you can start the implementation phase, which means that you will probably go through the edit-compile-run cycle a couple of times. Once all that is finished, you can let other people play your game. In many cases you will realize that some ideas in the game design do not really work out that well. So, you start again with changing the design, followed by changing the specification and finally a new implementation. You let other people play your game again, and then ... well, you get the idea. The edit–compile–run cycle is contained in a larger scale cycle: the design–specify–implement cycle.

2.7 What You Have Learned

In this chapter, you have learned:

- how computers work, and that they consist of processors to compute things, and memory to store things;
- how programming languages have evolved, from Assembler languages to modern programming languages such as Java and C#;
- how a computer translates a program written in a programming language into a language that the computer understands, using a compiler or an interpreter.

Chapter 3
Game Programming Basics

3.1 Introduction

In this chapter, we are going to cover the basic elements of programming games. This chapter provides a starting point for the chapters that follow it. First, we are going to talk about the basic skeleton of any game, consisting of a *game world* and a *game loop*. We will also show you what the basic structure of a game application in C# looks like, and how to create a simple application that changes the background color to illustrate how to use this structure. Finally, we will talk about clarifying your code by using comments, layout, and whitespace in the right places.

3.2 Building Blocks of a Game

3.2.1 The Game World

What makes games such a nice form of entertainment is that we can explore an imaginary world and do things there that we would perhaps never do in real life. We can ride on the back of a dragon, destroy entire solar systems, or create a complex civilization of characters that speak in an imaginary language. This imaginary world in which we play the game is called the *game world*. Game worlds can range from very simple worlds such as the Tetris world to complicated virtual worlds in games such as Assassin's Creed or World of Warcraft.

When a game is running on a computer or a console, the machine maintains an internal representation of the game world. This representation does not look anything like what you see on the screen when you play the game. It consists mostly of numbers describing the location of objects, how many hit points an enemy can take from the player, how many items the players has in his inventory, and so on. Fortunately, the machine also knows how to create a visually pleasing representation of this world that it displays on the screen. Otherwise, playing computer games would probably be incredibly boring, where the players have to sift through pages of

A. Egges et al., *Learning C# by Programming Games*,
DOI 10.1007/978-3-642-36580-5_3, © Springer-Verlag Berlin Heidelberg 2013

numbers to find out whether they saved the princess or died a horrible death. Players never see the internal representation of the game world, but the game developers do. When we want to develop a game, we also need to design how we will represent our game world internally. And part of the fun of programming your own games is that you have complete control over this.

Another important thing to realize is that just like the real world, the game world is changing all the time. Monsters move to different locations, the weather is changing, a car runs out of gas, enemies get killed, and so on. Furthermore, the player actually influences how the game world is changing! So simply storing a representation of the game world in the memory of a computer is not enough. A game also needs to register all the time what the player is doing and as a result *update* this representation. Finally, the game actually needs to *show* the game world to the player, either by displaying it on the monitor of a computer, on the TV, or on the screen of the smart phone. The process that deals with all this is called the *game loop*.

3.2.2 The Game Loop: Updating and Drawing

The game loop deals with all the dynamic aspects of a game. And lots of things happen while a game is running. The players press buttons on the gamepad, or they touch the screen of their device, there is a constantly changing game world, consisting of levels, monsters, and other characters, that needs to be kept up to date. There are also special effects such as explosions, sounds, and much more. All of these different tasks that need to be handled by the game loop can be organized in two different categories:

1. tasks related to updating and maintaining the game world, and
2. tasks related to visualizing the game world to the player.

The game loop continuously performs these tasks, one after the other. As an example, let us look at how we could handle user navigation in a simple game like Pacman. The game world mainly consists of a labyrinth with a couple of nasty ghosts moving around. Pacman is located somewhere in this labyrinth and is moving in a certain direction. In the first task (updating and maintaining the game world), we check whether the player is pressing an arrow key. If so, we need to update the position of pacman according to the direction that the player wants pacman to go in. Also, because of that move, pacman may have eaten a white dot, which increases the score. We also need to check whether it is the last dot in the level, because this means that the player has finished the level. Finally, if it is a larger white dot, the ghosts will need to be rendered inactive. Then, we need to update the rest of the game world. The position of the ghosts needs to be updated, we have to decide if fruit should be displayed somewhere for bonus points, and so on. We also need to check if pacman collides with one of the ghosts (if the ghost is not inactive), and so on. So you see that even in a simple game like Pacman, a lot of work needs to be done in this first task. From now on, we will call this collection of different tasks related to updating and maintaining the game world the Update method.

The second collection of tasks is related to visualizing the game world to the player. In the case of the Pacman game, this means drawing the labyrinth, the ghosts, pacman, but also information about the game that is important for the player to know, such as how many points he has scored, how many lives he has left, and so on. This information can be displayed in different areas of the game screen, such as the top or the bottom. This part of the display is also called the heads-up display (HUD). Modern 3D games have a much more complicated set of drawing tasks. These games need to deal with lighting and shadows, reflections, culling, visual effects like explosions, and much more. We will call the part of the game loop that deals with all the tasks related to visualizing the game world to the player the Draw method.

3.2.3 The Game Loop in XNA

In the first chapter of this book, we have already seen how we can create a simple game application by using the template provided on the website. The program that is supplied with this template is given in Listing 3.1. By looking at this program, you can already see that there is a part of the code called Update (lines 26–28) and a part called Draw (lines 30–33). These two parts correspond to the two main tasks of the game loop: updating the game world and drawing the game world. Every game that you are going to make in this book follows the same basic structure. When you run this program, the Update and Draw methods are continuously executed: update, draw, update, draw, update, draw, update, draw, update, draw, and so on. Furthermore, this happens at a very high speed. In the standard configuration of the game engine, it tries to do exactly sixty runs through the loop in one second. We also call this kind of loop a *fixed timestep* loop. It is possible to change this configuration so that, for example, the game engine tries to execute the loop as many times as possible instead of exactly sixty times per second.

Next to Update and Draw, game engines generally incorporate a few other useful methods. The most important method is LoadContent. This method is executed once, before the update-draw sequence of the game loop starts. The main thing that we do in this method is loading any game assets that are needed, such as sprites, sounds, or other files that the game needs. If we wanted to, we could also load the sprites and the sounds in the Update or Draw method. However, this would significantly affect the performance of our game, since we would load the files sixty times per second. Game assets are better loaded only once into the internal memory. After that, the Update and Draw methods read the information from the internal memory and update it, or draw it on the screen. The LoadContent method also has a counterpart UnloadContent that is called after the game loop ends (which happens when the player quits the game). In this method, you can clean up any memory that was allocated for game assets. Finally, there is another (similar) pair of methods, Initialize and Finalize. In Initialize you can perform initialization tasks needed for the game, such as setting up an input device or opening a network connection. The Finalize method can be

```
1    using Microsoft.Xna.Framework;
2    using Microsoft.Xna.Framework.Graphics;
3
4    class BasicGame : Game
5    {
6        GraphicsDeviceManager graphics;
7        SpriteBatch spriteBatch;
8
9        static void Main()
10       {
11           BasicGame game = new BasicGame();
12           game.Run();
13       }
14
15       public BasicGame()
16       {
17           Content.RootDirectory = "Content";
18           graphics = new GraphicsDeviceManager(this);
19       }
20
21       protected override void LoadContent()
22       {
23           spriteBatch = new SpriteBatch(GraphicsDevice);
24       }
25
26       protected override void Update(GameTime gameTime)
27       {
28       }
29
30       protected override void Draw(GameTime gameTime)
31       {
32           GraphicsDevice.Clear(Color.Olive);
33       }
34   }
```

Listing 3.1 A very basic game application

used for doing the things that are needed before the game application ends, such as storing the updated high-score list, or closing the network connection. This means that the basic set of methods to be supplied in an XNA game is (see also Fig. 3.1):

1. Initialize: here we can perform initialization tasks such as opening a network connection or setting up an input device;
2. LoadContent: here we can load all the game assets, such as sprites, sounds, or other assets needed for the game;

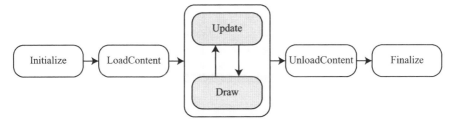

Fig. 3.1 The game loop and its associated methods in the XNA game engine

3. Update: here we update the game world according to the time passed or according to what the player is doing;
4. Draw: here we draw the game world onto the screen;
5. UnloadContent: here we can unload game assets if necessary;
6. Finalize: here we can perform any cleanup tasks needed, such as closing the network connection or storing the highscore list.

Not all of these methods are required in a game. For example in BasicGame, only LoadContent, Update, and Draw are used. In addition, you will see two other methods in the BasicGame program. One called BasicGame (lines 15–19) and one called Main (lines 9–13). We are going to look into these parts of the program later on in this chapter. For now, you can assume that the BasicGame part is also a kind of initialization, similar to the Initialize method, that every class has. The Main part tells the compiler which instructions to execute when the program starts, as we will see later on.

In this book, we are going to show you a lot of different ways of filling up all these different methods with the tasks that you need to perform in your game. During this process, we will also introduce a lot of programming techniques that are useful for games (and, indeed, for a lot of other applications). In the following section, we are going to look into the basic game application in more detail. Then, we are going to fill this basic skeleton of a game with some additional instructions.

3.3 The Structure of a Program

3.3.1 The Basic Game Application in More Detail

In the early days, many computer programs only wrote text to the screen and did not use any graphics at all. Such a text-based application is called a *console* application. In addition to printing text to the screen, these applications could also read text that a user entered on the keyboard. So, any communication with the user was done in the form of question/answer sequences ('Do you want to format the hard drive (Y/N?)'—'Are you sure (Y/N)?'—and so on). Before Windows-based OSes became popular, this text-based interface was very common for text editing programs, spreadsheets, math applications, and even games. These games were called text-based adventures and they described the game world in text form. The player could then enter commands to interact with the game world such as 'go west', 'pick up matches', or 'Xyzzy'. Examples of such early games are Zork and Adventure. Although they might seem dated now, these games are still a lot of fun to play!

It is still possible to write console applications in a modern language like C#: you can find an example of such an application (called HelloWorld) in the samples provided with this chapter. Although it is interesting to see how to write such applications, we prefer to focus on programming more modern games with graphics.

3.3.2 Other Types of Applications

The console application is only one example of a type of application that exists. Another very common type is the *Windows* application. This application shows a screen containing windows, buttons, and other parts of a *graphical user interface* (GUI). This type of application is often *event-driven*: it reacts to events such as clicking a button or selecting a menu item.

Another type of application is the *web application*, or *applet*. In this case, the program is stored on a server and the user runs the program in a web browser. There are many examples of such applications, think of web-based email programs or social network sites.

Yet another type is the *app*. This kind of application is run on a mobile phone or a tablet PC. Screen space is generally limited in these type of applications, but new interaction possibilities are available such as GPS to find out the location of the device, sensors that detect the orientation of the device, and a touch screen.

Finally, we have the *Game* application. A game is a graphical application, but with fast-moving images, and can be run on specialized hardware such as a game console or a mobile device (then it becomes a game app). Games often use a controller made specifically for the hardware, or the touch screen in the case of game apps. For a console application the keyboard is the most important interaction device, for games it generally plays a limited role (if it is used at all).

3.3.3 A Method: A Group of Instructions with a Name

Remember that in an imperative program the *instructions* are doing the actual job of the program: they are executed one after the other. This changes the memory and/or the screen, so that the user notices that the program is doing something. In the BasicGame program, not all lines in the program are actually instructions. One example of an instruction is the line GraphicsDevice.Clear(Color.Olive); which instructs the graphics device to clear the background and give it a color.

Because C# is a procedural language, the instructions are grouped in *methods*. Even though there are only a few instructions in our BasicGame program, we are obliged to group them in methods. *Every instruction in a program belongs to a method.* Grouping instructions is done with braces ({ and }). Such a block of instructions grouped together is called the *body* of a method. Above the body, we write the *header* of the method. An example of a method header is:

static void Main()

The header contains, among other things, the *name* of the method (in this case Main). As a programmer, you may choose any name for a method. However, every program *must* have exactly one method named Main. The Main method tells the compiler which instructions should be executed when the program starts. We have seen that the game loop consists of two parts: Update and Draw. In programming terms, these parts are modeled as *methods*, as you can see in the example program. Inside these methods, we then place the instructions that we want to execute in order to update or draw the game world.

3.3.4 A Class: A Group of Methods with a Name

Because C# is also an object-oriented language, methods, in turn, are grouped in *classes*. If you look more carefully at the BasicGame program, you see that there are five methods grouped in the class called BasicGame. Just like instructions, methods cannot be arbitrarily placed in a program. Instructions need to be part of the body of a method, and methods *must* be part of a class. Grouping methods is also done by using braces. This means that around our methods we place braces (this is called the *body* of the class) and above it we see the *header* of the class:

class BasicGame : Game

The class header consists of the word **class** and after that, the name of the class. As a programmer, you are allowed to choose any name for your class, which in this case is BasicGame. Sometimes, a class is a specialized version of another class. This is the case with our BasicGame class: we indicate behind the class name that we are building a *game*, and not a console application or a web application. We do this by using a colon and the name of another class (Game). We will come back to this later on.

3.3.5 Syntax Diagrams

Programming in a language such as C# can be quite difficult if you do not know the rules of the language. In this book, we will use so-called *syntax diagrams* to explain how the language is structured. The *syntax* of a programming language refers to the formal rules that define what is a valid program (in other words: a program that a compiler or interpreter can read). By contrast, the *semantics* of a program refers to the actual *meaning* of it. To illustrate the difference between syntax and semantic, take a look at the phrase "all your base are belong to us". Syntactically, this phrase is not valid (a compiler for the English language would definitely complain about it). However, the *meaning* of this phrase is quite clear: we apparently lost all of our bases to an alien race speaking bad English.

A compiler can check the syntax of a program: any program that violates the rules is rejected. Unfortunately, a compiler cannot check whether the semantics of the program correspond to what the programmer had in mind. So if a program is syntactically correct, this is no guarantee that it is semantically correct. But if it is not even syntactically correct, it cannot run at all. Syntax diagrams help us to visualize what the rules of a programming language such as C# are. To give an example of a syntax diagram, here is a simplified diagram that shows how to define a class in C#:

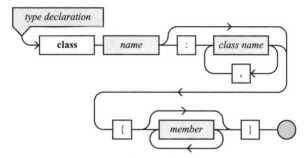

You can use syntax diagrams to construct C# code by starting in the top left of the diagram, in this case at the word 'top declaration', and following the arrows. When you reach the gray dot, your piece of code is complete. Here, you can clearly see that a class definition starts with the **class** keyword, and then we write the name of the class. After that, we then optionally write a colon with a number of different types separated by a comma. Then, we write a number of members (although we do not know yet what a member is . . .), all between braces. After that, we are done because we have reached the gray dot. Throughout this book, we will use these syntax diagrams to show how to structure your code according to the syntactical rules of the C# language.

3.3.6 Namespaces

Classes can be a part of a *namespace*. Namespaces are a way to group related classes together (just like methods are a way to group instructions together). We can use a syntax diagram to represent a *top level declaration* that consist of a namespace containing zero or more top level declarations. In other words, namespaces may contain other namespaces:

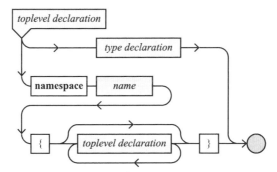

If there is no name space, the top level declaration consists of a *type declaration*. A type declaration can take a lot of forms, one example being a class definition (using the syntax diagram shown in the previous section). Name spaces are useful to group classes together that are related to each other without explicitly qualifying the library that they come from. For example, you could imagine that we create a namespace Graphics that contains all classes that have something to do with displaying things on the screen.

3.3.7 A Compilation Unit: A Group of Classes in a Text File

C# programs are stored in a text file, and we can put multiple classes in a text file if we want to. The class headers and the braces denote what methods belong to what class. A text file is compiled as a whole by the compiler, this is it is known as a *compilation unit*. In the BasicGame example, the compilation unit contains only one class. It is possible to spread the classes of a program over multiple compilation units, but because this example is quite basic, we do not yet need to do that.

3.3.8 Relying on Other Classes

The first lines of our compilation unit are not part of the class:

using Microsoft.Xna.Framework;
using Microsoft.Xna.Framework.Graphics;

With these lines, we indicate that the program may use other classes or methods which are available in other *libraries*. For example, we are using a class called GraphicsDevice which is in the library Microsoft.Xna.Framework.Graphics. The concept of libraries is very useful, because it allows us to *reuse* methods and classes written by other people. This way, we do not have to reinvent the wheel all the time. In our case, we use the Clear method to clear the window and give it a color. This method is not written by us, but we can still use it because we have indicated in the beginning of our program that we need things from the library Microsoft.Xna.Framework.Graphics.

So, a compilation unit consists of a number of **using** instructions followed by a number of top level declarations. We can again use a syntax diagram to describe this:

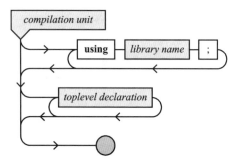

3.3.9 Subclasses: A Special Version of Another Class

Let us look at the class header again:

class BasicGame : Game

Game is in fact also a class, and it comes from the library Microsoft.Xna.Framework, hence the need for the **using** statement in the first line of the program. So why is it placed after the BasicGame class name? Although for now it is not yet so important to know what it means exactly, you can read this as: 'BasicGame is a special version of Game'. Game is a class, so it contains a group of methods as well. BasicGame is a *special version* of the Game class, so it *inherits* all of the methods that were in the Game class. We can then add our own methods to this class, or rewrite some of the methods that were in the original Game class, such as the Update method or the Draw method. If this seems a lot to take in, do not worry about it, we will discuss this in much more detail later on.

3.3.10 Calling a Method

When the instruction GraphicsDevice.Clear(Color.Olive); is executed, we can also say that we *call* the Clear method. In other words: we want the program to execute the instructions grouped in the method Clear. This group of instructions does exactly what we need for this example, namely clearing the screen and setting a background color. However, we need to give some extra information to this method, because it needs to know *which* color to set the background to. This extra information is also called a *parameter* of the method. A method can have more than one parameter, as we will see later on. The parameters are written between parentheses. When a method is called, we always write parentheses behind it, and within the parentheses are the parameters (if required).

> **Using methods**—Do we need to know which instructions are grouped together in the Clear method in order to use it? No, we do not! This is one of the nice things of grouping instructions together in methods. You (or other programmers) can use the method without knowing how it works. By smartly grouping instructions in methods, and methods in classes, it is possible to write reusable pieces of program that can be used in many different contexts. The Clear method is a good example of this. It can be used for a lot of different applications and you do not need to know how the method works in order to use it. The only thing you need to know is that it takes a Color as a parameter.

3.3.11 Update and Draw

Because the BasicGame class is a special version of the Game class, our application should have an Update method and a Draw method. Because a method is basically a group of instructions, every time the Update method is called, the instructions inside that method are executed. And the same goes for Draw.

As an example, imagine that we want a simple game where a balloon is drawn at the position of the mouse pointer. By moving the mouse around, the balloon moves along with the mouse. In terms of the Update and Draw methods, we could do this as follows. In the Update method we need to execute an instruction that retrieves the current position of the mouse pointer and that stores it in the memory. In the Draw method, we need to execute an instruction that displays a balloon image at the stored position. Of course, we do not yet know if these instructions exist (spoiler: they do!) and we do not yet know what these instructions look like. Also, you might wonder why this would work. We are not moving around the balloon, we are simply drawing it at a position that was stored in the Update method. Recall that in an XNA game, the Update and Draw methods are executed at a very high rate (sixty times per second). Because of this very high rate, drawing the balloon at different positions makes it look like the balloon moves (but it actually does not). This is how all game worlds are drawn and how the player is lured into thinking that there is movement in the world. In reality, we are just drawing the images very fast at different positions. Stay tuned, we are going to return to this example and actually make it work later on!

3.3.12 Different Kinds of Methods

We also see in the headers of both the Update and the Draw methods that there is a difference with respect to the Main method. Look at the Draw method for example:

protected override void Draw(GameTime gameTime)

There are some words: **protected**, **override** and **void**, then the name of the method (Draw) and then some stuff between parentheses. Not all of this is relevant for now, but the three words before the name of the method give some information about what kind of method it is and how it can be used. In particular, the **override** word means that this method is a *replacement* for a method, namely the method Draw in the Game class. Recall that BasicGame was a special version of the Game class? The Game class already has a method called Draw. But since we want to do something different in this method (such as setting a different background color), we want to make our *own version of this method*. The word **override** tells the compiler that we are replacing the original method in the Game class by a method of our own, like replacing an ingredient in a recipe to make it taste differently. Later on in this book, we will see many other examples of overriding methods and why this is useful. Let us leave those two other words (**protected** and **void**) a mystery for the moment. We will come back to it later.

Behind the name of the Draw method, we see parentheses with two words between them: GameTime and gameTime (note the case difference of the first character). These two words together define a *parameter* of a certain *type*. The type in this case is GameTime and in order to use this parameter inside the method, we have to give it a name, gameTime. The type is telling the compiler what *kind of information* needs to be given as a parameter when this method is called. In this case, we want a parameter that gives us the current time. But you could imagine that there are other types of parameters. For example, the Clear method needs a Color as a parameter. The reason that the compiler needs to know the type of a parameter is because that type determines how much memory is needed to store that particular information. Also, it would be silly to pass a color to a method that needs a time, or vice versa.

3.3.13 The Graphics Device

Before we can draw anything, we need to initialize the *graphics device*. This device controls the graphic capabilities of the game, so it is very important! In all your games built using the XNA engine, you will need to initialize the graphics device. Initializing the graphics device is something that we need to do before the actual game starts, otherwise, we cannot draw anything. Also, we need to do this initialization only once. Generally, we initialize the graphics device in the method called BasicGame (lines 15–19). The following instruction initializes the graphics device:

```
graphics = new GraphicsDeviceManager(this);
```

We are going to look into what this means exactly later on. In the Draw method, we can now use the graphics device to clear the screen and to set it to a particular color:

```
GraphicsDevice.Clear(Color.Olive);
```

Clear is a method of the GraphicsDevice class. In order to execute this method, we have to write in front of it what it belongs to. In this case, it is the graphics device. The graphics device and the method that belongs to it are separated by a dot. After the method name you see parentheses. We need to provide the values for the *parameters* that this method needs between these parentheses.

Let us look in a bit more detail at the parameter that we pass to this method. It represents the *color* to paint the window after it has been cleared. For this, we use another class, the Color class. This class is used to create different colors, such as olive in our example, but there are many more available, as we have already seen in the first chapter. You can even make your own color by combining red, green, and blue values. As you can see, we did not write Color.Olive() with parentheses. This is because Olive is not a method of the Color class, but it is called a *property*. There are a few differences between properties and methods. One is that a property does not take parameters, which is why we omit the parentheses. We will discuss what properties are in more detail later on. For now, let us just say that these properties give us *information* in the shape of a color. So Color.Olive results in information that describes the color 'olive'. Because the expression Color.Olive is placed inside the parentheses of the Clear method, this information is passed as a parameter to that method. So now, the Clear method knows that it needs to set the background color to olive and it can do its job.

Next to creating the graphics device, there is also another line of code in the BasicGame method:

```
Content.RootDirectory = "Content";
```

This instruction indicates where our game program can find sounds, images or other assets that are used in the game. At the right-hand side of the equals sign, you can see the word 'Content' between double quotes. If something is written between double quotes, the compiler interprets it as *text*. In this case, the text indicates the folder in which the game assets are located. Because the BasicGame program does not use any assets, we could also have left out this instruction from the program and it would still work fine. Similarly, there are a few other instructions that we will not deal with now, because they are related to loading and displaying game assets. In the next chapter, we will show why these instructions are needed and what they do.

3.4 Program Layout

3.4.1 Comments

For the human reader of a program (another programmer, or yourself in a couple of months, when you have forgotten the details of how your program worked), it can be very useful to add some clarifying comments to a program. These comments are completely ignored by the compiler, but it makes for a more understandable program. There are two ways in C# to mark comments in your code:

- everything between the symbol combination /∗ and ∗/ is ignored (can be multiple lines of comments)
- everything between the symbol combination // and the end of the line is ignored

It is useful to place comments in your code to explain groups of instructions belonging together, the meaning of parameters, or complete classes. If you use comments, do it to *clarify* the code, not to write the code again but in words: you can assume that the reader of your code knows C#. To illustrate this, the following comment line adds to the clarity of the instruction:

```
// Set the background color to olive green.
GraphicsDevice.Clear(Color.Olive);
```

This line is also a comment, but it does not clarify what the instruction does:

```
// Pass the value Color.Olive to the Clear method of the graphics device.
GraphicsDevice.Clear(Color.Olive);
```

While testing your program, you can also use comment symbols to temporarily remove instructions from the program. Do not forget to remove these parts of your code that are *commented out* once you finish the program, because they can lead to confusion when other developers look at your source code.

3.4.2 Layout

There are no strict rules about how to distribute the text of a C# program over the lines in a text file. Usually, we write every instruction on a separate line, even though this is not necessary for the compiler to understand the program. Sometimes, if it makes a program clearer, the programmer will write multiple instructions on a single line. Also, sometimes a single instruction that is very long (containing method calls, and many different parameters) can be distributed over multiple lines (we will see this later on in this book as well).

3.4.3 Whitespace and Indentation

As you can see in the BasicGame example, we use whitespace quite liberally. There is an empty line between each method, as well as spaces between an equals sign and the expressions either side of it. Spacing can help to clarify the code for the programmer. For the compiler, they have no meaning. The only place where a space is really important is between separate words. It is not allowed to write **protected override void** Update as protectedoverridevoidUpdate. And similarly, it is not allowed to write an extra space in the middle of a word. In text that is interpreted literally, spaces are also taken literally. There is a difference between:

```
Content.RootDirectory = "Content";
```

and

```
Content.RootDirectory = "C o n t e n t";
```

But apart from this, extra spaces are allowed everywhere. Good places to put extra whitespace are:

- behind every comma and semicolon (but not before),
- left and right of the equals sign (=), you can see an example of this in the instruction Content.RootDirectory = "Content";,
- at the beginning of lines, so that the bodies of methods and classes are indented (usually four positions) with respect to the braces enclosing the body.

The Visual Studio editor helps you a little bit by automatically performing the indentation for you. Also, the editor automatically places whitespace at certain spots in your code to increase readability.

3.5 What You Have Learned

In this chapter, you have learned:

- what the skeleton of a game is, consisting of the game loop and the game world that the loop acts upon;
- how to structure a game program, consisting of a Game subclass, setting up the graphics device and implementing the Draw method to change the background color;
- the basic layout rules of a program, including how to place comments in your code and where to put extra whitespace to improve readability of your code.

Chapter 4
Creating a Game World

4.1 Introduction

In this chapter, we will show you how to create a game world by storing information in the memory. We will introduce basic types and variables, and how they can be used to store or change information. Next, we will show you how to store more complicated information such as sprites and sounds, and how you can use them to draw a nice-looking game world with sounds.

4.2 Basic Types and Variables

In the previous chapters, we have discussed memory a couple of times. We have seen how we can execute a simple instruction like GraphicsDevice.Clear(Color.Olive); to clear a window and to set a background color. In the next example, we are going to use the *memory* to store information temporarily, in order to remember the results of a few simple calculations. The example that we are going to look at is the DiscoWorld example, in which we change the background color depending on the game time that has passed.

4.2.1 Types: Different Kinds of Structured Information

The previous examples used different kinds of information that were passed as parameters to methods. For example, the method GraphicsDevice.Clear wants as information a color, the Update method in the BasicGame class wants game time information, and the LoadContent method does not need any information at all. The compiler needs some way to distinguish between all these different kinds of information. For example, it is useful to know what kind of information a method expects, so that the compiler knows something is wrong when we try to execute the instruction

A. Egges et al., *Learning C# by Programming Games*,
DOI 10.1007/978-3-642-36580-5_4, © Springer-Verlag Berlin Heidelberg 2013

GraphicsDevice.Clear(gameTime). In order to do this, each kind of information used in a program is of a *type*. There are many types in C#, you can even make your own types!

4.2.2 Declaration and Assignment of Variables

Next to the type of information that needs to be stored, the compiler also needs to know what name we are going to use in the program when we want to use or modify this information. Together, the type and the name form the *declaration*. This is an example of a declaration:

int red;

In this example, *int* is the type of the location in memory, and *red* is the name used to refer to that place in memory. The type name is an abbreviation of *integer* and you can use this type to store a whole number. In programming languages, a place in memory with a name and a type is called a *variable*. So from now on, we will be talking about the *variable* red. After this declaration, we can visualize what the memory looks like:

red ☐

Now that we have told the compiler that some place in memory will be used for storing a number, and we call this place 'red', we can use that variable in our program to store a number in. Variables are given a value with an *assignment instruction*. This is done as follows:

red = 3;

The memory now looks like this:

red 3

The assignment instruction consists of the following parts:

- the name of the variable that should be assigned a value;
- the '=' sign;
- the new value of the variable
- a semicolon

We can recognize the assignment instruction by the equals-sign in the middle. However, it is better to think of this sign as 'becomes' rather than 'equals' in C#. After all, the variable is not yet equal to the value to the right of the '=' sign, it *becomes* that value after the instruction is executed. The syntax diagram describing the assignment instruction is given as follows:

So now we have shown one instruction for declaring a variable, and another instruction to store a value in it. But if you already know which value you want to store in a variable when you declare it, you can combine the declaration of a variable and the first assignment to it:

```
int red = 3;
```

Here are a few examples of more declarations and assignments of integer variables:

```
int age = 16;
int numberOfBananas;
numberOfBananas = 2;
int a, b;
a = 4;
int c = 4, d = 15, e = −3;
c = d;
numberOfBananas = age + 12;
```

In the fourth line of this example, you see that it is possible to declare multiple variables in one declaration. You can even perform multiple declarations with assignments in a single declaration, as can be seen in the sixth line of the example code. On the right hand side of the assignment, we can put other variables, or mathematical expressions, as you can see in the last two lines. The instruction c = d; results in the value stored in variable d being stored as well in variable c. Since the variable d contains the value 15, after this instruction is executed the variable c also contains the value 15. The last instruction takes the value stored in the variable age (16), adds 12 to it and stores the result in the variable numberOfBananas (which now has the value 28). In summary, the memory will look something like this after these instructions have been executed:

age	16	a	4	c	15	e	-3
numberOfBananas	28	b		d	15		

The syntax of declaring variables (with an optional initialization) is expressed in the following diagram:

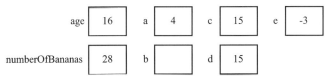

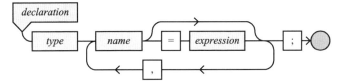

4.2.3 Instructions and Expressions

If you look at the elements in the syntax diagrams, you have probably noticed that we called the value or program fragment on the right-hand side of an assignment an *expression*. So what is the difference between an expression and an *instruction*? The difference between the two is that an *instruction* changes the memory in some way, whereas an *expression* has a value. Examples of instructions are method calls, or assignments, as we have seen in the previous section. Instructions often use expressions. Here are some examples of expressions:

```
16
numberOfBananas
2
a + 4
numberOfBananas + 12 − a
−3
Color.Olive
```

All these expressions represent a value *of a certain type*. Except for the last line, all expressions are of type *int*. The last line retrieves a property of the Color class and it returns a color value. The type of this color value is Color. So, although it may seem confusing, a class is actually also a type. How this works exactly is something that we will discuss later on.

4.2.4 Arithmetic Operators

In **int** expressions, the following arithmetic operators can be used:

- + add
- − subtract
- ∗ multiply
- / divide
- % remainder after division (pronounce as 'modulus')

For multiplication an asterisk is used, because the signs regularly used in mathematics ($\cdot$ or $\times$) are not on a computer keyboard. Completely omitting this operator, as is done also in mathematics (for example in the formula $f(x) = 3x$), is not allowed in C# because it introduces confusion with variables consisting of more than one character.

When the division operator / is used, the result is truncated, because a calculation with two **int** variables results in another **int** variable. For example, the result of the expression 14/3 is 4.

The special operator % gives the remainder after division. For instance, the result of 14%3 is 2, and the result of 456%10 is 6. The result will always lie between 0 and the value at the right side of the operator. The result is 0 if the result of the division is integral.

4.2.5 Priority of Operators

When multiple operators are used in an expression, the regular arithmetic rules of precedence apply: 'multiplication before addition'. The result of the expression $1 + 2 * 3$ therefore is 7, not 9. Addition and subtraction have the same priority, and multiplication and division as well.

If an expression contains multiple operators of the same priority, then the expression is computed from left to right. So, the result of $10 - 5 - 2$ equals 3, not 7. When you want to deviate from these standard precedence rules, parentheses can be used, for example $(1 + 2) * 3$ and $3 + (6 - 5)$. In practice, these expressions will generally also contain variables, otherwise you could have calculated the results (9 and 4) yourself.

Using more parentheses than needed is not forbidden: $1 + (2 * 3)$, you can go completely crazy with this if you want: $((1) + (((2) * 3)))$. However, your program will be a lot harder to read if you do.

In summary, an expression can be a constant value (such as 12), it can be a variable, it can be another expression in parentheses, or it can be an expression followed by an operator followed by another expression. As a result, this is the syntax diagram representing an expression:

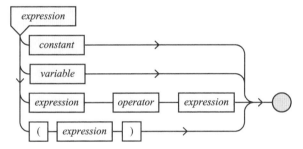

4.2.6 Other Numerical Types

Another numerical type is the **double** type. Variables of that type can contain numbers with decimals. After the declaration:

double d;

We can give the variable a value with the assignment operation:

d = 3.141592653;

Variables of type **double** can also contain whole numbers:

d = 10;

Behind the scenes, the computer will automatically place a zero behind the decimal point. Other than with the **int** type, dividing **double** variables results in only small rounding errors:

```
d = d / 3;
```

The variable d now contains the number 3.33333333.

Apart from **int** and **double** there are nine other types in C# for numerical variables. Eight of the 11 numerical types can be used for whole numbers. The difference between the types is the range of values that can be represented by a type. Some types allow for a bigger range of values to be represented, but the downside is that these types require more memory. Especially when you are developing a console game or a mobile game, memory is often limited. So when you have to store a number, think beforehand which type is best suited. For example, if you want to store the current level index, it makes no sense to use a **double** type, since level indices are whole numbers. In that case a type that only holds positive whole numbers would be more suited. There are types that can contain both negative and positive values, other types only contain positive values.

type	space	smallest value	largest value
sbyte	1 byte	−128	127
short	2 bytes	−32,768	32,767
int	4 bytes	−214,7483,648	2,147,483,647
long	8 bytes	−9,223,372,036,854,775,808	9,223,372,036,854,775,807
byte	1 byte	0	255
ushort	2 bytes	0	65,535
uint	4 bytes	0	4,294,967,295
ulong	8 bytes	0	18,446,744,073,709,551,615

The **long** type is only needed if you are planning to use extremely large or small values. The types **byte** and **short** are used if the range of the values is limited. In general, the memory that this saves is only relevant if a lot of these variables (thousands, or even millions) are required. The types **short**, **int** and **long** each have an 'unsigned' version, of which the name begins with a 'u'. Unsigned types can only contain positive values. The type **byte** already is unsigned by itself, and it has a 'signed' version called **sbyte**.

For non-whole numbers, there are three different types available. They do not only differ in the maximum value that can be stored, but also in precision after the decimal point.

type	space	significant digits	largest value
float	4 bytes	7	3.4×10^{38}
double	8 bytes	15	1.7×10^{308}
decimal	16 bytes	28	7.9×10^{28}

Here, the **float** type uses the least amount of memory. The **double** type can store very large numbers, and with high precision. The **decimal** type is even more precise, but it cannot contain values as high as the **float** or **double** types.

Every type has its own target application. The **decimal** type is useful for financial calculations, or in games for very precise physical calculations. The **double** type is used for many mathematical calculations. **float** is used if precision is not that important, but saving memory use is. When we write a numerical value in our program somewhere, we can explicitly indicate that it is of type **float**. For example:

float speed = 0.3f;

Here the f written behind the value 0.3 indicates that the value is of type **float**. This is useful, because we also want to store that value in a variable of type **float**. Suppose that we would have written the following:

float speed = 0.3;

This instruction would actually give a compiler error! Why? Because the compiler interprets the value 0.3 as being of type **double**, and by performing the assignment, this value would have to be stored in a variable of type **float**. Since **float** uses half of the memory as **double**, it does not fit, so the compiler complains. You may think that this is only to annoy the programmers. After all, the compiler should be able to understand that the **double** 0.3 value should be converted into a **float** value, and just do it automatically, right? If you think about it, that could lead to very dangerous situations. Suppose that you are a very rich person, and your bank uses C# to store how much money you have on your bank account:

double account = 12345678912345;

Now you want to transfer this money to another account. However, a not so smart programmer accidentally uses the **float** type for that:

float newaccount = account;

Now, because of the reduced precision of the **float** type, the value that is actually stored is 12,345,678,900,000. In other words, you just lost 12,345 dollars! When assigning a value to a variable may result in the loss of information, the compiler generates an error so that you are aware of it. If you still would like to perform the assignment, you have to state explicitly that you want to convert the value into a value of type **float**:

float newaccount = (**float**)account;

When you convert an expression of a certain type into an expression of another type, this is called a *cast*. A cast is performed by writing the type that we want to cast to between parentheses in front of the expression. Casting is only possible between related types. For example, you cannot cast a Color variable to a numerical type such as **float**.

All the numerical types are given in the following syntax diagram:

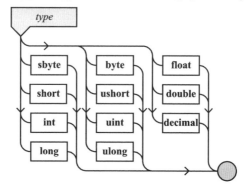

4.2.7 Declaration and Initialization of *const* Variables

Sometimes, it is useful to explicitly state that a variable will not be changed after it has been given a value. That way, it is clear to the readers of your program that this value will stay the same throughout the entire program. Furthermore, if you accidentally try to change it anyway, the compiler will complain about it. Often, things like mathematical constants are typically values stored in this way. Have a look at this example:

```
const float pi = 3.14159265f;
```

After this combined declaration and initialization, we are no longer allowed to change the variable. In other words, if we try to execute the following instruction:

```
pi = 12.0f;
```

the compiler will generate an error that it is not allowed to assign a value to the pi variable because it is a constant.

4.2.8 DiscoWorld: A Changing Background Color

In the previous sections, we talked about different variable types and how to declare and assign them. We have given several examples of how to declare and assign variables of type **int** or **double**. Next to the numerical types we have discussed there are many other types in C#. For example, GameTime is also a type and it represents the *game time*, in other words: the time that has passed since the game has started. As

```
1  using Microsoft.Xna.Framework;
2  using Microsoft.Xna.Framework.Graphics;
3
4  class DiscoWorld : Game
5  {
6      GraphicsDeviceManager graphics;
7      SpriteBatch spriteBatch;
8      Color background;
9
10     static void Main()
11     {
12         DiscoWorld game = new DiscoWorld();
13         game.Run();
14     }
15
16     public DiscoWorld()
17     {
18         Content.RootDirectory = "Content";
19         graphics = new GraphicsDeviceManager(this);
20     }
21
22     protected override void LoadContent()
23     {
24         spriteBatch = new SpriteBatch(GraphicsDevice);
25     }
26
27     protected override void Update(GameTime gameTime)
28     {
29         int red = gameTime.TotalGameTime.Milliseconds;
30         background = new Color(red, 0, 0);
31     }
32
33     protected override void Draw(GameTime gameTime)
34     {
35         GraphicsDevice.Clear(background);
36     }
37 }
```

Listing 4.1   A program that displays a changing background color

you can see in Listing 4.1, the Draw method has a parameter of type GameTime, and the name of this parameter is gameTime. Inside the method, we can use the parameter just like we use a variable. So, when we are executing instructions inside the Draw method, the current game time is stored somewhere in the memory, and we can access it with the name gameTime. The type of this parameter is GameTime, which is a much more complicated type than an integer. In fact, the GameTime type consists of several integer values, such as the number of seconds passed, the number of milliseconds passed, and so on. For example, this expression gives us the milliseconds fraction of the total time passed since the game has started:

gameTime.TotalGameTime.Milliseconds

For example, if 13 minutes, 12 seconds, and 345 milliseconds have passed since the game has started, the result of this expression will be 345. In this example, TotalGameTime is a property of the type/class GameTime and this gives us a variable of type TimeSpan, which in turn has a property called MilliSeconds. By the way, there is also a way to obtain the total passed game time in milliseconds, which would be 792,345 milliseconds $((13 * 60 + 12) * 1000 + 345)$. You can get this value with the following expression:

gameTime.TotalGameTime.TotalMilliseconds

Since the parameter gameTime is of type GameTime, we can make use of all these properties to obtain information contained within the variable. Once we have this information, we can store it in another variable (or do something else with it):

int red = gameTime.TotalGameTime.Milliseconds;

We are now going to use the variable red to create yet another variable, but one of the type Color. We will store a new color in this variable. Once we have done this, we can pass it as a parameter to the method Clear of the GraphicsDevice class. Let us first declare this variable:

Color background;

We name this variable background and the type of background is Color. Now that we have declared this variable, we can give it some value. Because the Color type is quite a complicated type, we cannot simply assign it a number like we did with the integer type. A Color variable needs to be *constructed* from three different numbers: the R (red), G (green), and B (blue) values. Constructing a value of a more complicated type is done with the keyword **new** and the name of the type written after it. We can then pass the information needed to construct the value as parameters between parentheses. For example, we can create the color *black* and store it in a variable as follows:

Color blackColor = **new** Color(0, 0, 0);

The three parameters given to construct this variable are separated by a comma and they are written between parentheses. After creating the blackColor variable, the memory will look like this:

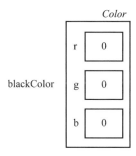

The Color type consists of three 'sub' variables: one for each color component.[1] In the image above, we write the type above the block containing the data so that it is clear we are dealing with a Color type. Other examples of colors are:

```
Color blueColor, greenColor, redColor, grayColor, whiteColor;
blueColor = new Color(0, 0, 255);
greenColor = new Color(0, 255, 0);
redColor = new Color(255, 0, 0);
grayColor = new Color(200, 200, 200);
whiteColor = new Color(255, 255, 255);
```

As you can see in these examples, the color intensity values range between 0 and 255, where 255 is the highest color intensity. By setting the 'red' value to 255 and the other two values to 0, we create the color red. We get the color white by setting all intensity values to 255. Similarly, the black color is created by setting all values to 0. Using these RGB values, it is possible to create a wide range of colors.

In our example, we want to use the passed game time to vary the color. We already stored the milliseconds value of the current game time in an integer variable:

```
int red = gameTime.TotalGameTime.Milliseconds;
```

Now, we use this value to create a new color:

```
background = new Color(red, 0, 0);
```

In the DiscoWorld example, we have done this work in the Update method, because basically the background color can be regarded as a very simple *game world*, and updating the background color, hence, the game world, needs to be done in the Update method. However, you can see that we placed the *declaration* of the background variable outside of the method, at the top in the class body (line 8). Why is this?

---

[1] In fact, the Color type consists of four elements: the R, G, and B values, as well as an A (alpha) value that stores the transparency. For now, we are only using the first three elements.

4.2.9 Scope of Variables

The place where we declare a variable has consequences on where we are allowed to use this variable. Take a look again at the variable red in the DiscoWorld program. This variable is declared (and assigned a value) in the Update method. Because it is declared in the Update method, we are only allowed to use it in this method. We are not allowed for example to use this variable again in the Draw method. Of course, we could declare another variable called red inside the Draw method, but it is important to realize that the red variable declared in Update would not be the same red variable declared in the Draw method. Alternatively, if we declare a variable at the *class body* level, then we can use it in the *entire class*. We need to use the background color in both the Update and Draw methods, because in the Update method, we update this background color, and in the Draw method, we use the updated color to paint the window using the Clear method. Therefore, the variable needs to be declared at the class level, so that all methods in the class can use this variable.

The places where a variable can be used are also called the *scope* of a variable. In this example, the scope of the variable red is the Update method, and the scope of the variable background is the DiscoWorld class. More officially, the scope of a variable is determined by the braces that enclose the declaration. In the case of the variable red, these braces are the delimiters of the Update method body. In the case of the variable background, the braces are the delimiters of the *class body*.

4.2.10 Setting the Background Color

After we have updated our color in the Update method, we can pass it as a parameter to the Clear method, which we call in the Draw method:

```
GraphicsDevice.Clear(background);
```

Try executing the program by pressing F5. You will see that the color changes from black to red, stays red for a while, then turns from red to black again, and so on. The Update and Draw methods are executed a number of times per second, and every time we look at what the current passed game time is, and we use the milliseconds component to create a color. This number of milliseconds starts with the value 0 (in the beginning of the game) and then rises to 1000. Once this value has been reached, the seconds counter is increased, and the milliseconds counter is reset to 0. Since we use the milliseconds counter to create the R value of the background color, we see the color changing on the screen.

You have probably noticed that the color stays red for a while, before starting from black again. Why is this? Remember that the range of RGB value is between 0 and 255? Since the milliseconds counter goes from 0 to 999, we are probably creating colors like **new** Color(260, 0, 0), **new** Color(378, 0, 0), or **new** Color(956, 0, 0). What happens when the color is created is that if the R value exceeds its maximum

Fig. 4.1 SpriteDrawing
project and its content
reference to Painter in the
solution explorer

value of 255, it is set to its maximum intensity. So, the expression **new** Color(835, 0, 0)
actually results in a color with RGB values of 255, 0, and 0. This means that for
about three quarters of a second, the displayed background color will be red, before
it turns black again.

4.3 Managing Game Assets

4.3.1 Introduction

In the previous sections, we have seen how to make a very basic game application by
writing our own class as a subclass of Game. We have seen how the graphics device
is initialized, and how we can use it to change the background color according to
the time passed. In this section, we will show how to draw images (or: sprites) on
the screen, which is the first step towards making a nice-looking game. Sprites are
generally loaded from a file. This means that any program that draws sprites is no
longer simply an isolated set of instructions, but it relies on *game assets* that are
stored somewhere. This immediately introduces a number of problems that we need
to take care of:

- How do we tell the game engine where to find sprites?
- How do we retrieve the information from an image file?
- How do we draw a sprite on the screen?

In this section we are going to deal with these questions.

4.3.2 Locating Sprites

Before a program can use any kind of asset, it needs to know where these assets are
located. Look at the project SpriteDrawing in the solution explorer (see also Fig. 4.1).
You see that it contains a folder called 'Content References'. Inside this folder you
see that there is a shortcut to another project in this solution called 'Painter'. If you
open that project, you see that it contains some image files. This is how game assets
are dealt with. Game assets are stored in a separate *Content project*. Other projects
can then *refer* to that project in order to access these assets. This means that it is
also possible to use the same assets for different projects in the same solution. This
is very handy, because when a number of projects use the same assets, we do not
need to copy them for each project.

The basic windows game template provided with this book does not deal explicitly with content references. The way to add your own content to a game is to create a Content project yourself. You can do this by going to File → New → Project and then select the 'Empty Content Project' template. You can give this content project a name and a location, just like any other project. Once you have done this, the content project will appear in your solution. Now you can link your own project with this content project by right clicking on the project in the solution explorer and selecting 'Add Content Reference'. You can then choose to link your content project with your game project. Adding assets to a content project is very easy. You can simply drag images or sounds to the content project and they will be added.

When you open the Painter content project, you see that it contains many different image and sound files. This is because that content project is also used for the first complete game that we will develop as a part of this book. Whenever a project has a reference to this content project, you can use all of these assets in the project. If you look again at the content project title, you will note that after the name of the project, there is another name (Content) between parentheses. This is the relative location where the assets will be available to the game project that refers to this content project. In this case, it is the directory 'Content'. When a project that refers to this content project is compiled, the assets will be automatically copied into a directory local to the program called 'Content'. However, we also need to indicate in our *source code* where the games assets are located.

As an example, have a look at the program SpriteDrawing in Listing 4.2. On line 19, you will find the code that tells the compiler in what directory the game assets are located:

```
Content.RootDirectory = "Content";
```

We are accessing a property called Content from the Game class. Since we are already inside the Game class (or actually a special version of it), we do not need to write anything in front of the property. The Content property, in turn, contains another property called RootDirectory, and we can assign a *text* value to it. In this case, the text is the name of the content folder. Here you see a value of a type we have not discussed before, namely a *string*, which is used to represent text. When we want to store text in a variable, we need to enclose the text by double quotation marks as you can see when we assign the value "Content" to the property RootDirectory.

4.3.3 Loading Sprites

Now that we have indicated the location of sprites, we can use XNA classes and methods to load a sprite and draw it. These classes are available in the library Microsoft.Xna.Framework.Graphics which we import with a **using** statement at the beginning of the program:

```
using Microsoft.Xna.Framework.Graphics;
```

```
 1   using Microsoft.Xna.Framework;
 2   using Microsoft.Xna.Framework.Graphics;
 3   using Microsoft.Xna.Framework.Media;
 4
 5   class SpriteDrawing : Game
 6   {
 7       GraphicsDeviceManager graphics;
 8       SpriteBatch spriteBatch;
 9       Texture2D balloon;
10
11       static void Main()
12       {
13           SpriteDrawing game = new SpriteDrawing();
14           game.Run();
15       }
16
17       public SpriteDrawing()
18       {
19           Content.RootDirectory = "Content";
20           graphics = new GraphicsDeviceManager(this);
21       }
22
23       protected override void LoadContent()
24       {
25           spriteBatch = new SpriteBatch(GraphicsDevice);
26           balloon = Content.Load<Texture2D>("spr_lives");
27
28           MediaPlayer.Play(Content.Load<Song>("snd_music"));
29       }
30
31       protected override void Draw(GameTime gameTime)
32       {
33           GraphicsDevice.Clear(Color.White);
34           spriteBatch.Begin();
35           spriteBatch.Draw(balloon, Vector2.Zero, Color.White);
36           spriteBatch.End();
37       }
38   }
```

Listing 4.2   A program that displays a sprite on a white background

Let us now look at how we can load a sprite from a file and store it somewhere in the memory (using a variable). We will need this variable in several different methods. In the LoadContent method, we have to load the sprite and store it in the variable. In the Draw method, we can access the variable in order to draw the sprite on the screen. Therefore, we declare this variable at the class body level, so that we can use it in all the methods. But what type should we give this variable? We have only seen simple types such as **int** or **float**, and they represent a number, not an image. Fortunately, the XNA game engine provides a type for storing sprites called Texture2D. So, let us declare a variable of that type:

Texture2D balloon;

Loading a sprite is done using the method Load<Texture2D> from the Content class. This method loads a sprite from a file and we can assign the loaded sprite to the balloon variable (which is of type Texture2D), as follows:

balloon = Content.Load<Texture2D>("spr_lives");

We now have declared and assigned a variable called balloon, which contains the sprite loaded from the file 'spr_lives.png'. As you can see, we do not have to provide the filename extension, the Load method automatically adds it for us.

4.3.4 Drawing Sprites

Loading a sprite and storing it in memory does not mean that the sprite is drawn on the screen. For that to happen, we need to do something in the Draw method. Drawing sprites can be done with the class SpriteBatch. But in order to use methods from that class, we first need a variable of the type SpriteBatch. In the template project, this work is already done for us. The variable is declared at the class body level and it is given a value in the LoadContent method:

spriteBatch = **new** SpriteBatch(GraphicsDevice);

As a parameter, we have to provide the graphics device (the same thing we used to set the background color in the previous example). This is needed, because the SpriteBatch class needs to know which graphics device it should use to draw the sprites.

Before we draw anything on the screen, we clear it so that any things previously drawn are removed. As usual, this is done by a simple call to the Clear method:

GraphicsDevice.Clear(Color.White);

Of course, you can choose any color here, or even use the code from the previous example to let the background color vary according to the current time.

Drawing a sprite on the screen is done using the Draw method from the SpriteBatch class, but before drawing anything, the class requires you to call the Begin method. Similarly after you have finished drawing, you need to call the End method. This means that drawing the balloon sprite on the screen consists of the following instructions:

Fig. 4.2 A screenshot of the SpriteDrawing program running

```
spriteBatch.Begin();
spriteBatch.Draw(balloon, Vector2.Zero, Color.White);
spriteBatch.End();
```

Before we start drawing anything, we have to make sure that the Begin method is called. In that method, the graphics device is prepared for drawing things on the screen. The End method tells the graphics device that we are done drawing, so things can be cleaned up for the next drawing batch. Neither the Begin nor the End methods need any parameters, therefore we leave the parentheses empty. The Draw method takes three parameters. The first parameter is the sprite that needs to be drawn. The second parameter is the position of the sprite on the screen. This position is given as a two-dimensional coordinate, where the coordinate $(0, 0)$ corresponds to the top left of the game screen. Just like Color.Chocolate is an expression that gives the color chocolate, the expression Vector2.Zero gives the two-dimensional vector $(0, 0)$. If we provide the top left point on the screen as a parameter to the Draw method, then the *top left point* of the sprite is drawn there. Finally we can provide a 'tint' to optionally change the color of the sprite. If the color Color.White is supplied, no tinting happens, which is what we want in this case. Figure 4.2 shows a screenshot of the program when running.

Just like with the Color class, we could also make a Vector2 variable that contains a position depending on the current time. Let us call this variable balloonPosition, and we declare it as follows:

```
Vector2 balloonPosition;
```

Where should we place this declaration? If you think about it, the balloon position is a part of the game world. We update the game world in the Update method, and we draw it in the Draw method. Because multiple methods need to access this variable, we therefore need to declare it at the class body level, and not in one of the methods. Now that is done, we can write the following instructions in the Update method:

```
protected override void Update(GameTime gameTime)
{
    int yposition = 480 - gameTime.TotalGameTime.Milliseconds / 2;
    balloonPosition = new Vector2(300, yposition);
}
```

In this example, we first store an expression containing the millisecond fraction of the current time in a variable called yposition. We then assign a value to the variable balloonPosition (which is of type Vector2) and in it we store the y-position that we just calculated. As an x-value, we choose 300 (which is about halfway horizontally on the screen). Because the x-position will always be 300 and the y-position is varying, the result will be a balloon flying from the bottom of the screen to the top of the screen. We need to slightly change the Draw method in order to actually draw the balloon at the right position. The call to the Draw method in the SpriteBatch class will then become:

```
spriteBatch.Draw(balloon, balloonPosition, Color.White);
```

Try to play around with the numbers used to calculate the new balloon position. Can you make the balloon move from left to right? Or diagonally across the screen?

4.3.5 Adding a Background Sprite

Building games with only a plain white background is somewhat boring, so we can also make it a bit more visually appealing by displaying a background sprite. This means we have to load another sprite in the LoadContent method and extend the Draw method in order to draw it. The final version of this program is called FlyingSprites and you can find the complete source code in the sample solution belonging to this chapter. If you run the program FlyingSprites from the samples, you see that now two sprites are drawn: a background, and on top of that, a balloon. In order to achieve this, we have introduced another variable of type Texture2D to contain the background sprite. Like the balloon variable, this variable is declared at the class level:

```
Texture2D balloon, background;
```

As you can see, just like with integers, we can declare multiple variables of the same type in a single instruction. Also, there are now two calls to the Draw method of the SpriteBatch class, instead of one:

```
spriteBatch.Draw(background, Vector2.Zero, Color.White);
spriteBatch.Draw(balloon, balloonPosition, Color.White);
```

The order in which these methods are called is very important! Because we want the balloon to appear on top of the background, we *first* have to draw the background, *then* we draw the balloon. If we did this the other way around, the background would be drawn over the balloon, and we would not see it anymore (try it yourself).

4.3.6 Music and Sounds

Another type of commonly used game asset is *sound*. Generally, we distinguish between two types of sound in games: background music, and sound effects. Sound effects are very useful to indicate to the player that something is done, or something has happened, for example when the player picks up a new weapon or when a level is completed. In XNA, it is very easy to play background music and sound effects. In order to use sound, we first need a sound file that we can play. In the SpriteDrawing program, we are going to play the file 'snd_music' which will serve as background music. As you can see, this file is located inside the content project. If you right click on this file and you select the properties, you can see that there is a field called 'content processor'. This indicates what kind of content we are dealing with. Select 'Song' as the content processor type. By doing this we can use the music file as background music. For sound effects, there is another related content processor type which (surprise!) is called 'Sound Effect'.

In order to play background music in our program, we need access to the *Media* library. This means that we have to add a **using**-instruction:

```
using Microsoft.Xna.Framework.Media;
```

In the LoadContent method, we can then load the sound file, and play it as background music:

```
MediaPlayer.Play(Content.Load<Song>("snd_music"));
```

We call the method Play from the MediaPlayer class, and we pass as a parameter the Song object that was loaded. As you can see, adding background music to your game is easy: it only requires a few lines of code. Playing a sound effect is also very easy. Sound effects are part of the *Audio* library, so we need the following **using**-instruction:

```
using Microsoft.Xna.Framework.Audio;
```

Loading the sound effect is done as follows:

```
SoundEffect mySound = Content.Load<SoundEffect>("scream");
```

And we play the sound effect by calling the Play method on the object:

mySound.Play();

In all the games that we develop in this book, we will use both types of sound (background music and sound effects) to make the games more exciting.

Sound and music—Most games contain sound effects and background music. These are important for various reasons. Sound effects give important cues to indicate to the user that something has happened. For example, playing a click sound when pressing a button provides feedback to the user that the button was indeed pressed. Hearing footsteps indicates that enemies might be nearby, even though the player might not see them yet. And hearing a bell ringing in the distance can give an indication that something is about to happen. The old game Myst was a classic in this respect because many cues on how to progress where passed to the player through sounds.

Atmospheric sound effects, like dripping water, wind in the trees, or the sound of cars in the distance enhance the experience and give a feeling of being present in the game world. They make the environment more alive, even when nothing is actually happening on the screen.

Music plays a crucial role in the way players experience the environment and the action. Music can be used to create tension, sadness, happiness, and many other emotions. However, dealing with music in games is a lot harder than in movies. In movies it is clear what is going to happen so the music can match that perfectly. But in games, part of the action is under control of the player. Modern games use adaptive music that constantly changes according to how the game story evolves.

4.4 What You Have Learned

In this chapter, you have learned:

- how to store information in the memory using variables;
- what the basic numerical types are in C#;
- how to load game assets such as sprites and sounds into the memory;
- how to use the Update method to change the game world through the variables and the Draw method to display the game world on the screen.

Part II
Creating Colorful Games

Fig. II.1 A screenshot of the game Painter

In the following chapters, we are going to develop a game called Painter (see Fig. II.1). While developing this game, we'll also introduce a few new techniques that are very useful when programming games, such as organizing instructions in classes and methods, conditional instructions, iteration, and much more.

The goal of the Painter game is to collect paint of three different colors: red, green and blue. The paint is falling from the sky in cans that are kept floating by balloons, and you must make sure that each can has the right color, before falling through the bottom of the screen. You can change the color of the paint falling down by shooting a paint ball of the desired color at the falling can. You can select the color that you shoot with by using the R, G, and B keys on the keyboard. You can shoot a paint ball by left clicking in the game screen. By clicking further away from the paint cannon, the ball is given a higher velocity. The place where you click also determines the direction in which the cannon shoots. For each can that lands in the right bin you get 10 points. For each wrongly-colored can, you lose a life (indicated by the yellow balloons in the top left of the screen). You can run the final version of this game by opening the solution belonging to Chap. 11. Press F5 and you can immediately start playing.

Chapter 5
Knowing What the Player Is Doing

5.1 Introduction

In the previous chapter, we have seen a few examples of loading and displaying sprites. We have also seen that we can use the current time information to change the position of a sprite. In this chapter, we will discuss how to deal with player input in our game. We will show how to retrieve what the player is doing and how the game world changes depending on that information. We will start with a simple extension of the FlyingSprites program, which draws the balloon at the position of the mouse pointer. In the next chapter, we will look into different types of input, such as keyboard or gamepad input.

5.2 A Sprite Following the Mouse Pointer

5.2.1 Retrieving the Mouse Position

Now that we know how to display sprites on the screen, let us see if we can use player input to control the position of a sprite. Have a look at the program Balloon1 (see Listing 5.1). Actually, there is not a lot of difference between this program and the FlyingSprites program. In the FlyingSprites program, we calculated the position of the balloon by using the milliseconds fraction of the passed game time:

```
int yposition = 480 − gameTime.TotalGameTime.Milliseconds / 2;
balloonPosition = new Vector2(300, yposition);
```

The position we calculated is stored in the variable balloonPosition. Now we want to create a program where the balloon position is not calculated based on the passed time, but we want the balloon position to be the same as the current mouse position. Getting the current mouse position is very easy. We have to use the class Mouse

```
 1   using Microsoft.Xna.Framework;
 2   using Microsoft.Xna.Framework.Graphics;
 3   using Microsoft.Xna.Framework.Input;
 4
 5   class Balloon : Game
 6   {
 7       GraphicsDeviceManager graphics;
 8       SpriteBatch spriteBatch;
 9       Texture2D balloon, background;
10       Vector2 balloonPosition;
11
12       static void Main()
13       {
14           Balloon game = new Balloon();
15           game.Run();
16       }
17
18       public Balloon()
19       {
20           Content.RootDirectory = "Content";
21           graphics = new GraphicsDeviceManager(this);
22       }
23
24       protected override void LoadContent()
25       {
26           spriteBatch = new SpriteBatch(GraphicsDevice);
27           balloon = Content.Load<Texture2D>("spr_lives");
28           background = Content.Load<Texture2D>("spr_background");
29       }
30
31       protected override void Update(GameTime gameTime)
32       {
33           MouseState currentMouseState = Mouse.GetState();
34           balloonPosition = new Vector2(currentMouseState.X, currentMouseState.Y);
35       }
36
37       protected override void Draw(GameTime gameTime)
38       {
39           GraphicsDevice.Clear(Color.White);
40           spriteBatch.Begin();
41           spriteBatch.Draw(background, Vector2.Zero, Color.White);
42           spriteBatch.Draw(balloon, balloonPosition, Color.White);
43           spriteBatch.End();
44       }
45   }
```

Listing 5.1 A program that shows a balloon following the mouse

for that. But before we can use the class, we have to place an additional **using**-instruction in the beginning of our program that tells the compiler that we will be needing some classes that provide methods for handling *input*:

using Microsoft.Xna.Framework.Input;

The Mouse class has a method called GetState. This method gives us the current mouse state. Using this current mouse state, we can find out where on the screen the mouse is, whether the player is clicking on one of the buttons, and so on. The *type* of the current mouse state is MouseState, and we can create a variable of that type to store the current mouse state that the GetState method gives us:

MouseState currentMouseState = Mouse.GetState();

Now that we have this variable, we can retrieve the *x* and *y*-position of the mouse in the screen using the properties X and Y of the variable of type MouseState. Just like in the FlyingSprites program, we store this position in the variable balloonPosition:

balloonPosition = **new** Vector2(currentMouseState.X, currentMouseState.Y);

So, in every call of the Update method, we retrieve the current mouse position, and we store this position in the variable balloonPosition. We then draw the balloon sprite at that position in the Draw method. The final effect of this is that the balloon is always drawn at the mouse position. If you press F5 and execute the program, you will see exactly this behavior.

5.2.2 Methods and Properties

A method call can be either an expression or an instruction. spriteBatch.Begin(); is an instruction, for example, but Mouse.GetState() is an expression, since the method has a result (the mouse state). Retrieving a property is always an expression (which, in turn, can be part of an instruction). We can extend the instruction syntax diagram with method calls and assignments to properties:

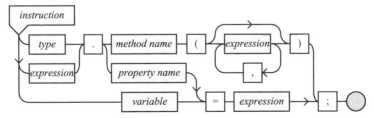

And similarly, we can extend the expression syntax diagram with the following part, which shows calling methods and properties as expressions, as well as creating an object such as Vector2 with the **new** keyword:

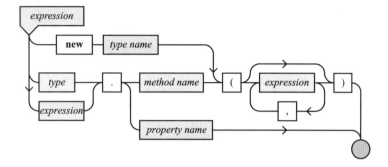

5.2.3 Changing the Origin of a Sprite

When you run the Balloon1 example, you will notice that the balloon is drawn such that the top left corner of the sprite is at the current mouse position. When we draw a sprite at a certain position, the default behavior is that the top left corner of the sprite is drawn at that position. If we execute the following instruction:

```
spriteBatch.Draw(someSprite, somePosition, Color.White);
```

the sprite named someSprite is drawn on the screen such that its top left corner is at position somePosition. You could also call the top left corner of the sprite the *origin* of the sprite. So what if we want to change this origin? For example, suppose that we would like to draw the *center* of the sprite someSprite at position somePosition? Well, we could calculate that by using the Width and Height properties of the Texture2D type. Let us declare a variable called origin and store the center of the sprite inside it:

```
Vector2 origin = new Vector2(someSprite.Width / 2, someSprite.Height / 2);
```

Now if we want to draw the sprite someSprite with this different origin we can do that as follows:

```
spriteBatch.Draw(someSprite, somePosition − origin, Color.White);
```

By subtracting the origin from the position, the sprite is drawn at an offset such that the position somePosition indicates the center of the sprite. The spriteBatch object also has a method for drawing a sprite using a different origin. This method is also called Draw, but it has more parameters than the Draw method we have been using until now. Here is an example of how to call this method:

```
spriteBatch.Draw(someSprite, somePosition, null, Color.White,
                 0.0f, origin, 1.0f, SpriteEffects.None, 0);
```

This version of the Draw method can draw a sprite at a position and with a blending color, just like the simpler version of the Draw method that takes only three parameters. However, you can see that one of the parameters is the origin variable, meaning that we can indicate to this method what the origin of the sprite is. As we have seen, it is also not a problem to calculate the position ourselves by subtracting the origin from the position, but this version of the method does that for us. Furthermore, there are a few other parameters that could be useful. For example, the fifth parameter of this method is a **float** value that indicates at which angle the sprite should be drawn. And the point that the sprite is rotated around is again the *origin*. The seventh parameter (also a value of type **float**) indicates a scaling factor. There are more parameters in this method, and a keyword that we have not seen before (**null**), but we will come to those later in the book.

Operators on more complex types—It is possible to calculate the origin of the someSprite sprite as follows:

```
Vector2 origin = new Vector2(someSprite.Width, someSprite.Height) / 2;
```

So, in some cases the division operation can be used on other types than basic types such as **int** or **double**. However, this only works on types where it makes sense. If you try this:

```
SpriteBatch halfASpriteBatch = spriteBatch / 2;
```

the compiler would not allow it, because 'half a sprite batch' does not make any sense. The programmers of the type Vector2 used a programming technique called *operator overloading*, which allows a programmer to define what the meaning is of the arithmetic operators when used in combination with that particular type. The Vector2 type also contains the definition of what several arithmetic operators do, thus defining the mathematical vector and how it behaves.

We can now use this more complicated Draw method to change the origin of the balloon sprite to its bottom center. To see this in action, have a look at the Balloon2 program. We declare an additional member variable where we store the origin of the balloon sprite:

```
Vector2 balloonOrigin;
```

In the LoadContent method, we can calculate the value of this vector once we have loaded the sprite. In order to do this, we use the Width and Height properties of the Texture2D class:

```
balloonOrigin = new Vector2(balloon.Width / 2, balloon.Height);
```

Why do we calculate this vector in the LoadContent method instead of for example in the Draw method? Here we touch upon a very important issue when programming games: *efficiency*. We can safely assume that the size of the balloon sprite will not change while the game is running. Therefore, it would not make sense to recalculate the bottom center of the image more than once. If we would calculate this vector in the Draw method, we would perform this calculation about sixty times per second as long as the game is running. In this example, it would probably not affect the performance of the application that much because the calculation is not that complicated. However, once your games start to become more complex, it is crucial to calculate things at the right place and that we are not wasting computation power when it is not needed. Therefore, we calculate the bottom center of the sprite in the LoadContent method, which is executed only once.

We can now use the nine-parameter version of the Draw method to draw the balloon at the origin that we calculated:

```
spriteBatch.Draw(balloon, balloonPosition, null, Color.White,
               0.0f, balloonOrigin, 1.0f, SpriteEffects.None, 0);
```

5.3 Classes, Types, and Objects

Let us reconsider some of the terms that have been introduced. We have seen that instructions are grouped into methods, and methods are grouped into classes. We have already seen quite a few examples of what a method looks like and that one of the instruction forms is *calling* a method. We have also discussed the difference between an *instruction* and an *expression*. An instruction changes memory, an expression has a value. For example, have a look at the following expression:

```
Mouse.GetState()
```

What happens here is that we call the method named GetState from the Mouse class. We said in the previous section that the *result* of calling this method is the current mouse state, which we can store in a variable. The *type* of that variable has to be MouseState. Let us look at another example of an expression:

```
new SpriteBatch(GraphicsDevice)
```

The result of this expression is a 'spritebatch' thing, which we can store in a variable of type SpriteBatch. But what does this mean exactly? If you hover your mouse pointer over the word SpriteBatch in the Visual Studio editor, you see a tool tip indicating that SpriteBatch is actually a class! This is also shown in Fig. 5.1.

Apparently, SpriteBatch is a class, but at the same time it is also a *type*. It seems that classes are more than just 'collections of methods'. Classes can be used as a type, and we can declare and initialize variables of that type. And next to grouping

Fig. 5.1 The tooltip that is shown when you hover over the word SpriteBatch

```
SpriteBatch spriteBatch = new SpriteBatch(GraphicsDevice);
class Microsoft.Xna.Framework.Graphics.SpriteBatch                ackground");
Enables a group of sprites to be drawn using the same settings.
```

together methods, classes themselves can also contain declarations. An example of a class that contains declarations is the Balloon class we programmed. This class declares among others a variable called spriteBatch and a variable called balloonPosition. Another example of a class that also declares variables is the Texture2D class, which is used to represent a sprite:

```
balloon = Content.Load<Texture2D>("spr_lives");
```

This instruction loads a texture from a file, and stores it in a variable of type Texture2D. Texture2D is a class, just like SpriteBatch and Balloon. You can verify this yourself by hovering over the word with your mouse pointer in the code editor. Next to a couple of methods, values of this class also contain variables because the image data have to be stored somewhere after they have been loaded. Probably these variables are quite complicated since an image contains a lot of information. We are not that interested in what these variables internal to this class look like. However, we do like to know how to use the methods in this class so we can do something with this variable of type Texture2D. The variable balloon has as a type Texture2D and therefore it contains the internal variables of the class Texture2D, as well as the *methods* that belong to the class. Variables such as balloon whose type is a class, are also called *objects*.

5.3.1 Methods and Properties Can Manipulate an Object

The Texture2D class has a couple of useful methods. For example, it has a method called SaveAsJpeg which allows us to save the loaded sprite as a JPEG image. This method probably contains a lot of instructions that open a file, compress the image information in the loaded sprite according to the JPEG standard, and that save the compressed information in the file. But which sprite should this method save to a JPEG file if we call the method? In the Balloon1 and Balloon2 programs, we have declared the following two variables (among others):

```
background = Content.Load<Texture2D>("spr_background");
balloon = Content.Load<Texture2D>("spr_lives");
```

Suppose that we would call the method SaveAsJpeg as follows:

```
Texture2D.SaveAsJpeg(...);
```

How can we indicate that we want to save the *balloon* image as a JPEG file, and not the background? The SaveAsJpeg method does not have a parameter where we can pass along the image that needs to be saved. This is because the method *manipulates an object*. For example, if we want this method to manipulate the object balloon, we can do this as follows:

balloon.SaveAsJpeg(...);

So instead of placing the name of the class before the dot, we place the object that we want to manipulate before the dot. Generally we cannot choose whether we want a method to manipulate an object, or simply call it from its class. For instance the SaveAsJpeg method *has* to be called on an object. It cannot be called directly from a class. If we would try to execute the instruction Texture2D.SaveAsJpeg(...);, the compiler would complain that the SaveAsJpeg method has to be called on an object (apart from the missing parameter values). Another example of a method that *has* to be called on an object is the Draw method from the SpriteBatch class. And here is another example:

spriteBatch.Begin();

Here we call the Begin method on the *object* spriteBatch. Just like the SaveAsJpeg method, the Begin method *has* to be called on an object. If we call the method without specifying which object it should manipulate, we get a compiler error:

SpriteBatch.Begin();

You cannot just call any method on any object. The Begin method is defined in the SpriteBatch class, so it can only manipulate objects of type SpriteBatch. Trying to have the Begin method manipulate a Texture2D object, like balloon, would result in a compiler error:

balloon.Begin();

To conclude, some methods manipulate objects, some methods do not. We have seen quite a few examples of the latter. For instance, the GetState method from the Mouse class does not need an object, we call it directly from the class. When a method does not manipulate an object but we call it directly from the class it is defined in, the method is called *static*. The method Main in the Balloon1 and Balloon2 programs is static, and you can see that it is static because the header of this method contains the keyword **static**. Since it is static, the Main method does not manipulate an object. The reason that the Main method has to be static is because it is the method that is executed when the program starts, and at that time no objects have been created yet, so there is no object to manipulate.

If you look at the Draw method in the Balloon class, you see that this method is not static (the **static** keyword is not written in its header). This means that this method manipulates an object. But which object does it manipulate? It manipulates the object that we created in the Main method:

```
Balloon game = new Balloon();
```

Here you see that we create an object of the class Balloon, which we then manipulate with the following instruction:

```
game.Run();
```

We call the Run method on the game object. The main thing task of this method is calling the game loop methods. It will call the LoadContent method once, and after that the Update and Draw methods sixty times per second. So, through the Run method, the object called game is manipulated.

Just like methods, properties also need an object. For instance, when we store the mouse position in the balloonPosition variable, we are using the properties X and Y which read information from the currentMouseState object:

```
balloonPosition = new Vector2(currentMouseState.X, currentMouseState.Y);
```

There also exist properties that do not manipulate an object, such as Vector2.Zero. This is a **static** property belonging to Vector2, so it does not need an object of type Vector2.

5.3.2 A Class Is a Blueprint for an Object

We have seen that it is possible to create an object of a certain class type. Just like we can declare and initialize multiple integer values, we can also declare and initialize multiple objects of the same class:

```
background = Content.Load<Texture2D>("spr_background");
balloon = Content.Load<Texture2D>("spr_lives");
```

In this example, the Load<Texture2D> method creates the Texture2D objects for us and we store them in two variables. We can also create objects ourselves, like we do in the case of the SpriteBatch class:

```
spriteBatch = new SpriteBatch(GraphicsDevice);
```

When we initialize an object of a certain class, we can also say that we have created an *instance* of the class. In this example, we have created an *instance* of the SpriteBatch class, and this instance is called spriteBatch. Whenever we want to explicitly create an instance of a class, we need to use the **new** keyword.

You could say that a class describes what an object looks like, or: a class is the *blueprint* for an object. Or to use a cooking analogy: a class is a recipe for an object. For example, the Texture2D class describes what an image consists of, and what methods are available to use or manipulate an image. When we create an instance of this class, such as balloon or background, we have an actual image stored somewhere in memory, which we can use or manipulate with the methods available from the Texture2D class.

5.3.3 A Constructor Describes How an Object Is Created

When a SpriteBatch object is created using the **new** keyword, we need to provide some information so that this object can be created, namely the graphics device. This information is passed as a parameter to a special method called the *constructor* method. Inside this method, we put all the instructions needed to initialize our object. A constructor method has a special header: it carries the same name as the class. The Balloon class contains a constructor method, which looks as follows:

```
public Balloon()
{
    Content.RootDirectory = "Content";
    graphics = new GraphicsDeviceManager(this);
}
```

Just like a normal method, the constructor method has parentheses which may contain parameters (in this case there are no parameters). And just like a normal method, a constructor method has a header and a body.

5.3.4 this: The Object We Are Currently Manipulating

When we create the instance of our Balloon class in the Main method, the Balloon constructor method will be called. Inside the constructor method, we set the root directory where all assets are placed, and we initialize the graphics device. The first line looks like we are accessing a property RootDirectory from the class Content. However, this is not what happens. In fact, Content is a *property* of the Game class, and because Balloon is a special version of that class, it also has the Content property. But if properties need an object, which object is this property manipulating? It manipulates the object that is currently created. So, in the Main method, we create an instance of the Balloon class and store it in the variable game. The instructions in the constructor method then manipulate this object.

   This object has a variable graphics. We assign the graphics device to that variable, which we create by constructing an instance of the GraphicsDeviceManager class. The constructor method of this class needs a variable of type Game, which we need to pass as a parameter. Of course, we want to pass our variable game to this constructor. However, if we would write the following line in the constructor, we would get a compiler error:

```
graphics = new GraphicsDeviceManager(game);
```

The reason for this is that the variable game is declared in the Main method, and because of the variable scope rule discussed in the previous chapter, we can *only access this variable in the method is was declared in*. What we in fact want to do is to somehow refer to 'the object we are currently manipulating'? In C#, and many other object-oriented programming languages, this is done by the keyword **this**, which always refers to the object we are currently manipulating. So, the graphics device is created as follows:

```
graphics = new GraphicsDeviceManager(this);
```

The object that **this** refers to is in this case the object that is stored in the variable game that we declared in the Main method. We can use the **this** keyword in many different cases. It is sometimes also useful to clarify that we are explicitly manipulating the object, instead of some unrelated variable. For example, we could also write the following instruction to set the content root directory:

```
this.Content.RootDirectory = "Content";
```

By explicitly writing **this** in front of the Content property, we clarify that we are accessing a property called Content and that this property manipulates the current object.

5.3.5 Properties: Retrieving or Changing Parts of an Object

Next to methods, we have seen that a class can also define *properties*. Properties are a way to access the data inside an object. Some of these properties allow only reading these data, other properties also allow you to write these data. For example, the Texture2D class has properties called Width and Height that we can use to retrieve the width and the height of a sprite. These two lines of code retrieve the width and the height of the balloon sprite and store them in two local variables of type **int**:

```
int width = balloon.Width;
int height = balloon.Height;
```

The Width and Height properties are *read-only*. We are not allowed to change them, which makes sense, because they reflect the size of the loaded sprite. Vector2 also has properties, namely X and Y. Look at the following example:

```
Vector2 v = new Vector2(3,4);
int xval = v.X;
v.Y = 12;
```

As you can see in this example, the X and Y properties can be read from as well as written to. After we have constructed the Vector2 object, we retrieve the *x*-value by using the X property. We set the *y*-value of the vector by using the Y property. Changing the value that a property represents is done by regular assignment, just like normal variables.

We have seen already quite a few examples of properties. For instance, the Content property inside the Game class. This property gives us an object of type ContentManager, which in turn has a property RootDirectory that can be written to. Another example is the GraphicsDevice property, which gives us an object of type GraphicsDevice and we can use that object to set a background color, or to pass as a parameter for creating a spritebatch:

```
spriteBatch = new SpriteBatch(GraphicsDevice);
```

Watch out: in the case of GraphicsDevice, the name of the property and the name of the type confusingly are the same. In the coming chapters, we will be using these properties a lot. They are a very useful tool to access the information inside an object in a structured way.

5.3.6 Member Variables and Local Variables

Until now, we have seen that classes are a collection of methods and properties. They can also be used as a type. A variable that has a class as a type is called an object. An object is also called an *instance* of class. Methods and properties manipulate the memory in some way. They can read it and write to it. But if we have an object, which 'memory' belongs to it, and how is it manipulated? This is done through *member variables*. We already have used member variables in our example programs. These are the variables that were declared at the *class level* and not at the method level. Member variables are like normal variables, except they belong to a *class* and not to a method. For example, the spriteBatch variable in the Balloon program is a member variable of that class.

An example of a variable that is *not* a member variable is the currentMouseState variable, because it is not declared on the class level, but in the Update method. Variables that are not member variables are also called *local variables*, because they can only be used in the method that they were declared in. Another example of a local variable is the yPosition variable in the FlyingSprites program. This variable is declared in the Update method, and it cannot be used outside that method.

5.4 Using the Mouse Position to Rotate the Cannon Barrel

One of the features of the Painter game is that it contains a cannon barrel that rotates according to the mouse position. We can now write the part of the program that does this, using the tools that we have discussed in this chapter. You can see this already working in the Painter1 program in the solution belonging to this chapter. We declare a few member variables for storing the background sprite, the cannon barrel sprite, the cannon barrel position and its origin:

Fig. 5.2 Calculating the
angle of the barrel based on
the mouse position

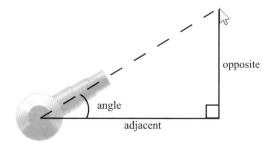

```
Texture2D background, cannonBarrel;
Vector2 barrelPosition, barrelOrigin;
```

We will draw the cannon barrel at an angle using the nine-parameter version of the
Draw method that we introduced in this chapter. This means that we need to store
the current angle of the barrel in a member variable as well:

float angle;

We will update the value of this angle in the Update method. In the LoadContent
method, we load the sprites and we assign a value to the barrelPosition variable, as
follows:

```
background = Content.Load<Texture2D>("spr_background");
cannonBarrel = Content.Load<Texture2D>("spr_cannon_barrel");
barrelPosition = new Vector2(72, 405);
```

The position of the barrel is chosen such that it fits nicely on the cannon base
that is already drawn on the background. The barrel image contains a circular part
with the actual barrel attached to it. We want the barrel to rotate around the center of the circular part. That means that we have to set this center as the origin.
Since the circle part is on the left part of the sprite, and the radius of this circle is cannonBarrel.Height / 2, we calculate the barrel origin as follows (also in the
LoadContent method):

barrelOrigin = **new** Vector2(cannonBarrel.Height, cannonBarrel.Height) / 2;

   In the Update method, we can now update the value of the angle based on the
current mouse position. The first step is to retrieve the current mouse position:

MouseState mouse = Mouse.GetState();

   Now we need to calculate at what angle the barrel should be drawn based on the
current mouse position. This situation is depicted in Fig. 5.2. We can calculate that
angle using the trigonometric *tangent* function, which is given as follows:

$$\tan(angle) = \frac{opposite}{adjacent}.$$

In other words, the angle is then given by

$$angle = \arctan\left(\frac{opposite}{adjacent}\right).$$

Calculating the length of the opposite and adjacent sides can be done by calculating the difference between the current mouse position and the position of the cannon barrel, as follows:

```
double opposite = mouse.Y − barrelPosition.Y;
double adjacent = mouse.X − barrelPosition.X;
```

Now we have to calculate the arc tangent using these values. How do we do this? Fortunately, the Math class can help us with that. In order to use this class, we need to place an extra **using** instruction at the top of our file since the Math class is contained in the System library:

using System;

The Math class contains many (static!) methods for basic mathematical calculations among which trigonometric functions like Sin, Cos, Tan and their inverses Asin, Acos, and Atan. However, there is a problem with calling Atan in a situation where the mouse is straight overhead of the barrel: a division by zero would occur because adjacent is zero.

Because this situation occurs often in games, there is an alternative arctangent method. Atan2 takes opposite and adjacent lengths as separate parameters, and returns the equivalent in radians of 90 degrees in this situation, as desired. We use this method to calculate the angle, as follows:

```
angle = (float)Math.Atan2(opposite, adjacent);
```

Note that we do a cast here from **double** to **float**. This is necessary because the Math.Atan2 method returns a value of type **double**, and we need to store it in a variable of type **float**. The angle variable has to be of type **float**, because the Draw method in the SpriteBatch class expects a **float** value to represent the angle. We call that method in the Draw method of our class and we pass along the right parameters:

```
spriteBatch.Draw(cannonBarrel, barrelPosition, null, Color.White,
                 angle, barrelOrigin, 1.0f, SpriteEffects.None, 0);
```

5.5 What You Have Learned

In this chapter, you have learned:

- how to read the current mouse position using the MouseState class and how to change the game world using the mouse position;

- that a class is a blueprint for an object (also called an instance of that class), and can therefore be used as a type;
- that the constructor method of a class responsible is for creating an instance of that class;
- the role of **this** as the object that we are currently manipulating in a method.

Chapter 6
Reacting to Player Input

6.1 Introduction

In this chapter, we will show you how your game program can react to mouse clicks and button presses. In order to do this, we need a instruction called **if** that executes an instruction (or a group of instructions) if a condition is met. We will also introduce enumerated types as another kind of primitive type.

6.2 Reacting to a Mouse Click

6.2.1 *ButtonState: An Enumerated Type*

In the previous examples, we have used the current mouse state to retrieve the mouse position. However, a MouseState object contains a lot of other information as well. For example, it can be used to find out whether a mouse button is pressed or not. For this, we can use the properties LeftButton, MiddleButton and RightButton. What these properties give is a value of type ButtonState. So we could save this value as follows:

```
ButtonState left = currentMouseState.LeftButton;
```

Primitive types—C# makes a distinction between the more complicated types representing a class and the very basic types representing things like integers or enumerations. The latter types are also called *primitive types*, because they form the building blocks of the more complicated *class types*.

You might guess that ButtonState is a class, however, it is actually an *enumerated type*. An enumerated type is very similar to the integer type, with the difference that instead of numeric values, the type contains words describing different states. In the case of the ButtonState type, these states are Pressed and Released, because a button is either pressed or released. Enumerated types are quite handy for representing a variable that can contain a few different meaningful states. For example, we might want to store the type of character that a player represents by using an enumerated type. We can decide ourselves what kind of different states there are in our type, so before we can use the enumerated type, we first have to define it:

enum CharacterClan { Warrior, Wizard, Elf, Spy };

The **enum** keyword indicates that we are going to define an enumerated type. After that follows the name of this type and, between braces, the different states that can be stored inside a variable of this type. This is the syntax diagram describing the **enum** *type definition*:

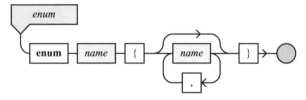

The type definition can be placed inside a method, but you may also define it at the class body level, so that all the methods in the class can use the type. You may even define it as a top-level declaration (outside of the class body). Here is an example of using the CharacterClan enumerated type:

CharacterClan myClan = CharacterClan.Warrior;

In this case, we have created a variable of type CharacterClan, which may contain one of four values: CharacterClan.Warrior, CharacterClan.Wizard, CharacterClan.Elf, or CharacterClan.Spy. In a very similar way, the ButtonState type is defined somewhere in a library probably looking something like

enum ButtonState { Pressed, Released };

Another example of using enumerated types would be to define a type for indicating the days in the week or the months in a year:

enum MonthType { January, February, March, April, May, June, July, August,
                September, October, November, December };
enum DayType { Sunday, Monday, Tuesday, Wednesday, Thursday, Friday, Saturday };
MonthType currentMonth = MonthType.February;
DayType today = DayType.Tuesday;

6.2.2 The if-Instruction: Executing an Instruction Depending on a Condition

As a simple example of how we can use the mouse button state to do something, let us make a simple extension of the Painter1 program, where we only calculate the new angle of the cannon barrel if the left mouse button is down. This means that we have to change the instructions in the Update method, because that is where we calculate the barrel angle.

Until now, all the instructions we have written had to be executed all the time. For example, drawing the background sprite and the cannon barrel sprite always needs to happen. But calculating the barrel angle only has to happen *sometimes*, namely when the player presses the left mouse button. In broader terms, we want to execute an instruction only if some condition holds true. This kind of instruction is called a *conditional instruction*, and it uses a new keyword: **if**.

With the **if**-instruction, we can provide a condition, and execute a block of instructions if this condition holds (in total, this is sometimes also referred to as a *branch*). Examples of conditions are:

1. the number of seconds passed since the start of the game is larger than 1000, or
2. the balloon sprite is exactly in the middle of the screen, or
3. the monster has eaten my character.

These conditions can either be **true** or **false**. A condition is an *expression*, because it has a value (it is either **true** or **false**). This value is also called a *boolean* value. It is associated with a type called **bool**, which we will talk about more later on. With an **if**-instruction, we can execute a block of instructions if a condition is **true**. Take a look at this example:

```
if (mouse.X > 200)
{
    spriteBatch.Draw(background, Vector2.Zero, Color.White);
}
```

This is an example of an **if**-instruction. The condition is always placed in parentheses. After that, a block of instructions follows, enclosed by braces. In this example, the background is only drawn if the mouse *x*-position is larger than 200. This means that if you move the mouse too far to the left of the screen, the background is not drawn anymore. We can place multiple instructions between the braces if we want:

```
if (mouse.X > 200)
{
    spriteBatch.Draw(background, Vector2.Zero, Color.White);
    spriteBatch.Draw(cannonBarrel, Vector2.Zero, Color.White);
}
```

If there is only one instruction, you may omit the braces to shorten the code a bit:

```
if (mouse.X > 200)
    spriteBatch.Draw(background, Vector2.Zero, Color.White);
```

In our example, we want to update the cannon barrel angle only when the player presses the left mouse button. This means that we have to check if the state of the left mouse button currently is pressed. This condition is given as follows:

```
mouse.LeftButton == ButtonState.Pressed
```

The == operator compares two values and returns **true** if they are the same, and **false** otherwise. On the left hand side of this comparison operator, we find the left mouse button state. On the right hand side, we find the state ButtonState.Pressed. So, this condition checks whether the left button is currently pressed. We can now use it in an **if**-instruction as follows in the Update method:

```
if (mouse.LeftButton == ButtonState.Pressed)
{
    double opposite = mouse.Y − barrelPosition.Y;
    double adjacent = mouse.X − barrelPosition.X;
    angle = (float)Math.Atan2(opposite, adjacent);
}
```

So, only if the left mouse button is pressed, we calculate the angle and store its value in the angle member variable. In order to see this program working, run the Painter1a example in the solution belonging to this chapter.

6.3 Boolean Values

6.3.1 Comparison Operators

The condition in the header of an **if**-instruction is an expression that returns a truth value: 'yes' or 'no'. When the outcome of the expression is 'yes', the body of the **if** instruction is executed. In these conditions you are allowed to use comparison operators. The following operators are available:

- < smaller than
- <= smaller than or equal to
- > larger than
- >= larger than or equal to
- == equal to
- != not equal to

These operators may be used between two numbers. On the left hand side and the right hand side of these operators you may put constant values, variables, or complete expressions with additions, multiplications and whatever you want, provided that they are of the same type. Again, watch out that testing the equality of two values is done using a double equals sign (==). This is needed, because the single equals sign is already used for assignments. The difference between these two operators is very important:

  x=5;   this instruction means: **assign** the value 5 to x!
  x==5   this expression means: **is** x equal to 5?

6.3.2 Logic Operators

In logical terms, a condition is also called a *predicate*. The operators that are used in logic to connect predicates ('and', 'or', and 'not') can also be used in C#. These operators have a special notation in C#:

- && is the logical 'and' operator
- || is the logical 'or' operator
- ! is the logical 'not' operator

We can use these operators to check for complicated logical statements, so that we can execute instructions only in very particular cases. For example, we can draw a 'You win!' overlay only if the player has more than 10,000 points, the enemy has a life force of 0, and the player life force is larger than 0:

```
if (playerPoints > 10000 && enemyLifeForce == 0 && playerLifeForce > 0)
spriteBatch.Draw(winningOverlay, Vector2.Zero, Color.White);
```

6.3.3 The Boolean Type

Expressions that use comparison operators, or that connect other expressions with logical operators also have a type, just like expressions that use arithmetic operators. After all, the result of such an expression is a value: one of the two truth values: 'yes' or 'no'. In logic, these values are called 'true' and 'false'. In C#, these truth values are represented by the **true** and **false** keywords.

Next to being used for expression a condition in an **if**-instruction, logical expressions can be applied for a lot of different things. A logical expression is similar to an arithmetic expression, except that it has a different type. For example, you can store the result of a logical expression in a variable, pass it as a parameter, or use that result again in another expression.

The type of logical values is called **bool**. This is one of the primitive types of C#. The type is named after the English mathematician and philosopher George Boole (1815–1864). Here is an example of a declaration and an assignment of a boolean variable:

```
bool test;
test = x>3 && y<5;
```

In this case, if x contains, for example, the value 6 and y contains the value 3, then the boolean expression x>3 && y<5 will evaluate to **true** and this value will be stored in the variable test. We can also store the boolean values **true** and **false** directly in a variable:

```
bool isAlive = false;
```

Boolean variables are extremely handy to store the status of different objects in the game. For example, you could use a boolean variable to store whether or not the player is still alive, or if the player is currently jumping, or if a level is finished, and so on. We can use boolean variables as an expression in an **if**-instruction:

```
if (isAlive)
    do something
```

In this case, if the expression isAlive evaluates to **true**, the body of the **if**-instruction is executed. You might think that this code generates a compiler error, and that we need to do a comparison of the boolean variable, like this:

```
if (isAlive == true)
    do something
```

However, this extra comparison is not necessary. A conditional expression like in the **if**-instruction *has to evaluate* to **true** or **false**. Since a boolean variable already represents either one of these two values, we do not need to perform the comparison anymore. In fact, if the previous comparison would be needed, then we also would need to compare that outcome again with a boolean value:

```
if ((isAlive == true) == true)
    do something
```

And this gets worse:

```
if (((((((isAlive == true) == true) == true) == true) == true) == true) == true)
    do something
```

In summary: do not make things more complicated than they are. If the outcome is already a boolean value, we do not have to compare it to anything anymore.

We can use the **bool** type to store complex expressions that are either **true** or **false**. Let us look at a few additional examples:

```
bool a = 12 > 5;
bool b = a && 3+4==8;
bool c = a || b;
if (!c)
    a = false;
```

Before you read on, try and find out what the value is of the variables a, b, and c
after these instructions have been executed. In the first line, we declare and initialize
a boolean a. The truth value that is stored in this boolean is evaluated from the
expression 12 > 5, which evaluates to **true**. So, variable a has the value **true**. In the
second line, we declare and initialize a new variable b, in which we store the result
of a more complex expression. The first part of this expression is the variable a,
which contains the value **true**. The second part of the expression is a comparison
3+4==8. This comparison is not true (3 + 4 does not equal 8), so this evaluates to
false, and therefore the logical 'and' also results in **false**. Therefore, the variable b
contains the value **false**.

The third line stores the result of the logical 'or' operation on variables a and b
in variable c. Since a contains the value **true**, the outcome of this operation is also
true, and it is assigned to c. Finally, there is an **if**-instruction, which assigns the value
false to variable a, but only if !c evaluates to **true**, that is, c evaluates to **false**. In this
particular case, c is **true**, so the body of the **if** instruction is not executed. Therefore,
after all the instructions are executed, a and c contain the value **true**, and b contains
the value **false**.

6.4   More on if-Instructions

6.4.1   An if-Instruction with an Alternative

We can use the **if**-instruction to check if the left mouse button is down. If so, we
update the angle of the cannon barrel:

```
if (mouse.LeftButton == ButtonState.Pressed)
{
    double opposite = mouse.Y − barrelPosition.Y;
    double adjacent − mouse.X − barrelPosition.X;
    angle = (float)Math.Atan2(opposite, adjacent);
}
```

In the Painter1a example, the angle stays the same when the left mouse button is not
pressed. But suppose that we want to have the angle set to zero again once the player
releases the left mouse button. We could add another **if**-instruction, like this:

```
if (mouse.LeftButton != ButtonState.Pressed)
    angle = 0f;
```

However, there is a nicer way of dealing with this: by using an **if**-instruction with
an alternative. The alternative instruction is executed when the condition in the **if**-

instruction is *not* true, and we use the **else** keyword for that:

```
if (mouse.LeftButton == ButtonState.Pressed)
{
    double opposite = mouse.Y − barrelPosition.Y;
    double adjacent = mouse.X − barrelPosition.X;
    angle = (float)Math.Atan2(opposite, adjacent);
}
else
    angle = 0f;
```

This instruction does exactly the same thing as the two **if**-instructions before, but we only have to write down the condition once. Execute the Painter1b program and see what it does. You will note that the angle of the cannon barrel is zero as soon as you release the left mouse button.

The syntax of the **if**-instruction with an alternative is represented by the following syntax diagram:

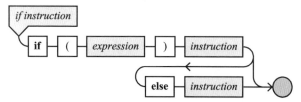

The reason that the body of an **if**-instruction can consist of multiple instructions between braces is that an instruction can also be a *block* of instructions, which is defined in the following syntax diagram:

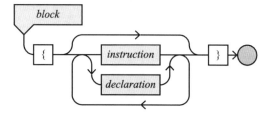

6.4.2 A Number of Different Alternatives

When there are multiple categories of values, you can find out with **if**-instructions which case we are dealing with. The second test is placed behind the **else** of the first **if**-instruction, so that the second test is only executed when the first test failed. A possible third test would be placed behind the **else** of the second **if**-instruction.

The following fragment determines within which age segment a player falls, so that we can draw different player sprites:

```
if (age<4)
    spriteBatch.Draw(babyPlayer, playerPosition, Color.White);
else if (age<12)
        spriteBatch.Draw(youngPlayer, playerPosition, Color.White);
    else if (age<65)
            spriteBatch.Draw(adultPlayer, playerPosition, Color.White);
        else
            spriteBatch.Draw(oldPlayer, playerPosition, Color.White);
```

Behind every **else** (except the last one), there is another **if**-instruction. For babies, the babyPlayer sprite is drawn, and the rest of the instructions are ignored (they are behind the **else** after all). Old players on the other hand, go through all the tests (younger than 4? younger than 12? younger than 65?) before we conclude that we have to draw the oldPlayer sprite.

We used indentation in this program to indicate which **else** belongs to which **if**. When there are many different categories, the text of the program becomes less and less readable. Therefore, as an exception to the usual rule that instructions after the **else** should be indented, we allow for a simpler layout with such complicated **if**-instructions.

```
if (age<4)
    spriteBatch.Draw(babyPlayer, playerPosition, Color.White);
else if (age<12)
    spriteBatch.Draw(youngPlayer, playerPosition, Color.White);
else if (age<65)
    spriteBatch.Draw(adultPlayer, playerPosition, Color.White);
else
    spriteBatch.Draw(oldPlayer, playerPosition, Color.White);
```

The additional advantage here is that using this layout, it is a lot easier to see which cases are handled.

6.4.3 Toggling the Cannon Barrel Behavior

As a final example of using the **if**-instruction to handle mouse button presses, let us try to handle a mouse button *click* instead of a mouse button press. We know how to check with an **if** instruction if the mouse button is currently pressed, but how do we find out if the player has clicked (meaning pressing and then releasing the mouse button)? Have a look at the program Painter1c. In this program, the cannon barrel rotation follows the mouse pointer after you click the left button. When you click again, the cannon stops following the mouse pointer.

The issue with this kind of 'toggle' behavior is that we only know the current status of the mouse in the Update method. This is not enough information for determining when a 'click' happens, because a click is partly defined by what happened the previous time we were in the Update method. We can say that a player has clicked the mouse button if these two things happen:

- the player did not press the mouse button during the last Update method;
- in the current Update method, the player presses the mouse button.

In order to solve this, we need to store the *previous mouse state*, so that we can compare it with the current mouse state the next time we are in the Update method. Let us therefore store the previous and the current mouse state in two member variables:

MouseState currentMouseState, previousMouseState;

Getting the current mouse state is easy, we have done it before:

currentMouseState = Mouse.GetState();

Now, how do we get the 'previous mouse state'? There is no way of doing this directly by calling a method from the Mouse class. However, we do know that what is now the current mouse state will be the previous mouse state in the next Update call. So, we can solve this problem by assigning the value of the current mouse state to the previous mouse state before we get the new mouse state. Therefore, our Update method will look something like:

```
protected override void Update(GameTime gameTime)
{
    previousMouseState = currentMouseState;
    currentMouseState = Mouse.GetState();
    Here we do something with the mouse state
}
```

Now, we can write the code needed to toggle the cannon barrel behavior by looking at the previous and current mouse state. We check this by using an **if**-instruction:

```
if (currentMouseState.LeftButton == ButtonState.Pressed
        && previousMouseState.LeftButton == ButtonState.Released)
    calculateAngle = !calculateAngle;
```

The conditional expression in this case checks that the state of the left mouse button currently is 'pressed', while its state was 'released' the previous time we retrieved the mouse state. If this condition evaluates to **true**, we toggle the calculateAngle variable. This is a member variable of type boolean (so it is either true or false). In order to get the toggling behavior, we make use of the logical 'not' operator. The result of the 'not' operation on the variable calculateAngle is stored again in the variable calculateAngle. So, if that variable contained the value **true**, we will store in the same variable the value **false** and vice versa. The result of this is that the value of the calculateAngle variable toggles every time we execute that instruction.

We can now use that variable in another **if**-instruction to determine whether we should update the angle or not:

```
if (calculateAngle)
{
    double opposite = currentMouseState.Y − barrelPosition.Y;
    double adjacent = currentMouseState.X − barrelPosition.X;
    angle = (float)Math.Atan2(opposite, adjacent);
}
else
    angle = 0.0f;
```

6.5 Handling Keyboard and Gamepad Input

6.5.1 Basics of Handling Keyboard Input

Handling keyboard and gamepad input is dealt with in a very similar way to dealing with mouse input. Instead of getting the mouse state, we have to get the *keyboard* or *gamepad* state. This can be done as follows:

```
KeyboardState currentKBState = Keyboard.GetState();
GamePadState currentGPState = GamePad.GetState();
```

Also, just like the mouse state, these variables have several methods for checking if the player presses a key on the keyboard, or a button on the gamepad. For example, we can check if the player presses the 'A' button on the gamepad by calling currentGPState.IsButtonDown(Buttons.A). Similarly, we check if the 'A' key on the keyboard is pressed by calling currentKBState.IsKeyDown(Keys.A). The classes Buttons and Keys provide a number of properties for defining the available keys and buttons.

6.5.2 A Multicolored Cannon

The program Painter2 is an extension of the Painter1 program. It also features a rotating cannon, but now the player can also select the color of the cannon by pressing different keys (R, G, or B). The current color of the cannon is displayed on the screen by drawing a colored ball in the center of the rotating barrel. The cannon can be either red, green, or blue. So, we will need three images of a ball, one for each of the three colors:

```
Texture2D colorRed, colorGreen, colorBlue;
```

To make things a bit more convenient, we will declare an extra Texture2 variable called currentColor, in which we keep track of what the current color of the cannon is:

Texture2D currentColor;

Finally, we need a variable for storing the origin of the ball:

Vector2 colorOrigin;

Now that we have our member variables in place, let us have a look at the LoadContent method. In this method, we need to load a few extra sprites, and store them in the member variables that we just declared:

```
colorRed = Content.Load<Texture2D>("spr_cannon_red");
colorGreen = Content.Load<Texture2D>("spr_cannon_green");
colorBlue = Content.Load<Texture2D>("spr_cannon_blue");
```

At the start of the program, we assume that the cannon is blue, so we assign the blue sprite to the currentColor variable:

currentColor = colorBlue;

Finally, we calculate the origin of the ball sprite which we choose as its center:

colorOrigin = **new** Vector2(currentColor.Width, currentColor.Height) / 2;

6.5.3 Handling the Keyboard Input

For handling the keyboard input, we will need the keyboard state. For completeness, we will store the previous and current state for both the keyboard and the mouse. so, we need the following member variables:

```
MouseState currentMouseState, previousMouseState;
KeyboardState currentKeyboardState, previousKeyboardState;
```

When we enter the Update method, we have to first update all these member variables so that they contain the right values when we are actually going to handle the player input. We follow the same procedure for the keyboard states as for the mouse states:

```
previousMouseState = currentMouseState;
previousKeyboardState = currentKeyboardState;
currentMouseState = Mouse.GetState();
currentKeyboardState = Keyboard.GetState();
```

If we want to know if the player has pressed the 'R' key, we use both the current and previous keyboard states, like we did with the mouse state:

```
if (currentKeyboardState.IsKeyDown(Keys.R)
        && previousKeyboardState.IsKeyUp(Keys.R))
    currentColor = colorRed;
```

If the player did press the 'R' key, we assign the red colored ball sprite to the currentColor variable. We follow the same procedure for the 'G' and 'B' keys, which gives us the following **if**-instruction:

```
if (currentKeyboardState.IsKeyDown(Keys.R)
        && previousKeyboardState.IsKeyUp(Keys.R))
    currentColor = colorRed;
else if (currentKeyboardState.IsKeyDown(Keys.G)
        && previousKeyboardState.IsKeyUp(Keys.G))
    currentColor = colorGreen;
else if (currentKeyboardState.IsKeyDown(Keys.B)
        && previousKeyboardState.IsKeyUp(Keys.B))
    currentColor = colorBlue;
```

Finally, we only need to add an additional drawing call to the Draw method so that the current colored ball is drawn on top of the cannon:

```
spriteBatch.Draw(currentColor, barrelPosition, null, Color.White, 0f,
                colorOrigin, 1.0f, SpriteEffects.None, 0);
```

Try to run the Painter2 program now, and see how the program responds to moving the mouse and pressing the 'R', 'G' or 'B' keys.

6.6 What You Have Learned

In this chapter, you have learned:

- what an enumerated type is;
- how to react to mouse clicks and button presses using the **if**-instruction;
- how to formulate conditions for these instructions using boolean values;
- how to use **if**-instructions with different alternatives;
- how to deal with keyboard and gamepad input.

Chapter 7
Basic Game Objects

7.1 Introduction

In this chapter, we are going to start organizing the source code of the Painter game. This is necessary because the source code of a game contains many lines of code. If we want to understand what such a complicated program is doing, we need to organize it.

7.2 Structuring the Game World

7.2.1 The Basics

In the Painter2 version of the game, we already had quite a few member variables:

```
GraphicsDeviceManager graphics;
SpriteBatch spriteBatch;
Texture2D background, cannonBarrel;
Vector2 barrelPosition, barrelOrigin;
float angle;
Texture2D colorRed, colorGreen, colorBlue;
Texture2D currentColor;
Vector2 colorOrigin;
MouseState currentMouseState, previousMouseState;
KeyboardState currentKeyboardState, previousKeyboardState;
```

Some of these member variables are used for running the game in general (such as spriteBatch and graphics), others are for representing the colored cannon, and there are some variables for handling player input. You can imagine that this list will become even longer when we add the flying ball and the falling paint cans to this game. And then Painter is just a basic game! Once we start building more complicated games, having a huge list of member variables will result in code that is impossible

A. Egges et al., *Learning C# by Programming Games*,
DOI 10.1007/978-3-642-36580-5_7, © Springer-Verlag Berlin Heidelberg 2013

to manage. In this chapter, we will look at various ways to organize the code to keep things manageable.

7.2.2 The HandleInput Method: Organizing Instructions in Methods

Take a look at the Painter3 program belonging to this chapter. A difference between the Painter2 program and the Painter3 program is that the Painter class contains another method called HandleInput. This method was created by the programmer of this game, as opposed to the others, which are required by the framework in some way. Generally, programmers define methods in such a manner that they logically divide the instructions into related 'chunks' of instructions. By grouping our instructions in methods, we can more easily recognize which instructions do what. A second advantage is that if we structure these instructions in methods in a smart way, we can reuse the same instructions in different contexts. This is what the HandleInput method looks like:

```
public void HandleInput()
{
    previousMouseState = currentMouseState;
    previousKeyboardState = currentKeyboardState;
    currentMouseState = Mouse.GetState();
    currentKeyboardState = Keyboard.GetState();

    code for handling the player input
}
```

Inside this method, we placed all the instructions for handling player input (both mouse and keyboard). The HandleInput method is then called from the Update method:

```
protected override void Update(GameTime gameTime)
{
    HandleInput();
}
```

Currently, the Update method does not do anything else, but this will change in the later versions of the game. It is very useful to put all input handling into a separate method, because when we need to change how the game responds to player input, we immediately know where to look. Furthermore, we can now clearly see the difference between dealing with player input and updating the game world. Although in the current version we do not need to update the game world in any way, a more complicated game will need to do a lot of different things: handle collisions between game objects, calculate speed and positions of objects, update the current score, and much more. So, in order to make everything clearer, we use methods to separate instructions into chunks that belong together.

In C#, you can add an arbitrary number of methods to your class. Of course, it is a good idea to think beforehand about how you want to structure your instructions into methods. Some of these methods are required by the framework and their header cannot be changed, such as the Main method in your application class. Other methods can be fully designed by yourself. When you add a method to a class, think about why you do it. For example, it would probably not be very useful to add a method that loads the background sprite, because that method would only contain one instruction and we can just as well write that instruction directly. Furthermore, this method would solve only one very specific problem (loading the background sprite) and it would be called only once.

It is a good idea to group instructions together that have some logical connection, such as the instructions that handle all the input, or instructions for drawing sprites on the screen. Finally, when you have created your own method, give it a logical name. The name HandleInput gives an idea of what this method is doing. If you name your method ILikeMashedPotatoes then, although we would have some insight into your food preferences, it would be very difficult later on to deduce what the method is actually doing.

7.2.3 Different Kinds of Methods: With or Without Parameters, with or Without a Result

We have seen and used already quite a few different kinds of methods. For example, there is a clear difference between the Update method in our class, and the HandleInput method: the latter one does not have any parameters, whereas the first one does (the game time). Additionally, some methods can have a *result* object that can be used in the instruction that does the method call, for example, by storing the result in a variable:

```
currentKeyboardState = Keyboard.GetState();
```

Here, we call the GetState method from the Keyboard class, and we store its result in the member variable currentKeyboardState. The HandleInput method does not provide a result that we can store in a variable. Of course, the method does have an effect of some sort, since it interprets the input from the player and changes the member variables accordingly. However, when we talk about the *result of a method*, we do not mean that the method has some effect on an object. We mean that the *method call* returns a value that can be stored in a variable. This is also called the *return value* of a method. In mathematics, it is quite common that a method (or: 'function' in mathematics) has a result. A mathematical function $f(x) = x^2$ takes as parameter an x-value and it returns its square as a result. We could actually write this mathematical function in C# as a part of our class if we wanted to:

```
public float Square(float x)
{
    return x*x;
}
```

If we look at the header of this method, we see that it takes one parameter of type **float**. The type **float** is also written in front of the method name. This means that the *type of the return value* is **float**, i.e., when we call this function, we can store the result in a variable of type **float**:

```
float f = Square(10.0f);
```

After this instruction is executed, the variable f will contain the value 100. So, the type indicator in front of the method name tells us which type the return value of this method has. Inside the method body, we can indicate using the keyword **return** what the actual value is that the method returns. In the case of Square, the method returns the outcome of the expression x*x. Of course, the type of the expression after the **return** keyword needs to be the same type as the type written in front of the method name, which in this case is **float**. Note that executing the **return** instruction also terminates executing the rest of the instructions in a method. Any instructions placed *after* the **return** instruction will not be executed. For example, consider the following method:

```
public int SomeMethod()
{
    return 12;
    int tmp = 45;
}
```

In this example, the second instruction (**int** tmp = 45;) will never be executed because the instruction before it will end the method. This is a very handy feature of the **return** instruction, and we can use it to our advantage:

```
public float SquareRoot(float f)
{
    if (f < 0.0f)
        return 0.0f;
    Calculate the square root, we are now sure that f ≥ 0.
}
```

In this example, we use the **return** instruction as a safeguard against wrong input by the user of the method. We cannot calculate the square root of a negative number, so we handle the case where f is negative before we do any calculations.

An example of a method that does not have a return value is the HandleInput method. Let us have a look at its header:

```
public void HandleInput()
{
    do something...
}
```

Instead of a type like **float** or **bool**, the keyword **void** is written in front of the method name. **void** means that the method does *not have a return value*, meaning that we cannot store the outcome of this method in a variable. For example, the following line would result in a compiler error:

```
float oops = HandleInput();
```

Also, because this method does not have a return value, we do not need to use the **return** keyword inside the body of the method (although it can sometimes be useful, as we will see). You will notice that whenever a method with no return value is called, it has no result that can be stored in a variable and whenever a method does have a return value, this value is used in some way. We can use the value to store it in a variable, like in this example:

```
currentMouseState = Mouse.GetState();
```

The method GetState in the Mouse class has a return value of type MouseState, so we can store it in a member variable of the same type. The following example shows the calling of two methods neither of which has a return value:

```
GraphicsDevice.Clear(Color.White);
spriteBatch.Begin();
```

A return value does not necessarily have to be stored in a variable. We can also directly use it in an **if**-instruction, like we do in the HandleInput method:

```
if (currentKeyboardState.IsKeyDown(Keys.R) &&
    previousKeyboardState.IsKeyUp(Keys.R))
    currentColor = colorRed;
```

Here, the IsKeyDown and IsKeyUp methods return a value of type **bool**. The difference between things that have a value and things that do not have a value is something we have seen before: it is the same difference we saw between *instructions* (which do not have a value) and *expressions* which *do* have a value. So, this means that IsKeyDown(Keys.K) is an *expression*, whereas HandleInput(); is an *instruction*. A second difference between these two things is that expressions never end with a semicolon, and instructions always end with a semicolon, except if the instruction is a block.

7.2.4 Declarations Versus Parameters

Declarations of variables have a lot in common with parameters that are written in the method header. In fact, those parameters also are declarations, but there are a few differences:

- variables are declared in the body of the method, parameters are declared between the parentheses in the method header;
- variables get a value by using an assignment instruction, parameters automatically get a value when the method is called;
- in a variable declaration you can declare multiple variables of the same type and write down the type name only once, in parameter declarations the type needs to be written down for every parameter (even if the type is the same);
- variable declaration end with a semicolon, parameter declarations do not.

7.2.5 Why Declarations Are Useful

Declarations are useful for different reasons:

- the compiler knows what the type of each variable is, so the compiler can decide whether a method call makes sense (calling the Draw method on a SpriteBatch object makes sense, but is impossible with object types such as Texture2D or **int** values);
- the compiler can check whether the parameters passed to a method call are of the correct type: if you were to switch the sprite object and the Vector2 object in a call to the Draw method, the compiler would warn you;
- if there is a typo in the name of a variable (e.g., you wrote screenHeigth instead of screenHeight), the compiler will find out because the variable is not declared.

7.3 Classes and Objects

7.3.1 An Object Is a Group of Variables with Methods and Properties

In the Painter3 example, we have seen that we can add our own methods to a class that group instructions that belong together. This helps us to organize our source code, since we create groups of instructions that belong together, and we give these groups a name as a method. Although this helps avoid long lists of instructions, it does not do anything about the long list of member variables that are declared in a class. For that, we need to move to the next level of code organization: grouping member variables into *objects*.

We have talked about objects before and we have already seen quite a few examples of them. For instance, each sprite that is loaded is represented by an object of type Texture2D. We have a *spriteBatch* object that can draw sprites on the screen. One purpose of these objects is to group data that belong together. For example, the Texture2D objects will contain all the pixels in the sprite that it represents. The SpriteBatch object will contain all the data needed to draw things on the screen. The Painter object will contain all the data needed for the 'Painter' game. These data are represented in the objects by *variables*. And if we want to access these variables from another object, we can do that by using *properties* such as the Width property in the Texture2D class.

In addition to data, objects also have *behavior*. This behavior is encoded in the methods. For example, the behavior of a Painter object is mainly encoded in the Update and Draw methods, which determine how the game behaves. A SpriteBatch object has several Draw methods that allow the object to do what it needs to do. The methods and properties that an object knows determine how the data inside the object are changed. For example, the HandleInput method in the Painter object changes the color of the cannon based on player input.

7.3.2 Objects in the *Painter* Game

It actually is quite logical to try and structure the game world into different *objects*, where each object corresponds to an object in the game. Which objects are present in the Painter game? We have three cans that fall down, a ball, and a cannon. Because C# is an *object-oriented* language, we can represent these game objects also as objects in our code.

In C#, the blueprints for objects are *classes*. Therefore, we need to add a class for each kind of object we have in our game. As a first step, let us add a class Cannon that represents the cannon object in the game.

7.3.3 Adding Classes to Your Project

It is very easy to add a class in the Visual C# development environment. Right-click on the project that you want to add a class to and select Add → Class. You will see the window depicted in Fig. 7.1. Select the 'Class' template and choose an appropriate name for the class. We will start with a class for the cannon game object, and call it Cannon. In order to do that, choose Cannon.cs for the name of the file. After you have clicked on 'Add', you will see that a new file called Cannon.cs has been added to your project. Double click on that file to open it. The contents of the file will look like this:

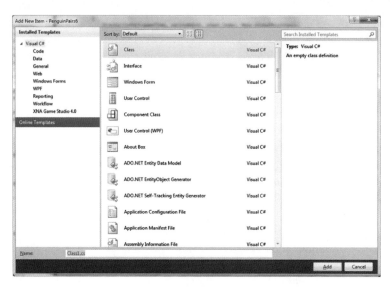

Fig. 7.1 Adding a new class to a project

```
using System;
using System.Collections.Generic;
using System.Linq;
using System.Text;

namespace Painter
{
    class Cannon
    {
    }
}
```

Every class that is added to the project by default gets its own file. The name of this file is the same as the name of the class that it contains. You may name the files differently, and you may also put multiple classes below one and other in a single file. However, your project becomes a lot messier if you do that, and it will be much more difficult to find everything. Therefore, keep every class in a single file, and name the file the same as the class. Visual Studio already puts the class in a common project namespace, and there are a couple of **using** instructions that it thinks might be of use. We will only need the first one (**using** System;) so leave that one in, and remove the others. Also remove the namespace because we do not use it in the Painter program.

As you can see, the Cannon class is completely empty. Even if a class does not yet contain any member variables or methods, we can already use it by declaring a

Fig. 7.2 The two roles of the 'class' concept

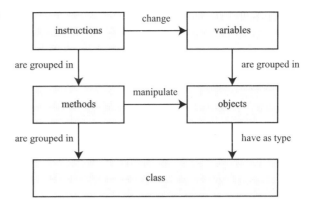

variable that is of its type. To try this, add the following member variable declaration to the Painter class, just below the large list of existing variables:

Cannon cannon;

And add the following line at the end of the LoadContent method:

cannon = **new** Cannon();

We have now created an *instance* of our own class! Of course, since this class is empty, the cannon object that we have created does not have any data, properties or behavior yet. We are going to have to add this ourselves.

7.3.4 Classes Can Be Used as a Type

Earlier in this book, we defined the term 'class' as a group of methods with a name. A method should always belong to a class: the Draw method for example belongs to the SpriteBatch class. However, classes also fulfill another role: they are the type of objects. In that case, the name of the class is used as the type of a variable, just like you can use built-in types such as **int**:

int x; Cannon c;

Both of these roles that a class plays are strongly connected. After all, methods change an object (the object before the dot in a method call). This object consists of variables that can be changed by the instructions in the method. Objects that have a class as a type can be modified by methods from that class. In other words: methods of a class can change objects that have that class as a type. Figure 7.2 shows the relation between the concepts instruction, variable, method, object and class, where the double role of the class is clearly visible.

7.4 The Cannon Class

7.4.1 Data in the Cannon Class

The goal of the Cannon class is to group the data and behavior belonging to the cannon game object together. In the Painter3 example, there were a few member variables associated with the cannon: the variable containing the cannon barrel sprite, three variables containing the different color indication discs, another Texture2D variable to maintain the current color, and variables for storing the position, origin and angle of the cannon barrel. We are going to put all these member variables inside the Cannon class, since they are all belong with the cannon *game object*:

```
Texture2D cannonBarrel;
Texture2D colorRed, colorGreen, colorBlue;
Texture2D currentColor;
Vector2 position;
Vector2 barrelOrigin, colorOrigin;
Color color;
float angle;
```

We have also added a member variable color to indicate the current color of the cannon. Although this variable is redundant, it will be convenient later on for retrieving and setting the current cannon color.

Now that we have added these declarations to our Cannon class, every time we create an instance of this class, the object that has been created will contain these variables. However, we did not yet provide any information about which *values* these variables should have when the object is created. For this, we need to define a *constructor* method in the class. The constructor method is a special kind of method that tells the compiler what to do when an object of type Cannon is created. Often, constructor methods will mainly contain instructions for assigning values to the variables that are a part of the object. Not all of these values are known inside of the Cannon class. For example, we need to assign a value to the cannon_barrel variable. Normally, we would load the sprite using the Content property. However, we cannot do that inside the Cannon class, because there is no Content property in that class. So how can we access the content manager in this case? Fortunately, constructors can have *parameters* just like other methods. The variable that the Content property gives us is of type ContentManager, so we add a parameter to the Cannon constructor of that type. In order to use the ContentManager type, we have to add an additional **using**-instruction at the top of the Cannon.cs file, so that the compiler can recognize the type:

using Microsoft.Xna.Framework.Content;

The header of the Cannon constructor method is then defined as follows:

public Cannon(ContentManager Content)

You can recognize that this is a constructor method and not a normal method because of two things:

- the name of the constructor method is the same as the name of the class;
- constructor methods never have a return type, not even **void**.

> **Multiple constructor methods**—You may notice that we used the plural form: constructor *methods*. It is possible to define multiple constructor methods in the same class, but only if they have different kinds of parameters, otherwise the compiler does not know which constructor to use when you create an instance. This can be useful when you want to offer different ways of constructing an instance of your class. For example, the Vector2 type offers a constructor without parameters, a constructor with a single parameter which is assigned to both the *x* and *y* values of the vector, and a constructor that takes two parameters.
>
> It is possible in C# to define a class without providing a constructor method, as you will see later on. In that case, the compiler will automatically add a *default constructor*. This constructor does not have any parameters, and does not do anything. However, as soon as you add your own constructor to the class the default constructor will be gone. So if your class has a single constructor method with one parameter, using that constructor method will be the only way to create an instance of that class.

Since the Cannon constructor contains a parameter, we need to provide the value of this parameter when the cannon object is created. This value is available here as the Content property. In the LoadContent method of the Painter class, we have access to that property since Painter is an extension of Game. So, we retrieve the content manager using the Content property, and pass it as a parameter to the Cannon constructor in order to create the cannon instance:

cannon = **new** Cannon(Content);

Inside the constructor method of the Cannon class, we need to tell the compiler how to create the Cannon object. One thing that needs to be done is the loading of the sprites using the content manager that was passed as a parameter. We can do this with a sequence of instructions:

```
this.cannonBarrel = Content.Load<Texture2D>("spr_cannon_barrel");
this.colorRed = Content.Load<Texture2D>("spr_cannon_red");
this.colorGreen = Content.Load<Texture2D>("spr_cannon_green");
this.colorBlue = Content.Load<Texture2D>("spr_cannon_blue");
```

Next to assigning values to the sprite member variables, we also need to add the instructions that give the remaining variables an initial value. For one, we need to set the default color of the cannon to blue. The following two instructions achieve that:

```
this.currentColor = colorBlue;
color = Color.Blue;
```

We also need to define the position and the origins of the barrel and the color indicator disc, we do this as follows:

```
barrelOrigin = new Vector2(cannonBarrel.Height, cannonBarrel.Height) / 2;
colorOrigin = new Vector2(currentColor.Width, currentColor.Height) / 2;
position = new Vector2(72, 405);
```

Now all the member variables of the Cannon instance have a value, and the object creation is complete. Note that we have not assigned a value to the angle member variable explicitly. Because angle is of type **float**, which is a primitive type, it gets assigned a default value of 0 by the compiler.

7.4.2 Adding Methods to the Cannon Class

Just like in the Painter class, it is possible to add our own methods to the Cannon class. A very useful method is one that resets a game object to its initial state. Such methods are especially useful in games. When the player restarts a game or a level in a game, we simply reset all the game objects to their initial states by calling the reset method. In order to provide for this, let us add a method called Reset to the Cannon class.

The Reset method does not have any parameters. It simply sets the member variables in our class to some initial value. We do not have to reset all the member variable values, only the ones that will be changed while playing the game. For example, we do not have to give the cannon_barrel variable an initial value, since it will not change while playing the game. The angle variable, however will change, so we have to reset it. Also, we have to reset the color, since that may also change while playing the game. As a result, we add the following Reset method to the Cannon class:

```
public void Reset()
{
    currentColor = colorBlue;
    color = Color.Blue;
    angle = 0.0f;
}
```

The Reset method is an example of a method that *changes* the object that it works on. This is the general goal of methods: define behavior that modifies the member variables, or that extracts some meaningful information from them for the caller of the method. Methods can manipulate multiple member variables. For example, the Reset method changes the color of the cannon, as well as the angle of the barrel.

Next to the Reset method, we also add a method called Draw that will draw the cannon on the screen at its position, in the desired color. Because the SpriteBatch object is defined inside the Painter class, we need to pass it as a parameter. And since the Draw method in the Painter class also gets a GameTime parameter, we pass this parameter along to the Draw method in the Cannon class. The outline of the Draw method is then given as follows:

```
public void Draw(GameTime gameTime, SpriteBatch spriteBatch)
{
    // draw the cannon sprites
}
```

Inside the Draw method, we need to draw the cannon barrel at an angle, and the color indicator disc. We simply copy the two draw instructions that do this from the previous version of the game, so then the complete Draw method is as follows:

```
public void Draw(GameTime gameTime, SpriteBatch spriteBatch)
{
    spriteBatch.Draw(cannonBarrel, position, null, Color.White, angle, barrelOrigin,
                1f, SpriteEffects.None, 0);
    spriteBatch.Draw(currentColor, position, null, Color.White, 0f, colorOrigin,
                1f, SpriteEffects.None, 0);
}
```

Now we can call this Draw method in the Painter class. The Draw method is not static, which means we have to call it on an object. The logical candidate for this is of course the cannon object that we created in the LoadContent method. So, the following instructions in the Painter.Draw method will draw everything on the screen:

```
GraphicsDevice.Clear(Color.White);
spriteBatch.Begin();
spriteBatch.Draw(background, Vector2.Zero, Color.White);
cannon.Draw(gameTime, spriteBatch);
spriteBatch.End();
```

We let the cannon draw itself, so to speak. As you can see, the Draw method inside the Cannon class specifies what we are going to *do* with the member variables. In this case, we are going to draw them on the screen. Methods work on objects, and this is a very clear example of that. Also, what we are slowly working toward is a software design where each game object deals with its own stuff. For instance, the Cannon class has to deal with loading the sprites that are part of it, as well as drawing and resetting itself. In a later stage, we will add more capabilities to the Cannon class, such as handling input.

7.4.3 Accessing the Data in the *Cannon* Class

We have shown how to define a class that describes an object in the game. This object groups together the data that belongs to the game object. These data can be accessed by the methods that are part of the class. For example, the Reset method assigns initial values to the member variables. However, sometimes we need to access this data directly from other classes. For example, we may need to retrieve the current position of the cannon, or we may need to know what the color of the cannon is so that we can change the color of the ball that we are shooting. In the Painter2 program, we could obtain this information easily because there was only one class and all the member variables were in a single long list. Now, if we want for example to access the color variable that belongs to the cannon object in the Painter class, we could try something like this:

```
Color cannonColor = cannon.color;
```

Unfortunately, this is not allowed; the compiler will generate an error that the color variable is not accessible. This is because by default, member variables are only accessible to methods that are inside the same class. So we can access the color variable in the Reset method because they are both in the Cannon class, but the same variable is not accessible in the HandleInput method, because that method is in the Painter class.

   This sounds like it is a bad thing. How are we going to change the color of the cannon in the HandleInput method if this data is not accessible? We could add a method called SetColor to the Cannon class that would get the color as a parameter and that would change it:

```
public void SetColor(Color col)
{
    this.color = col;
}
```

And we could add another method to the class called GetColor to retrieve the color of the cannon:

```
public Color GetColor()
{
    return this.color;
}
```

Sometimes, programmers call these kinds of methods *getters* and *setters*. In many object-oriented programming languages, methods are the only way to access the data inside an object, so for each member variable that needs to be accessible outside of the class, programmers added a getter and a setter. As C# is a more modern language, it provides a feature that is relatively new to object-oriented programming languages, called *properties*. A property is a replacement for a getter and a setter. It defines what happens when we retrieve data from an object, and what happens when we assign a value to data inside an object. So, let us now add a property for getting and setting the color of the cannon object.

7.4.4 Retrieving the Color of the *Cannon* Object

Adding a property to a class is actually quite similar to adding a method, but a property has a slightly different header and body. In the header of a property, we need to indicate what the type is of the data that the property accesses. We also have to provide a name, just like with a method. For accessing the color of a Cannon object, we need a property of type Color, and we will call this property Color. Although the name of the property happens to be the same as its type, this is not a problem for the compiler. Similarly, the property GraphicsDevice from the Game class also carries the name of the type of data that it controls (which is an object of type GraphicsDevice). Generally, it is better to choose another name for the property, but in some cases it makes sense, especially when the object involved only has *one* thing of that type. In these examples, a game will have only one graphics device, and a cannon will have only one color at a time. The header of the Color property is given as follows:

public Color Color

An important difference between methods and properties, is that properties can consist of a **get** part and a **set** part. The **get** part contains the instructions to retrieve the data, and the **set** part contains the instructions for modifying the data. Not every property contains both a **get** and a **set** part. If a property only contains a **get** part, it is called a *read-only* property, meaning that we cannot use the property to *modify* the data, only *read* it.

The **get** part of a property is indicated by the keyword **get**, followed by a sequence of instructions placed between braces. Just as for a method that has a return value, we use the **return** keyword to indicate what value the property should return. In this case, we want to return the data contained in the member variable color. So, the Color property is given as follows:

```
public Color Color
{
    get { return color; }
}
```

We can now use this property to access the color of the cannon. For example, we can store it in a variable, like this:

```
Color cannonColor = cannon.Color;
```

We also want to be able to assign a value to the cannon color. For that, we have to define the **set** part of the property. In that part, we need to modify the value of the color variable. This value is provided when the property is used in another method. For example, it could be an instruction like this:

cannon.Color = Color.Red;

So how do we access the right-hand side of this assignment in the property? This is done with the **value** keyword. Therefore, we can write down the **set** part of this property as follows:

set { color = **value**; }

But when we set the color of the cannon, we also have to change the current color indicator sprite. For that, we have to first check what the new color is, and based on that we change the currentColor variable. So, the complete Color property is then given as follows:

```
public Color Color
{
    get { return color; }
    set
    {
        color = value;
        if (color == Color.Red)
            currentColor = colorRed;
        else if (color == Color.Green)
            currentColor = colorGreen;
        else if (color == Color.Blue)
            currentColor = colorBlue;
    }
}
```

Now, suppose that someone would use the class, and do the following:

cannon.Color = Color.Black;

What would happen? Not much actually. Because of the conditions in the **if** instruction, the currentColor variable would not change. But the color variable would contain the value Color.Black. So, the cannon object will now be *inconsistent*. Although this will not lead to immediate problems in this case, it is better to avoid these kinds of inconsistency. But what stops other users of the Cannon class from assigning incorrect colors? Well, nothing. Of course, you could periodically contact all the programmers in the world that use your Cannon class and verify that they assign the right color to the cannon instances, but that would be a lot of work. A better way would be to program the properties to make sure that the object remains consistent. For example, we can make a more secure version of the Color property by modifying the **set** part as follows:

```
set
{
    if (value != Color.Red && value != Color.Green && value != Color.Blue)
        return;
    color = value;
    if (color == Color.Red)
        currentColor = colorRed;
    else if (color == Color.Green)
        currentColor = colorGreen;
    else if (color == Color.Blue)
        currentColor = colorBlue;
}
```

So if someone would execute the following instruction:

```
cannon.Color = Color.Black;
```

the color would not change. You might wonder why this is useful. After all, you are the one writing the instructions that use this class, right? That is true in this case, but if you plan to work in a team with other developers later on (which is quite normal in the game industry), then the developers that use your classes may do things that they are not supposed to do. By building these kinds of security into your classes, you know for certain that the cannon will never be any other color than red, green, or blue. The problem in this case is that there is no way to warn the other developers that they are not supposed to use any other colors. There are several ways to solve this: you can either document the conditions in the software documentation, but there is also another way, which depends on a coding mechanism called *exception handling*. For now it is too early to get into that topic, but later on in this book, we are going to see how this is done.

   Now that we have this Color property, we can use it in the HandleInput method to manipulate the current color of the cannon object:

```
if (currentKeyboardState.IsKeyDown(Keys.R) &&
        previousKeyboardState.IsKeyUp(Keys.R))
    cannon.Color = Color.Red;
else if (currentKeyboardState.IsKeyDown(Keys.G) &&
        previousKeyboardState.IsKeyUp(Keys.G))
    cannon.Color = Color.Green;
else if (currentKeyboardState.IsKeyDown(Keys.B) &&
        previousKeyboardState.IsKeyUp(Keys.B))
    cannon.Color = Color.Blue;
```

7.4.5 Adding More Properties

Now that we are at it, we could add a few more properties to the Cannon class to access other data members. For example, we also want to be able to modify the angle of the cannon barrel. Let us add another property for doing that to the Cannon class. This property also has a get and a set part, and we define it as follows:

```
public float Angle
{
    get { return angle; }
    set { angle = value; }
}
```

As an exercise, can you make a more secure version of this property, which only allows angle values between 0 and 2π radians? In the HandleInput method, we use this property to update the angle of the cannon:

```
cannon.Angle = (float)Math.Atan2(opposite, adjacent);
```

For fun, we will do another one. Let us add a read-only property to the Cannon class for accessing the position of the cannon:

```
public Vector2 Position
{
    get { return position; }
}
```

Since this property only has a **get** part, we cannot modify the data through this property. For example, the following instruction would result in a compiler error (try it):

```
cannon.Position = Vector2.Zero;
```

As you can see, adding properties to a class is very easy! And they provide a great means to control how data inside an object is changed from the outside. As an exercise, can you add a property to the Cannon class that allows reading the cannon barrel sprite? How about writing it? Can you also add a property to the Painter class that gives access to the spriteBatch object?

7.4.6 Properties Do Not Always Directly Correspond to Data

The properties that we added to the cannon class correspond directly to member variables: they get and set the values of the position, color, and angle variables. However, there is no particular restriction on properties that they can only directly correspond to member variable values. A property may also use one or more member variables to calculate a *new* value. For example, we could add a property called Bottom, which calculates the bottom of the cannon barrel. This (read-only!) property would return a **float** value, which is computed every time the property is called. The header and body of this property would be given as follows:

```
public float Bottom
{
    get { return position.Y + barrelOrigin.Y; }
}
```

As you can see, this property uses the position and barrelOrigin member variables to calculate the **float** value. Of course, another option would be to add an extra member variable to the Cannon class called bottom and compute it only once, in the constructor. The advantage of calculating the bottom of the game object in the property itself instead of doing it in the constructor of the class is that it makes for less redundant data in our class. We only store the position of the object and the height of the cannon barrel sprite once, in the cannonBarrel object and the position variable. The counter side of this argument is that recomputing the bottom every time the property is accessed will make our code less efficient. This is a *design choice* that you have to make as a developer. There are many ways to design classes and their member variables, methods and properties, and it is important to realize what your goals are and who is going to use the class. Unfortunately, there is no 'perfect' design that caters for all possible needs. Make your design choices carefully, be aware of them, and make sure that everyone who uses your classes knows which design choices you made and how they impact the use of your class.

7.5 Reorganizing the Class Structure

7.5.1 A Class for Handling Input

Now that we have seen how to create our own class, let us think about the class structure of our program. In the Painter3 project, we have two classes: the Painter class that handles initializing the graphics device, loading sprites, and so on, and the Cannon class for representing the cannon game object. Not only game objects are suitable to put in a separate class. Also, other parts of the program could be grouped together in a class, making the total program easier to read. In the Painter4 example, we have added two classes to the program: the GameWorld class and the InputHelper class. We have added the GameWorld class to make a clear separation between things that need to be done for running an XNA game (initializing the graphics device, creating the sprite batch, running the game, and so on) and the structure and behavior of the actual game world (consisting of a number of game objects such as a cannon, a ball and three paint cans).

The goal of the InputHelper class is to make dealing with input somewhat easier. Up until now, if we wanted to check if a player pressed a key, we needed to store the previous and current keyboard state and use a fairly complicated **if**-instruction. For example:

```
if (currentKeyboardState.IsKeyDown(Keys.R) &&
    previousKeyboardState.IsKeyUp(Keys.R))
    cannon.Color = Color.Red;
else if (currentKeyboardState.IsKeyDown(Keys.G) &&
        previousKeyboardState.IsKeyUp(Keys.G))
    cannon.Color = Color.Green;
else if (currentKeyboardState.IsKeyDown(Keys.B) &&
        previousKeyboardState.IsKeyUp(Keys.B))
    cannon.Color = Color.Blue;
```

The same kind of thing happens for checking a mouse button press. In order to make input handling a bit easier, we are going to create a *helper class* (called InputHelper) that will provide us with a few simple, but very useful methods and properties. We can then use this class to make input handling in the game a lot easier. This helper class will have two tasks:

1. maintain the previous and current mouse and keyboard states, and
2. provide methods and properties that allow for easy access of mouse and keyboard information.

Once we have written this helper class, we can make an instance of it in our game and use it in our HandleInput method. The InputHelper class needs to store the current and previous keyboard and mouse state, so we at least need the following member variables:

```
MouseState currentMouseState, previousMouseState;
KeyboardState currentKeyboardState, previousKeyboardState;
```

Also, these states need to be updated at the beginning of every update. We therefore add an Update method to this class that copies the last 'current' mouse and keyboard state to the previous state and that retrieves the current state:

```
public void Update()
{
    previousMouseState = currentMouseState;
    previousKeyboardState = currentKeyboardState;
    currentMouseState = Mouse.GetState();
    currentKeyboardState = Keyboard.GetState();
}
```

In the Painter class, we create an instance of the InputHelper class in the constructor that we store as a member variable:

```
inputHelper = new InputHelper();
```

This inputHelper object is updated in the first instruction of the Update method of the Painter class:

```
inputHelper.Update();
```

Now that the inputHelper object is created and updated, we can add a few convenient methods and properties to encode some behavior and to access the data contained in the input helper object. A very convenient method is one that checks if a particular key has been pressed. This method returns a boolean value (**true** or **false**) indicating whether the key has been pressed. The key that needs to be checked is passed as a parameter. This method is given as follows:

```
public bool KeyPressed(Keys k)
{
    return currentKeyboardState.IsKeyDown(k) && previousKeyboardState.IsKeyUp(k);
}
```

As you can see, it does not do much, except check a condition that the given key is currently down, while it was not down in the previous state. Now that we have this method, our **if**-instruction for checking if the player presses the R, G, or B key becomes much simpler:

```
if (inputHelper.KeyPressed(Keys.R))
    color = Color.Red;
else if (inputHelper.KeyPressed(Keys.G))
    color = Color.Green;
else if (inputHelper.KeyPressed(Keys.B))
    color = Color.Blue;
```

A similar thing can be done for checking if the player clicked the left mouse button. We call this method MouseLeftButtonPressed. This method does not need any parameters, and it also returns a value of type **bool**. The complete method is given as follows:

```
public bool MouseLeftButtonPressed()
{
    return currentMouseState.LeftButton == ButtonState.Pressed
        && previousMouseState.LeftButton == ButtonState.Released;
}
```

Finally, we add a property MousePosition that gives us a Vector2 containing the current mouse position. Since this is a read-only property, we only need to write a **get** part:

```
public Vector2 MousePosition
{
    get { return new Vector2(currentMouseState.X, currentMouseState.Y); }
}
```

So, now we have a simple InputHelper class that updates the mouse and keyboard states and that provides a few convenient methods and properties for accessing the information. Note that this class is far from ready to be used in any complicated game. You can imagine adding a lot of useful things to this class such as handling dragging and dropping, selecting, handling special key combinations such as Shift-F7, and even managing other input devices such as a multi-touch screen or a gamepad. However, for the Painter game, the current version is sufficient. In the remaining chapters of this book, we will keep using and improving this class.

If you look at the file containing the class definition, you will see that the InputHelper class does not contain a constructor. So what happens when we create the object as follows?

```
inputHelper = new InputHelper();
```

The compiler does not generate an error complaining that it cannot construct the object because there is no constructor. The reason is that there actually *is* a constructor: the *default constructor*. Whenever you define a class and you do not provide a constructor, the compiler adds a default, empty constructor:

```
public InputHelper()
{
}
```

The default constructor is an empty constructor method that does not take any parameters and that does not contain any instructions.

7.5.2 The GameWorld Class

The goal of the GameWorld class is to manage all the game objects. Managing a game object means: creating it, updating it, and drawing it. Currently, the game world is quite basic. It only consists of a background sprite, and a cannon.

Next to the game objects, what else could we say is part of the game world? One part of the game world is its border. In the case of this game, the border is determined by the width and height of the playing screen. The background image is also part of the game world. Therefore, we will declare in any case the following member variables:

```
Texture2D background;
Cannon cannon;
```

Now we need to manage the game objects that are inside this game world. The first step is creating the objects. Like in any class, this is done in the constructor method. One of these game objects is the cannon. In order to create a Cannon instance, we need to pass along the content manager to the constructor. But since we are in the GameWorld constructor, and not in the Painter class, we need to get access to the content manager by using a parameter, just like we did with the Cannon class. We, therefore, pass the content manager as a parameter to the GameWorld constructor.

The header of the constructor then becomes

public GameWorld(ContentManager Content)

In the Painter class, we then define a member variable gameWorld that will contain an instance of the GameWorld class. In the Painter program, there will only be a single game world. And we will be accessing that instance later on in many other classes. Let us therefore find a way to easily access this instance. One thing that we can do is to make it static. That way, we will not need an actual Game object to access the game world instance. This leaves us with only a few member variables in the Painter class:

```
GraphicsDeviceManager graphics;
SpriteBatch spriteBatch;
InputHelper inputHelper;
static GameWorld gameWorld;
```

The graphics variable contains the graphics device manager as usual, there is a spriteBatch variable that is used for drawing sprites, the inputHelper object gives a few convenient methods and properties for player input handling, and the gameWorld variable contains the game world. This variable is assigned a value in the LoadContent method of the Painter3 class. This cannot be done earlier since the GameWorld object needs to load sprites. This assignment is given as follows:

gameWorld = **new** GameWorld(Content);

Then, we can add a *static property* to the Painter class to access this game world. This property is given as follows:

```
public static GameWorld GameWorld
{
    get { return gameWorld; }
}
```

Now, whenever we want to access the game world, we can get it with the expression Painter.GameWorld. We do not need an actual object. This is very useful, because the GameWorld object is going to provide the means for game objects to *interact with each other*, as we will see in later chapters.

7.5.3 Managing the Game Objects

There are basically three things that the gameWorld object should do to manage the game objects: make sure that the game objects handle player input, make sure that they are updated, and finally draw them on the screen. For now, the only game objects are the background, and the cannon. Both of these objects need to be drawn, but they do not need to be updated in this example. However, for the Cannon object, we need to handle some player input. Since this is a task relevant only for the cannon, let us add a HandleInput method to the Cannon class that handles any input relevant for a cannon object. In order to be able to handle input, the cannon object needs the instance of the InputHelper class. So, we pass this as a parameter. Then, inside the HandleInput method, we check if the player has pressed the R, G, or B key and we update the color and angle of the cannon:

```
public void HandleInput(InputHelper inputHelper)
{
    if (inputHelper.KeyPressed(Keys.R))
        Color = Color.Red;
    else if (inputHelper.KeyPressed(Keys.G))
        Color = Color.Green;
    else if (inputHelper.KeyPressed(Keys.B))
        Color = Color.Blue;
    double opposite = inputHelper.MousePosition.Y − position.Y;
    double adjacent = inputHelper.MousePosition.X − position.X;
    angle = (float)Math.Atan2(opposite, adjacent);
}
```

For handling input in the game world, we add a HandleInput method to the GameWorld class. This method basically tells all the game objects to handle their input using the inputHelper object, therefore this method also has a parameter for passing this object. Since the only game object that deals with player input is the cannon, we only need to call that object's HandleInput method. This is what the HandleInput method in the GameWorld class looks like:

```
public void HandleInput(InputHelper inputHelper)
{
    cannon.HandleInput(inputHelper);
}
```

In a very similar way, we may need to update all the game objects. For that, we add an Update method to the GameWorld class. Since there are no objects yet to update, we leave this method empty for now.

Both the HandleInput and Update methods in the GameWorld class are called from the Update method in the Painter class. So, including updating the inputHelper object, there are in total three instructions in the Painter.Update method:

```
inputHelper.Update();
gameWorld.HandleInput(inputHelper);
gameWorld.Update(gameTime);
```

As you can see, because the game objects themselves deal with their own behavior, the task of the GameWorld object becomes very easy. The same goes for drawing the game objects. We add a Draw method to the GameWorld class, which is called from the Painter class, where we pass a sprite batch as a parameter. The Draw method in the Painter class then contains only a few instructions:

```
protected override void Draw(GameTime gameTime)
{
    GraphicsDevice.Clear(Color.White);
    gameWorld.Draw(gameTime, spriteBatch);
}
```

The Draw method in the GameWorld class then basically asks all the game objects to draw themselves. Before drawing the game objects, the background sprite is drawn. So, the instructions in the Draw method are:

```
spriteBatch.Begin();
spriteBatch.Draw(background, Vector2.Zero, Color.White);
cannon.Draw(gameTime, spriteBatch);
spriteBatch.End();
```

You may think it is overkill to define a separate GameWorld class for these few tasks. We could choose to leave them in the Painter class. Again, this is a design choice. Why did we do this? One reason is because it separates the handling of the actual game objects from generic game management such as initializing the graphics device and creating a sprite batch. This is a good thing, because later on in this book, both tasks are going to become more complicated. There will be extra game management code (for example for going to full screen mode and back), and the later game examples will have many more game objects.

> **Use static objects sparingly**—Making the gameWorld object static is another design choice that makes it easier to access the object in different classes later on. If we did not declare the object as static, we would have to pass it as a parameter to every method that would need it. This would needlessly complicate the way that the other classes are designed, because it would introduce an extra parameter in all of these methods. So, why not make every variable static then? We would not need parameters at all! This is not a good idea. By making every variable static, we create the impression that we will only ever need a single instance of that type. As a result, you are basically ignoring half of the power that object-oriented programming offers. Actually, you can use the fact that an object is not always easily accessible to your advantage. For instance, we have chosen not to make the inputHelper object static, but pass it along as a parameter to the HandleInput methods. By doing that, we enforce a

software design where input handling *has to be done* in the HandleInput method and not elsewhere, because that is the only place where there is access to the inputHelper object. Of course, there are ways around it, but the programmer has to do extra work for that. Similarly, the spriteBatch object is only available in the Draw method. We do not want the programmer to draw things on the screen in the Update method: it is not intended for that by design.

Define variables as static sparingly. They can be useful if it is an variable containing an object that is accessed from many different places and it is completely logical that there is only a single instance of that object in your program. In all other cases, do not define a variable as static.

7.6 Objects and Types

7.6.1 Copy by Value or by Reference

Before we finish this chapter, let us have a look at how objects and variables are actually dealt with in memory. When dealing with basic types such as **int** or **float**, the variables are directly associated with a place in memory. For example, look at the following instructions:

int i = 12;

After this instruction has been executed, the memory will look like this:

$$i \quad \boxed{12}$$

Now, we can create a new variable j, and store the value of variable i in that variable:

int j = i;

The memory now looks like this:

If we assign another value to the j variable, for example by executing the instruction j = 24, this is what happens in memory:

Now let us have a look at what happens when we use variables of a more complicated type, such as the Cannon class. Look at the following code:

```
Cannon cannon1;
cannon1 = new Cannon(cannonSprite);
Cannon cannon2 = cannon1;
```

Looking at the example using the **int** type, you would expect that there are now two cannon objects in the memory: one stored in the variable cannon1, and one stored in cannon2. However, this is not the case! Actually, both cannon1 and cannon2 *refer to the same object*. After the first instruction (creating the Cannon object), the memory looks like this:

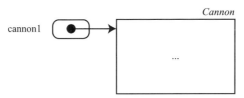

Here, you see that there is a big difference between how a basic type such as **int** or **float** is represented in memory and more complicated types such as the Cannon class. In C#, all objects of a class type are stored as *references* as opposed to values. This means that a variable such as cannon1 does not directly contain the Cannon object, but it contains a reference to it. If we now declare the cannon2 variable and we assign the value of cannon1 to it, the memory looks like this:

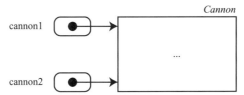

The result is that if we would change the color of the cannon as follows:

```
cannon2.Color = Color.Red;
```

then the expression cannon1.Color would be Color.Red, since both cannon1 and cannon2 refer to the same object! This also has an effect on how objects are passed around in methods. For example, in the Draw method of the Cannon class, we pass a SpriteBatch object as a parameter. Because SpriteBatch is a class, we pass this parameter as a *reference*. The result of this is that we can *change* the SpriteBatch object in our method (for example, by drawing in it). Passing basic types such as **float** as parameters to method happens *by value*, so changing the value inside the method has no effect. Consider the following method:

```
void Square(float f)
{
    f = f * f;
}
```

And now the following instructions:

```
float someNumber = 10.0f;
Square(someNumber);
```

After executing these instructions the value of someNumber still is 10.0f (and not 100.0f). Why is this? It is because when the Square method is called, the **float** parameter is passed *by value*. The variable f is a local variable inside the method that initially contains the value of the someNumber variable. Inside the method, the local variable f is changed to contain f * f, but this does not change the someNumber variable, because it is another location in memory. Because class objects are passed by *reference*, the following example will change the object's color:

```
void ChangeColor(Cannon cannon)
{
    cannon.Color = Color.Red;
}
...
Cannon cannon1 = new Cannon(cannonSprite);
ChangeColor(cannon1);
// The object referred to by cannon1 now has a red color.
```

7.6.2 The null Keyword

So if variables whose type is a class contain references to objects, instead of direct values, what happens when we declare a variable of that type? Suppose that we declare a member variable of type Cannon:

```
Cannon anotherCannon;
```

At this point, we have not yet created an object (using the **new** keyword) that this variable points to. So what does the memory look like? It looks like this:

anotherCannon   (null)

The variable is not yet pointing to anything. We indicate this with the keyword **null**. It is even possible to check in a C# program whether a variable is pointing to an object or not, like this:

```
if (anotherCannon == null)
    anotherCannon = new Cannon(cannonSprite);
```

In this example, we check if the variable is equal to **null** (not pointing to an object). If so, we create a Cannon instance using the **new** keyword. After that, the memory looks like this:

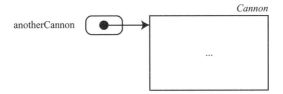

7.6.3 Different Kinds of Object Types

We have seen that a class is used as a blueprint for creating objects. Also, a big difference between primitive types and classes is that variables of a primitive type are passed by value, whereas variables of a class type are passed by reference. Next to the class for creating objects, C# also knows another object type called a **struct**. As opposed to classes, structs are also passed by value, just like the primitive types. Structs are generally used for more basic kinds of objects. You have already used struct objects without knowing it. For example, the Vector2 type is a struct, as is the Color type. Consider the following declaration:

Vector2 position;

After this declaration, the memory looks something like this:

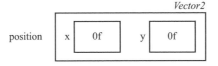

Generally, classes can be quite complicated when represented in memory. They can contain variables of other class, struct or primitive types. Any of these types may in turn consist of other variables, and so on.

Figure 7.3 shows an impression of what the memory could look like when we create a new instance of a Cannon object. You can see the different kinds of objects that are in a Cannon instance. The Vector2 objects are structs, and therefore they are part of the Cannon instance. Texture2D is a class, so the Cannon instance contains *references* to Texture2D objects. In some cases, the references point to the same object as is the case with colorBlue and currentColor. When you create your classes, it can sometimes be helpful to draw these kinds of diagrams to get a feeling of which object belongs where and at which places references to these objects are stored.

7.7 What You Have Learned

In this chapter, you have learned:

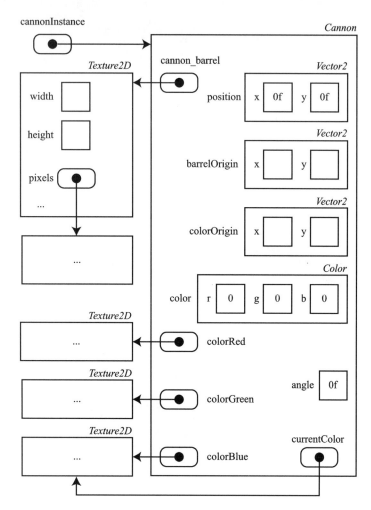

Fig. 7.3 An impression of the memory structure of a Cannon instance

- how to organize instructions in different methods and classes;
- how to write your own methods and properties;
- what the difference is between values and references and what the **null** keyword means in that context;
- what the difference is between a class and a struct.

Chapter 8
Adding Interaction

8.1 Introduction

In the previous chapter, we laid out the basic class structure for the Painter game. We have defined a simple input helper class and a class for representing the game world. We have already filled part of that game world by adding a background image, a cannon, and doing some basic input handling for changing the color of the cannon and rotating the cannon barrel. In this chapter, we will add the other game objects (the ball and the paint cans) to the program and look into how they interact with each other. For each different kind of game object, we will add a class to the program.

8.2 The Ball Class

8.2.1 Structure of the Class

We will setup the Ball class in a very similar fashion as the Cannon class. In the program Painter5, you will see a version of the Painter game where we added a ball to the game world. The ball can be shot from the cannon by clicking anywhere in the game screen. Furthermore, the ball changes color together with the cannon. Just like the Cannon class, the Ball class will also contain a few Texture2D objects to contain the sprite in the three different colors, a sprite pointing to the current sprite that we want to draw, a color, and a position. However, since the ball moves, we also need to store its *velocity*. This velocity is a vector that defines how the position of the ball changes over time. For example, if the ball has a velocity of $(0, 1)$ then every second, the y-position of the ball will have increased with 1 pixel (meaning that the ball will fall down). Finally, the ball can be in two states: it is either flying through the air because it was shot from the cannon, or it is waiting to be shot (so it is not moving). For that, we add an extra boolean

A. Egges et al., *Learning C# by Programming Games*,
DOI 10.1007/978-3-642-36580-5_8, © Springer-Verlag Berlin Heidelberg 2013

member variable shooting. In total, the Ball class will have the following member variables:

```
Texture2D colorRed, colorGreen, colorBlue;
Texture2D currentColor;
Vector2 position, velocity;
Color color;
bool shooting;
```

In the games that we develop in this book, most of the objects will have a position and a velocity. Since we only concern ourselves with 2D games, both the position and the velocity will always be of type Vector2. When we update these game objects, we need to calculate the new position based on the velocity vector and the time that has passed. Later on, we will see how we can do that using the parameter gameTime that is passed to the Update method of the game object.

8.2.2 Initializing the Ball

In the constructor method of the Ball class, we have to assign values to the member variables, just as in the case of the Cannon class. We pass the content manager as a parameter, so that we can load the required sprites in the constructor. Then, we assign values to the other member variables. When the game starts, the ball should not be moving. Therefore, we set the velocity of the ball to zero (Vector2.Zero). Also, we initially set the ball to a position so that it is hidden behind the cannon. That way, when the ball is not moving, we do not see it. Of course, we have to make sure that the ball is drawn before the cannon in that case. We initially set the color of the ball to blue (Color.Blue), and we set the shooting member variable to **false**. The complete constructor then becomes

```
public Ball(ContentManager Content)
{
    this.colorRed = Content.Load<Texture2D>("spr_ball_red");
    this.colorGreen = Content.Load<Texture2D>("spr_ball_green");
    this.colorBlue = Content.Load<Texture2D>("spr_ball_blue");
    position = new Vector2(65, 390);
    velocity = Vector2.Zero;
    shooting = false;
    Color = Color.Blue;
}
```

As you can see in the last instruction of the constructor, we use the Color property. We added this property to the Ball class so that we can retrieve and change the color of the ball. And just like the Cannon class, we added a Reset method so that we can reset the ball to its initial state. Have a look at the source code in the Painter5 program to see the complete Ball class.

Inside the GameWorld class, we store a member variable of the type Ball:

Ball ball;

And in the GameWorld constructor method, we create an instance of the Ball class:

ball = **new** Ball(Content);

8.2.3 Shooting the Ball

The player can click the left mouse button in the game screen to shoot a ball of
paint. The speed of the ball and the direction in which it is moving is determined
by the position where the player clicks. The ball should move in the direction of
that position, and the further away a player clicks from the cannon, the higher the
speed of the ball will be. In order to handle input, we add a HandleInput method to
the Ball class. Inside this method, we can check whether the player clicks with the
left button by using the input helper:

if (inputHelper.MouseLeftButtonPressed())
    do something...

However, since there can only be a single ball in the air at any moment, we only
want to do something if the ball is not already in the air. This means that we have to
check what the shooting status of the ball is. If the ball is already shooting, we do
not have to handle the mouse click. So, we extend our **if**-instruction with an extra
condition that the ball currently is not shooting as follows:

if (inputHelper.MouseLeftButtonPressed() && !shooting)
    do something...

As you can see, we are using several logical operators (&& and !) in conjunction here.
Because of the logical 'not' (!) operator, the entire condition in the **if**-instruction
will only evaluate to **true** if the shooting variable has the value **false**, or: the ball is
currently not shooting.

Inside the **if**-instruction, we need to do a couple of things. We know that the
player has clicked somewhere and that the ball has to be shot from the cannon. The
first thing that we need to do is set the variable shooting to the correct value, because
the status of the ball will need to be changed to 'currently shooting':

shooting = **true**;

In the Reset method, we have already given the ball an initial position. What we now
need to do is give the ball a *velocity*. This velocity will be a vector in the direction of
the place where the player has clicked. We can calculate this direction by subtracting
the ball position from the mouse position. For this, we will use the handy property

MousePosition from the InputHelper class:

velocity = inputHelper.MousePosition − position;

By calculating the velocity in this way, we will also have the desired effect that when we click further away from the cannon, the velocity will be bigger, because then the difference between the mouse position and the ball position will also be bigger. However, if we were to play the game now, the ball would move a bit slowly. Therefore, we multiply this velocity with a constant value that gives the ball a velocity that is usable in the context of this game:

velocity = (inputHelper.MousePosition − position) ∗ 1.2f;

The constant value of 1.2 is chosen after testing the gameplay with different values. Each game will have a number of these *gameplay parameters* that will need to be tweaked while play-testing the game to determine their optimal value. Finding the right values for these parameters is crucial for a balanced game that plays well, and you need to make sure that the values that you choose for these parameters do not make the game overly easy or difficult. For example, if we would choose a constant value of 0.3 instead of 1.2, the ball would move much slower. This would make the game much more difficult, and it might even make the game unplayable because the ball might never be able to reach the furthest can.

   If we add the HandleInput method, it will not automatically be called. We need to do that explicitly in the GameWorld class. Therefore, we add an extra instruction to the HandleInput method of that class:

```
public void HandleInput(InputHelper inputHelper)
{
    cannon.HandleInput(inputHelper);
    ball.HandleInput(inputHelper);
}
```

8.2.4 Updating the Ball

A big advantage of grouping related member variables and behavior together in classes is that we can keep each class relatively small and clear. We have chosen to design a class structure that more or less reflects the various kinds of game objects in the game. In our case, we have a class for the cannon, as well as a class for the ball. Our goal is that each of these game objects deals with player input relevant for that object. We also want the game objects to update and draw themselves. Therefore, we add an Update method and a Draw method to the Ball class, so that we can call this method from the GameWorld class.

   Inside the Update method of the ball, we need to define what the behavior of the ball is. The ball behavior is different depending on whether it is currently shooting or not. This is the complete method:

```
public void Update(GameTime gameTime)
{
    if (shooting)
    {
        velocity.X *= 0.99f;
        velocity.Y += 6;
        position += velocity * (float)gameTime.ElapsedGameTime.TotalSeconds;
    }
    else
    {
        Color = Painter.GameWorld.Cannon.Color;
        position = Painter.GameWorld.Cannon.BallPosition − Center;
    }
    if (Painter.GameWorld.IsOutsideWorld(position))
        Reset();
}
```

As you can see in the header of the Update method, it has one parameter: the game time. Having the current time is very useful in many games. In this case we are going to use the passed time to calculate what the new position of the ball should be.

Looking at the body of the method, we can see that the first part consists of an if-instruction. The condition of the if is that the shooting member variable should have the value **true**. So, if the ball is currently shooting, then the body of the if-instruction will be executed. This body again consists of three instructions. The first two instructions update the velocity, the last one updates the position. The first instruction updates the x direction of the velocity. We multiply the velocity with a value of 0.99, the effect of which is that the velocity slowly decreases. This is done to simulate air friction. The second instruction slightly increases the y velocity in each update. This is done to simulate the effect that *gravity* will have on the ball. Together, the velocity changes in the x and y direction result in plausible ball behavior. Finally, the current position of the ball is updated by adding the velocity to it.

Of course, in the real world, the gravity is not 6 and the same goes for the air friction. But then again, our real world does not consist of pixels either. Physics in game worlds does not always accurately represent physics in the real world. When you want to incorporate some form of physics in your game (be it very simple or extremely complex), the most important part is not that the physics is realistic, but that the *game is playable*. These parameters have a huge influence on the gameplay. Try, for example, to give them different values and see what happens. You will note soon that the range of values that produce a game that is playable is not very big.

The next line is very important:

```
position += velocity * (float)gameTime.ElapsedGameTime.TotalSeconds;
```

Here, we calculate the new position of the ball based on the velocity and the time that has passed since the last update. We access the time that was passed through the ElapsedGameTime property, which gives us the time that was elapsed since the last update. This property is found in the GameTime type, and it gives us an object of type TimeSpan. The TimeSpan type has a property called TotalSeconds which gives us a **double** representing the total time span in seconds. Because the velocity is of type Vector2, and Vector2 contains **float** members, we need to cast this **double** value to a **float** value. Then, we multiply the velocity by this amount, and we add the outcome to the current position. Now, if for some reason the last update took a bit longer than expected, the ball will still have the correct position. Taking the elapsed time into account is really important. Some older games did not do this and simply updated the position of an object with a constant velocity factor. As a result, when computers became faster, these games became more and more difficult to play! Players do not like this. Therefore: always take the elapsed time into account when calculating things like velocities or positions.

If the ball is not currently shooting, we are allowed to change the color of the ball. In this case, we do that by simply copying the color of the cannon to the color of the ball. That way, we are sure that the color of the ball always matches the color of the cannon. We can access the color value through the Cannon property of the GameWorld object. We have access to the GameWorld object through the static GameWorld property that we added to the Painter class. Here, you can see that the game world serves as a basic means for objects to interact with each other. In the case of the ball, the color of the cannon needs to be retrieved so that the ball has the same color. Furthermore, we also update the position of the ball, as follows:

```
position = Painter.GameWorld.Cannon.BallPosition − Center;
```

Why do we change the position? When the ball is not shooting, the player can modify the shooting position of the ball by rotating the barrel of the cannon. Therefore, we need to calculate the correct ball position here, to ensure that it matches the current orientation of the cannon barrel. Also, since the ball is drawn behind the cannon we need to update its position so that it stays behind the cannon after its barrel is rotated. In order to do this, we add a new property called BallPosition to the Cannon class, in which we calculate the position of the ball based on the barrel orientation. Using the sine and cosine functions, we calculate the new position as follows:

```
public Vector2 BallPosition
{
    get
    {
        float opposite = (float)Math.Sin(angle) ∗ cannonBarrel.Width ∗ 0.5f;
        float adjacent = (float)Math.Cos(angle) ∗ cannonBarrel.Width ∗ 0.5f;
        return position + new Vector2(adjacent, opposite);
    }
}
```

As you can see, we multiply the opposite and adjacent sides with a value of 0.5 so that the ball is drawn halfway up the rotated barrel.

The second part of the Update method also is an **if**-instruction:

```
if (Painter.GameWorld.IsOutsideWorld(position))
    Reset();
```

This part of the method deals with the event that occurs when the ball goes outside of the game world. In order to calculate if this is true, we added a method called IsOutsideWorld to the GameWorld class. The goal of this method is to check if a given position is outside of the game world. We define the boundaries of the game world by a few simple rules. Remember that the top left of the screen is the origin. An object is outside the game world if its x-position is smaller than zero, or larger than the width of the screen. An object is also outside the game world if its y-position is larger than the height of the screen. Note that we do not say that an object is outside of the world if its y-position is smaller than zero. Why not? We chose to do this so that it is possible for a player to shoot a ball in the air and let the ball be momentarily above the screen before falling down again. Often, you see a similar effect in platform games, where a character can jump up to disappear partly outside of the screen, as opposed to falling through the bottom of the screen which generally means instant death of the character.

If you look at the header of this method, you see that it has a return value of type **bool**:

```
public bool IsOutsideWorld(Vector2 position)
```

Furthermore, this method has one input parameter of type Vector2 which indicates the position that needs to be checked.

If we want to check if a position is outside of the screen, we need to know the width and height of the screen. Unfortunately, this information is only available in the Painter class, since that class inherits from the Game class and it has a graphics device which can provide that kind of information. Passing along the width and height of the screen constantly to all methods that need it is also not really convenient. Since there will most probably only be a single screen width and height, we could decide to store this information in a static Vector2 variable in the Painter class:

```
static Vector2 screen;
```

When the graphics device is created, we assign a value to this vector. For example, this could be done once in the LoadContent method. For retrieving the screen dimensions, we can use the Viewport property of the graphics device, as follows:

```
screen = new Vector2(GraphicsDevice.Viewport.Width,
                     GraphicsDevice.Viewport.Height);
```

And accessing this variable is then done through a static property, just like we did for the game world:

```
public static Vector2 Screen
{
    get { return screen; }
}
```

Now that we have done that preparatory work, we can go back to the IsOutsideWorld method, and use the static Screen property. The body of the method consists of a single instruction using the keyword **return** to calculate a boolean value. The logical 'or' operation is used to cover the different cases in which the position is outside of the game world:

```
return position.X < 0 || position.X > Painter.Screen.X || position.Y > Painter.Screen.Y;
```

As you can see, we do not mind if the y coordinate is smaller than zero. This allows us to have the ball ending up above the screen and falling back in again.

Let us return to the Update method in the Ball class. The second **if**-instruction calls the IsOutsideWorld method in its condition, and if this method returns the value **true**, then the Reset method is executed. Or in simpler terms: if the ball flies out of the screen, it is placed at the cannon, ready to be shot again by the player. Here we see another advantage of grouping instructions in methods: methods such as Reset can be *reused* in different parts of the program, which saves development time and results in shorter, better readable programs.

Finally, in order to call the Update method of the ball, we add an instruction to the (until now empty) GameWorld.Update method:

```
public void Update(GameTime gameTime)
{
    ball.Update(gameTime, this);
}
```

8.2.5 Drawing the Ball on the Screen

Finally, for drawing the ball on the screen, we also add a Draw method. Here, we do not have to do anything in particular, we simply draw the ball sprite in the current color on the screen at the desired position. For the complete example, see the Painter5 program and the other classes in the project.

8.3 The PaintCan Class

8.3.1 A Class with Multiple Instances

In this section, we will add paint cans to our game. We will base this section around the Painter6 example, which adds a PaintCan class. Both the Cannon class and the Ball class were associated with a single instance in the previous version of the Painter game. The game only needs one ball, and one cannon. In the case of the paint cans, we are going to need *three* instances. We will reuse these instances and reset them once they fall out of the bottom of the screen, so we will not need more than three. This also shows a big difference between a *class* and an **object** (instance). A class is a blueprint for an object. This means that one class can have multiple instances. In the PaintCan class, we define what a paint can is and what its behavior is. Then, we can create multiple instances of this class. Inside the GameWorld class, we store these instances in three different member variables:

```
PaintCan can1, can2, can3;
```

Another difference between the PaintCan class and the Ball and Cannon classes is that each paint can has a *target color*. For example, the leftmost can has a red target color. The goal of the game is to make each paint can falling down have its target color before it falls out of the screen. Therefore, we need two member variables of type Color: one for storing the target color, and one for storing the current color. Furthermore, we are going to let the paint cans fall down with a certain velocity. How we are going to set this velocity is something that we will deal with later. In order to calculate that velocity, we want to know what the minimal velocity is that a paint can should have, so that it does not fall down too slowly. For this, we add a member variable minVelocity that contains this value. In total, the PaintCan class will have the following member variables:

```
Texture2D colorRed, colorGreen, colorBlue;
Texture2D currentColor;
Vector2 position, velocity;
Color color, targetcolor;
float minVelocity;
```

In the constructor of the PaintCan class, we assign values to these member variables. The constructor takes three parameters: the content manager (for loading the sprites), the desired position, and the target color of the paint can. Just like in the Ball and Cannon classes, we use the content manager to load the three sprites in the PaintCan constructor. Then, we assign values to the other member variables. Initially, we set the *y* position of the paint can such that it is drawn just outside of the top of the screen, so that later on in the game, we can see it fall down. The complete constructor is then given as follows:

```
public PaintCan(ContentManager Content, float positionOffset, Color targetcol)
{
    this.colorRed = Content.Load<Texture2D>("spr_can_red");
    this.colorGreen = Content.Load<Texture2D>("spr_can_green");
    this.colorBlue = Content.Load<Texture2D>("spr_can_blue");
    targetcolor = targetcol;
    minVelocity = 30;
    Color = Color.Blue;
    position = new Vector2(positionOffset, −currentColor.Height);
    velocity = Vector2.Zero;
}
```

Inside the GameWorld class, we call this constructor three times to create the three PaintCan objects, each with a different x-offset and target color.:

```
can1 = new PaintCan(Content, 450.0f, Color.Red);
can2 = new PaintCan(Content, 575.0f, Color.Green);
can3 = new PaintCan(Content, 700.0f, Color.Blue);
```

Because the paint cans do not handle any input (only the ball and the cannon do this), we do not need a HandleInput method for this class. However, the paint cans do need to be updated. One of the things that we want to do is to have the paint cans fall down at random moments and at random speeds. But how can we do this?

8.3.2 Randomness in Games

One of the most important parts of the paint can behavior is that some aspects of it should be *unpredictable*. We do not want every can falling down at a predictable speed or time. We want to add a factor of *randomness* to it, so that every time the player starts a new game, the game will be different. Of course, we also need to keep this randomness in control. We do not want one can to take three hours to fall from top to bottom while another can takes only 1 millisecond. The speed should be random, but within a *playable range of speeds*.

What does randomness actually mean? Generally, random events or values in games and other applications are managed by a *random number generator*. In object-oriented programming languages like C#, this is often implemented as a class of which we can make an instance. This instance then has methods that generate random numbers according to different parameters. But then you might wonder: how do you actually generate a completely random number? And you may even wonder if randomness exists at all in reality. After all, is not randomness just a manifestation of behavior that we cannot yet fully predict and therefore we call it 'random'? Well, let us not get too philosophical here. In game worlds and in computer programs, we actually *can* predict precisely what is going to happen, because a computer can only do exactly what we tell it to do. Therefore, strictly speaking, a computer is not capable of producing a completely random number. One way to pretend that we can produce random numbers is by picking a number from a predefined, very large table of numbers. Because we are not really producing random numbers, this is called a *pseudo-random number generator*. Most random number generators can generate a number between a range, such as 0 or 1, but they often can also generate an arbitrary number or a number between another range. Each number within the range has an equal chance of being generated as any other number. In statistics, such a distribution is called a *uniform distribution*.

Suppose that when we start the game, we start generating 'random' numbers by walking through the table. Because the number table does not change, it means that every time we play the game, the same sequence of random numbers would be generated. In order to avoid this problem, we can indicate in the beginning that we should start at a *different* position in the table. The position where we start in the table is also called the *seed* of the random number generator. Often, we take a value for the seed that is different every time we start the program, such as the current system time.

So how do we use this random number generator to create randomness in our game world? Suppose that we want to spawn an enemy 75 % of the times that a user steps through a door. In that case, we generate a random number between 0 and 1. If the number is smaller or equal to 0.75, we spawn an enemy, otherwise we do not. Because of the uniform distribution this will lead exactly to the behavior that we require. If we want to calculate a random speed between $\frac{1}{2}$ and 1, we generate a random number between 0 and 1, we divide this number by 2, and we add $\frac{1}{2}$. Let us look how we can incorporate randomness in our Painter game.

In C#, generating a random number is done by using the Random class from the System library. Therefore, in order to use this class, we need an extra **using** instruction:

```
using System;
```

In order to use the random number generator, we need an instance of the Random class. It is likely that this instance needs to be accessed by different classes, and we can also assume that a game only needs one random number generator. Therefore, we again add a static member variable random to the Painter class, together with a static property Random to access it. Have a look at the Painter class in the Painter6 program to see the actual code.

After that, we can access the random object to generate random numbers for us. We can use the method NextDouble from the Random class for that. This method returns a random value of type **double** that is between 0.0 and 1.0.

```
double someRandomNumber = Painter.Random.NextDouble();
```

The variable someRandomNumber now contains a value between 0.0 and 1.0.

8.3.3 Calculating a Random Velocity and Color

Each time a can falls down, we want to create a random velocity and color for it. We can use the random variable to help us do this. Let us first look at creating a random velocity. For neatness, we are going to do this in a separate method inside the PaintCan class called CalculateRandomVelocity. We can then call this method when we want to initialize the velocity of the can. Because we express velocity as an object of type Vector2, the *return value* of this method is of the same type. Here we will use the member variable minVelocity to define the minimum velocity that paint cans have when they fall down. This variable is given an initial value in the constructor method:

```
minVelocity = 30;
```

We use this minimum velocity value when we calculate a random velocity, which we do in the CalculateRandomVelocity method:

```
public Vector2 CalculateRandomVelocity()
{
    return new Vector2(0.0f, (float)Painter.Random.NextDouble() * 30 + minVelocity);
}
```

As you can see, the return type of this method is indeed Vector2. The method contains only a single instruction, which returns a new Vector2 object, with an x-velocity of zero and a y-velocity that is calculated using the random number generator. Because the random number generator creates a value of type **double**, we need to explicitly convert it to a value of type **float** so that we can store it in a Vector2 object. After that, we multiply it by 30 and add the value stored in the member variable minVelocity in order to get a positive y-velocity between minVelocity and minVelocity+30.

For calculating a random color, we also use the random number generator, however we do not use the NextDouble method but the Next method. This method gives an integer value, and we can specify a maximum value or a range of possible values. For example, the call Painter.Random.Next(10) will give a random number between 0 and 9 (so 10 is excluded). By using an **if**-instruction, we can then select a color based on the randomly generated number. This is what the method looks like:

```
public Color CalculateRandomColor()
{
    int randomval = Painter.Random.Next(3);
    if (randomval == 0)
        return Color.Red;
    else if (randomval == 1)
        return Color.Green;
    else
        return Color.Blue;
}
```

The header of the method shows that it returns a value of type Color and that the method has no parameters. The first line in the body of the method generates a random integer that is either 0, 1, or 2. We then check with an **if**-instruction which of these three numbers was selected and we return the associated color.

Now that we have programmed these two methods for generating random values, we are going to use them when we define the behavior of the paint can.

8.3.4 Updating the Paint Can

The Update method in the PaintCan class should do at least the following things:

1. set a randomly created velocity and color if the can is currently not yet falling down,
2. update the can position by adding the velocity to it, and
3. check if the can has fallen down completely and reset it in that case.

For the first task, we can use an **if**-instruction to check if the can is currently not moving, e.g. if the velocity equals zero. Furthermore, we want to introduce a bit of unpredictability for when the can appears. In order to achieve that effect, we only assign a random velocity and color if some generated random number is smaller than a threshold of 0.01. This means that because of the uniform distribution only in approximately one out of a hundred random numbers, the number will be smaller than 0.01. As a result, the body of the **if**-instruction will only be executed sometimes, even when a can's velocity is zero. Inside the body of the **if**-instruction, we use the two methods we defined earlier for generating a random velocity and a random color:

```
if (velocity.Y == 0.0f && Painter.Random.NextDouble() < 0.01)
{
    velocity = CalculateRandomVelocity();
    color = CalculateRandomColor();
}
```

The next step is to update the can position by adding the current velocity to it, again taking into account the elapsed game time:

```
position += velocity * (float)gameTime.ElapsedGameTime.TotalSeconds;;
```

Now that we have initialized the can and updated its position, we need to handle the 'special cases'. For the paint can, we have to check if it has fallen outside of the game world. If so, we need to reset it. The nice thing is that we already wrote a method for checking if a certain position is outside of the world. This was the IsOutsideWorld method in the GameWorld class. We can now use that method again to check if the position of the can is outside of the world. If this is the case, we need to reset the can so that it is placed at the top outside of the screen again. The complete

if-instruction then becomes

```
if (Painter.GameWorld.IsOutsideWorld(position))
                Reset();
```

Finally, in order to make the game a bit more challenging, we slightly increase the minimum velocity that the cans get each time we go through the update loop:

```
minVelocity += 0.001f;
```

Because the minimum velocity is slightly increasing all the time, the game gets more difficult as time progresses.

8.3.5 Drawing the Cans on the Screen

For drawing the paint cans on the screen, we add a Draw method to the PaintCan class. Inside the GameWorld class, we can now call the Update and Draw methods on the different game objects. So, the new Update method contains the following instructions:

```
ball.Update(gameTime);
can1.Update(gameTime);
can2.Update(gameTime);
can3.Update(gameTime);
```

And the GameWorld.Draw method is given as follows:

```
public void Draw(GameTime gameTime, SpriteBatch spriteBatch)
{
    spriteBatch.Begin();
    spriteBatch.Draw(background, Vector2.Zero, Color.White);
    ball.Draw(gameTime, spriteBatch);
    cannon.Draw(gameTime, spriteBatch);
    can1.Draw(gameTime, spriteBatch);
    can2.Draw(gameTime, spriteBatch);
    can3.Draw(gameTime, spriteBatch);
    spriteBatch.End();
}
```

The complete program (Painter6) is available in the example solution belonging to this chapter.

8.4 Handling Collisions Between the Ball and the Cans

In the Painter7 program, we have extended the example by also handling collisions between the ball and the cans. If two objects collide, we have to handle this collision in one of the two object's Update method. In this case, we can choose to handle collisions in the Ball class or in the PaintCan class. We have chosen to handle the collision in the PaintCan class, because if we were to do it in the Ball class, we would need to repeat the same code three times, one for each paint can. By handling collisions in the PaintCan class, we get this behavior automatically, since each can will check for itself if it collides with the ball.

Although collision checking can be done in many different ways, we are going to use a very simple method here. We define that there is a collision between two objects if the distance between their centers is smaller than a certain value. The position of the center of the ball at any time in the game world is computed by adding the center of the ball sprite to the position of the ball. Similarly, the center of the paint can we are currently updating is given by position + Center. Therefore we can calculate a vector expressing the distance as follows:

```
Vector2 distanceVector = (Painter.GameWorld.Ball.Position
                    + Painter.GameWorld.Ball.Center) − (position + Center);
```

Note that not all the parentheses are obligatory (which ones are not?). We wrote them here, so that it is clear what we are doing. Now that we have calculated this vector, we have to check if its length in both the x and y directions is smaller than some given value. If the absolute value of the x component of the distance vector is smaller than the x value of the center, it means that the ball object is within the x range of the can. The same principle holds for the y direction. If this holds for both the x and y components, we can say that the ball collides with the can. We can write an **if**-instruction that checks this condition:

```
if (Math.Abs(distanceVector.X) < Center.X && Math.Abs(distanceVector.Y) < Center.Y)
{
    Handle the collision.
}
```

We use the Math.Abs method to calculate the absolute value. If there is a collision between the ball and the can, we need to change the color of the can to the color of the ball. Next, we have to reset the ball so that it can be shot again. The following two instructions do exactly that:

```
Color = Painter.GameWorld.Ball.Color;
Painter.GameWorld.Ball.Reset();
```

The full Painter7 example is again available in the solution provided with this chapter.

8.5 What You Have Learned

In this chapter, you have learned:

- how to add interaction between different game objects;
- how to add randomness to your game to increase replayability;
- how to handle basic collisions between game objects.

Chapter 9
A Limited Number of Lives

9.1 Introduction

In this chapter, we are going to make the game more interesting by giving the player a limited number of lives. If the player misses too many paint cans, she/he dies. In this chapter, we will discuss how to deal with that, and how to display the current number of lives to the player. In order to do the latter, we introduce a few programming constructs for repeating a group of instructions several times.

9.2 The Number of Lives

9.2.1 Maintaining the Number of Lives

In order to introduce some danger in the game, we would like to limit the number of paint cans in the wrong color that the player can allow to fall through the bottom of the screen. In the Painter8 example, you can see this effect worked out. We set this limit to 5. In order to store this limit, we add an extra member variable to the GameWorld class, as well as a property for modifying it:

```csharp
int lives;

public int Lives
{
    get { return lives; }
    set { lives = value; }
}
```

We initially set this value to 5 in the constructor of the GameWorld class. Now we can update this value whenever a paint can falls outside of the screen. We perform this check in the Update method of the PaintCan class. Therefore, we have to add a

A. Egges et al., *Learning C# by Programming Games*,   141
DOI 10.1007/978-3-642-36580-5_9, © Springer-Verlag Berlin Heidelberg 2013

few instructions in that method to deal with this. The only thing we need to do is check if the color of the paint can is the same as its target color when it falls through the bottom of the screen. If that is the case, we decrement the lives counter in the GameWorld class through the Lives property:

```
if (Painter.GameWorld.IsOutsideWorld(position))
{
    if (color != targetcolor)
        Painter.GameWorld.Lives--;
    Reset();
}
```

As you can see, we use the −− operator here to decrease the number of lives by 1, but we also could have written a longer version as follows (more about that later):

```
Painter.GameWorld.Lives = Painter.GameWorld.Lives − 1;
```

9.2.2 Indicating the Number of Lives to the Player

Obviously, the player would like to know how he/she is doing. So we have to indicate somehow on the screen how many lives the player still has. In the Painter game, we do that by displaying a number of balloons in the left top corner of the screen. Using the knowledge that we have, we could use an if-instruction for that:

```
if (lives == 5)
{
    Draw the balloon sprite 5 times in a row
}
else if (lives == 4)
{
    Draw the balloon sprite 4 times in a row
}
else if (lives == 3)
And so on...
```

This is not a very nice solution. It leads to a lot of code, and we would have to copy the same instruction a lot of times. Fortunately, there is a better solution for that: *iteration*.

9.3 The while-Instruction: Executing Instructions Multiple Times

Iteration in C# is a way to repeat instructions a number of times. Have a look at the following code fragment:

```
int val = 10;
while (val >= 3)
    val = val − 3;
```

The second instruction is called a *while*-loop. This instruction consists of a kind of header (**while** (val >= 3)) and a body (val = val − 3;). The header consists of the word **while** followed by a *condition* between parentheses. The body itself is an instruction. In this case, the instruction subtracts 3 from a variable. However, it could just as well have been another kind of instruction such as a method call or accessing a property. This is the syntax diagram of the **while**-instruction:

When the **while**-instruction is executed, the body is executed multiple times. In fact, as long as the *condition* in the header yields **true**, the body will be executed. In this example, the condition is the val variable contains a value that is at least 3 or higher. In the beginning, the variable contains the value 10, so it is certainly higher than 3. Therefore, the body of the **while**-instruction is executed, and the variable val then contains the value 7. The condition is then evaluated again. The variable still is higher than 3, so the body is executed once more, after which the variable val contains the value 4. Again, the value is higher than 3, so the body is executed again and val will contain the value 1. At that point, the condition is evaluated, but it is no longer **true**. Therefore, the repeating instruction comes to an end. So, after this piece of code is executed, the variable val contains the value 1. In fact what we have programmed here is the integer division operator using the **while**-instruction.

Of course, it is easier to simply use the division operator in this case, but if we want to draw the number of lives of the player on the screen, we can use a **while**-instruction to do this quite efficiently:

```
int i = 0;
while (i < lives)
{
    spriteBatch.Draw(livesSprite, new Vector2(i * livesSprite.Width + 15, 20),
                    Color.White);
    i = i + 1;
}
```

In this **while**-instruction, the body is executed as long as the variable i contains a value smaller than numberOfLives. Every time the body is executed, we draw the sprite on the screen, and then we increment i by 1. The result of this is that we draw the sprite on the screen exactly numberOfLives times! So in fact, we are using the variable i here as a *counter*. As you can see, the body of a **while**-instruction may contain more than a single instruction. If the body contains more than one instruction, the instructions need to be placed between braces, just like with the **if**-instruction.

The position at which we draw the sprites depends on the value of i. This way, we can draw each sprite a bit further to the right, so that they are nicely placed in a row. The first time we execute the body, we draw the sprite at x-position 15, because i is 0. The next iteration, we draw the sprite at x position livesSprite.Width + 15, the iteration after that at 2 * livesSprite.Width + 15, and so on. In this case, we use the counter not only to determine how often we will execute instructions, but also to *change what the instructions do*. This is a very powerful feature of an iteration instruction such as **while**. Because of the looping behavior, a **while**-instruction is also called a **while**-*loop*.

9.3.1 A Shorter Notation for Incrementing Counters

Many **while**-instructions, especially those that use a counter, have a body that contains an instruction for incrementing a variable. This can be done with the instruction:

i = i + 1;

(As a side note, especially because of these kinds of instructions, it is unwise to pronounce the assignment as 'is'. The value of i can of course never be the same as i+1, but the value of i *becomes* the old value of i, plus 1.) These kinds of instructions are very common in programs, therefore a special, shorter notation exists that does exactly the same thing:

i++;

The '++' can be pronounced as 'is incremented'. Because this operator is placed after the variable that it operates on, the '++' operator is called a *postfix operator*. For incrementing a variable with more than 1, there is another notation:

i += 2;

which means the same as

i = i + 2;

9.4 The for-Instruction: A Compact Version of while

Many **while**-instructions use a counting variable, and therefore have the following structure:

```
int i;
i = begin value ;
while (i < end value )
{
    do something useful using i
    i++;
}
```

Because this kind of instruction is quite common, a more compact notation is available for it:

```
int i;
for (i = begin value ; i < end value; i++ )
{
    do something useful using i
}
```

The meaning of this instruction is exactly the same as the earlier **while**-instruction. The advantage of using the **for**-instruction in this case is that everything that has something to do with the counter is nicely grouped together in the header of the instruction. This reduces the chance that you forget the instruction to increment the counter (resulting in an endless loop). In the cases where 'do something useful using i' consists of only a single instruction, you can leave out the braces, which makes the notation even more compact. Also, you can put the declaration of the variable i in the header of the **for**-instruction as well. For example, have a look at the following code fragment:

```
for (int i=0; i < lives; i++)
    spriteBatch.Draw(livesSprite, new Vector2(i * livesSprite.Width + 15, 20),
                    Color.White);
```

This is a very compact instruction that increments the counter and draws the sprite at different positions. This instruction is equivalent to the **while**-instruction:

```
int i = 0;
while (i < numberOfLives)
{
    spriteBatch.Draw(livesSprite, new Vector2(i * livesSprite.Width, 20), Color.White);
    i = i + 1;
}
```

And another example:

```
for (int i = lives − 1; i >= 0; i−−)
    spriteBatch.Draw(livesSprite, new Vector2(i * livesSprite.Width + 15, 20),
                    Color.White);
```

To which **while**-instruction is this **for**-instruction equivalent? For completeness, here is the syntax diagram of the **for**-instruction:

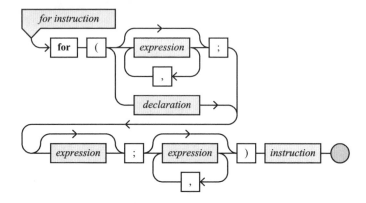

9.5 A Few Special Cases

9.5.1 No Repeat at All

Sometimes, it can happen that the condition in the header of a **while**-instruction is already **false** in the beginning. Look at the following code fragment:

```
int x = 1;
int y = 0;
while (x < y)
    x++;
```

In this case, the body of the **while**-instruction is not executed, not even once! Therefore, in this example the variable x retains the value 1.

9.5.2 Infinite Repeat

One of the dangers of using **while**-instructions (and to a lesser extent **for**-instructions) is that they might never end, if you do not take care. We can easily write such an instruction:

```
while (1+1 == 2)
    x = x+1;
```

In this case, the value of x is incremented without end. This is because the condition 1 + 1 == 2 always yields **true**, no matter what is done in the body of the instruction. Now this example is quite easy to avoid, but often a **while**-instruction ends in an infinite loop because of a programming error. Consider the following example:

```
int x = 1;
int n = 0;
while (n < 10)
    x = x*2;
    n = n+1;
```

The intention of this code is that the value of x is doubled ten times. However, unfortunately the programmer forgot to put the two instructions in the body between braces. This intention is suggested by the layout of the program, but the compiler does not care about that. Only the x=x*2; instruction is repeated, so the value of n will then never be greater or equal to ten. After the **while**-instruction, the instruction n=n+1 will be executed, but the program never gets there. What the programmer actually meant was:

```
int x = 1;
int n = 0;
while (n < 10)
{
    x = x*2;
    n = n+1;
}
```

It would be a pity if you had to throw away your computer or console after it was put into a coma because you forgot to write braces around your **while**-instruction. Fortunately, the operating system can stop the execution of a program by force, even if it has not finished. The program is stopped immediately in that case, and you can start to look for the cause of the program hanging. Consoles generally do not have this kind of process management, so you will have to restart the console the old-fashioned way. Although such hang-ups occur occasionally, it is your job as a game programmer to make sure that once the game is sold to the customers, these kinds of programming errors have been removed from the game code. This is why proper testing is so important.

In general, if the program you wrote does not seem to do anything on startup, or if it hangs indefinitely, check out what is happening in the **while**-instructions. A very common mistake is to forget incrementing the counter variable, so the condition of the **while**-instruction never becomes **false**, and the **while** loop continues indefinitely.

9.5.3 Nested Repeats

The body of a **while**-instruction or a **for**-instruction is also an instruction itself. This instruction can be an assignment, a method call, or a block of instructions delimited

Fig. 9.1 Balloons in a
triangle shape

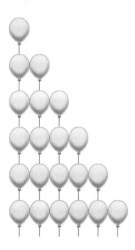

by braces. For example:

```
int x, y;
for (y=0; y<7; y++)
    for (x=0; x<y; x++)
        spriteBatch.Draw(livesSprite,
                    new Vector2(livesSprite.Width * x, livesSprite.Height * y),
                    Color.White);
```

In this fragment, the variable y counts from 0 to 7. For each of these values of
y, the body is executed, which itself consists of a **for**-instruction. This second **for**-
instruction uses the counter x, which has as a upper limit the value of y. Therefore,
in each progression of the outer **for**-instruction, the inner **for**-instruction will go on
longer. The instruction that is repeatedly repeated is drawing a yellow balloon sprite
at the position calculated by using the values of the x and y counters. The result of
this loop is a number of balloon placed in the shape of a triangle (see Fig. 9.1).

The first line in this shape contains zero balloons. The reason for this is that the
value of y is still zero at that point, which means that the inner **for**-instruction is
executed zero times.

9.6 Restarting the Game After the Game Is Over

When the player has lost all of his/her lives, the game is over. How do we deal with
this? In the case of the Painter game, we would like to show a 'game over' screen.
The player can press the space bar which would restart the game. In order to add
this to the game, we load an extra sprite in the GameWorld class that represents the
game over screen:

```
gameover = Content.Load<Texture2D>("spr_gameover");
```

Now we can use an **if**-instruction in each of the game loop methods to determine what we should do. If the game is over, we do not want the cannon and the ball to handle input anymore, we simply want to listen if the player presses space. If the player presses the space bar, we reset the game. So, our new HandleInput method contains the following instructions:

```
if (lives > 0)
{
    cannon.HandleInput(inputHelper);
    ball.HandleInput(inputHelper);
}
else if (inputHelper.KeyPressed(Keys.Space))
    Reset();
```

We added a Reset method to the GameWorld class, so that we can reset the game to its initial state. This means resetting all the game objects. We also need to reset the allowed number of missed cans to 15 again. Finally, we need to reset the minimal velocity of each paint can to its original value. For that, we added an extra method ResetMinVelocity to the PaintCan class. The full Reset method in the GameWorld class then becomes

```
public void Reset()
{
    lives = 5;
    cannon.Reset();
    ball.Reset();
    can1.Reset();
    can2.Reset();
    can3.Reset();
    can1.ResetMinVelocity();
    can2.ResetMinVelocity();
    can3.ResetMinVelocity();
}
```

For the Update method, we only need to update the game objects if the game is not over. Therefore, we first check with an **if**-instruction if we need to update the game objects. If not (in other words: the number of lives is zero or less), we return from the method:

```
if (lives <= 0)
    return;
ball.Update(gameTime);
can1.Update(gameTime);
can2.Update(gameTime);
can3.Update(gameTime);
```

Finally, in the Draw method we draw the game objects, and the game over screen if the player has no more lives left. This results in the following structure:

```
public void Draw(GameTime gameTime, SpriteBatch spriteBatch)
{
    spriteBatch.Begin();
    Draw the game world...
    if (lives <=0)
        spriteBatch.Draw(gameover,
                        new Vector2(Painter.Screen.X − gameover.Width,
                                Painter.Screen.Y − gameover.Height) / 2,
                        Color.White);
    spriteBatch.End();
}
```

You can see here that we use the dimensions of the screen and the dimensions of the 'game over' overlay to position it nicely in the center of the screen.

9.7 What You Have Learned

In this chapter, you have learned:

- how to store and display the number of lives that a player currently has;
- how to repeat a group of instructions using the **while** or **for** instruction;
- how to restart the game after the player has died.

Chapter 10
Organizing Game Objects

10.1 Introduction

We have seen in the previous chapter how we can use classes to group variables that belong together. In this chapter, we are going to look at the similarities between the different types of game objects, and how we can express these similarities in C#.

10.2 Similarities Between Game Objects

If we look at the different game objects in our Painter game, we can see that they have a lot of things in common. For example, the ball, the cannon and the paint cans all have three sprites that represent each of the three different colors. Also, most objects in the game have a position and a velocity. Furthermore, all game objects need a method to draw them, some of the game objects have a method for handling input, some of them have an Update method, and so on. Now, it is not really a problem that these classes have similarities. The compiler will not complain about that. However, it is a pity that we have to copy code all the time. To give an example, both Ball and the PaintCan) class have the following method:

```
public void Draw(GameTime gameTime, SpriteBatch spriteBatch)
{
    spriteBatch.Draw(currentColor, position, Color.White);
}
```

The code is exactly the same, but it is copied in both the classes. And every time we want to add a different kind of three colored game object, we need to copy this method again. In this case, the method is fortunately not that complicated, but in our application we are copying around a lot of other things as well. For example, all the game objects in the Painter game share the following member variables:

A. Egges et al., *Learning C# by Programming Games*,   151
DOI 10.1007/978-3-642-36580-5_10, © Springer-Verlag Berlin Heidelberg 2013

```
Texture2D colorRed, colorGreen, colorBlue;
Texture2D currentColor;
Vector2 position;
Color color;
```

Also, both the paint can and the ball have a Center property:

```
public Vector2 Center
{
    get { return new Vector2(currentColor.Width, currentColor.Height) / 2; }
}
```

Again, the code is exactly the same in the different classes, and we copy it every time we make a new kind of game object. And the same goes for the Position or the Color property. In general, it is better to avoid copying around a lot of code. Why is that? Because if at some point you realize there is a mistake in that part of the code, you have to correct it everywhere you copied it to. In a small game like Painter, this is not a big issue. But when you develop a commercial game with hundreds of different game object classes, this becomes a serious mainte-nance problem. In order to solve this problem, we need to think about how the different kinds of game objects are similar, and if we can group these similarities together, just like we grouped the member variables together in the previous chap-ters.

Conceptually speaking, it is easy to say what is similar between balls, paint cans and cannons: they are all *game objects*. Basically they can all be drawn at a certain position, they all have a velocity (even the cannon, but its velocity is zero), and they all have a color that is either red, green or blue. Furthermore, most of them handle input of some kind and are updated.

10.3 Inheritance

With object-oriented programming, it is possible to group these similarities together in a generic class, and then define other classes that are a *special version* of this generic class. In object-oriented jargon, this is called *inheritance* and it is a very powerful language feature. We have already used this feature before, but we did not know yet that it was called inheritance. Our Painter game class is defined as follows:

```
class Painter : Game
{
    ...
}
```

When you look at the class header, you see the name of the class (Painter), but also the class name Game. We did not really explain what this meant before, except that the Painter class was a special version of the Game class. This is in fact an example of inheritance. The Game class contains a lot of methods and properties (such as Content), and because we *inherit* from this class, we can use them in the Painter class as well, since Painter is basically the same as Game, except that it is a special version of it. You could also say that Painter is a *subclass* of Game, or that Game is the *superclass*, or the *base class* of Painter. The inheritance relationship between classes is widely used and in a good class design, it can be interpreted as 'is a kind of'. For example, Painter is a kind of Game. You can also say that Painter is a *subclass*, or a *derived class* of Game.

10.3.1 Game Objects and Inheritance

The 'is a kind of' relationship also holds for the game objects in the Painter game. A ball is a kind of game object, and so are the paint cans and the cannon. We can make this inheritance relationship explicit in our program by defining a generic class called ThreeColorGameObject, and then have our actual game object classes inherit from that generic class. We can then put everything that defines what a three color game object is inside that class, and the ball, the cannon, and the paint can will be special versions of that class.

10.3.2 The *ThreeColorGameObject* Class

So let us now have a look at this ThreeColorGameObject class in more detail. We are going to put all the member variables that are used by all the different types of game objects in our game, into this class. So, we can define a basic skeleton of our class as follows:

```
class ThreeColorGameObject
{
    Texture2D colorRed, colorGreen, colorBlue;
    Texture2D currentColor;
    Vector2 position, velocity;
    Color color;
    ...
}
```

As a first step, let us define the constructor method of this class. Each game object that inherits from this class will load different sprites for representing the three different colors. Therefore, we add three parameters to the ThreeColorGameObject constructor: one for each of the sprites. Inside the constructor, we then assign these parameter values to the member variables:

```
public ThreeColorGameObject(Texture2D colorRed, Texture2D colorGreen,
                            Texture2D colorBlue)
{
    this.colorRed = colorRed;
    this.colorGreen = colorGreen;
    this.colorBlue = colorBlue;
    Color = Color.Blue;
    position = Vector2.Zero;
    velocity = Vector2.Zero;
}
```

Note that there is a difference between **this**.colorRed and colorRed. The expression colorRed refers to the *parameter* that was passed. If we want to access the member variable carrying the same name, we have to explicitly write **this**. in front of it. If we had written the following instruction:

```
colorRed = colorRed;
```

the member variable **this**.colorRed would still point to **null** since we assigned the parameter value to itself!

Since we want to be able to reset every game object, we add a Reset method to the ThreeColorGameObject that resets the game object to its original state, in this case that means resetting the color of the object to blue:

```
public void Reset()
{
    Color = Color.Blue;
}
```

Now, we would like to define the basic methods for handling input, updating the game object, and drawing the game object. The method for drawing the game object is rather straightforward:

```
public void Draw(GameTime gameTime, SpriteBatch spriteBatch)
{
    spriteBatch.Draw(currentColor, position, Color.White);
}
```

The problem is that we do not know yet how a three colored game object should handle input. A cannon will handle input differently than a ball. The only thing that we know is that the position of the object should be updated according to the velocity. So for now, let us leave the HandleInput method empty, and the Update method contains a single instruction that updates the current position of the game object:

```
public void HandleInput(InputHelper inputHelper)
{
}
```

```
public void Update(GameTime gameTime)
{
    position += velocity * (float)gameTime.ElapsedGameTime.TotalSeconds;
}
```

Finally, we can add a few convenient properties for getting and setting the color, position or velocity. For the complete ThreeColorGameObject class, see the example project Painter9 belonging to this chapter.

10.4 Creating Special Versions of Game Objects

Now that we have created a very basic game object class, we can reuse this basic behavior for the actual game objects in our game by *inheriting* from this class, just like we inherited from the generic Game class.

10.4.1 The *Cannon* Class

Let us first have a look at the cannon game object. Since we now have the basic ThreeColorGameObject class, we can create the Cannon class, and inherit from the ThreeColorGameObject class:

```
class Cannon : ThreeColorGameObject
{
    ...
}
```

Now we need to add a constructor method to this class. Before we start writing the code for this constructor, let us first think about what it means when we create an instance of Cannon. In the previous version of the Painter game, the Cannon instance can be depicted as in Fig. 10.1.

In the new version of the Cannon class, it is no longer a class that stands on its own, but it inherits from the ThreeColorGameObject class. This means that Cannon is basically a special version of a ThreeColorGameObject instance. From the point of view of the compiler, this means that when a Cannon instance is created, this instance consists of a ThreeColorGameObject instance and the extensions that make it a Cannon object. Next to the member variables that are already in the ThreeColorGameObject class, a Cannon object also has a barrel that is drawn at a certain angle. As a result, we need two additional member variables:

```
Texture2D cannonBarrel;
float angle;
```

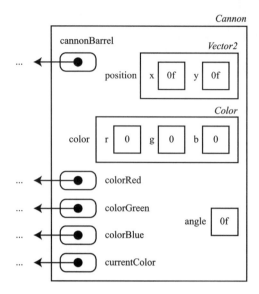

Fig. 10.1 Structure of a Cannon instance

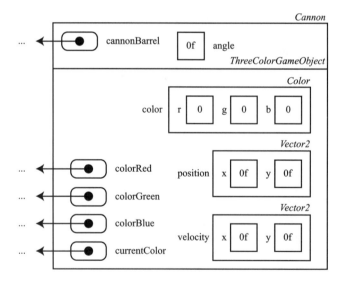

Fig. 10.2 Structure of a Cannon instance that inherits from ThreeColorGameObject

These member variables belong to Cannon and not to ThreeColorGameObject. We can now depict the structure of the version of a Cannon object that inherits from ThreeColorGameObject, see Fig. 10.2.

Now let us go back to the Cannon constructor. We need to pass the content manager to the constructor so that we can load all the sprites. So, we can initially write down the header of this constructor as follows:

```
public Cannon(ContentManager Content)
```

Inside the constructor, we have to load the different sprites and assign them to the member variables, just like we did in the original class. However, we also wrote part of that code in the ThreeColorGameObject constructor. That is because this constructor is responsible for creating the ThreeColorGameObject part of the Cannon instance. How can we tell the compiler that the constructor of the base class should be called? Have a look at the following code:

```
public Cannon(ContentManager Content)
        : base(Content.Load<Texture2D>("spr_cannon_red"),
             Content.Load<Texture2D>("spr_cannon_green"),
             Content.Load<Texture2D>("spr_cannon_blue"))
   {
     ...
```

We use the keyword **base** to denote that we call the constructor of the *base class* of this class, in other words: the class that we are inheriting from. We will see another use of this keyword later on. Because the constructor of the ThreeColorGameObject class expects three Texture2D object parameters, we call the Content.Load method to load the sprites and pass them along as a parameter. The body of the Cannon constructor consists only of setting the position and loading the cannon barrel sprite:

```
this.cannonBarrel = Content.Load<Texture2D>("spr_cannon_barrel");
position = new Vector2(72, 405);
```

The rest of the work (assigning the three color sprites and resetting the object) is done for us inside the ThreeColorGameObject constructor!

10.4.2 Overriding Methods from the Base Class

Now that we have written the constructor of the Cannon class, we have to think about how a cannon is different from a generic three color game object. As we have seen initially, the ThreeColorGameObject class has an empty method body for the HandleInput method, whereas the cannon needs to change its color depending on the user input. This means that we need to *replace* the original method from the ThreeColorGameObject class with a method specific for cannon input handling. We can also say that we want to *override* the HandleInput method. Suppose that we add the following method to the Cannon class:

```
public void HandleInput(InputHelper inputHelper)
{
    if (inputHelper.KeyPressed(Keys.R))
        Color = Color.Red;
    else if (inputHelper.KeyPressed(Keys.G))
        Color = Color.Green;
    else if (inputHelper.KeyPressed(Keys.B))
        Color = Color.Blue;

    double opposite = inputHelper.MousePosition.Y − position.Y;
    double adjacent = inputHelper.MousePosition.X − position.X;
    angle = (float)Math.Atan2(opposite, adjacent);
}
```

This method has the exact same header as the one in the ThreeColorGameObject class, except that the body is different. However, the C# compiler does not automatically assume that we want to replace the original HandleInput method. This is not because the compiler is stupid, but it is because overriding a method has quite a big impact on the behavior of a class, so it is better to be very explicit about it. This is why we have to use the **override** keyword to indicate that we are overriding a method. The header of the HandleInput method in the Cannon class then becomes:

public override void HandleInput(InputHelper inputHelper)

But does this mean that any class that inherits from the GameObject class can override all its methods without any problem? No, in fact we can indicate in the GameObject class which methods we are allowed to override. Only the methods that carry the keyword **virtual** can be overridden. This means that if we want subclasses to override the HandleInput method from GameObject, we need to change the header in the ThreeColorGameObject class to

public virtual void HandleInput(InputHelper inputHelper)

As you can see in the ThreeColorGameObject class definition provided in the example, all of its methods are virtual. This means that any of its methods can be overridden. This mechanism is very important to govern what a class can do when it inherits from another class, because in some cases it is not desirable that a subclass can override any method it likes. For example, the Game class allows you to override its Update and Draw methods, but not the Run method. The reason is that the Run method does all kinds of low-level things that we do not want any subclasses to mess around with. By making this distinction between methods that are virtual and methods that are not, we can shield parts of the base class from the subclasses so that the programmer of the subclass cannot do any serious harm when overriding methods and extending the base class.

10.4.3 Accessing Member Variables from the Base Class

So how about accessing member variables that are declared in the base class? As you can see in the overridden HandleInput method, we access the position member variable which is declared in the ThreeColorGameObject class. So does that mean that a subclass can access any member variable it likes? No. Also in this case, the base class decides who can access its member variables. For this, there are three different keywords that are used: **public**, **private** and **protected**. These keywords are also called *access modifiers* since they change how members of a class can be accessed. If we use the **private** access modifier, only the class itself can access the member variable. This member variable is then called a *private member variable*. A class can never access private member variables of another class.

A protected member variable can be accessed from within the class in which it is declared, or from within any class that inherits from that class, but not from any other (unrelated) classes. Finally, a public member variable can be accessed by anyone (including unrelated classes). Let us look at an example to see how this works. Consider the following classes:

```
class Base
{
    public int publicVar;
    protected int protectedVar;
    private int privateVar;

    void someMethod()
    {
        A
    }
}

class Derived : Base
{
    void someOtherMethod()
    {
        B
    }
}

class SomeGame : Game
{
    Other member variables and methods

    protected override void Update(GameTime gameTime)
    {
        Derived d = new Derived();
        C
    }
}
```

In this example, we have a Base class that has three member variables, each with different access modifiers. Inside the someMethod method (point A), we can execute the following instructions without any problem:

```
publicVar = 10;
protectedVar = 5;
privateVar = 1;
```

This is because within the class where a member variable is declared, we can always access this member variable. Now suppose that we are inside the someOtherMethod (point B), which is defined in the Derived class. Since Derived inherits from Base, it contains a Base instance. This means that Derived also has three member variables which it has inherited from Base. However, we can only execute the following two instructions inside the someOtherMethod method:

```
publicVar = 10;
protectedVar = 5;
```

If we try to access the privateVar variable here, it will result in a compiler error, because this variable was declared **private**, meaning that *only the class in which it was declared* can access it directly. However, we do have access to both the publicVar and protectedVar variables, because public variables can be accessed by anyone, and protected variables can be accessed within the base class, or within any method of a derived class. Finally, we can only access the publicVar variable in the Update method (point C):

```
d.publicVar = 10;
```

Trying to access either protectedVar or privateVar in the d object would result in a compiler error, because the SomeGame class is unrelated to the Base and Derived classes, it only uses them.

In the ThreeColorGameObject class, we did not yet provide any access modifiers for the member variables. If there is no access modifier before a member variable declaration, the C# compiler assumes that the member variable is private. So,

```
Texture2D currentColor;
```

is equivalent to

private Texture2D currentColor;

In our case, we would like that classes that inherit from ThreeColorGameObject can access the member variables. Therefore, we declare the member variables in ThreeColorGameObject as follows:

```
protected Texture2D colorRed, colorGreen, colorBlue;
protected Texture2D currentColor;
protected Vector2 position, velocity;
protected Color color;
```

10.4.4 Access Modifiers and Methods/Properties

Access modifiers such as **public** or **private** can also be used on methods and properties. Just like with member variables, we can control who can call a method or a
property in a class. For example, if we look at the header of the Update method in the
Game class, we see that it is a *protected* member. This means that the Update method
can only be called by the Game class or any class that inherits from the Game class.
This makes sense, because the Update method forms a part of the game loop, and
we would not want any random class to be able to call this method. So declaring
methods as private or protected helps us to control what level of access a user has to
a class.

In the classes that we have defined so far, all the methods have the **public** access
modifier, meaning that everyone can access the method. Just like with member variables, if no access modifier is provided, the compiler assumes that the method is
private.

10.4.5 The Final *Cannon* Class

We have seen how to construct the Cannon class constructor and how to override the
HandleInput method. As such, the Cannon class is complete (for the complete class,
see Listing 10.1). As you can see, the class definition is now much smaller and easier
to read than in the previous version, since all the generic game object members
are placed in the GameObject class. Organizing your code in different classes and
subclasses helps to reduce copying code around and results in generally cleaner
designs. There is a caveat however: your class structure (which class inherits from
which other class) has to be right. Remember that classes should only inherit from
other classes if there is a 'is a kind of' relationship between the classes. To illustrate
this, suppose that we would like to add an indicator at the top of the screen that
shows which color the ball currently is. We could make a class for that and let it
inherit from the Cannon class since it also needs to handle input in a similar way:

```
class ColorIndicator : Cannon
{
    ...
}
```

```
1   using System;
2   using Microsoft.Xna.Framework;
3   using Microsoft.Xna.Framework.Content;
4   using Microsoft.Xna.Framework.Graphics;
5   using Microsoft.Xna.Framework.Input;
6
7   class Cannon : ThreeColorGameObject
8   {
9       Texture2D cannonBarrel;
10      float angle;
11
12      public Cannon(ContentManager Content)
13          : base(Content.Load<Texture2D>("spr_cannon_red"),
14              Content.Load<Texture2D>("spr_cannon_green"),
15              Content.Load<Texture2D>("spr_cannon_blue"))
16      { this.cannonBarrel = Content.Load<Texture2D>("spr_cannon_barrel");
17          position = new Vector2(72, 405);
18      }
19
20      public override void HandleInput(InputHelper inputHelper)
21      { if (inputHelper.KeyPressed(Keys.R))
22              Color = Color.Red;
23          else if (inputHelper.KeyPressed(Keys.G))
24              Color = Color.Green;
25          else if (inputHelper.KeyPressed(Keys.B))
26              Color = Color.Blue;
27          double opposite = inputHelper.MousePosition.Y − position.Y;
28          double adjacent = inputHelper.MousePosition.X − position.X;
29          angle = (float)Math.Atan2(opposite, adjacent);
30      }
31
32      public override void Draw(GameTime gameTime, SpriteBatch spriteBatch)
33      { spriteBatch.Draw(cannonBarrel, position, null, Color.White, angle,
34              new Vector2(34, 34), 1.0f, SpriteEffects.None, 0);
35          spriteBatch.Draw(currentColor, position − new Vector2(currentColor.Width,
36              currentColor.Height) / 2, Color.White);
37      }
38
39      public override void Reset()
40      { base.Reset();
41          angle = 0.0f;
42      }
43
44      public Vector2 BallPosition
45      { get
46          { float opposite = (float)Math.Sin(angle) ∗ cannonBarrel.Width ∗ 0.5f;
47              float adjacent = (float)Math.Cos(angle) ∗ cannonBarrel.Width ∗ 0.5f;
48              return position + new Vector2(adjacent, opposite);
49          }
50      }
51  }
```

Listing 10.1 The final Cannon class

However, this is a very bad idea. A color indicator is certainly not a kind of cannon, and designing your classes in this way makes it very unclear what the supposed use is of your classes. Every time you write a class that inherits from another class, ask yourself whether that class really is 'a kind of' the class that you inherit from. If it is not, then you have to rethink your design.

10.5 The Ball Class

10.5.1 Outline of the Class

We can define the Ball class in a very similar fashion as the Cannon class. Just like the Cannon class, we inherit from the ThreeColorGameObject class. The only difference is that we have to add an extra member variable that indicates if the ball is currently shooting.

```
class Ball : GameObject
{
    bool shooting;
    ...
}
```

When a Ball instance is created, we need to call the ThreeColorGameObject constructor, just as we did with the Cannon class. Next to that, we need to give the shooting variable an initial value of **false**, and set the position. However, for now we are not going to set these variables explicitly in the constructor. We will deal with this later on. This means that the constructor is given as follows:

```
public Ball(ContentManager Content)
    : base(Content.Load<Texture2D>("spr_ball_red"),
          Content.Load<Texture2D>("spr_ball_green"),
          Content.Load<Texture2D>("spr_ball_blue"))
{
}
```

The ball should do a couple of things. First, it should handle input from the player, so we have to override the HandleInput method. Also, the ball needs to be updated, therefore the Update method also needs to be overridden. Finally, the Reset method needs to be overridden, because the shooting member variable needs to be reset as well when this method is called. Overriding the HandleInput and Update methods is rather straightforward. Both the headers need the **override** keyword, and we can fill them in with the right instructions. You can have a look at the complete Ball class definition given in Listing 10.2.

```
1   using Microsoft.Xna.Framework;
2   using Microsoft.Xna.Framework.Content;
3   using Microsoft.Xna.Framework.Graphics;
4
5   class Ball : ThreeColorGameObject
6   {
7       bool shooting;
8
9       public Ball(ContentManager Content)
10          : base(Content.Load<Texture2D>("spr_ball_red"),
11                 Content.Load<Texture2D>("spr_ball_green"),
12                 Content.Load<Texture2D>("spr_ball_blue"))
13      {
14      }
15
16      public override void HandleInput(InputHelper inputHelper)
17      {
18          if (inputHelper.MouseLeftButtonPressed() && !shooting)
19          {
20              shooting = true;
21              velocity = (inputHelper.MousePosition − position) * 1.2f;
22          }
23      }
24
25      public override void Update(GameTime gameTime)
26      {
27          if (shooting)
28          {
29              velocity.X *= 0.99f;
30              velocity.Y += 6;
31          }
32          else
33          {
34              Color = Painter.GameWorld.Cannon.Color;
35              position = Painter.GameWorld.Cannon.BallPosition − Center;
36          }
37          if (Painter.GameWorld.IsOutsideWorld(position))
38              Reset();
39          base.Update(gameTime);
40      }
41
42      public override void Reset()
43      {
44          base.Reset();
45          position = new Vector2(65, 390);
46          velocity = Vector2.Zero;
47          shooting = false;
48      }
49  }
```

Listing 10.2   The final Ball class

10.5.2 The Reset Method

When the ball object is reset, it needs to be placed at the start position, the shooting variable should be set to **false**, and its velocity should be set to zero, and for completeness, we set the color to blue. We could override the Reset method from GameObject as follows:

```
public override void Reset()
{
    Color = Color.Blue;
    position = new Vector2(65, 390);
    velocity = Vector2.Zero;
    shooting = false;
}
```

However, we are again copying code from the ThreeColorGameObject class and we argued a few pages ago that copying code is generally a bad idea. The problem here is that we do not only want to override the Reset method, we want to *extend* it. What we actually would like to do is to first call the original Reset method defined in ThreeColorGameObject, and then set the start position and velocity of the ball and its shooting status. But how do we call the 'original version' of the Reset method if it is overridden? Here, the **base** keyword proves its use again.

10.5.3 base Versus this

The **base** keyword can be used in a similar way to the **this** keyword. As you recall, **this** refers to the current instance that the method is being called on. Similarly, **base** also refers to the current instance, but it *refers to the part of that instance that forms the base class*. So in our example, **base** refers to the ThreeColorGameObject instance that is a part of the Ball instance. This means that if we want to call the version of the Reset method that is a part of the ThreeColorGameObject class, we can call it through the **base** instance as **base**.Reset(). The Reset method in the Ball class then becomes

```
public override void Reset()
{
    base.Reset();
    position = new Vector2(65, 390);
    velocity = Vector2.Zero;
    shooting = false;
}
```

So, first the part of the instance representing ThreeColorGameObject is reset, and then we perform the reset operation specific to the ball (setting it at a particular position and setting the shooting status to **false**).

Something similar is happening in the Update method of the Ball class. At the end of that method, we call the Update method of the ThreeColorGameObject class, so that the position is changed according to the velocity. You can also see an example of this in the new PaintCan class, which is also a subclass of ThreeColorGameObject.

10.5.4 Polymorphism

Because of the inheritance mechanism, there are now some interesting things happening. Since a cannon object is a three colored game object, this instruction is allowed:

```
ThreeColorGameObject cannon = new Cannon(...);
```

Now suppose that we would then execute the following instruction:

```
cannon.Reset();
```

Which version of the Reset method would be called? The one in the Cannon class or the one in the ThreeColorGameObject class? Although the variable cannon is of type ThreeColorGameObject, it actually refers to an object of type Cannon. When you run the program, the compiler maintains a so-called *vtable* which contains for each object in the program to which inheritance tree it belongs and what that tree looks like. Whenever a virtual method is called, like what happens here in the case of the Reset method, the compiler looks in the table to find out which version of the method should be called. In this case, it will see that we're dealing with a Cannon object, so it will call the version of the Reset method that is defined in the Cannon class.

This effect is called *polymorphism* and it comes in very handy sometimes. Another example where polymorphism is responsible for the behavior of the program is when we call the Run method on the game variable. The Run method is defined inside the Game class. This method does not know that it happens to work with a Painter object. Because of polymorphism, when, for instance, the Update method is called from within the Run method, automatically the right version of the method is called, which would be the Update method that we defined in the Painter class.

Another example of where polymorphism is useful is when a game company wants to release an extension of their game. For example, they might want to introduce a few new enemies, or skills that a player can learn. They can provide these extensions as subclasses of generic Enemy and Skill classes. The actual game engine would then use these objects without having to know which particular skill or enemy it is dealing with. It simply calls the methods that were defined in the generic classes.

10.5.5 Sealed Methods

If you do not want a subclass of the class that you programmed to be able to override a virtual function, you can define the method with the keyword **sealed**. Sealed methods cannot be changed anymore by a subclass. For example, suppose the header of the HandleInput method of the Ball class would be given as follows:

public sealed override void HandleInput(InputHelper inputHelper)

In this case, we can no longer override the method in a subclass of Ball. So if we were to try this in the class BouncingBall (which inherits from Ball), we would get a compiler error.

10.6 Hierarchies of Classes

10.6.1 A Subclass 'Is a Kind of' Base Class

We've seen several examples of classes inheriting from a base game object class in this chapter. A class should only inherit from another class if the relationship between these two classes can be described as 'is a kind of'. For example: a Ball is a kind of ThreeColorGameObject, and a Painter is a kind of Game. In fact, the hierarchy does not end there. We could write another class that inherits from the Ball class, such as BouncingBall, which could be a special version of a standard ball that bounces off canisters instead of only colliding with them. And we could make another class BouncingElasticBall that inherits from BouncingBall, which is a ball that deforms according to its elastic properties when it bounces against a canister. Every time we inherit from a class, we get the data (encoded in member variables) and the behavior (encoded in methods and properties) from the base class for free.

Commercial games will have a class hierarchy of different game objects with many different levels. For example, you could imagine that for a game that takes place in a city with a harbor, we would need many different classes for objects commonly occurring in such an environment:

class GameObject {*a very generic class for describing game objects with a position and a velocity.*}
class StationaryGameObject : GameObject {...}
class Tree : StationaryGameObject {...}
class House : StationaryGameObject {...}
class MovingGameObject : GameObject {...}
class Vehicle : MovingGameObject {...}
class MotorizedVehicle : Vehicle {...}
class Car : MotorizedVehicle {...}
class Truck : MotorizedVehicle {...}

class Motorbike : MotorizedVehicle {...}
class Bicycle : Vehicle {...}
class Airplane : MovingGameObject {...}
class Boat : MovingGameObject {...}
class MotorBoat : Boat {...}
class SteamBoat : MotorBoat {...}
class SpeedBoat : MotorBoat {...}
class SailBoat : Boat {...}

Figure 10.3 shows the inheritance structure, using arrows to indicate an inheritance relation between classes. At the very base of the inheritance tree is a GameObject class. This class contains only very basic information such as the position or the velocity of the game object. For each subclass, new members (variables, methods or properties) can be added, which are of relevance for the particular class and its subclasses. For example, the variable numberOfWheels typically belongs in the Vehicle class and not in MovingGameObject (since boats do not have wheels). The variable flightAltitude belongs in the Airplane class and the variable bellIsWorking belongs to the Bicycle class.

10.6.2 Designing Class Hierarchies

When you determine the way that your classes are structured, you have to make many decisions. There is not a single 'best' hierarchy and, depending on the application, one hierarchy might be more useful than another. For instance, in this example we have opted to first divide the MovingGameObject class according to the

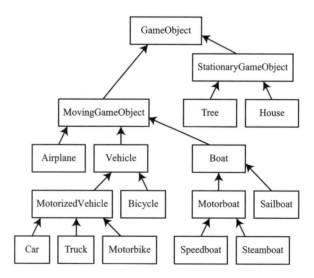

Fig. 10.3 A complicated hierarchy of classes

medium that the object uses to displace itself: land, air, or water. After that, we divide the classes in different subclasses: motorized or not motorized. We could have chosen to do this the other way round. For some classes, it is not entirely clear where in the hierarchy they belong: do we say that a motorbike is a special type of bike (namely one with a motor), or is it a special kind of motorized vehicle (namely one with only two wheels)?

However, the relationship between the classes themselves should always be clear. A sailboat is a boat, but a boat is not always a sailboat. A bicycle is a vehicle, but not every vehicle is a bicycle.

10.7 What You Have Learned

In this chapter, you have learned:

- how to use inheritance to structure related classes in a hierarchy;
- how to override methods in a subclass to provide specific behavior for that class;
- what the difference is between **private**, **protected**, and **public** modifiers;
- what the difference is between **base** and **this**;
- how to use polymorphism to automatically call the right version of the method.

Chapter 11
Finishing the Game

11.1 Introduction

In this chapter, we will finish the Painter game by adding a few extra features, such as motion effects, sounds and music, and maintaining and displaying a score. In order to do the latter, we introduce the **string** and **char** types.

11.2 Adding Motion Effects

In order to make the game more visually appealing, we can introduce a nice rotational effect in the movement of the paint cans to simulate the effect of wind and friction on the falling down motion. In the Painter10 program, you can find the final version of the game where we added this motion effect to the cans. Adding such an effect is not very complicated, only a single line needs to be changed in the Draw method. In order to achieve such an effect, we use the Math.Sin method. By letting the value depend on the current position of the can, we get different values depending on the position of can. We use this value to apply a *rotation* on the sprite object. In order to draw the rotated paint cans on the screen, we use the extended version of the Draw method in the SpriteBatch class that we also used in the Cannon class. We call this method as follows:

```
spriteBatch.Draw(currentColor, position, null, Color.White,
            (float)Math.Sin(position.Y / 50.0) * 0.05f,
            Vector2.Zero, 1.0f, SpriteEffects.None, 0);
```

You can see in this instruction that we use the *y* coordinate of the paint can position to get different rotation values. Furthermore, we divide it by 50 to get a nice slow movement, and we multiply the outcome with 0.05 to reduce the amplitude of the sine, so that the rotation looks more or less realistic.

A. Egges et al., *Learning C# by Programming Games*,
DOI 10.1007/978-3-642-36580-5_11, © Springer-Verlag Berlin Heidelberg 2013

Creating sprites—Even if you are not an artist, it still helps to be able to make simple sprites yourself. It enables you to quickly make a prototype of the game. And maybe you will find out there also is an artist inside you.

To create sprites you first of all need good tools. Most artists use painting programs like Adobe Photoshop or vector drawing programs like Adobe Illustrator. But others work with such simple tools as Microsoft Paint or the more extensive and free GIMP. Every tool requires practice. Work your way through some tutorials and make sure you get some insight into the many different features. Often, the things that you want can be achieved in an easy way.

Preferably create very large images of your game objects and then scale them down to the required size. The advantages are that you can change the required size in your game later on and that you get rid of the aliasing effects because colors are blended. Keep the outside transparent and when scaling, the border pixels will automatically become partially transparent. Only if you want to create the classic pixel style should you create the sprites in the actual size required.

Finally, look around on the web. There are lots of sprites that you can use for free. You can then use these as a basis for your own sprites. But in the end, realize that the quality of your game probably increases a lot when you work together with an experienced artist.

11.3 Adding Sounds and Music

Another way to make the game more enjoyable is by adding some sound. In this game, we will use both background music and sound effects. For the background music, we simply added the following lines to the main Game subclass:

```
MediaPlayer.IsRepeating = true;
MediaPlayer.Play(Content.Load<Song>("snd_music"));
```

We also want to play sound effects. For example, when the player shoots a ball, we want to hear it! So, we load a SoundEffect object, just like we would load a sprite, and we store this object in a member variable in the Ball class:

```
ballShot = Content.Load<SoundEffect>("snd_shoot_paint");
```

Then, we can play this sound effect when we start shooting the ball. This is dealt with in the HandleInput method of the Ball class:

```
public void HandleInput(InputHelper inputHelper)
{
    if (inputHelper.MouseLeftButtonPressed() && !shooting)
    {
        shooting = true;
        velocity = (inputHelper.MousePosition − position) * 1.2f;
        ballShot.Play();
    }
}
```

Similarly, we also play a sound when a paint can of the correct color falls out of the screen.

11.4 Maintaining a Score

Scores are often a very effective way of motivating players to continue playing. Especially *highscores* work very well in that regard, because they introduce a competitive factor into the game: you want to be better than 'AAA' or 'XYZ'.[1] In the Painter game, we add a member variable score to the GameWorld class to store the current score in. This member variable is of type **int**, and it is given an initial value of 0 in the constructor method:

```
score = 0;
```

We also add a property to the GameWorld class, so that game objects can update the score when needed:

```
public int Score
{
    get { return score; }
    set { score = value; }
}
```

The player starts with a score of zero. Each time a paint can falls outside of the screen, the score is updated. If a can of the correct color falls out of the screen, 10 points are added to the score. If a can does not have the right color, the player loses a life.

The score is a part of what we call the *economy* of a game. The economy of a game basically describes the different costs and merits in a game and how they interact. When you make your own game, it is always useful to think about its economy. What do things cost, and what are the gains of executing different actions as a player? And are these two things in balance with each other?

---

[1] A lot of early arcade games allowed only three characters for each name in the high score list, leading to a lot of very imaginative names.

We update the score in the PaintCan class, where we can check if the can falls outside of the screen. If so, we check if it has the right color and update the score and the number of player lives accordingly. Finally, we reset the paint can object so that it can fall down again:

```
if (Painter.GameWorld.IsOutsideWorld(position))
{
    if (color == targetcolor)
    {
        Painter.GameWorld.Score += 10;
        collectPoints.Play();
    }
    else
        Painter.GameWorld.Lives--;
    Reset();
}
minVelocity += 0.001f;
```

Whenever a can of the right color falls off the screen, we play a sound. This sound is again a SoundEffect instance that is passed along as a parameter in the constructor and stored as a member variable in the PaintCan class.

11.5 Drawing Text on the Screen

Next to drawing the sprites on the screen, we also want to draw the current score on the screen (otherwise it would not make much sense to maintain it). For this, we can use the DrawString method. Instead of drawing a sprite on the screen, this method can draw *text* on the screen. Just like the Draw method from the SpriteBatch class requires a sprite, the DrawString method requires a *font*. This font is loaded just like a sprite, in the GameWorld constructor, and it is stored in a variable of type SpriteFont:

```
gameFont = Content.Load<SpriteFont>("GameFont");
```

The file describing the font is located in the same place as the sprites: in the content project. Open the Painter content project and double click on the file 'Game-Font.spritefont'. You will see a text file containing a lot of information describing the font. In this file, you can change the size and type of the font, among other things. Try, for example, to change the size to 30 and run the game again to see what happens. Or try to change the font name to 'Courier New' or 'Times New Roman'. You can add your own fonts to the content project by right clicking on the project name in the solution explorer and choosing Add → New Item. Then, choose the template called 'SpriteFont' and type an appropriate name. When you click 'Add', the font file is created for you and it is added to the content project. After that, you can modify the font file as desired and use it in your game application.

Drawing text on the screen is quite easy using the DrawString method. For example, this draws some green text in the top left of the screen:

```
spriteBatch.DrawString(gameFont, "Hello, how are you doing?",
                    Vector2.Zero, Color.Green);
```

11.6 Characters, Strings and Type Conversion

11.6.1 The char Type

The text that we draw on the screen using the DrawString method has a type called **string**. The **string** type is used in C# to represent text (consisting of multiple characters, punctuation marks and so on). There is also a primitive type called **char**. This type contains only a single character. Just like the other primitive types like **int** or **double**, **char** values can be stored in variables, they can be passed as a parameter to a method, they can be part of an object, and so on. There is a special kind of notation to indicate that something is a **char** value: by enclosing the character in *singe quotes*. This is different from **string** values, which use *double quotes*:

```
char asterisk;
string dashes;
asterisk = '*';
dashes = "--------";
```

Between single quotations you can place only a single symbol; between double quotations you can place multiple symbols, or a single symbol, or even no symbols at all. Next to **char** and **string** values, other constant values can be numbers, boolean values, or **null**, as expressed in this syntax diagram:

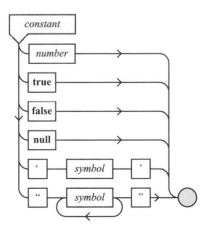

11.6.1.1 History of char

The number of different symbols that can be stored in a **char** variables has become bigger throughout the years in different programming languages:

- In the 1970s, programmers thought that $2^6 = 64$ symbols would be enough: 26 letters, 10 numbers, and 28 punctuation marks (comma, semicolon, and so on). Although this meant that there was no distinction between normal and capital letters, it was not a problem at the time.
- In the 1980s, people used $2^7 = 128$ different symbols: 26 capital letters, 26 normal letters, 10 numbers, 33 punctuation marks, and 33 special character (end-of-line, tabulation, beep, and so on). The order of these symbols was known as ASCII: the American Standard Code for Information Interchange. This was nice for the English language, but it was not sufficient for other languages such as French, German, Dutch, Spanish and more.
- As a result, in the 1990s new code tables were constructed with $2^8 = 256$ symbols, where the most common letters for a country were represented as well. The symbols from 0–127 were the same as in ASCII, but the symbols 128–255 were used for special characters belonging to a given language. Depending on the language (English, Russian, Indian), a different code table was used. The West-European code table was 'Latin1' for example. For Eastern-Europe, another code table was used (Polish and Czech have many special accents for which there was no more place in the Latin1 table). Greek, Russian, Hebrew, and the Indian Devangari-alphabet all had their own code table. This was a reasonable way of dealing with the different languages, but things became complicated once you wanted to store a text in different languages at the same time. Also, languages containing more than 128 symbols (such as Chinese) were impossible to represent using this format.
- In the beginning of the 21st century, the coding standard was extended again to a table containing $2^{16} = 65,536$ different symbols. This table could easily contain all the alphabets in the world, including many different punctuation marks and other symbols. This code table is called *Unicode*. The first 256 symbols of Unicode are the same symbols as the Latin1 code table.

In C#, **char** values are stored using the Unicode standard. Not all computers or all fonts can actually display all these symbols, but at least we will not have to change our programs when they can.

11.6.1.2 Using Single and Double Quotes

When using **string** and **char** values, you have to be careful which type of quotes you use (if any). If you forget the quotes, you are not writing text or characters anymore, but a piece of a C# program! There is a big difference between:

- the string "hello" and the variable name hello
- the string "bool" and the type name **bool**

- the string "123" and the **int** value 123
- the **char** value '+' and the operator +
- the **char** value 'x' and the variable name x
- the **char** value '7' and the **int** value 7

11.6.1.3 Special char Values

Special symbols are, simply because they are *special*, not always possible to indicate easily using a single character between single quotes. So, a number of special symbols have special notations, using the backslash symbol:

- '\n' for the end-of-line symbol
- '\t' for the tabulation symbol

This introduces a new problem: how to indicate the backslash character itself? The backslash character is indicated using the *double backslash*. In a similar way, the backslash symbol is used to represent the character for the single and double quotes themselves:

- '\\' for the backslash symbol
- '\'' for the single quote character
- '\"' for the double quote character

In these cases there are two symbols between the single quotes, but together, they indicate a single **char** value. These special symbols are specified in the syntax diagram that describes the symbol syntax:

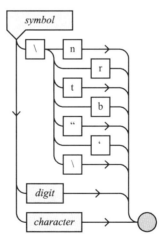

11.6.1.4 Calculating Things with char

The symbols in the Unicode table are ordered: every symbol has its own number. For example, the number of the capital letter 'A' is 65, the number for 'a' is 97.

The number for the symbol '0' is not 0, but 48. Also the space (' ') does not have code 0, but code 32. The symbol that does have code 0 is a special symbol that does not have any visible representation. You can find out what the code of a **char** is by assigning the **char** value to an **int** value:

```
char c; int i;
c = '*';
int i = c;
```

Or even directly:

```
int i = '*';
```

This is always possible. After all, there are only 65,536 different symbols, while the largest **int** value is more than 2 billion. This assignment trick also works the other way around, but then you have to tell the compiler explicitly that you agree with any unexpected conversions in case the **int** value is too big. You do this by indicating explicitly that you want to convert the **int** value to a **char** value as follows:

```
c = (char) i;
```

This allows you to perform calculations with symbols. The symbol after 'x' is (**char**)('x' + 1), and the capital letter c is (**char**)(c−'A'+1). This conversion notation is called a cast, as we have also seen in Sect. 4.2.6. Casts are very useful. For example, you can also use a cast to remove the decimals:

```
double d; int i;
d = 3.14159;
i = (int) d; // now contains the value 3
```

11.6.2 String Operations

In the Painter game, we use **string** values in combination with the DrawString method to draw text of a certain color in a desired font somewhere on the screen. In our case we want to write the current score in the top left of the screen. The score is maintained in an integer member variable called score. This variable is increased or decreased in the Update method. So how can we construct the text that should be printed on the screen, since a part of this text (the actual score) is changing all the time? The solution is called *string concatenation*, or: gluing one piece of text after another. In C# (and in many other programming languages as well), this is done using the plus sign. For example, the expression "Hi, my name is "+ "Arjan" results in the string "Hi, my name is Arjan". In this case, we concatenated two pieces of text. It is also possible to concatenate a piece of text and an integer value. For example, the expression "Score: "+ 200 results in the string "Score: 200". Instead of using a fixed integer value, we can even use a variable. So if the variable score contains the value 175, then the expression "Score: "+ score evaluates to "Score: 175". By writing this expression as a parameter of the DrawString method, we always draw the current score on the screen. The final call to the DrawString method then becomes (see the GameWorld class):

```
spriteBatch.DrawString(gameFont, "Score: " + score, new Vector2(20, 18), Color.White);
```

Watch out: concatenation only makes sense when we are dealing with text. For example, it is not possible to 'concatenate' two numbers: the expression 1 + 2 will result in 3 and not 12. Of course, we can concatenate *numbers represented as text*: "1"+ "2" will result in "12". Making the distinction between text and numbers is done by using the double quotes.

In fact, what we have secretly done in the expression "Score: "+ 200 is a *cast*. The integer value 200 was casted to the **string** "200" but we did not have to write this explicitly as "Score: "+ (**string**)200. The reason is that it is clear to the compiler we want to convert the integer value to a string value. Similarly, an implicit cast is also performed if we execute the instruction i = '*'. As soon as a cast is no longer trivial, or there are special cases that the compiler has to deal with, we have to state explicitly that we want to perform a cast:

```
c = (char) i;
```

If we want to convert a **string** value to a **double** or an **int** value, things get a bit more complicated. This is not an easy operation to perform by the compiler, and not all strings can be converted to a numerical value. For this, the primitive types have a special method associated with them called Parse. Here is an example of how to use this special method:

```
int result = int.Parse("10");
double otherResult = double.Parse("3.14159");
```

Who plays games?—You might think that games are primarily played by young males, but that is not true at all. A huge percentage of the people play games. In 2012 in the US there were 157,000,000 active gamers, which is half of its total population (including babies). They play games on many different devices. For example, more than 70 % played casual games on websites. Most time though was spent on console games.

If you develop a game you would better first think about the audience you want for your game. Games for young kids are rather different from games for middle-aged women. The games should have a different kind of gameplay, a different visual style, and different goals.

While console games tend to take place in large 3D worlds, casual games on websites and mobile devices are often 2D and are limited in size. Also, console games are designed such that they can (and need to be) played for hours and hours, while casual games are often designed to be playable in sessions of just a few minutes. Then there are many types of *serious game*, which are games that are used for training of professionals, such as firemen, mayors or doctors.

Realize that the games you like are not necessarily the games your target audience likes.

11.7 What You Have Learned

In this chapter, you have learned:

- how to add music and sound effects to your game;
- how to maintain and display a score;
- how to use the **string** and **char** types for representing and dealing with text.

Part III
Structures and Patterns

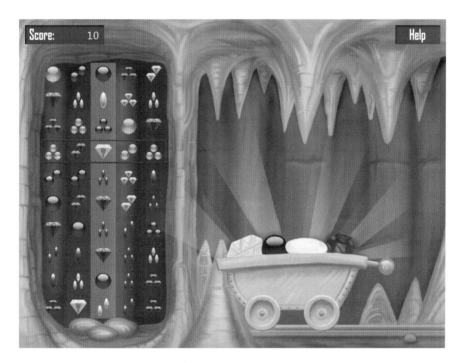

Fig. III.1 A screenshot of the game Jewel Jam

Deep, deep down in the mines, you are looking for your fortune. You know that the priceless gems are there, but they are all mixed up and you have to collect as many as possible before the cart that can transport them leaves. Can you make as many sets of jewels as possible before your time is up?

Jewel Jam is a puzzle game where combinations of jewels need to be found. A screenshot of this game can be seen in Fig. III.1. There is a limited amount of time, though.

A jewel cart is moving slowly away. Once this cart is out of the screen, your time is up. Every time the player makes a valid combination of jewels, he/she gains points and the jewel cart is moved back a few steps. The playing board consists of ten rows and five columns. There are different jewels on the playing field. The jewels are different according to three different properties: they can have a different color (red, blue or yellow), they can be different shapes (diamond-shaped, sphere-shaped and ellipse-shaped) and they can be different numbers (one, two or three jewels).

The player can shift rows to the left or to the right using the arrow keys, and the goal is to find matching combinations of three adjacent jewels in the middle column. A combination of three jewels is valid if each of the properties is either the same for all objects, or different for all objects. For example, a yellow single diamond object, a blue single diamond object, and a red single diamond object is a valid combination of objects, since the color is different for each object, and the shape and number is the same for all objects. A yellow sphere object, a yellow double diamond object and a yellow triple ellipse object is also a valid combination, because all objects have the same color, they all have a different shape, and they all have a different number. The combination yellow diamond, red double sphere and blue double ellipse is not a valid combination, because although the color and the shape is different for each object, the number for the diamond object is different from the other two. The combination yellow diamond, red double sphere and blue triple ellipse on the other hand, is valid. Once the player has found a valid combination by shifting the rows around, he/she presses the space bar and the jewels that form a valid combination disappear, upon which the remaining jewels fall down to fill the empty slots, and three new jewels fall down from the top of the screen. When there are two or three combinations at the same time in the middle column when the player presses the space bar, extra points are awarded and an overlay is shown on the screen for some time to indicate that a double or triple combination was made.

In the following chapters, we will be developing this game. If you want to play the complete version of the game to get a feel for how the game works, open the solution belonging to Chap. 18 and run the JewelJam project.

Chapter 12
Collections of Game Objects

12.1 Introduction

After reading the overview of the game Jewel Jam, I am sure you are eager to find out how to build it in C#. However, before we start creating this game, we have to introduce a few new programming aspects that we are going to use, in particular: how to deal with large collections of game objects. In this chapter, we will introduce collections and arrays, and show that they are a very powerful tool for making game code scalable and more flexible.

12.2 Many Game Objects

When looking back at our previous examples, we have avoided using many game objects of the same type on purpose. For example, in the Painter game, there are only three paint cans and one ball. Because of these limited numbers of game objects, we could simply declare the variables as follows:

```
PaintCan can1, can2, can3;
Ball ball;
```

Suppose that we wanted to create a game where the player could shoot more than one ball at a time? Or what about having more than three paint cans? Of course, we could still expand the list of member variables and deal with it that way:

```
PaintCan can1, can2, can3, can4, can5, can6, can7, can8;
Ball ball1, ball3, ball4, ball5, ball6;
```

Adding many more balls and paint cans would surely lead to a lot of duplicate code in your game, but if you are a very stubborn developer, you could still get away with it. However, at some point, simply declaring more and more member variables will no longer provide a solution to the problem. The following example will surely discourage any developer to use this technique!

A. Egges et al., *Learning C# by Programming Games*,
DOI 10.1007/978-3-642-36580-5_12, © Springer-Verlag Berlin Heidelberg 2013

Fig. 12.1 A lot of snow this year in the Swiss mountains

12.3 Snowflakes

In the beautiful Swiss mountains, it regularly snows (see Fig. 12.1). Obviously, the game company in charge of developing the (slightly gory) first-person shooter game 'Sauerkraut Zombies' wants to display snow to the players as realistically as possible. In order to simulate snow falling from the sky, the lead game designer has determined that there should be about 400–500 snowflakes visible on the screen. Since the developer of this game has only read this book up until the previous chapter, the first version of the game has the following member variables (among others):

```
SnowFlake snowflake1, snowflake2, snowflake3, snowflake4, snowflake5, snowflake6,
          snowflake7, snowflake8, snowflake9, snowflake10, snowflake11, snowflake12,
          snowflake13, snowflake14, snowflake15, snowflake16, ...
```

Guess who was fired the next day? Of course, in this case it makes no sense at all to try and declare hundreds of variables of the same type, all with more or less the same behavior. For such kinds of cases, C# has something called *Collections*.

12.4 Collections of Objects

Instead of storing a separate member variable for each object, we can store an entire collection of similar objects using one of the *Collection* classes. In order to use any of the collection classes, an extra **using**-instruction is required:

using System.Collections.Generic;

A very useful collection class is the List class, and we can use it as follows:

List<Snowflake> snowflakes;

As you can see, a List declaration expects the *type* between < and > characters (angled brackets). This is needed, because List needs to know what kind of objects it stores so that it can reserve enough memory for it (an Elephant object is bigger than a Mouse object). We have seen the angled brackets before when using the Content.Load method which also needs a type to know what kind of asset it should load.

A List object is initialized as follows:

snowflakes = **new** List<Snowflake>();

After this initialization, snowflakes represents an empty list. We can add objects to the list as follows:

snowflakes.Add(**new** Snowflake(sprite));
snowflakes.Add(**new** Snowflake(sprite2));
snowflakes.Add(**new** Snowflake(sprite3));

Each item added to the list has its own index, which can be used to access the item. This is done using brackets ([and]):

Snowflake first = snowflakes[0];
Snowflake last = snowflakes[2];

Note that the first object in a List has index 0, not 1! This is something very easy to forget and accessing a List outside its allowed values will lead to an error (not a compiler error, but a runtime error; which we will see later on). Another useful feature of the List class is the Count property, which counts the number of items currently in the list:

if (snowflakes.Count == 0)
    do something...

Okay, the List class seems very useful. So let us now add 500 snowflakes to it:

snowflakes.Add(**new** Snowflake(sprite));
snowflakes.Add(**new** Snowflake(sprite));
snowflakes.Add(**new** Snowflake(sprite));
snowflakes.Add(**new** Snowflake(sprite));
snowflakes.Add(**new** Snowflake(sprite));
snowflakes.Add(**new** Snowflake(sprite));
snowflakes.Add(**new** Snowflake(sprite));
snowflakes.Add(**new** Snowflake(sprite));
snowflakes.Add(**new** Snowflake(sprite));
and so on...

Alright, maybe that is not the right way to do it. Here, we can use again the power of iteration instructions, such as **while** and **for**. Using a **while**-loop, we can easily add 500 snowflakes, as follows:

```
List<Snowflake> snowflakes = new List<Snowflake>();
while (snowflakes.Count < 500)
    snowflakes.Add(new Snowflake(sprite));
```

Another place where loops are very useful is for iterating through a list and performing some operation on each element in the list. Look at the following example:

```
int i=0;
while (i < snowflakes.Count)
{
    snowflakes[i].Draw(gameTime, spriteBatch);
    i++;
}
```

With the **while**-instruction, we have many ways of controlling how the loop runs. The following example only draws the items with an even index:

```
int i=0;
while (i < snowflakes.Count)
{
    snowflakes[i].Draw(gameTime, spriteBatch);
    i = i + 2;
}
```

Or instead of drawing the first item in the list first, we can also walk through the list backwards:

```
int i = snowflakes.Count − 1;
while (i >= 0)
{
    snowflakes[i].Draw(gameTime, spriteBatch);
    i = i − 1;
}
```

Or when using a **for**-loop:

```
for (int i = snowflakes.Count − 1; i >= 0; i−−)
    snowflakes[i].Draw(gameTime, spriteBatch);
```

Check for yourself what happens when these varieties of **while**-instructions are executed. Can you modify the last **for**-instruction so that it draws the items with even indices only? Or that it only draws items with indices divisible by 5?

12.5 The IList Interface

It is possible that in the future, someone will write a class that has exactly the same methods as List, but it offers some advantages: the methods are faster, or the objects take up less space in memory (or even both, but that is a lot to ask). Let us say that in a few years a new class FastList becomes available. Because it is so much better, we want to change our SnowFlakes program to take advantage of this new class. That is not a problem. We have to change the declaration of the member variable snowflakes:

FastList<Snowflake> snowflakes;

and in the constructor, we modify the initialization to:

snowflakes = **new** FastList<Snowflake>();

The rest of the program can stay as it is, if the FastList class offers exactly the same methods as List.

   However, generally it is not so easy to change the program. For example, if the list is passed as a parameter to methods, we also need to change the declarations of the parameters in these methods. Then we also have to make sure that when the methods are called, the parameter is indeed a FastList object instead of a List object. This can be a lot of trouble.

   One way to avoid this problem is to try and predict the future. When we declare the member variables and the parameters, we will not say that we are going to use a List or a FastList (because the latter does not exist yet). Instead, we declare our variables of type IList. The IList type is not a class, but an *interface*. An interface is a specification of which methods and properties objects of that type should have, without already implementing these methods and properties. Therefore, it is not possible to make an instance of an interface-type, because the interface does not specify what the objects look like, only what they should be capable of doing. When we initialize a variable of an interface-type, this means we have to make a choice, for example:

IList<Snowflake> snowflakes;
snowflakes = **new** List<Snowflake>();

When a new, better version of the List class becomes available, we can leave the declaration as is, and we only have to change the initialization. As you can see in this example, we can assign an object of type List to the member variable of type IList. This is possible because the List class promises in its header that it is an *implementation* of the interface IList. In other words: all the methods that were promised in the interface, exist in the List class. And the compiler verifies this.

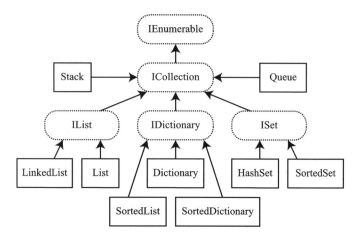

Fig. 12.2   An overview of the classes and interfaces related to collections

12.6 The Collection Interface

The library System.Collection.Generic contains more than only IList and List. Figure 12.2 shows an overview of the interfaces and classes that are part of the library. There is a distinction between two kinds of interface:

- ISet, for data where the order does not matter;
- IList, for ordered data.

These are a number of methods (not all of them) that are specified in the interface ICollection:

```
interface ICollection<E>
{
    void Add (E x);
    bool Remove (E x);
    bool Contains (E x);
    int Count {get;}; // a read−only property
    void Clear ();
}
```

All methods where an index is needed (in other words: methods requiring *ordered* data), are in the sub-interface IList:

```
interface IList<E> : ICollection<E>
{
    E this [int n] {get; set;}; // this is the notation for defining indexing
    int IndexOf (E x);
    void Insert (int n, E x);
    void RemoveAt (int n);
}
```

There are classes, such as HashSet that are an implementation of ICollection but not of IList. As a result, you can add, remove or search for an element in a HashSet, but it is impossible to add elements 'at the end'. A HashSet does not have an identifiable 'end' since all the elements are on a big heap instead nicely of in a row.

12.7   The ISet Interface

Another sub-interface of ICollection is ISet. In this interface, the Add method is special. In an ISet, the Add method guarantees that each element is placed at most one time in the collection. Equality is tested using the == operation. If the element is already in the set, then it will not be added. Except for this particular behavior of Add, the ISet interface has a few methods for calculating the overlap between different ISet objects. Furthermore, the ISet interface does not have any indexing methods, so the data in the set are not ordered in any particular way.

12.8   The IDictionary Interface

Imagine that in a list we did not indicate the elements using an integer index, but with a **string**. That could be useful for games that are published in different countries and different languages. You could use this for example to create a translation table between different languages, by using as index the English word and as value the same word in the desired language. In order to translate a word you only have to look in the table at the right place.

   Such a translation table is exactly what is specified by the IDictionary interface. It resembles an IList, but where an IList indexes its elements with integers, the IDictionary can use any type. In practice, the IDictionary is used most with **string** values as indices. So, the IDictionary is generic for both the key type K and the element type E. The interface specifies among others the following methods:

```
interface IDictionary<K,E>
{
    E Remove (K key);
    bool Add (K key, E value)
}
```

   Next to the list, set, and dictionary collection types, the library has a few classes that are collections but that do not inherit from either IList, ISet, or IDictionary. An example is the Queue class, which implements a queue data structure that allows you to place elements at the end of the queue and remove them from the front. For instance, in games queues can be useful for handling messages that are sent between players. When a message arrives, it is added to the queue. Messages are processed by removing them one by one from the front of the queue and handling them in order. A variation of this kind of data structure is the Stack class, which allows you to push elements onto the stack, and pop elements from the top again.

12.9 The Array: A Simpler Version of the List

Next to the collection classes, C# also has a more basic data structure called an *array*. An array basically is a simplified version of a List object. For example, we can declare an array of integers as follows:

```
int[] table;
```

The brackets indicate in this case that we are not declaring a single integer variable, but an *array* of **int** variables. Declaring the array is not enough to be able to use it. We have to initialize it beforehand:

```
table = new int[5];
```

We can assign values to the items in the array as follows:

```
table[3] = 4;
table[0] = 1;
```

As you can see, arrays also start from index 0. The elements in an array can also be used in an expression, such as:

```
int x = table[3] + 12;
```

Furthermore, arrays have a property called Length which allows us to determine the size of the array:

```
if (table.Length > 10)
    do something...
```

When looking at the array declaration, we immediately see the disadvantage of using an array over a List: when we initialize an array, we need to specify its size, and this size cannot be changed afterwards. So if we initialize our table array with size 5, but later on in the game we realize that we need a larger size, then there is only one way to do it: copy the entire array into a temporary array, create a new (larger) array, and copy all the elements back. A List on the other hand, has a dynamic size: we can add elements to it or remove elements from it once it has been initialized.

So why should we use arrays at all? One of the times when arrays are very useful is when we need a multidimensional structure such as a grid. For example, we can declare a two-dimensional array as follows:

```
int[,] grid;
```

Initializing this array is done as follows:

```
grid = new int[5,10];
```

Again, the actual size of the grid is fixed because of the limitation of arrays, but in general, this is not a problem for grids, which are often used to represent structures of fixed size such as playing boards. Once we have initialized the array, we can assign values to it and read from it as follows:

```
grid[0,1] = 12;
int g = grid[0,1] * grid[0,1];
```

The Length property is available for multidimensional arrays as well:

```
int length = grid.Length;
```

But what does it mean in the case of multidimensional arrays? In this case, Length will return the size of the first dimension. So in the case of grid, grid.Length will yield 5. How do we get access to the length of the other dimensions? For this, there is the GetLength method:

```
int dim0length = grid.GetLength(0);
int dim1length = grid.GetLength(1);
```

The array type is not restricted to one- or two-dimensional arrays, for example we can also declare three- or four-dimensional arrays, if we wish so:

```
int[,,] grid3d = new int[10,10,10];
int [,,,] grid4d = new int[10,10,10,10];
```

Although this is all possible to do with arrays, you will probably not use such complicated data structures very often. Also note that such structures start using a lot of memory. For example, the four-dimensional grid in the previous example does not look so big (I mean, it is only 10 by 10 by 10 by 10), but it actually contains 10,000 integer variables! With integers this still does not take up a lot of space, but if you use a more complicated type, such as, say a GameObject, things might look very different.

We can now extend the syntax diagram representing the different types by including the array, as well as classes, structs, and generics such as List:

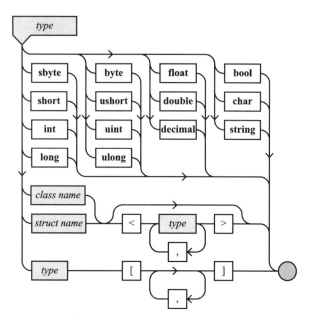

12.9.1 Strings: A Special Kind of Array

The **string** class has a lot of similarities to an array: it consists of a list of characters, it has a length, and we can access the individual characters using brackets, just like an array. The **string** class has among others the following methods and properties:

- **int** Length: determines the length of the string;
- **string** SubString(**int** x,**int** y): selects a part of the string indicated by two positions and returns it as a result;
- **string** Concat(**object** s): glues a second string behind it, and returns it as a result. If the parameter is something other than a string, the method ToString is called on the object first.
- **bool** Equals(**string** s): compares the string character-by-character to another string and yields **true** if all characters are the same;
- **int** IndexOf(**string** s): determines at which spot s in **this** appears for the first time;
- **string** Insert(**int** p, **string** s): insert s into the string at position p.

In all cases where a string is returned as a result, it is a new string. The original string is not changed in any way. This is a conscious choice by the designers of the class. The **string** type is *immutable*, in other words: once an object of that type is created it cannot be modified anymore. Of course it is possible to make a modified *copy*, which is exactly what SubString, Concat and Insert do.

Apart from methods, the **string** class also defines operators.

- The + operator with a left **string** argument does exactly the same as the Concat method. This allows concatenating strings as "Hello"+ name.

- The == operator is redefined and does the same as the Equals method. This is a smart move: without this redefinition, the == operator would compare the references and not the content of the objects. There are situations where two **string** references to different object contain the same value. Thanks to the redefinition the comparison will then still yield **true**. In languages such as Java and C this is not done, so you have to watch out when you are comparing strings.

With the SubString method you can select a part of the string, for example the first five characters:

```
string head;
head = s.SubString(0,5);
```

The numbering of the positions in a string is—just like arrays and lists—a bit special: the first character is position 0, the second character position 1, and so on. As parameters to the SubString method, you provide the position of the first character that you need, and the position of the first character that you do not want anymore. Therefore, the call s.SubString(0,5) gives the characters at positions 0, 1, 2, 3, and 4; in other words the first five characters.

Just like arrays, you can access the individual elements in a string using an *indexer*. However, you cannot *change* this element since the **string** type is immutable. The individual elements of a string are of the primitive **char** type, so you can store them directly in a variable:

```
char first;
first = s[0];
```

12.10 foreach: Do Something with All the Items in a List or an Array

Traversing a list to perform some operation on each item in the list is so common, that for that purpose, a special iteration instruction is available called **foreach**. For example, the following **foreach**-instruction draws all the snowflakes in the list on the screen:

```
foreach (Snowflake s in snowflakes)
    s.Draw(gameTime, spriteBatch);
```

The **foreach**-instruction does away with the counter variable altogether. In each iteration, a local variable s represents the item that we are currently working on. Although this is a very compact notation for iterating through a list, it is less powerful than the full-fledged **for**-instruction, since we do not have control over which items in the list are processed and in which order. The **foreach**-instruction can be used on both arrays and lists. Here is the syntax diagram for the **foreach**-instruction:

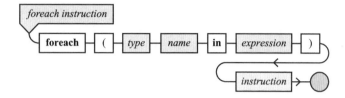

12.11 Iterating with an Iterator

For traversing all the elements in an ICollection, there is another way apart from
foreach. For this purpose, there is a method available in ICollection. Or actually: in
the super-interface from which ICollection inherits:

```
interface IEnumerable<E>
{
    ...
    IEnumerator<E> GetEnumerator ();
}
```

This method GetEnumerator delivers an IEnumerator object, which is also called an
iterator. From this object you can call the property Current and the method MoveNext.
In other words: this object is itself an implementation of the interface IEnumerator:

```
interface IEnumerator<E>
{
    E Current {get;}; // a read—only property
    bool MoveNext (); // gives false if there is no next element anymore
}
```

These two methods are exactly what you need in a **while**-loop:

```
IEnumerator<Snowflake> e;
e = snowflakes.GetEnumerator();
while (e.MoveNext())
    doSomethingWith(e.Current);
```

Or even more compact with a **for**-instruction:

```
for (IEnumerator<Snowflake> e = snowflakes.GetEnumerator(); e.MoveNext(); )
    doSomethingWith( enum.Current );
```

In an ICollection, the data are not in a particular order. Therefore, there is no guarantee
that the IEnumerator provided by GetEnumerator will return the elements in the same
order as they were added. However, you are guaranteed to traverse all of them. By
the way, this is exactly what happens behind the scenes when you use the **foreach**
syntax. The program will therefore not be faster or slower if you use an IEnumerator
instead of **foreach**.

12.12 What You Have Learned

In this chapter, you have learned:

- how to store multiple objects of the same type in a collection or array;
- how the library of collection classes in C# is structured using interfaces;
- how to traverse a collection and perform operations on its elements using the **foreach**-instruction;
- how strings are similar to arrays.

Chapter 13
Fullscreen Games

13.1 Introduction

In this chapter, we are going to deal with viewing games in full screen mode. We will start developing the Jewel Jam game by adding some methods for switching between full screen and window mode. All the examples we have seen until now were drawn in a window. If you really want to involve your players in your game, you do not want them distracted by emails, pop ups, other windows or that nice desktop background of a game of a competitor of yours. So, the solution is to go into full screen mode. This is not that hard to do, but there are a couple of things to think about.

13.2 Setting the Resolution

When displaying something in full screen, the full screen resolution often will not match the desired resolution of the game. This means that we have to scale everything up or down when we go into full screen mode. Downscaling everything might sometimes even be necessary when we are not in full screen mode, for example, if the maximum resolution of the screen is lower than the desired resolution of the game. As we will see later on, the XNA game engine has a few classes and methods that we can use to achieve this.

Before we start adding fullscreen capabilities to our game, we first need to define what the desired resolution of our game is. Setting the resolution of the game is not that hard, we can use the graphics device manager for that. For example, the following two lines set a resolution of 1024 × 768 pixels:

```
graphics.PreferredBackBufferWidth = 1024;
graphics.PreferredBackBufferHeight = 768;
```

If we are viewing the game in a window (like in the Painter game), the game engine will automatically resize the window so that it can display 1024 × 768 pixels. If we

A. Egges et al., *Learning C# by Programming Games*,   197
DOI 10.1007/978-3-642-36580-5_13, © Springer-Verlag Berlin Heidelberg 2013

want to be sure that the graphics device is not in fullscreen mode, we can add the
following instruction:

graphics.IsFullScreen = **false**;

Once we have changed the resolution, we need to tell the graphics device manager
that it should update the window. This is done by calling the ApplyChanges method:

graphics.ApplyChanges();

This way of setting the resolution does not take into account the actual screen dimensions. So let us try to come up with a method that handles this nicely. Especially
when we are in full screen mode, chances are that the actual resolution of the screen
is probably different from the desired resolution, we need to keep track of what the
desired resolution is and with what factor we should scale the sprites so that everything is drawn correctly. In order to do that, we declare a member variable screen
inside the JewelJam class, together with a property to access it. We will use the type
Point for that, which is similar to a Vector2D type, except that it does not have vector manipulation methods, and the type of the coordinates is **int**. The declaration is
given as follows:

protected static Point screen;

Since there will probably be only one screen resolution in the game, we made this
variable and its associated property *static*. Inside the LoadContent method, we assign
a value to the screen member variable:

screen = **new** Point(1440, 1080);

Now we need to inform the graphics device that we would like to use this screen
resolution and we need to indicate if we want to run the game in full screen mode
or not. For that, we will add a method to the JewelJam class called SetFullScreen.

13.3 Updating the Graphics Device

The SetFullScreen method will have the following structure:

```
public void SetFullScreen(bool fullscreen = true)
{
    ...
    if (!fullscreen)
    {
        Deal with non fullscreen mode
    }
```

```
    else
    {
        Deal with fullscreen mode
    }
    graphics.ApplyChanges();
    ...
}
```

There are a few interesting things happening in this method. First, if you look at the parameter, you see that it is assigned a value. This is a feature in the C# programming language allowing us to define *default values* for parameters. In this case, the default value for the parameter is **true**. This means that we could call the method as **this**.SetFullScreen();, which would be equivalent to **this**.SetFullScreen(**true**);. Default values can come in handy sometimes, since you can avoid defining a lot of parameters that you do not care about, making your code easier to read.

In the **if** instruction, we deal with the two cases: windowed mode, or fullscreen mode. After that, we apply the changes to the graphics device. Also, we store the actual screen resolution by accessing the width and height of the viewport. We need to get this information from the viewport instead of simply storing the resolution, because in some cases, the two can be different, especially when we are in fullscreen mode. Also in some other cases, the graphics device manager may choose to use another resolution than the one we specify because of limitation of the graphics device. That is why a property used to set the resolution are called PreferredBackBufferWidth and not simply BackBufferWidth.

When we want to determine if we have to scale anything, we first have to find out what the current screen resolution is. For that, we can use the GraphicsAdapter class that is provided by XNA. For example, we can get the current width using GraphicsAdapter.DefaultAdapter.CurrentDisplayMode.Width. We can use this to calculate with what factor we should scale the x game screen width to match the actual total width of the screen:

```
float scalex = GraphicsAdapter.DefaultAdapter.CurrentDisplayMode.Width /
               (float)screen.X;
```

The value that we calculate here is either less than 1 (so, we need to scale down in order to fit the desired size on the screen), equal to one (the screen size matches the desired size), or greater than 1 (we need to scale up the image in order to fit on the screen). Similarly, we calculate this value for the y direction:

```
float scaley = GraphicsAdapter.DefaultAdapter.CurrentDisplayMode.Height /
               (float)screen.Y;
```

If we want to maintain the correct aspect ratio, we need to choose one of these scales and use it to scale the image. Let us store this scale in a local variable finalscale, which will initially be one (no scaling):

```
float finalscale = 1;
```

Now we have to handle the two cases (fullscreen or not). If we are not in fullscreen mode, then we want to scale down if the window does not entirely fit on the screen. If the desired x screen size is larger than the display screen, the scalex variable will contain a value smaller than 1. And the same goes for the y screen size. In other words, if either the scalex or scaley variable is smaller than 1, we want to scale down the size of the window so that it fits on the screen. And to ensure the window always fits on the screen, we would have to choose the smallest scale in that case:

```
if (!fullscreen)
{
    if (scalex < 1f || scaley < 1f)
        finalscale = Math.Min(scalex, scaley);
}
```

In case we are in fullscreen mode, we will either scale up or down (or not scale at all in very few cases). We want to scale the image as little as possible to avoid too much distortion, so we want to choose the scale that is closest to 1. We can do that as follows:

```
float finalscale = scalex;
if (Math.Abs(1 − scaley) < Math.Abs(1 − scalex))
    finalscale = scaley;
```

Here we use the Math.Abs method which returns the absolute value of a numerical type value passed as a parameter. So, in this **if** instruction we check if the difference between the y scale and 1 is smaller than the difference between the x scale and 1. If so, we choose the y scale as the final scaling value. Now that we have calculated which scale we are going to use, we apply this scale to calculate what the new width and height should be, and set that as the desired screen size:

```
graphics.PreferredBackBufferWidth = (int)(finalscale ∗ screen.X);
graphics.PreferredBackBufferHeight = (int)(finalscale ∗ screen.Y);
```

Then, we set the mode to either fullscreen or not, depending on the value of the variable passed as a parameter, and we apply the changes to the graphics device:

```
graphics.IsFullScreen = fullscreen;
graphics.ApplyChanges();
```

13.4 Correcting the Mouse Position

Now that we have changed the resolution of the game, we need to solve a couple of things. One thing now is that the mouse position will no longer always be correct, since we will be scaling the sprites later on. Therefore, we also need to scale the mouse position. We are going to extend the InputHelper class for that. First, we add a Vector2 member variable in that class to store the current scale:

```
protected Vector2 scale;
```

We also define a property Scale to be able to read and write the member variable:

```
public Vector2 Scale
{
    get { return scale; }
    set { scale = value; }
}
```

Then, we have to modify the MousePosition property to take this scale into account:

```
public Vector2 MousePosition
{
    get { return new Vector2(currentMouseState.X, currentMouseState.Y) / scale; }
}
```

In the SetFullScreen method, we then set the properties to the right values:

```
inputHelper.Scale = new Vector2((float)GraphicsDevice.Viewport.Width / screen.X,
                                (float)GraphicsDevice.Viewport.Height / screen.Y);
```

Note that we recalculate what the scale is using the GraphicsDevice property. We do this to ensure that we get the right scale values. Remember that setting the PreferredBackBufferWidth property does not *guarantee* that the game will indeed get this particular resolution. The game engine may decide that the final screen size is slightly different depending on the limitations of the graphics output device.

13.5 Scaling the Sprites

Now that we set the right resolution, we will need to scale the sprites when we draw them so that they correspond to the scaled resolution. If we did not do this, our viewport resolution would be correct, but the sprites would be drawn at their original size. Scaling the sprites sounds a lot more complicated than it is. XNA provides a very simple way to scale everything up or down, using the Matrix class (this refers to the mathematical construction, not the movie). First, we declare a member variable spriteScale and then we use the CreateScale method to create a scaling matrix:

```
spriteScale = Matrix.CreateScale(inputHelper.Scale.X, inputHelper.Scale.Y, 1);
```

The only thing left to do now is tell the SpriteBatch object that we want it to apply a scaling factor to all the drawing operations. We can do this by calling another version of the Begin method that takes a few different parameters, one of them being the scale that we want to apply. We do this in the Draw method of the JewelJam class:

```
GraphicsDevice.Clear(Color.Black);
spriteBatch.Begin(SpriteSortMode.Deferred, null, null, null, null, null, spriteScale);
spriteBatch.Draw(...);
```

Now, our sprites will be nicely scaled in fullscreen mode.

13.6 Making Sure We Can Still Quit the Game

If a game is in fullscreen mode, we have no more means to close the program, except by force using the Windows task manager. Clearly, this is not really a desirable 'feature' of our game, so let us add a simple extension that will allow us to press the Escape button to quit the game. In order to do that, we add the following lines to the Update method:

```
if (inputHelper.KeyPressed(Keys.Escape))
    this.Exit();
```

Furthermore, we would like to be able to easily switch between windowed mode and fullscreen mode by pressing the F5 key. In order to do this, we add the following **if** instruction to the Update method:

```
if (inputHelper.KeyPressed(Keys.F5))
    SetFullScreen(!graphics.IsFullScreen);
```

Now we are done. In the JewelJam1 program, you can see the complete code. In the next section, we will expand the JewelJam1 program to draw a grid of game objects.

13.7 What You Have Learned

In this chapter, you have learned:

- how to retrieve and set the screen resolution;
- how to display a game in fullscreen mode;
- how to scale sprites and correct the mouse position.

Chapter 14
Game Objects in a Structure

14.1 Introduction

In Chap. 12, we have seen how we can maintain a list of game objects. In the Snow example, these objects (snowflakes) were placed arbitrarily on the screen. However, games often require that game objects are adhering to some kind of structured game world. Many board or puzzle games have this requirement. These games impose a set of rules, which binds the playing pieces to certain positions or configurations on the playing board. For example, in a chess game, the pieces can only be placed (meaningfully) on the white and black squares on the playing board. It is not allowed to place your queen halfway two squares. In computer games, these kinds of restrictions are easier to enforce, you just have to make sure that the position where you place your game object is a valid one.

In this chapter, we will look into incorporating these kind of structures into computer games.

14.2 Game Objects in a Grid

14.2.1 Grids in Games

Often, board games and puzzle games are based on placing objects in some kind of grid. There are many examples of such games: Chess, Tetris, Tic-tac-toe, Sudoku, Bejeweled, and many more. Often the goal in these games is to modify the configuration of the grid in some way to achieve points. In Tetris, completely filled rows have to be constructed, and in Sudoku, numerical properties must hold for rows, columns, and sub grids. Our game Jewel Jam also uses a grid structure. The question is: how do we represent these kinds of grid-like structures in our games?

First let us have a look at a simplified case, where we want to draw a background sprite, and on top of that, a grid of ten rows times five columns, where each location in the grid is filled with a sprite. The program that does this is called JewelJam2 and you can find it in the example solution belonging to this chapter.

A. Egges et al., *Learning C# by Programming Games*,
DOI 10.1007/978-3-642-36580-5_14, © Springer-Verlag Berlin Heidelberg 2013

14.2.2 Using a Grid to Draw Sprites

In Chap. 12, we have seen how we can create a two-dimensional array. Now let us put this feature to use in our next example for creating a two-dimensional playing field. The program JewelJam2 contains the instructions to create a game world consisting of a grid of sprites that can be manipulated. Because there will only be three different sprites in this example, we do not store the actual sprites in the grid, but an *integer that represents them*. We load these three sprites in the LoadContent method:

```
jewel1 = Content.Load<Texture2D>("spr_single_jewel1");
jewel2 = Content.Load<Texture2D>("spr_single_jewel2");
jewel3 = Content.Load<Texture2D>("spr_single_jewel3");
```

We also initialize the two-dimensional grid and assign random integer values in the domain [0, 2] to them:

```
grid = new int[5, 10];
for (int x = 0; x < 5; x++)
    for (int y = 0; y < 10; y++)
        grid[x, y] = random.Next(3);
```

As you can see, we use a *nested* **for**-loop to initialize all the items in the array to a random value. The outer **for**-loop traverses the different x-indices, while the inner **for**-loop traverses the y-indices. If you do not yet feel familiar with these kinds of loops, try to follow step-by-step what is happening in this code fragment. We can use the same nested **for**-loop in the Draw method to draw the sprites on the screen:

```
for (int x = 0; x < 5; x++)
    for (int y = 0; y < 10; y++)
    {
        Vector2 position = new Vector2(85 + x * 85, 150 + y * 85);
        if (grid[x, y] == 0)
            spriteBatch.Draw(jewel1, position, Color.White);
        else if (grid[x, y] == 1)
            spriteBatch.Draw(jewel2, position, Color.White);
        else
            spriteBatch.Draw(jewel3, position, Color.White);
    } spriteBatch.Draw(symbol3, position, Color.White);
```

In this code, you can see the advantage of using a grid. By using the indices, we can calculate the position of the sprite in a very convenient way. The whole grid should be drawn at an offset of (85, 150), so we add 100 to both the x and y values of the local position variable. In order to calculate the actual position of the sprite, we multiply the indices by 85 (which is the width and height of the sprite) to get the final position. Finally, we determine which sprite to draw (jewel1, jewel2 or jewel3) by using an **if**-instruction to link the integer value in the grid to the sprite drawing method.

14.2.3 Grid Operations

Because we have organized part of the game world in a grid, we can now use **for**-loops in a smart way to add some *behavior* to this grid. In this example, we will add a feature for moving each row down one row. This means that the last row disappears and we need to generate new (random) values for the first row. Let us add a method called MoveRowDown that does this for us. So what does it mean to 'move down' a row? Basically, we simply have to copy the values in the row at index *y* to the row at index *y* + 1. Let us try and put this in a **for**-loop:

```
for (y = 0; y < 9; y++)
    for (x = 0; x < 5; x++)
        grid[x, y + 1] = grid[x, y];
```

The outer **for**-loop iterates of the rows 0 until 8. This means that the last row will not be moved downwards. This is actually what we want, because there is no row below the last row! The inner **for**-loop iterates over the columns (from 0 until 4) and copies the value at location (x, y) to location $(x, y + 1)$. This means that after this inner **for**-loop has finished, the contents of row *y* has been copied to row *y* + 1. However, if you try to run this **for**-loop, you will notice that it does not have the behavior that we want. No, in fact what happens is that the contents of the first row seem to be copied to all the rows below it! How is this possible?

Here you see an example of why it is important to think through how these loops work. The problem in this case is that we forgot that loops are *sequential*. Let us have a look at what is happening. The first time we enter the loop, we copy the contents of row 0 to row 1. The second time we enter the loop, we copy the contents of row 1 to row 2. However, row 1 was already replaced by the contents of row 0 the previous time we entered the loop, so in fact, we are copying (indirectly) the contents of row 0 to row 2!

So how can we solve this issue? Actually, we only have to make a simple change to our algorithm. Instead of starting with row 0 and continuing until we reach the last row, we start with the last row and continue upward until we reach the first row. This modified algorithm looks like this:

```
for (y = 8; y >= 0; y−−)
    for (x = 0; x < 5; x++)
        grid[x, y + 1] = grid[x, y];
```

In this case, we start with the row at index 8 and copy its contents to the row at index 9. After that, we copy row 7 to row 8, and so on. As opposed to the previous version of the algorithm, this approach does work, because we work from the bottom upwards and we only make modifications to rows that we no longer have to consider: once we have copied the values from row 7 to row 8, we do not look at row 8 anymore in the remainder of our algorithm.

After we have moved all the rows down, the only thing left to do is generate new random values for the first row. This can be done by a single **for**-instruction that retrieves a random number for each item in the row:

```
for (x = 0; x < 5; x++)
    grid[x, 0] = random.Next(3);
```

14.2.4 More Possibilities with Grids

You can find the complete listing of the JewelJam2 program in the samples provided with this chapter. In order to get acquainted with how multi-dimensional arrays work, you can try to program some other grid operations on your own. For example, can you write a method **void** RemoveRow(**int** i) that removes a row at a given index and that creates new values for the top row? Or can you write a method that performs a round-robin operation on the rows (so: all rows move down and the last row becomes the first row)? Or how about moving rows up? Or moving columns? You can imagine that it is possible to create many different operations on a grid like this. These operations can be useful for many different games. For example, removing a row from a grid is an operation that is used a lot in Tetris games. In a game like Bejeweled, operations are needed that can remove a number of items from a row or a column and fill the grid up again.

Next to the operations that we can perform on grids, we also have to think about the items that a grid contains. In this example, we have used a two-dimensional grid containing integers. For more complicated games, it is probably useful to have a grid of *game objects* instead, so that we can add more behavior and interaction to the objects that are a part of the grid.

14.3 Hierarchy of Game Objects

14.3.1 Anatomy of a Game Object

Most of the games have quite a complicated structure of game objects. First, there might be a background consisting of various layers of moving objects (mountains, air, trees, and so on). Then, there are various objects moving around that the player can interact with. These objects can be enemies of the player so they need some level of intelligence, these objects can also be more static such as power-ups, trees, doors, or ladders. Sometimes, objects do not even have a physical appearance in the shape of a sprite. For example, you could imagine that the current score of the player is also a game object, but it does not have a sprite associated with it, but a font in which the current score should be displayed somewhere. Or you could imagine a game where there is an invisible enemy that has to be defeated, whose position can only be seen by the effect that this enemy has on its surroundings. We can also think of game objects that are even more complex: game objects that consist of other game objects. Suppose that we have a game object that represents a house. However, this game object might consist of many other game objects, such as a door, stairs, windows, and a kitchen (which itself, in turn, consists of different game objects). In the case of puzzle games, the grid that represents the playing field could also be considered a game object that consists of a grid of other game objects. Given these different types of game objects and the relations between them, we could say that game objects generally form part of a *hierarchy*. This hierarchy can be completely flat, as was the case in our first example game Painter, but the complete Jewel Jam game explained in the following chapters has quite a complicated hierarchy of game objects.

Many games use such a hierarchy of game objects. Especially in 3D games, such a hierarchy is very important because of the complexity of three dimensional environments. Objects in 3D games will normally not be represented by sprites, but by one or more 3D models. The advantage of a hierarchy is that these objects can be grouped together, so that if you pick up a vase that contains a scroll with magic writings on it, the scroll moves along with the vase. Such hierarchies of games are also called *scene graphs* since they present the scene (the environment) as a graph-like structure.

In the Painter game, our basic type of game object was represented by the ThreeColorGameObject class. It is clear that not all game objects will have three possible colors, a current position and a current velocity. Until now, this is how we have represented game objects, simply because it was sufficient for the basic examples that we were using. If we want to develop bigger, more complicated games, we have to let go of the basic premise that a game object is a three colored sprite. But then, what is a game object? In a sense, a game object can be anything we want. So we could define the following class to represent a game object:

```
class GameObject
{
}
```

Okay, this is maybe going a bit too far. For now, let us assume that any game object has a position and a velocity, but how the game object appears (if it appears) is something that we do not yet want to say anything about. So if we want to define a generic GameObject class, it will in any case have the following two member variables:

```
protected Vector2 position, velocity;
```

Note that we used the **protected** keyword to make sure that classes inheriting from GameObject have direct access to these two member variables. If we want to have a game object that is represented by a sprite, we can inherit from this base class and add the necessary member variables.

We also add the main game loop methods: HandleInput, Update, and Draw. Since we do not know yet how the game object should handle input, and how it should be drawn on the screen, we leave these two methods empty. In the Update method, just like we did in the ThreeColorGameObject class, we update the current position of the game object according to its velocity and the elapsed time.

14.3.2 Relations Between Game Objects

If we want to establish a certain hierarchy between game objects, we need to identify which game object *is a part of* which other game object. In terms of hierarchies, this means that we need to establish that a game object can have a *parent game object*. For the game object itself, it is very useful to know who your parent is. Therefore, we need to store a GameObject variable that refers to the parent of the game object as well:

protected GameObject parent;

For example, you can image that there is a object called 'playing field' that contains all the elements part of the playing field (jewels, row selection object, and so on). The 'playing field' object can then be considered the *parent* of these elements. But not all game objects have a parent. For example, the root object does not have a parent. How can we indicate that a game object does not have a parent? We need to set the value of the parent member variable to 'nothing', or in C# programming terms: **null**.

parent = **null**;

Now that we have added a parent to our game object class, we will have to deal with a few administrative hassles in order to make sure that the parent-child relationship between game objects is properly maintained, but we will get back to that later on. Because of this hierarchy of game objects, there are now a few things that we have to make decisions about.

14.3.3 Local Versus Global Positions

As we know, each game object has a variable containing its position. Until now, each game object was directly positioned in the game world. Although this approach works just fine, it might not be the ideal solution. Consider the playing field game object. In order to align the playing field to the background sprite, we want to place it at position (85, 150). However, all the child objects (the jewels in the grid, a sprite for selecting a different row) will probably also have this same position offset of (85, 150). In fact, we had to apply this offset to all of the items in the grid in the previous example:

Vector2 position = **new** Vector2(85 + x ∗ 85, 150 + y ∗ 85);

Although it is a bit of work to apply that offset to all game objects that are a child of the playing field object, this is still doable. It becomes more problematic once the child objects become more complicated and have child objects themselves that also need to be positioned correctly. Furthermore, what happens if we change the position of the playing field? We would have to update the position of all the game objects that hang under it. There is a better way to do this: we have to differentiate between *local and global positions*. The *global position* of a game object is its absolute *x*- and *y*-coordinates in the game world. The *local position* of a game object is its position with respect to the position of the parent game object. So, do we need to store both these positions in each game object? No, in fact we only need to store the *local position*. We can calculate the global position by adding the local position of the game object to the position of the parent. If there is no parent, then the local position is the same as the global position. We can write a property that does this work for us:

```
public virtual Vector2 GlobalPosition
{
    get
    {
        if (parent != null)
            return parent.GlobalPosition + this.Position;
        else
            return this.Position;
    }
}
```

Using this property, we can now obtain both the local position of the game object (which is stored in the position member variable), as well as the global position, which is accessed through the GlobalPosition property. As you can see, we calculate the global position by adding the local position to the global position of the parent. The global position of the parent is, again, calculated by taking its local position and adding it to the global position from its parent. This goes on, until we reach a game object that does not have a parent, in which case the local position becomes the global position. As an example, the global position of the row selection object is calculated by adding the (local) position of the root object, the local position of the playing field object plus its own local position. This is exactly the behavior that we get when we access its GlobalPosition property. It may seem a bit strange that we are calling the GlobalPosition property inside the GlobalPosition property itself, but this is perfectly valid C# code. In fact, we are using a programming technique here called *recursion* (we will talk more about that later on).

14.3.4 Layers of Game Objects

When we want to draw a game object, we can use the GlobalPosition property as a convenient way to find out where to draw the game object on the screen. The only problem is that we do not have any idea in which order the game objects in the hierarchy should be drawn. When looking at the Jewel Jam game, we clearly want the background to be drawn before the playing field is drawn, otherwise, the player will only see the background.

It would be nice if we can indicate somehow as a part of the game object when it should be drawn. One way to do this is to introduce *layers*. We can assign a layer to each game object, and the layer which they have been assigned determines when the object should be drawn. We can represent these layers in a very simple way by using integers. Lower layer numbers indicate that the object will be drawn earlier. So, we could assign layer 0 to the background sprite game object, and layer 1 to the playing field game object, making sure that the background is drawn before the playing field. Storing a layer is done directly in the GameObject class by using an integer variable:

protected int layer;

A minor drawback of using layers is that there is no guarantee about the order in which objects in the same layer are drawn. So as a programmer, if you want that one object is always drawn after another, that object has to be in a higher layer.

For a complete view of the GameObject class, see the code in the JewelJam3 example. Of course, simply adding a layer member variable to the GameObject class is not enough, we have to *do something* with this information. In the next section, we will have a look at a few different game object subclasses. One of these classes is the GameObjectList class, which is a class that consists of multiple other game objects. In this class, we will show how the layer variable can be used to draw the objects in the right order.

14.4 Different Kinds of Game Objects

14.4.1 A Sprite Game Object

One of the most commonly appearing game objects is a sprite with a position and a velocity. Since the position and velocity are two member variables available already in the GameObject class, we can inherit from this class and then we only have to add a single member variable to store the sprite. In the constructor of this class we have to pass the sprite as a parameter. Because we are inheriting, we have to call the constructor of the base class so that the GameObject part of the object is constructed as well. This constructor expects an integer value denoting the layer. Finally, we have to override the Draw method. This method is empty in GameObject, because we decided that game objects do not necessarily have a sprite attached to them. Inside the overridden Draw method, we draw the sprite on the screen, and we use the GlobalPosition property to calculate the actual position of the sprite on the screen. For the complete class, see Listing 14.1.

```
1   using Microsoft.Xna.Framework;
2   using Microsoft.Xna.Framework.Graphics;
3
4   class SpriteGameObject : GameObject
5   {
6       protected Texture2D sprite;
7
8       public SpriteGameObject(Texture2D spr, int layer = 0)
9           : base(layer)
10      {
11          sprite = spr;
12      }
13
14      public override void Draw(GameTime gameTime, SpriteBatch spriteBatch)
15      {
16          if (visible)
17              spriteBatch.Draw(sprite, this.GlobalPosition, Color.White);
18      }
19  }
```

Listing 14.1   A sprite-based game object

14.4.2 A List of Game Objects

The next type of game object that we want to introduce is the game object that consists of a list of other game objects. This is a very useful type, because it allows us to create hierarchical structures of game objects. For example, the 'root' game object will need to be a list of other game objects, since it contains the background sprite game object, as well as the playing field. The playing field itself will also be a list of game objects because it contains an overlay, a grid, and a row selector object. To represent a game object containing a list of other game objects, we introduce a class called GameObjectList (see also Listing 14.2). This class inherits from the GameObject class, so a list of game objects is, itself, also a game object. This way, we can treat it as a normal game object and give it a position, a velocity, a drawing layer, or a parent game object. In order to manage a list of game objects, we need to add the following member to the class:

protected List<GameObject> gameObjects;

In the constructor, we initialize this variable, so that the list is ready to be filled with game objects.

One of the goals of the GameObjectList class is to take care of the game objects that are in its list. This means that, if we call the Draw method of a GameObjectList instance, this instance will draw all the game objects that are in its list. The same

```
 1   using System.Collections.Generic;
 2   using Microsoft.Xna.Framework;
 3   using Microsoft.Xna.Framework.Graphics;
 4
 5   class GameObjectList : GameObject
 6   {
 7       protected List<GameObject> gameObjects;
 8
 9       public GameObjectList(int layer = 0) : base(layer)
10       { gameObjects = new List<GameObject>();
11       }
12
13       public void Add(GameObject obj)
14       { obj.Parent = this;
15           for (int i = 0; i < gameObjects.Count; i++)
16               if (gameObjects[i].Layer > obj.Layer)
17               {
18                   gameObjects.Insert(i, obj);
19                   return;
20               }
21           gameObjects.Add(obj);
22       }
23
24       public void Remove(GameObject obj)
25       { gameObjects.Remove(obj);
26           obj.Parent = null;
27       }
28
29       public override void HandleInput(InputHelper inputHelper)
30       { foreach (GameObject obj in gameObjects)
31               obj.HandleInput(inputHelper);
32       }
33
34       public override void Update(GameTime gameTime)
35       { foreach (GameObject obj in gameObjects)
36               obj.Update(gameTime);
37       }
38
39       public override void Draw(GameTime gameTime, SpriteBatch spriteBatch)
40       { if (!visible)
41               return;
42           List<GameObject>.Enumerator e = gameObjects.GetEnumerator();
43           while (e.MoveNext())
44               e.Current.Draw(gameTime, spriteBatch);
45       }
46
47       public override void Reset()
48       { foreach (GameObject obj in gameObjects)
49               obj.Reset();
50       }
51   }
```

Listing 14.2 The GameObjectList class

procedure needs to be followed if the HandleInput method is called or if the Update method is called. For example, the only instruction that is inside the HandleInput method is

```
foreach (GameObject obj in gameObjects)
    obj.HandleInput(inputHelper);
```

So, GameObjectList itself does not define any behavior, it simply manages the behavior of the game objects it contains. Similarly, the Update method simply calls the Update method of all the game objects in the list. Note that we used the **foreach**-instruction for convenience. For HandleInput and Update, we do not care in what order the game objects handle their input or update themselves. For the Draw method, we have to do it slightly differently, since we want to draw the game objects with the lowest layer number first.

This means that we cannot use the **foreach** loop here, because it does not allow us to control the order in which the elements of a collection are traversed. The most robust way to do it would be to sort the list of game objects in the beginning of each call to the Draw method. After that, we can use a regular **for**-loop to draw the game objects one after the other, according to their ordering inside the list. The body of the Draw method would then look something like this:

```
sort the list of game objects
...
for (int i = 0; i<gameObjects.Count; i++)
    gameObjects[i].Draw(gameTime, spriteBatch);
```

Because sorting can be quite complex, we will use another technique that is a bit less robust, but also much faster, since we do not have to perform a sorting operation every time we want to draw the objects. For this, we are going to write a very smart Add method in our GameObjectList class. We are going to write this method in such a way that we can ensure that, after this method has added the game object to the list, the list is already sorted! This can be done by putting the game object in the list at the right location. So, if the list contains three objects at layer 0, and two at layer 3 and we want to add a game object at layer 1, we *insert this object* between the objects at layer 0 and the objects at layer 3.

To make things easy for us, the List class already has a method called Insert which can insert an object at a certain index of the list. In order to achieve this behavior, we construct a **for**-instruction that walks through the list. If we arrive at a point where the current object has a layer with a higher number than the object that we want to add, we insert the object. This **for**-instruction is given as follows:

```
for (int i = 0; i < gameObjects.Count; i++)
    if (gameObjects[i].Layer > obj.Layer)
    {
        gameObjects.Insert(i, obj);
        return;
    }
```

In order to ensure that we insert the object only once, we return from the method after inserting the object. However, we are not done yet. What happens if the list does not contain any objects, or if it contains only objects with a lower layer number than the layer number of the object we want to add? In these cases, the condition in the **if**-instruction will never be **true**, so the game object will not be added at all. This is not what we want. If we reach the end of the **for**-instruction without having added any object, we *still* want to add the object to the list, but then we can simply add it at the end. Therefore, we add the following instruction after the **for**-loop:

```
gameObjects.Add(obj);
```

Now, there is still one thing to do. When a game object is added to the list, it means that the list object should become its parent. So we have to add the following instruction as well:

```
obj.Parent = this;
```

This instruction is the *first* instruction of the Add method, because then we are sure that the parent will always be properly set, whether the game object is inserted somewhere in the list or added at the end. The complete Add method is shown in Listing 14.2. Because we ensure that the game objects are added at the right positions, the Draw method simply consists of a **for**-loop (also see Listing 14.2). But why did we say that this version was slightly less robust than sorting the game list at every call of the Draw method? Imagine the following code fragment:

```
SpriteGameObject obj1 = new SpriteGameObject(spr, 1);
SpriteGameObject obj2 = new SpriteGameObject(spr, 2);
GameObjectList objects = new GameObjectList();
objects.Add(obj1);
objects.Add(obj2);
obj2.Layer = 0;
```

In this fragment, we create two sprite game objects, and add them to a list of game objects. The Add method call makes sure that they are added at the right position (in this case, the order of adding happens to coincide with the layer ordering). However, after that we change the layer index of object obj2, but the list of game objects is not changed, meaning that obj1 will still be drawn before obj2. A way to solve this would be to change the Layer property of a game object so that it removes itself from its parent and adds itself again. However, there are no guarantees that any subclasses of the GameObject class that override this property will remember to take care of this. So, the system is clearly less robust. However, it is a lot faster, and we do not have to bother writing a sorting algorithm (although this is easier than you think, especially with the collection classes of C#).

For the sake of completeness, the GameObjectList class also contains a Remove method. This method is a lot simpler than the Add method. It removes the object from the list, and because the object is not part of the list anymore, its parent is set to **null**.

We can now profit from the layered drawing mechanism we have created, as well as the hierarchical structure. For example, take a look at the following code fragment:

```
gameWorld = new GameObjectList();

Texture2D background = Content.Load<Texture2D>("spr_background");
gameWorld.Add(new SpriteGameObject(background));

GameObjectList playingField = new GameObjectList(1);
playingField.Position = new Vector2(85, 150);
gameWorld.Add(playingField);
```

Here is a part of the code needed to recreate the hierarchy of the Jewel Jam game. We first create a GameObjectList instance. Then, we add a SpriteGameObject instance with layer 0 to this list. After that, we create another GameObjectList instance called playingField, but with layer index 1. As a result, the playing field will be drawn on top of the background. Because playingField is, again, a list of game objects, we can add more game objects to it. In this way, we create a hierarchy of related game objects that are automatically updated and drawn in the right order!

14.4.3 A Grid of Game Objects

Just like we created a class GameObjectList for representing a list of game objects, we can also create a class GameObjectGrid for representing a *grid* of game objects. There is, however, a big conceptual difference between these two classes. For one, the GameObjectList class says nothing about the positions of the game objects that it contains. The GameObjectGrid class, on the other hand, relates all the game objects to a grid, which in turn means that they all have a position on the grid. However, each game object itself also has a position member variable. So how should we deal with this?

Actually, this is not really a problem, but a feature (where did we hear that before?). The positions dictated by the grid can be considered as 'anchor positions' of the game objects (or: the positions to where they belong). The *actual* positions of the game objects can be different, though. By using the anchor position in combination with the actual game object position, we can achieve nice motion effects, where game objects move smoothly over the grid while still belonging to certain grid positions. An example of a game where this kind of effect can be used quite a lot is Tetris: the player can move the Tetris blocks to different positions on the grid, but because the grid anchor position is different from the actual game object position, the blocks move smoothly. Also in the program JewelJam3, this effect is demonstrated.

Our GameObjectGrid class inherits again from GameObject, which makes it easy to incorporate the grid into any hierarchy of game objects. Obviously, there is a member variable for storing a grid of game objects:

```
GameObject[,] grid;
```

As you can see, we refer to the actual game objects in the grid, as opposed to using integers like in the previous version. The advantage is that we can now store any kind of game object as a part of the grid. Because we need to be able to calculate anchor positions, we also need to know the size of a single element in the grid. Therefore we also add two member variables to store the size of a single cell in the grid:

```
protected int cellWidth, cellHeight;
```

In order to modify the cell size, we add two properties to the GameObjectGrid class: CellWidth and CellHeight. The constructor of the class needs three parameters: the number of rows and columns in the grid, and the drawing layer. Inside the constructor, we initialize the two-dimensional array according to the size and we store the value null in each of the grid locations so that it is clear that the entire grid is empty on creation. The complete GameObjectGrid constructor is given as follows:

```
public GameObjectGrid(int rows, int columns, int layer = 0) : base(layer)
{
    grid = new GameObject[columns, rows];
    for (int x = 0; x < columns; x++)
        for (int y = 0; y < rows; y++)
            grid[x, y] = null;
}
```

Now we need to write a method for adding a game object. For now, we are going to keep things extremely basic. Let us just assume that the Add method simply looks for the first empty position in the grid and inserts the game object there. This means that we do not have any control over where objects are placed, but for the example game, this behavior is sufficient. So, inside the Add method, we place a nested for-instruction to walk through the elements in the array. Once we find an empty spot, we insert the game object there and we return from the method. Next to adding the object, we also set a few parameters inside the game object. For example, we have to set the parent of the game object to the grid object, just like we did in the GameObjectList class. We also set the position of the game object to its anchor position in the grid. Then, the complete Add method becomes

```
public void Add(GameObject obj)
{
    for (int x = 0; x < Columns; x++)
        for (int y = 0; y < Rows; y++)
```

```
        if (grid[x, y] == null)
        {
            grid[x, y] = obj;
            obj.Parent = this;
            obj.Position = new Vector2(x * cellWidth, y * cellHeight);
            return;
        }
}
```

14.4.4 A Grid of Jewels

For the Jewel Jam game, we would like to perform a couple of basic operations on the grid. For one, we would like to be able to go to a row and shift the elements in the row to the left or to the right. For example, when the player selects the third row in the grid and presses the left button, all elements except the leftmost one should shift to the left, and the leftmost element becomes the rightmost one. Since this kind of operation is not something that we need in every game that uses a grid, let us create a class JewelGrid that inherits from GameObjectGrid and then we add the operations we need to that class. The basic structure of this class is given as follows:

```
class JewelGrid : GameObjectGrid
{
    public JewelGrid(int rows, int columns, int layer = 0)
        : base(rows, columns, layer)
    {
    }

    // here we add the row shifting methods
}
```

The way we implement shifting the columns in a row to the left, is by storing the first element in a temporary object, then moving the other objects one column to the left, and finally placing the element stored in the temporary object in the last column. We add a method ShiftRowLeft that does exactly this. Because the method is only applied to one row, we have to pass the row index as a parameter. The complete method is given as follows:

```
public void ShiftRowLeft(int rowIndex)
{
    GameObject firstObj = grid[0, rowIndex];
    for (int x = 0; x < Columns - 1; x++)
        grid[x, rowIndex] = grid[x + 1, rowIndex];
    grid[Columns - 1, rowIndex] = firstObj;
    firstObj.Position = new Vector2(Columns * objsize, rowIndex * objsize);
}
```

In addition, we change the position of the object that was changed from being the leftmost object to the rightmost object. The result of this positional change is a nice motion effect, as we will see later on. The method ShiftRowRight is quite similar to this method, have a look for yourself.

We also want to add a method that gives us the anchor position in the grid for any game object. This method is going to be useful later on. As a parameter, this method expects a game object, and it returns a Vector2 object containing the anchor position. Here is the complete method:

```
public Vector2 GetAnchorPosition(GameObject s)
{
    for (int x = 0; x < Columns; x++)
        for (int y = 0; y < Rows; y++)
            if (grid[x, y] == s)
                return new Vector2(x * cellWidth, y * cellHeight);
    return Vector2.Zero;
}
```

This method uses (again) a nested **for**-instruction to look for the game object that was passed as a parameter. Once this object has been found, we calculate its anchor position based on the x and y indices in the grid, together with the cell size. If the object was not found, we return the zero vector (Vector2.Zero). Since this method is useful for almost all grids, we added this method to the GameObjectGrid class.

Because the GameObjectGrid class inherits from GameObject, we need to define what the different game loop methods do. In this case, it is quite straightforward. The nice thing in C# is that we can actually use **foreach** on arrays as well, even if they are multidimensional. So, for instance the Update method becomes

```
public override void Update(GameTime gameTime)
{
    foreach (GameObject obj in grid)
        obj.Update(gameTime);
}
```

Both the HandleInput method and the Draw method do something very similar. Note that when drawing the objects in a grid, we do not take the drawing layer of each game object into account, to keep things simple. Can you extend the Draw method of this class so that it does take care of it? Hint: copy the game objects from the grid to a list, and add them in the same fashion as we did in the GameObjectList class.

14.4.5 Moving Smoothly on the Grid

For our objects to move smoothly on the grid, we are going to use the velocity and the position member variables that are a part of the GameObject class. We are going to use the anchor position that we can retrieve from the GameObjectGrid to calculate the velocity of the game object belonging at that position. The effect of this is that when the game object is not exactly at the anchor position, it automatically starts moving towards that position.

For doing this, we introduce another class called Jewel which represents a game object inside the grid (in this case a kind of jewel). This game object is a subclass of SpriteGameObject. The only thing we need to change in this game object is the Update method, since drawing the sprite is already properly handled in the base class.

So what needs to be done in the Update method? First we need to find out what the anchor position of this game object is. We can do this by calling the getAnchorPosition from the parent (which normally should be a GameObjectGrid instance). However, if we try the following, the compiler complains:

```
Vector2 anchorPosition = this.Parent.GetAnchorPosition(this);
```

Why? Because **this**.Parent returns a GameObject instance, and the GameObject class does not contain a method called getAnchorPosition. What we should do instead is tell the compiler that the parent game object is in fact a GameObjectGrid instance. This is done through *casting*. Casting is something that we have already seen when dealing with basic types such as **float** or **string**, but it can also be done with classes. For example, this is how we can cast a GameObject to a GameObjectGrid instance:

```
GameObjectGrid parentGrid = (GameObjectGrid)this.Parent;
```

A problem with doing this occurs in the case when **this**.Parent is not an instance of GameObjectGrid. In this case, the casting operation will cause an exception, which—if not handled—will result in ending the program. Later on in this book, in Chap. 25, we will discuss exceptions in more detail. There is another way to perform this cast, by using the **as** keyword::

```
GameObjectGrid parentGrid = this.Parent as GameObjectGrid;
```

This does exactly the same thing as the previous casting operation, except that if **this**.Parent cannot be casted to a GameObjectGrid instance, the result is **null**. This means that we can check if the cast was successful. If so, we modify the velocity of the game object so that it moves toward the anchor position, and we update the object position by calling the Update method of the base class:

```
if (parentGrid == null)
    return;
Vector2 targetPosition = parentGrid.GetAnchorPosition(this);
velocity = (targetPosition − position) * 8;
base.Update(gameTime);
```

As you can see, we calculate the velocity by taking the difference between the target position (which equals the anchor position), and the current position. In order to get a faster motion effect, we multiply this value by 8. Then, we add this velocity to the position vector (taking into account the elapsed game time), so that the game object moves toward the target position. For the complete Jewel class, see the JewelJam3 project.

14.4.6 Selecting Rows in the Grid

The final game object that we want to discuss in this chapter is the game object that is used for selecting different rows in the grid. This game object is represented by a rectangular sprite which is drawn around the currently selected row. Because of that, we need to keep track of the currently selected row inside the class that defines the row selector game object. Finally, the row selection object needs to access the grid, so that it can call the row shifting operation on it. Since the row selection game object basically is a sprite that is drawn at a certain position, we are going to design the class RowSelectGameObject as a subclass of SpriteGameObject. In the constructor, we set the selected row to be the first one, we store a reference to the grid that the selection object works on, and we call the base constructor. The complete RowSelectGameObject constructor is given as follows:

```
public RowSelectGameObject(JewelGrid grid, Texture2D selector_frame, int layer = 0)
    : base(selector_frame, layer)
{
    selectedRow = 0;
    this.grid = grid;
}
```

The row-selection game object will be part of the playing field, just like the grid. Therefore, we can express the local position of the row-selection game object relative to the local position of the grid. The only thing we have to do in this class is override the HandleInput method so that we can react to what the player is doing and perform an action accordingly.

First, we check if the player has pressed the up or down arrow key, and increment or decrement the selectedRow variable accordingly. Once that is done, we have to make sure that the selected row is within the range of the grid. We can use the Clamp method from the MathHelper class for that, as follows:

```
if (inputHelper.KeyPressed(Keys.Up))
    selectedRow--;
else if (inputHelper.KeyPressed(Keys.Down))
    selectedRow++;
selectedRow = (int)MathHelper.Clamp(selectedRow, 0, grid.Rows - 1);
```

This way, we are sure that the selected row always is a valid row in the grid. Now that we know what the currently selected row is, we can calculate the position of the row selection game object relative to the grid:

this.position = **new** Vector2(−10, grid.CellHeight ∗ selectedRow − 10);

We place the row selection object 10 pixels to the left and to the top to account for the space between the jewels and the row selection object.

   If the player presses the left or right arrow key, we call the ShiftRowLeft or ShiftRowRight method, and we pass along the currently selected row to these methods so that they know which row to shift. These instructions are rather straightforward:

```
if (inputHelper.KeyPressed(Keys.Left))
    grid.ShiftRowLeft(selectedRow);
else if (inputHelper.KeyPressed(Keys.Right))
    grid.ShiftRowRight(selectedRow);
```

14.5 Creating the Game Objects

Now that we have shown how different game object classes can be constructed, the only thing left to do is create these objects, and the rest will be dealt with by the objects themselves. First we create the gameWorld object, and we add the background image at layer 0 (which is the default layer value). Then we create the playingField object and add it to the gameWorld object as well. For this object, we set the layer index to 1, to ensure that it is drawn on top of the background:

```
gameWorld = new GameObjectList();

Texture2D background = Content.Load<Texture2D>("spr_background");
gameWorld.Add(new SpriteGameObject(background));

GameObjectList playingField = new GameObjectList(1);
playingField.Position = new Vector2(85, 150);
gameWorld.Add(playingField);
```

Then, we create the grid and the row selection object. Both of these objects are added to the playingField object:

```
JewelGrid grid = new JewelGrid(10, 5);
playingField.Add(grid);

Texture2D selectorFrame = Content.Load<Texture2D>("spr_selector_frame");
RowSelectGameObject rowSelector = new RowSelectGameObject(grid,
                                              selectorFrame, 1);
playingField.Add(rowSelector);
```

Finally, we create all the Jewel instances that need to be added to the grid. Every time we create an instance, we randomly select between three different sprites, in

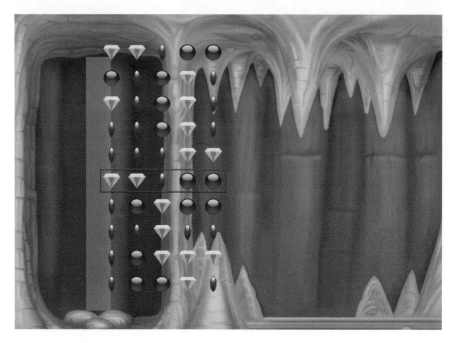

Fig. 14.1 Moving the playing field to another position

order to introduce some variety. Because we do not care about where these objects
are placed in the grid, a nested **for**-instruction is not necessary. We simply have to
create grid.Rows∗grid.Columns objects and add them to the grid:

```
Texture2D jewel1 = Content.Load<Texture2D>("spr_single_jewel1");
Texture2D jewel2 = Content.Load<Texture2D>("spr_single_jewel2");
Texture2D jewel3 = Content.Load<Texture2D>("spr_single_jewel3");

for (int i = 0; i < grid.Rows ∗ grid.Columns; i++)
{
    int val = random.Next(3);
    Jewel obj;
    if (val == 0)
        obj = new Jewel(jewel1);
    else if (val == 1)
        obj = new Jewel(jewel2);
    else
        obj = new Jewel(jewel3);
    grid.Add(obj);
}
```

Now, the only thing left to do is to call the game loop methods of the gameWorld object at the right time. Because of the hierarchy of game objects, the game loop calls

are automatically propagated to all the game objects in the hierarchy. Another nice thing that we can now do because of this hierarchical structure is modify the position of a parent object, and the child objects will automatically be moved accordingly. For example, try to place the playingField object at another position:

```
playingField.Position = new Vector2(300, 100);
```

The result of this change is seen in Fig. 14.1. As you can see, all the child objects are nicely moved along, the row selection mechanism works just as well as the row shifting operations. Here you see the true power of placing game objects in such a hierarchy: we have a lot of control over how the objects are placed on the screen. We could even go completely crazy and give the playing field object a velocity so that it moves around the screen!

14.6 What You Have Learned

In this chapter, you have learned:

- how to organize game objects in a scene graph;
- how to create structured collections of game objects, such as a grid or a list;
- what the difference is between local and global positions;
- how to make the scene graph an integral part of the game by using it for drawing and updating the game objects.

Chapter 15
Redesigning the Game World

15.1 Introduction

Many things change over the course of running a game: many levels are completed, the player's character may change, new quests and enemies are introduced, and so on. In terms of programming games, this translates into more classes and changing relations between instances of these classes. There are, however, also a couple of things that will not change at all while a game is running. For example, the process for loading sprites and sounds will probably stay the same throughout the game, so the class that deals with this will not really change. Another process that is not likely to change while a game is running is the random number generator. While these processes might not change, a lot of different game objects use them. Some objects need to access sprites or sounds, other objects might need the random number generator to initialize themselves. We have already proposed some solutions for these problems. For example, we made the game world object and the random number generator static member variables of the JewelJam class so that they can be easily accessed everywhere. However, the way that we deal with sprites currently is rather cumbersome. We have to pass the content manager to all the constructor methods of the game objects, and as a result, some sprites will be loaded multiple times. In this chapter, we will investigate how to setup a class for dealing with various assets in a game, an instance of which is accessible to all the objects that need assets such as sprites and sounds.

15.2 Better Asset Management

15.2.1 Moving Sprites Around

In the game engine used in this book, assets such as sprites and sounds are loaded by the content manager as follows:

A. Egges et al., *Learning C# by Programming Games*,
DOI 10.1007/978-3-642-36580-5_15, © Springer-Verlag Berlin Heidelberg 2013

Texture2D background = Content.Load<Texture2D>("background");

We have to make a software design decision about where the sprites belonging to the game should be loaded. In the Painter game, some sprites (such as the background sprite) were loaded in the GameWorld class, others were loaded in the classes that defined the objects related to those sprites, such as Ball or Cannon. The disadvantage of loading the sprites in different classes is that we need to pass around the content manager in order to be able to call the Load<Texture2D> method everywhere. A way to avoid that would be to simply load all the sprites when the game starts, and then pass these sprites as parameters to the different objects that are created. In the Painter game, the logical place to do this is the GameWorld class:

```
Texture2D cannonBarrel = Content.Load<Texture2D>("spr_cannon_barrel");
Texture2D cannonColorRed = Content.Load<Texture2D>("spr_cannon_red");
Texture2D cannonColorGreen = Content.Load<Texture2D>("spr_cannon_green");
Texture2D cannonColorBlue = Content.Load<Texture2D>("spr_cannon_blue");
Texture2D ballColorRed = Content.Load<Texture2D>("spr_ball_red");
Texture2D ballColorGreen = Content.Load<Texture2D>("spr_ball_green");
Texture2D ballColorBlue = Content.Load<Texture2D>("spr_ball_blue");
Texture2D canColorRed = Content.Load<Texture2D>("spr_can_red");
Texture2D canColorGreen = Content.Load<Texture2D>("spr_can_green");
Texture2D canColorBlue = Content.Load<Texture2D>("spr_can_blue");
```

```
cannon = new Cannon(cannonBarrel, cannonColorred, cannonColorGreen,
                    cannonColorBlue);
ball = new Ball(ballColorRed, ballColorGreen, ballColorBlue, ballShot);
can1 = new PaintCan(canColorRed, canColorGreen, canColorBlue, 450.0f,
                    Color.Red, collectPoints);
can2 = new PaintCan(canColorRed, canColorGreen, canColorBlue, 575.0f,
                    Color.Green, collectPoints);
can3 = new PaintCan(canColorRed, canColorGreen, canColorBlue, 700.0f,
                    Color.Blue, collectPoints);
```

However, a disadvantage of loading the sprites in the GameWorld instance is that the game world has to know which assets its game objects use. It is much more logical that the game objects *themselves* load their sprites. But of course, then we would have to pass around the content manager everywhere again. As a solution to this problem, we will introduce a new class, the AssetManager class.

15.2.2 The Asset Manager

The goal of the asset manager is to keep track of any assets that have been loaded, and make them available to game objects that want to use these assets. The idea is that the asset manager provides a simple way to access assets used in the game. The asset manager needs a method that load and returns an asset, given an identifier. In our example, we will use strings for these identifiers. The asset manager is going to be a static member of the JewelJam class, so that any game object can access it through a AssetManager property. So, we add the following declaration and property to the JewelJam class:

protected static AssetManager assetManager;

public static AssetManager AssetManager
{
    get { **return** assetManager; }
}

The asset manager object is created in the JewelJam constructor. Because the asset manager needs a reference to the content manager, we pass it along as a parameter:

assetManager = **new** AssetManager(Content);

15.2.3 Loading and Retrieving Assets

Loading and retrieving a sprite asset is done in the GetSprite method. First, this method checks if the string identifier that was passed along is not empty. If it is not, we call the Load method of the content manager to retrieve the sprite. The Load method is quite smart. It loads a sprite only once and it keeps track of which sprites are already loaded in the game. Therefore, if you would call the Load method a thousand times with the same sprite name, the sprite would get loaded only once. For the complete AssetManager class, see Listing 15.1.

Designing games—Although in game development teams the programmer is normally not responsible for the design of the game, it is still very useful to have a basic understanding of this process. The programmer must turn the game design into code and must be able to advise the designer on what will work and what will be difficult to achieve. For this collaboration to be successful, everyone has to speak the same language.

Designing a game primarily consists of defining the game mechanics, the setting of the game and the levels. Game mechanics involve such things are the rules of the game, the way players control the game, the goals and challenges, and the reward structure. Psychology and educational science play an important role here. They help you to understand how players get in the flow (the mood in which they are fully committed to playing the game), how goals, challenges and rewards can support each other, and how to vary and adapt the difficulty of the game.

```
 1   using Microsoft.Xna.Framework.Audio;
 2   using Microsoft.Xna.Framework.Content;
 3   using Microsoft.Xna.Framework.Graphics;
 4   using Microsoft.Xna.Framework.Media;
 5
 6   public class AssetManager
 7   {
 8       protected ContentManager contentManager;
 9
10       public AssetManager(ContentManager Content)
11       {
12           this.contentManager = Content;
13       }
14
15       public Texture2D GetSprite(string assetName)
16       {
17           if (assetName == "")
18               return null;
19           return contentManager.Load<Texture2D>(assetName);
20       }
21
22       public ContentManager Content
23       {
24           get { return contentManager; }
25       }
26   }
```

Listing 15.1 A basic class for managing assets

The setting of the game deals with the story, the characters, and the virtual world in which the game takes place. A good story can be a strong motivator for the players and discovering the story while playing can be a very satisfying task. Characters need to evoke empathy from the player to give meaning to the tasks that must be performed. And the game world enhances these aspects and adapts the game to certain demographics.

Level design is sometimes done by special level designers but in smaller teams it is often the responsibility of the game designer. Careful level design leads to a good learning curve. It keeps the player challenged and motivated. And it should result in pleasant surprises.

Many books have been written about game design and you are strongly encouraged to read some of them. Furthermore, you can find lots of information on all aspects of game development on sites like http://www.gamasutra.com/.

```
 1   using Microsoft.Xna.Framework;
 2
 3   class JewelJamGameWorld : GameObjectList
 4   {
 5       public JewelJamGameWorld()
 6       {
 7           this.Add(new SpriteGameObject("spr_background"));
 8
 9           GameObjectList playingField = new GameObjectList(1);
10           playingField.Position = new Vector2(85, 150);
11           this.Add(playingField);
12
13           JewelGrid grid = new JewelGrid(10, 5, 0);
14           playingField.Add(grid);
15
16           playingField.Add(new RowSelectGameObject(grid, 1));
17       }
18   }
```

Listing 15.2 The class for representing the game world in the JewelJam game

15.3 Accessing the Game World

In the JewelJam game, we do not have a separate GameWorld class anymore. This is because the GameObjectList class is now basically the basis for creating the game world consisting of a hierarchy of game objects that are drawn in a certain order. However, creating all the game objects is now done in the JewelJam class because of that. This is not a very nice software design, because now the basic initialization tasks are mingled with the game-specific object creation tasks. We can separate them by creating a new class called JewelJamGameWorld which will be a subclass of the GameObjectList class. In the constructor of this class, we write all the instructions for filling the game world. Now we only have to make an instance of that class in the JewelJam class, and call the game loop methods on the JewelJamGameWorld object. The complete JewelJamGameWorld class can be found in Listing 15.2. You can find the new version of the JewelJam class in the JewelJam4 program belonging to this chapter.

15.4 Game Objects Using the Asset Manager

15.4.1 The SpriteGameObject Class

Since we want our objects to retrieve their assets themselves, we do not want to pass a Texture2D object anymore as a parameter. For example, the sprite game object should get the name of the asset that it represents as a parameter, and then retrieve the sprite itself from the resource manager. The resource manager is a static member variable that is available from the JewelJam class. As a result, the new SpriteGameObject constructor is given as follows:

```
public SpriteGameObject(string assetname, int layer = 0)
    : base(layer)
{
    sprite = JewelJam.AssetManager.GetSprite(assetname);
}
```

15.4.2 The RowSelectGameObject Class

The game object responsible for selecting different rows also needs to be changed slightly so that it retrieves the sprites that it needs on its own. For this, we need to modify the constructor, just like for the SpriteGameObject class:

```
public RowSelectGameObject(JewelGrid grid, int layer = 0)
    : base("spr_selector_frame", layer)
{
    selectedRow = 0;
    this.grid = grid;
}
```

Since RowSelectGameObject is a subclass of SpriteGameObject, the only thing we need to do here is passing the image name as a parameter to the base constructor, so that the sprite is properly loaded.

15.4.3 The Jewel Class

In order to prepare the Jewel class a bit more for the game that it is going to be used for, we are going to change a couple of things in this class. The biggest change is that we want to introduce more variety in the sorts of jewels that this object can represent. Basically, there will be three variations: the jewel's shape can vary, the color of the jewel can vary, and the number of jewels can vary (one, two or three jewels). So, we have three kinds of properties that a jewel can have (shape, color and number). Also, for each property there are three variations: there are three different shapes, three different colors and three different numbers. In total, that means there are $3 \times 3 \times 3 = 27$ possible jewel configurations (see also Fig. 15.1).

Instead of creating 27 different image files, we will store all the different varieties in a single image file which is loaded when we create the first Jewel object (again, see

Fig. 15.1 The different jewels used in the game Jewel Jam

Fig. 15.1 for the image). The ordering of these jewels in the image file is important, as we will show later on. Inside our object, we randomly choose which jewel we represent by storing a random number between 0 and 26 (to cover the 27 varieties) in a member variable variation. Therefore, the constructor becomes:

```
public Jewel(int layer = 0)
    : base("spr_jewels", layer)
{
    variation = JewelJam.Random.Next(27);
}
```

Because the Jewel class knows which sprite it is going to use, we pass the string ("spr_jewels") directly to the base class constructor.

Now the only thing that needs to be modified is the Draw method, since we do not want to draw the entire sprite, but only a part of it: the part that contains the jewel that this object represents. For this, we use a more complicated version of the Draw method in the SpriteBatch class that allows us to draw only part of a sprite. The part that we want to draw is indicated by a Rectangle object. We can calculate the position of this rectangle by using the value of the variation member variable:

```
Rectangle source = new Rectangle(variation * sprite.Height, 0,
                                 sprite.Height, sprite.Height);
```

Here we assume that the segment we want to draw is a square shape that has the same width and height as the height of the original sprite. The position of the rectangle (given by the first two parameters in the Rectangle constructor) is calculated by multiplying the height of the sprite with the variation index. As a result, the higher the variation index, the further to the right the rectangle is moved. Finally, a call to the Draw method of the sprite batch shows the symbol on the screen:

```
spriteBatch.Draw(sprite, GlobalPosition, source, Color.White);
```

15.5 What You Have Learned

In this chapter, you have learned:

- how to design an asset manager that is accessible from different classes;
- how to create specific game object classes such as Jewel that use the asset manager.

Chapter 16
Gameplay Programming

16.1 Introduction

In this section we are going to look into the gameplay programming of the Jewel Jam game. First, we will talk about interaction between game objects. Then, we will introduce a few new game objects that are used in the game. Finally, we will tackle the main gameplay element of this game: finding combinations of jewels and properly handling them.

16.2 Interaction Between Game Objects

16.2.1 Finding Other Game Objects

In the previous chapter, we have presented the game world as a list of game objects. Each of these game objects may process user input, and may exhibit some kind of behavior. For example, the row selector game object checks if the player has pressed any of the arrow keys, and it moves to another row, or it performs a row shifting operation on the playing grid. This is a typical example of how many game objects in games will be designed. They process input from the player, and they react to it, either by doing something themselves (move to another row), or by influencing other game objects (shift a row in the grid). In the Painter game, we saw that the ball and the paint cans interacted with each other in a similar fashion. In more complicated games, many different game objects will interact with each other.

The problem is: how do these game objects find each other? In the case of the Painter game, the GameWorld class had a specific property for retrieving the Ball object. This is not a very good solution, since it makes the GameWorld class completely dependent on the game that it is a part of. However, in the JewelJamGameWorld we only have a list of GameObjects, which makes it much more complicated to find a particular game object.

A. Egges et al., *Learning C# by Programming Games*,
DOI 10.1007/978-3-642-36580-5_16, © Springer-Verlag Berlin Heidelberg 2013

We would like to design our classes in such a way that they can be used in many different games. In the last version of the game Jewel Jam, the row selector object interacts with the grid object. We have achieved this by passing the grid object as a reference to the row selector object, so that the row selector can directly access any information it needs from the grid. However, this is not an ideal solution either. Once game objects start to become more complex, we would have to pass many different parameters to the constructors of these objects, making them overly complicated and difficult to manage. What we need is a way to find objects in the game world, without making the game world rely on code specific to our game.

16.2.2 Assigning Identifiers to Game Objects

One way of solving this problem in a more generic way is to assign *identifiers* to our game objects. Not all of the objects need identifiers, generally only the ones that interact with other objects do. In our example, we have chosen to use strings as identifiers for game objects. Although this may not be the most performance-efficient approach, it is very easy to implement, as well as easy to understand for humans. After all, "pass me the salt, please" is a lot easier to grasp than "pass me the object with id 4815162342, please". All we need to do is extend our game object classes so that we can assign an identifier to them. We will start with the GameObject class. In this class, we add a member variable to store its ID:

```
protected string id;
```

In order to store an id when we create a game object, we also add a parameter to the GameObject constructor. The header then becomes

```
public GameObject(int layer = 0, string id = "")
```

Because not all game objects need an ID, we have set the empty string as a default value. Inside the constructor, we assigned the parameter value to the member variable. We also add a property ID to have easy access to the ID of a game object:

```
public string ID
{
    get { return id; }
}
```

Because all game objects inherit from the GameObject class, this means that they will now also have an identifier. In many cases, we have to update the constructor of the GameObject subclasses so that they pass along the identifier to the constructor of the base (GameObject) class. For example, the updated SpriteGameObject constructor is given as follows:

```
public SpriteGameObject(string assetname, int layer = 0, string id = "")
    : base(layer, id)
{
    sprite = JewelJam.AssetManager.GetSprite(assetname);
}
```

Similar to this example, most of the GameObject subclasses have been updated in this way. Take a look at the JewelJam5 project to see how this is done for all the different game object types.

16.2.3 Finding Game Objects

Although assigning identifiers to game objects might be a good idea, it is only useful if we also provide a way to *find* these game objects. To see how this can be done, let us add a method Find to the GameObjectList class that will look through the list of game objects to see if any of these game objects have the requested identifier. If the game object is found, the method returns a reference to this game object, otherwise, it returns **null**. The header of our method is then given as follows:

```
public GameObject Find(string id)
```

The only thing we have to do now is write the *algorithm* that examines the game objects in the list and that returns the game object matching the identifier, if it is contained in the list. We will use the **foreach**-instruction to do this, although you could use either the **for**-instruction or the **while**-instruction to do the same thing. Inside the **foreach**-instruction, we check if the current game object's identifier matches the requested identifier passed as a parameter to the method. If so, we return that object. If we did not return from the method in the body of the **foreach**-instruction, it means that none of the game objects in the list had the requested ID, so the method returns **null**. The body of the Find method then becomes

```
foreach (GameObject obj in gameObjects)
    if (obj.ID == id)
        return obj;
return null;
```

Note that once the **return** instruction is executed, we return immediately from the method. This means that the remaining game objects are not checked anymore. Furthermore, we do not check if game objects have duplicate IDs. If there are multiple game objects that carry the same ID, this method returns the first one that it finds.

16.2.4 Recursion: A Method Calling Itself

There is one thing that we did not take into account. It is, of course, possible that one or more of the game objects in the list is itself of the type GameObjectList. If that game object contained a game object with the ID that we seek, then this method would not find it, since it only checks the game objects that are stored in the list of the current object (**this**). So how can we solve this? First, we need to check if an object is of a certain type. For that, we can use the **is** keyword:

```
if (obj is GameObjectList)
    do something
```

Before the **is** keyword, we put the object to be checked, and after the keyword we place the type. If the object is of the given type, then the expression yields **true**. If not, the result is **false**. Therefore, we can use it in an **if**-instruction like in the example above. If we know that the object is of type GameObjectList, we can *cast* it and then try to find the game object that we are looking for in the casted game object list. The following code does exactly that:

```
foreach (GameObject obj in gameObjects)
{
    if (obj.ID == id)
        return obj;
    if (obj is GameObjectList)
    {
        GameObjectList objlist = obj as GameObjectList;
        foreach (GameObject obj2 in objlist.gameObjects)
            if (obj2.ID == id)
                return obj2;
    }
}
return null;
```

So, now we check for each game object to determine if it is of type GameObjectList. If so, we traverse that list's gameObjects variable and look for the game object in there. Are we done now? Well, not really. What if one of the game objects in objlist *also* is of type GameObjectList? It means that we have to add another layer that checks if one of the game objects in *that* list perhaps corresponds to the ID that we are looking for. But one of those game objects could also be of type GameObjectList. Obviously, this approach is not ideal. However, we can do something to avoid this kind of infinite search problem. Why not use the Find method in objlist? Look at the following code:

```
foreach (GameObject obj in gameObjects)
{
    if (obj.ID == id)
        return obj;
```

```
    if (obj is GameObjectList)
    {
        GameObjectList objlist = obj as GameObjectList;
        GameObject subobj = objlist.Find(id);
        if (subobj != null)
            return subobj;
    }
}
return null;
```

This may look a bit strange. We are actually calling the method that we are currently writing. So why does this work? Think about what is happening exactly when the Find method is called on an object. If the game object that we are looking for is inside the list, then this method returns that object. Furthermore, the method calls the Find method on every object that is also of type GameObjectList. If none of those method calls find the object, the method returns **null**. And each of the Find method calls themselves also call the Find method on the objects that belong to them that are of type GameObjectList. At some point however, this big 'tree' of Find method calls end, when we reach the bottom of the game object hierarchy. In other words, at some point there will be no more lists, only game objects. Then, the results of all the Find method calls (either **null** or a game object) are sent back through the return values. Finally, the first caller of the method gets the object (if it was found somewhere in the tree), or **null** if no object carrying the requested ID was found. This kind of search strategy is also called *depth-first*, since we call the Find method on the child object, before examining the rest of the objects in our own list.

When a method calls itself, this is called *recursion*. Recursion is a very powerful tool, because it allows us to perform these kinds of complicated search algorithms without having to write a lot of code. However, watch out with recursion, because you could end up with writing a method that calls itself indefinitely. Suppose that we want to use recursion to compute the product of two (positive) integers by adding them up:

```
public int Product(unsigned int a, unsigned int b)
{
    return (b + Product(a−1, b));
}
```

Here, we forgot to check that the product should return 0 if a == 0. So, the method calls itself indefinitely, resulting in an endless loop, similar to what can happen if you forget to increment the counter in the **while**-instruction. The correct version of this recursive method is, of course:

```
public int Product(unsigned int a, unsigned int b)
{
    if (a == 0)
        return 0;
```

```
    else
        return (b + Product(a−1, b));
}
```

The key here is that the recursive method should have a *termination condition* some-where, so that in some cases, the method does not call itself but does something else. In this example, the termination condition is a == 0. In that case, the method does not call itself, but it simply returns 0 (which is correct, since any number multiplied by 0 results in 0).

16.2.5 Finding the Game World

Although we can look for a game object with a particular ID in a GameObjectList in-stance, we are going to need access to the object representing the game world. The variable that refers to this object is declared in the JewelJam class, and there is no real easy way to access it. One way to solve it would be to use the same approach as we did in the Painter game: make the game world a static member variable and add a property, so the expression JewelJam.GameWorld would yield the game world. However, this is not an ideal solution for several reasons. As we have said before, it is better to avoid static variables when possible. A variable should only be static when you are sure that there will only ever be a single meaningful instance belong-ing to the class that contains the member variable. Although we only have a single game world in both the Painter and JewelJam games, this is certainly not the case for more complicated games. Each level in a game could be a separate game world. Even a single level could contain several different game worlds. So, it is wise to al-ready prepare ourselves so that the classes that we write will also be useful in these cases. A second problem with accessing the game world as a static variable from the JewelJam class is that all the game objects now use a game-specific class (JewelJam) to access the game world. If we would like to use our game object classes in another game, we would have to go through the code and replace all the calls to the JewelJam class with calls to the class specific for that game.

Clearly, we need a better solution to get access to the game world that is useful across different games. In order to do that, we are going to rely on the parent-child relationship that is encoded into the generic GameObject class. For each game object, we can assume that if we get to the root of the hierarchy that the game object belongs to, that this root is the game world. Therefore, we can easily retrieve the game world by walking through the list of parents to get to the root. We add a property called Root to the GameObject class that does exactly this, and it relies on recursion:

```
public GameObject Root
{
    get
    {
        if (parent != null)
```

```
            return parent.Root;
        else
            return this;
    }
}
```

The code inside the property is very simple. If our current parent is not **null** (meaning we have a parent), we ask that parent for the root game object. If the parent is **null** it means that the game object we are currently manipulating is at the root of the hierarchy, meaning that it is the game world. For convenience, we add an extra property to retrieve the game world as a GameObjectList instance which relies on the Root property:

```
public GameObjectList GameWorld
{
    get
    {
        return Root as GameObjectList;
    }
}
```

Assumptions in software design—We made quite a few assumptions in these last paragraphs. For one, we assume that every game object is part of a hierarchy so that we can use that hierarchy to find the game world. This can lead to problems. For example, suppose that you already need access to the game world in the constructor. Chances are that the game object we are constructing is not yet added to a hierarchy so its parent will still be **null**. In the current design, there is no way to access the game world in the constructor, unless we explicitly pass it along as a parameter. Here you see that we made a trade-off in the software design. We will not have to declare the game world as a static variable using our technique, but the price we pay is that we sometimes may have to pass the game world as a parameter to a method. Another assumption is that the object at the root of the hierarchy always is of type GameObjectList. However, you could image that someone would like to use the GameObjectGrid type as the root of a game world. Our current design does not cater for this. One way to solve it would be to redesign the GameObjectGrid class so that it inherits from the GameObjectList class. We would not use a two-dimensional array in that case to store the grid, but we would need to write a few instructions that deal with the translation between two-dimensional coordinates and their actual index in the gameObjects member variable. Even better would be to make a distinction between the hierarchy that game objects are in, and the *layout* that they should follow. In the GameObjectGrid class, these two are currently mixed since it serves both as a game object container, and as a description of the layout for the game objects (which is a grid).

16.2.6 Updating the **RowSelectGameObject** Class

We can now give the playing grid an identifier "grid", so that later on, we can find the grid again in the game objects that use it:

```
JewelGrid grid = new JewelGrid(10, 5, 0, "grid");
playingField.Add(grid);
```

Let us update our existing classes so that they use the identifier system. As an example of how to do this, we will look at the RowSelectGameObject class. This class needs to access the grid object because it has to apply a row shifting operation to it. Because we can retrieve the grid object based on its identifier, we do not have to pass it along to the constructor anymore or store it in a member variable. For example in the HandleInput method, we can retrieve the grid object as follows:

```
JewelGrid grid = GameWorld.Find("grid") as JewelGrid;
```

Here, the GameWorld property comes in handy. We use it transparently to retrieve the grid by calling the Find method. Using that method, we can find any game object that has a unique ID, which is very useful for handling input and updating the state of game objects that depend on other game objects.

As an extra advantage, the RowSelectGameObject class has become simpler, since we do not need to store the grid as a member variable anymore. We can simply look for it when we need it. For the new version of the row selection game object class, see Listing 16.1.

16.3 Introducing a Couple of New Game Object Types

16.3.1 The **ScoreGameObject** Class: Maintaining the Current Score

The next step in making this game more interesting is to add a few game objects that relate to the way that the game is played and how rewards are handed to the player. In this game, we express the reward given to the player by a number of points: the *score*. Every time the player finds a valid combination of symbols, the player gains 10 points. This current score should be stored in a variable or an object somewhere. Also, the score should be written on the screen, so that the player knows how many points he/she currently has obtained.

Now we see another advantage of not specifically assuming that every game object is represented by a sprite. The 'score' game object uses a *font* to display itself on the screen. To make this even a bit more generic, we are first going to introduce a class called TextGameObject, which simply writes some text on the screen at a certain position. This class is very similar to the SpriteGameObject class, except that we draw text on the screen instead of a sprite. In order to do that, we need to store the text to

```
 1    using Microsoft.Xna.Framework;
 2    using Microsoft.Xna.Framework.Input;
 3
 4    class RowSelectGameObject : SpriteGameObject
 5    {
 6        protected int selectedRow;
 7
 8        public RowSelectGameObject(int layer = 0, string id = "")
 9            : base("spr_selector_frame", layer, id)
10        {
11            selectedRow = 0;
12        }
13
14        public override void HandleInput(InputHelper inputHelper)
15        {
16            JewelGrid grid = GameWorld.Find("grid") as JewelGrid;
17
18            if (inputHelper.KeyPressed(Keys.Up))
19                selectedRow——;
20            else if (inputHelper.KeyPressed(Keys.Down))
21                selectedRow++;
22            selectedRow = (int)MathHelper.Clamp(selectedRow, 0, grid.Rows — 1);
23            this.position = new Vector2(−10, grid.CellHeight ∗ selectedRow − 10);
24
25            if (inputHelper.KeyPressed(Keys.Left))
26                grid.ShiftRowLeft(selectedRow);
27            else if (inputHelper.KeyPressed(Keys.Right))
28                grid.ShiftRowRight(selectedRow);
29        }
30    }
```

Listing 16.1 A new version of the row selection game object that uses the identifier system to find game objects in the game world

be written and the font that is used. Finally, we also want to be able to change the *color* of the text that is displayed. Therefore, the TextGameObject class has at least the following member variables:

```
protected SpriteFont spriteFont;
protected Color color;
protected string text;
```

We can then override the Draw method to write text on the screen, which is done by calling the DrawString method from the SpriteBatch class:

```
public override void Draw(GameTime gameTime, SpriteBatch spriteBatch)
{
    if (visible)
        spriteBatch.DrawString(spriteFont, text, this.GlobalPosition, color);
}
```

Again, we are using the *global position* here, so that text-based game objects can also be a part of the hierarchy. It can be useful to use a different origin for displaying text, just as we did with some of the sprites in the Painter game. We, therefore, add a member variable origin of type Vector2 to the TextGameObject class, as well as a property to access and modify it. We then call the extended version of the Draw method from the SpriteBatch class to take the origin into account.

Now, we define a ScoreGameObject class that inherits from the TextGameObject class. We add one member variable to this class which holds the current score:

```
protected int score;
```

Furthermore, we add a property Score that allows to retrieve or modify the current score. We override the Update method to update the text that should be displayed on the screen. For easier text drawing, we want to set the origin of the text to the bottom right. This results in the text being right-aligned, and the position is independent of the font size. Setting the origin is done using the Origin property we added to the TextGameObject class, and we can determine what the origin should be by calculating the size of the text. The SpriteBatch class has a very useful method for that called MeasureText. So, we add another property called TextSize to the TextGameObject class that calculates the text size for us:

```
public Vector2 TextSize
{
    get { return spriteFont.MeasureString(text); }
}
```

Now we can use that property in the Update method of the score game object to set the right origin. For the complete ScoreGameObject class, see Listing 16.2. We now only have to create an instance of this class and add it to the game world. Inside the JewelJamGameWorld class, we place the instructions needed for creating the object. We also add a frame upon which we can draw the current score. These instructions do all the work:

```
SpriteGameObject scoreframe = new SpriteGameObject("spr_scoreframe", 1);
scoreframe.Position = new Vector2(20, 20);
this.Add(scoreframe);

ScoreGameObject score = new ScoreGameObject(2, "score");
score.Position = new Vector2(270, 80);
this.Add(score);
```

```
 1   using Microsoft.Xna.Framework;
 2
 3   class ScoreGameObject : TextGameObject
 4   {
 5       protected int score;
 6
 7       public ScoreGameObject(int layer = 0, string id = "")
 8           : base("ScoreFont", layer, id)
 9       {
10       }
11
12       public override void Update(GameTime gameTime)
13       {
14           this.Text = score.ToString();
15           this.Origin = this.TextSize;
16       }
17
18       public override void Reset()
19       {
20           base.Reset();
21           score = 0;
22       }
23
24       public int Score
25       {
26           get { return score; }
27           set { score = value; }
28       }
29   }
```

Listing 16.2 A game object for maintaining and displaying the current score

We assign the score game object to layer 2, so that it is drawn on top of the background and the score frame. We also choose appropriate positions for the frame and the score. Finally, we have assigned an ID "score" to the score game object, so that other objects can retrieve it when needed.

16.3.2 A Moving Jewel Cart

In order to make the game a bit more exciting, we want to add a feeling of pressure for the player. In the Jewel Jam game, this is done by drawing a jewel cart that slowly moves out of the screen. Once the jewel cart is outside of the screen, the game is over. Every time the player finds a correct combination of jewels, the jewel cart is moved backed a little bit.

The jewel cart is represented in the JewelCart class. We define a couple of things. First, we define how much the jewel cart should be moved back when the player finds a correct combination. This is stored in the push member variable. We also want to set a minimal x position, so that the jewel cart will never be drawn over the playing field. This we do in the minxpos variable, which is accessed by a property carrying the same name. We add a Push method that can be called when the player finds a correct combination of jewels. For the complete class, see Listing 16.3.

We add an instance of this class to the game world as follows:

```
JewelCart jewelcart = new JewelCart(1, "jewelcart");
jewelcart.Position = new Vector2(410, 230);
jewelcart.MinXPos = 410;
this.Add(jewelcart);
```

The jewel cart object also gets an ID, so that we can find it later on when it needs to be pushed. Furthermore, we set its position and its minimal x position to appropriate values. As you can see in Listing 16.3, we assign a positive x velocity to the cart. Because JewelCart is a subclass of SpriteGameObject, which in turn is a subclass of GameObject, the Update method will update the cart position according to its velocity for us (assuming that this method is called from somewhere else).

16.4 Finding Combinations of Jewels

16.4.1 Handling the Combinations

Whenever a player has constructed a valid combination in the middle column using the arrow keys, the player can press the space bar to let the game check if the combination is valid, and if so, add points to the score and push the jewel cart back. The question is: in which object should we handle the event that the player presses the space bar? Since we have many game objects, we could do it in any of their HandleInput methods. For example, we could do it in the RowSelectGameObject class, because we already handle row selection in there. However, that would not be very logical. Checking for valid combinations of jewels is something that fits much better in the JewelGrid class, since that is were the grid of jewels is stored. Therefore, we are going to add a HandleInput method to that class to deal with finding combinations of symbols. In this method, we will check if the player has pressed space. Therefore, the skeleton of the method is given as follows:

```
public override void HandleInput(InputHelper inputHelper)
{
    if (!inputHelper.KeyPressed(Keys.Space))
        return;
    do something...
}
```

```
 1   using Microsoft.Xna.Framework;
 2
 3   class JewelCart : SpriteGameObject
 4   {
 5       protected float push;
 6       protected float minxpos;
 7
 8       public JewelCart(int layer = 0, string id = "")
 9           : base("spr_jewelcart", layer, id)
10       {
11           velocity.X = 6;
12           push = 50.0f;
13       }
14
15       public void Push()
16       {
17           position.X = MathHelper.Max(position.X - push, minxpos);
18       }
19
20       public float MinXPos
21       {
22           get { return minxpos; }
23           set { minxpos = value; }
24       }
25   }
```

Listing 16.3 A game object for displaying a slowly moving jewel cart

16.4.2 Finding Valid Combinations of Jewels

Inside the HandleInput method, we need to check for all groups of three adjacent
jewels to see if they form a valid combination. In order to help us do that, we are
going to add a method IsValidCombination, which has the following header:

public bool IsValidCombination(Jewel a, Jewel b, Jewel c)

This method takes three Jewel objects, and it returns a boolean value indicating if the
three jewels form a valid combination or not. So now the question is: how can we
evaluate whether three jewels form a valid combination? To recall: a valid combination means that for each property (color, shape, number), each jewel should have
either the same or a different value. In order to make things a bit easier, let us *encode*
each symbol by using three integers between 0–2. Let us say that the first integer
represents the color (yellow, blue, or red), the second integer the shape (diamond,
oval or round), and the last integer the number of jewels (one, two or three). Using this encoding scheme, we can, for example, encode the blue oval-shaped single

jewel as $(1, 0, 0)$. The yellow round single jewel is then defined as $(0, 2, 0)$, and the red oval-shaped triple jewel is defined as $(2, 1, 2)$.

Now let us see if we can use this encoding scheme to find valid combinations of three jewels (let us call them jewel A, B, and C). For each jewel, we have to compare their color, the shape, and the number. Each of these properties has to be either the same for all jewels, or all different. Using the encoding, this means that if A has encoding value 0 for the color, B has encoding value 0, and C also has encoding value 0, then for the color the condition holds, since all symbols have the same color (yellow). The same goes if the symbols all have the blue color (A-color $= 1$, B-color $= 1$, C-color $= 1$) or the red color (A-color $= 2$, B-color $= 2$, C-color $= 2$). Finally, the condition holds if all their colors are different, or: there is an ordering of A-color, B-color and C-color that yields 0, 1, and 2. If we look at the sum of these different combinations, we see an interesting property: $0 + 0 + 0 = 0$, $1 + 1 + 1 = 3$, $2 + 2 + 2 = 6$, and $0 + 1 + 2 = 3$, in other words: *the sum is divisible by three*. Also, it happens to be the case that any of the other possible combinations of values is *not* divisible by three. Therefore, we can say that for each property (color, shape, and number): the *sum of the encoding values of each jewel must be divisible by three*. If this sum is represented by a variable sum, then in C# code the condition sum % 3 == 0 must hold! So, if we calculate this sum for each property and check that it is divisible by three, we have found a valid combination of three jewels.

The only thing left to do now is to retrieve the encoding from each jewel. As of now, we only have a single number: the offset of the jewel in the sprite. This is a number between 0–26. If you take a look again at Fig. 15.1, you will see that the first 9 symbols are yellow, the following 9 are blue and the last 9 are red. Therefore, if we divide the variation number by 9, we will get a value between 0 and 2 that represents the color! The rest of that division will be a number between 0–8. If we divide that number by 3, we will again get a number between 0 and 2 that represents the shape. The rest of that division is a number between 0 and 2, and it represents the number of jewels. By using this concept, we can construct an algorithm that calculates these values for each property and that checks if the sum of the properties is divisible by 3. Have a look at the following algorithm:

```
int curra = a.Variation;
int currb = b.Variation;
int currc = c.Variation;
int divider = 9;
for (int i = 0; i < 3; i++)
{
    if ((curra / divider + currb / divider + currc / divider) % 3 != 0)
        return false;
    curra %= divider;
    currb %= divider;
    currc %= divider;
    divider /= 3;
}
return true;
```

First, we retrieve the value that represents which jewel we are dealing with, using the Variation property. Then we define a divider number that is equal to 9 (we are first going to divide by 9). We then define a **for**-instruction that runs three times. In the body of the **for**-instruction, we place a condition that the sum of the three variation indices divided by divider should be divisible by 3. If this is not the case, we return **false** since the combination condition does not hold for one of the properties. We then assign the rest of the division by the divider to each of the variables containing the current variation index. We then divide the divider by 3. If we exit the **for**-instruction, it means that in all cases, the condition in the **if**-instruction was **true**, meaning that we found a valid combination. Since we found a valid combination, we return the value **true**.

16.4.3 Removing Jewels from the Grid

Inside the HandleInput method, we can now use the IsValidCombination method to determine if a valid combination exists. For this, we use a **while**-instruction that evaluates all sequences of three symbols in the middle column:

```
int middleCol = this.Columns / 2;
int i = 0;
while (i < this.Rows − 2)
{
    if (IsValidCombination((Jewel)grid[middleCol, i],
                           (Jewel)grid[middleCol, i + 1],
                           (Jewel)grid[middleCol, i + 2]))
    {
        do something...
    }
    else
        i++;
}
```

When we find a valid combination, we need to remove these jewels from the grid, and insert new jewels. For this, we define a method called ReplaceJewel, which removes a jewel from the grid, and inserts a new one. Because we want to create a nice 'falling down' motion, we place these jewels in different positions above the grid. We pass the desired *y*-location as a parameter to the ReplaceJewel method so that it knows where the new jewel should be located. The complete method then becomes

```
public void ReplaceJewel(int x, int y, int newYPosition)
{
    this.Clear(x, y);
    Jewel s = new Jewel();
    this.Add(s);
    s.Position = new Vector2(x * cellWidth, newYPosition);
}
```

As you see, this is rather straightforward. Inside the HandleInput method, we call ReplaceJewel three times to remove the three symbols that formed a valid combination:

```
ReplaceJewel(middleCol, i, −cellHeight);
ReplaceJewel(middleCol, i + 1, −cellHeight * 2);
ReplaceJewel(middleCol, i + 2, −cellHeight * 3);
```

Now, the grid is updated again. The position difference between the jewel objects and their target location on the grid results in a nice 'falling down' effect. Finally, since introducing new jewels could mean that there now is a new valid combination of three jewels, we reset the counter i to zero with the instruction i = 0;.

16.4.4 Updating Other Game Objects

Now that the grid has been updated, we can focus on the other game objects that need to be updated. The first game object that needs to be updated is the score game object, since the score should be increased if we handle a valid combination. We use the Find method again to retrieve the score object, and we add 10 points to the score, as follows:

```
ScoreGameObject score = GameWorld.Find("score") as ScoreGameObject;
score.Score += 10;
```

Also, because we found a valid combination, we push back the jewel cart:

```
JewelCart jewelCart = GameWorld.Find("jewelcart") as JewelCart;
jewelCart.Push();
```

For the complete program, have a look at the JewelJam5 example belonging to this chapter.

16.5 What You Have Learned

In this chapter, you have learned:

- how to organize game objects and assign IDs to them;
- how to program gameplay aspects and interaction between game objects;
- how to detect valid combinations of symbols in the Jewel Jam game.

Chapter 17
Game States

17.1 Introduction

In the previous chapter, we have programmed the main gameplay elements of the
Jewel Jam game. However, the game as it stands is still far from being complete. For
example, nothing happens when the jewel cart disappears from the screen. Also,
when you start the program, the game immediately begins without any warning.
What is still needed is a way to incorporate menus and overlays in the game so
that the player can change settings, get help, or start playing the game. When the
player is, for example, in a menu screen, the type of interaction with the game is
very different from when the player is solving a level or trying to survive as long as
possible. When programming a game, you have to think about how you are going
to incorporate these different *game states* in your game and how you will switch
between them.

Modern games will have many different game states, such as menus, maps, in-
ventories, splash screens, intro movies, and much more. In this chapter, we are going
to show how to add different game states to the Jewel Jam game. Because this game
is not yet very complicated, we can get away with using a few simple extensions
to our current classes. However, as you will see in the later game examples in this
book, game state management is something that needs to be handled properly if we
want to build a commercial game, and later on in the book, we will discuss a software design using classes that can handle game states in a very nice and generic
way.

17.2 Adding a Title Screen

One of the first things we are going to do to make the game more complete is
add a title screen. The title screen allows the player to get ready for playing the
game instead of being immediately launched into it. We are going to extend the
JewelJamGameWorld class so that it loads and displays a title screen. The title screen

A. Egges et al., *Learning C# by Programming Games*,
DOI 10.1007/978-3-642-36580-5_17, © Springer-Verlag Berlin Heidelberg 2013

in our example consists of a single image that we have to load and display. We create a SpriteGameObject instance for that, which we store in a member variable title and we add it to the game world:

```
title = new SpriteGameObject("spr_title", 100);
this.Add(title);
```

We choose a high value for the layer (100) so that we can be sure that the title is drawn on top of everything. But we have to do a little extra work to properly handle input and update the game world, since we want the game to start only once the title screen is no longer visible. We can do that by adding a few instructions to the HandleInput method to distinguish between two states: the state in which we show the title screen and the state in which we are playing the game:

```
if (title.Visible)
{
    if (inputHelper.KeyPressed(Keys.Space))
        title.Visible = false;
}
else
    base.HandleInput(inputHelper);
```

Looking at the **if** instruction, you can see that if the title screen is visible, we only react when the player presses space. In that case, we set the title screens visibility flag to **false** so that it is not drawn anymore. If the title screen is not visible, we call the HandleInput method on all the game objects in the game world, in other words, the game will react to the player as it should.

We follow very much the same procedure for the Update method, where we only update the game world if the title is not visible:

```
if (!title.Visible)
    base.Update(gameTime);
```

When we start the game, the player now gets to see a title screen before the game starts. We are not done yet. In the next section, we are going to add a simple button GUI element for showing a help frame.

17.3 Adding a Button for Showing the Help Frame

In this section, we will explain how you can add a simple button to a game, which we will use to display a help frame. In order to do that, we are going to add another class, Button, to our program. We will inherit from the SpriteGameObject class, and add some simple behavior for checking if the player pressed a button or not. In the Button class, we declare a boolean member variable that indicates whether the button was pressed or not. Then, we override the HandleInput method to check if the player has clicked the left mouse button. If the mouse position is within the boundaries of the sprite at that time, we know that the player has pressed the button and we set the value of the member variable to **true**. How can we check if the mouse position is within the boundaries of the sprite? For that, we can use the Rectangle class. As a first step, we construct a Rectangle object that encompasses the sprite, as follows:

```
Rectangle rect = new Rectangle((int)GlobalPosition.X, (int)GlobalPosition.Y,
                               sprite.Width, sprite.Height);
```

We pass four parameters to the Rectangle constructor. The first two indicate at which position the rectangle is located. Note that we use the *global* position here, because we want to check if the mouse pointer is within the sprite at its actual, global position. The second two parameters provide the width and height of the rectangle, which is the same as the width and height of the sprite. Then, we can simply use the Contains method to find out if the current mouse position is within the rectangle boundaries. The Contains method returns a boolean value, which we store in the member variable:

```
pressed = inputHelper.MouseLeftButtonPressed() &&
          rect.Contains((int)inputHelper.MousePosition.X,
                        (int)inputHelper.MousePosition.Y);
```

Finally, we add a property Pressed to the Button class, that indicates if the button is currently pressed or not. For the complete class, see Listing 17.1.

Now that we have a button class, we can add a help button to the game world (see the JewelJamGameWorld class):

```
helpButton = new Button("spr_button_help", 2, "help_button");
helpButton.Position = new Vector2(1268, 20);
this.Add(helpButton);
```

Since we want to display a help frame when the player presses the help button, we also add a help frame to the game world. We set its visibility flag to **false** so that it is not yet visible:

```
helpFrame = new SpriteGameObject("spr_frame_help", 2, "help_frame");
helpFrame.Position = new Vector2(636, 120);
helpFrame.Visible = false;
this.Add(helpFrame);
```

Now we have to make sure that when the player presses the help button, the help frame visibility is toggled. We can do this using the following **if**-instruction in the HandleInput method of the JewelJamGameWorld class:

```
if (helpButton.Pressed)
    helpFrame.Visible = !helpFrame.Visible;
```

```
 1   using Microsoft.Xna.Framework;
 2
 3   class Button : SpriteGameObject
 4   {
 5       protected bool pressed;
 6
 7       public Button(string imageAsset, int layer = 0, string id = "")
 8           : base(imageAsset, layer, id)
 9       {
10           pressed = false;
11       }
12
13       public override void HandleInput(InputHelper inputHelper)
14       {
15           Rectangle rect = new Rectangle((int)GlobalPosition.X, (int)GlobalPosition.Y,
16                                   sprite.Width, sprite.Height);
17           pressed = inputHelper.MouseLeftButtonPressed() &&
18                       rect.Contains((int)inputHelper.MousePosition.X,
19                                   (int)inputHelper.MousePosition.Y);
20       }
21
22       public bool Pressed
23       {
24           get { return pressed; }
25       }
26   }
```

Listing 17.1 A simple class for representing a button

When the help frame is visible, we want to be able to remove it by pressing the space bar. So, our final **if**-instruction is slightly more complicated:

```
if (helpButton.Pressed || (helpFrame.Visible && inputHelper.KeyPressed(Keys.Space)))
    helpFrame.Visible = !helpFrame.Visible;
```

Finally, we have to make sure that the game is not updated when the help frame is displayed. We can do that in the Update method by only updating the game objects if the help frame is not visible:

```
if (!helpFrame.Visible && !title.Visible)
    base.Update(gameTime);
```

17.4 Overlays

A very common way of presenting information to the player is by using *overlays*. Overlays are basically images that can be displayed on top of the game world to present information or to provide a user interface such as a menu, a mini map, status information and more.

Overlays can present an entirely new game state (such as a 'game over' overlay), but they can also supplement the game world by only providing information to the player. For example, many strategy games provide information about the number of units selected, the available resources, ongoing building processes, items gathered, and so on. These kinds of overlays are generally always present on the screen, and together they are called the *Heads-Up Display* or: HUD.

Jewel Jam has a very basic HUD. It consists of a frame where the score is displayed, and it has a help button that can be pressed to view a frame with help information.

Next to the HUD, we want to show a 'game over' overlay when the jewel cart moves out of the screen. We add this overlay to the game world as well, and set its visibility to **false**:

```
gameover = new SpriteGameObject("spr_gameover", 100, "gameover");
gameover.Visible = false;
gameover.Position = JewelJam.Screen/2 − gameover.Center;
this.Add(gameover);
```

Also, we add a property to the JewelJamGameWorld class to check if the jewel cart is outside of the screen:

```
public bool GameOver
{
    get
    {
        JewelCart jewelCart = Find("jewelcart") as JewelCart;
        return (jewelCart.Position.X > JewelJam.Screen.X);
    }
}
```

We can then use that property in the HandleInput method, so that the player can press the space bar to restart the game, as follows:

```
if (this.GameOver)
{
    if (inputHelper.KeyPressed(Keys.Space))
        this.Reset();
}
```

We override the Reset method because we need to do a little extra work when the game restarts. Notably, we have set the visibility of some of the overlays to **false** so that they are not shown on the screen when the game restarts. Apart from that, we simply call the Reset method on the **base** object so that all game objects are reset:

```
public override void Reset()
{
    base.Reset();
    title.Visible = false;
    helpFrame.Visible = false;
    gameover.Visible = false;
}
```

Now there is only one thing left to do. If the game is over, we have to set the visibility of the overlay to **true**. We do this in the Update method of JewelJamGameWorld:

```
if (this.GameOver)
    gameover.Visible = true;
```

17.5 What You Have Learned

In this chapter, you have learned:

- how to add an HUD and overlays to the game;
- how to define a simple button.

Chapter 18
Finishing the Game

18.1 Introduction

In this chapter, we will finish the game Jewel Jam. As a first step, we are going to give the player extra points when he/she makes two or three valid combinations of three jewels at the same time. Secondly, we are going to add a nice visual effect by showing glitters on the jewels in the game. Finally, we will add sound and music to the game.

18.2 Extra Points for Multiple Combinations

We want to give the player extra points when the player finds multiple combinations at once. Because a column contains 10 different jewels, the player can make at most three combinations of three jewels at once. So, we award the player extra points in case of two or three multiple combinations. In order to do that, we have to count how many combinations a player finds. We do this in the JewelGrid class, by introducing an extra variable nrCombis:

```
int nrCombis = 0;
```

Every time we find a valid combination, we increment this variable. Now we can check with an **if**-instruction when we should award extra points:

```
if (nrCombis == 2)
{
    score.Score += 50;
}
else if (nrCombis == 3)
{
    score.Score += 100;
}
```

We also would like to give a message to the player that he/she got extra points in the case of a double combination or a triple combination. For that, we want to show an overlay for a couple of seconds. As a first step, let us load two overlays for that and add them to the game world in the JewelJamGameWorld class:

```
SpriteGameObject doubleOverlay = new SpriteGameObject("spr_double", 1);
doubleOverlay.Position = new Vector2(800, 400);
this.Add(doubleOverlay);

SpriteGameObject tripleOverlay = new SpriteGameObject("spr_triple", 1);
tripleOverlay.Position = new Vector2(800, 400);
this.Add(tripleOverlay);
```

What we want to do now is that as soon as the player finds multiple combinations, we want to show this overlay on the screen for a couple of seconds. In order to be able to do that, we first need to understand a bit more about how we deal with time in games.

18.3 Time in Games

Time is a very important concept in games. For example, it is used to measure how fast a player executes a task, to update positions of objects according to their velocity, to keep track of the last time that the player beat an enemy, to determine if it is currently day or night in the game, and so on. In order to accommodate for these things, a game engine will generally contain many classes to deal with different aspects of time. Because time is so important in games, the game loop methods in the Game class all have as a parameter a GameTime object. The game time does not have to be the same as the time in the real world. In the game, time can go three times as fast, or ten times as slow, or whatever the game designer wants. For example, a game designer could decide that in a simulation game, time at night goes much faster because not much happens at night. Also, the game time begins only after the game has started. Furthermore, the game time can also be interrupted. For example, if the player is moving the application window, the game time is paused (whereas the real time continues).

When the game starts, the game time is zero. So: zero hours, zero minutes and zero seconds will have passed. Every time the Update and Draw methods are executed we get as a parameter a GameTime object. The GameTime class is made to give a lot of information about how much time has passed. For example, you can retrieve how much (game) time has passed since the last call to the Update method using the ElapsedGameTime property. Also, you can retrieve how much game time has passed since the start of the game using the TotalGameTime property. Similar properties exist for accessing the *real* time, such as ElapsedRealTime or TotalRealTime. Finally, the GameTime object can also be used to check if the game is running slowly. This can happen if a part of the game is very resource-hungry. We can retrieve this information using the IsRunningSlowly property. If the game is running slowly, we can for example decide to temporarily switch off or simplify a part of the game code.

18.3.1 Other Useful Classes for Managing Time

Next to the GameTime class, another important type is the TimeSpan struct. For example, the ElapsedGameTime property in the GameTime class returns a TimeSpan object. The TimeSpan struct is very useful for representing a time interval, such as the time passed since the last update. You can retrieve the time information from the TimeSpan object in a variety of ways: in hours, seconds, minutes, or 'ticks'. A tick is a time unit used by a computer, and at the same time it is the smallest time unit that a computer can measure. One tick stands for 100 nanoseconds. We can retrieve the time interval size in ticks using the Ticks property.

Just like the GameTime class, the TimeSpan struct cannot represent *dates* such as 'June 8, 1977'. To express a moment in time, we use another struct called DateTime. This struct has a number of useful ways to deal with dates. There are easy ways to retrieve the month, year or day, and we can use the DateTime type to format the date as a string. For example, if we want to format the total elapsed game time as a string containing the passed time in minutes and seconds, we can do this as follows:

```
DateTime gameTime = new DateTime(gameTime.TotalGameTime.Ticks);
string passedTime = gameTime.ToString("mm:ss");
```

You can see that each time-related class or struct has its own pros and cons. Watch this when you are using these classes, and be sure to use the right class for the right job!

18.3.2 A Timer for Controlling Visibility of a Game Object

What we are going to do in this section is create a class that controls the visibility of a game object based on a timer. Let us call this class VisibilityTimer. The idea of this class is that we can assign it a target game object, of which it will set the visibility to **false** by default, but when we start the timer, the target object becomes visible until the timer has reached its maximum value. We can then use such a timer and connect it to an overlay in order to show that overlay on the screen for a while. The complete VisibilityTimer class is given in Listing 18.1.

A visibility timer object needs to keep track of a couple of things. For one, we need to store the target object of which we are going to control the visibility. Also, we will store how much time in total this object should be visible for when the timer is started. Finally, when the timer is running we have to maintain how time is still left before it stops. This value will be updated every time the Update method is called. Therefore, the VisibilityTimer class inherits from the GameObject class.

When the timer is created, we assume that the timer is not running, so the time left is set to 0. We also set the total time that the timer should run to 1 second:

```
totaltime = 1;
timeleft = 0;
```

In the Update method, we then subtract the elapsed game time in seconds from the timeleft variable. If this variable contains a value less than zero, we set the target visibility to **false**. Finally, we add a method called StartVisible that assigns the total time to the timeleft variable.

Now we can use the VisibilityTimer class to control the visibility of the double and triple combination overlays in the Jewel Jam game. When we create overlay objects, we also create VisibilityTimer instances with these overlays as their target:

```
VisibilityTimer doubleTimer = new VisibilityTimer(doubleOverlay, 0, "doubleTimer");
this.Add(doubleTimer);
VisibilityTimer tripleTimer = new VisibilityTimer(tripleOverlay, 0, "tripleTimer");
this.Add(tripleTimer);
```

When the player finds two or three combinations of jewels, we start the visibility timer of that particular overlay. For example, this is what the code looks like for the double combination (see the Update method of the JewelGrid class):

```
if (nrCombis == 2)
{
    score.Score += 50;
    VisibilityTimer doubleTimer = GameWorld.Find("doubleTimer") as VisibilityTimer;
    doubleTimer.StartVisible();
}
```

You can see the timer in action by running the JewelJam7 program.

18.4 A Field of Glitters

In this section, we are going to add some eye-candy to the game. Currently, the jewels in the game are sprites displayed on the screen. We are going to add a nice visual effect to them: glitters. Let us try to do this in a generic way: we want to be able to designate a rectangle on the screen inside which these glitters are drawn at random positions. We also want to be able to indicate how *dense* this rectangle of glitters is. Then, we can create different rectangles of different sizes and attach them to game objects in our game. So, let us create a GlitterField class that allows us to do this. This class inherits from the GameObject class.

```
1    using Microsoft.Xna.Framework;
2
3    class VisibilityTimer : GameObject
4    {
5        protected GameObject target;
6        protected float timeleft;
7        protected float totaltime;
8
9        public VisibilityTimer(GameObject target, int layer=0, string id = "")
10           : base(layer, id)
11       {
12           totaltime = 1;
13           timeleft = 0;
14           this.target = target;
15       }
16
17       public override void Update(GameTime gameTime)
18       {
19           timeleft −= (float)gameTime.ElapsedGameTime.TotalSeconds;
20           if (timeleft <= 0)
21               target.Visible = false;
22       }
23
24       public override void Reset()
25       {
26           base.Reset();
27           timeleft = 0;
28       }
29       public void StartVisible()
30       {
31           timeleft = totaltime;
32           target.Visible = true;
33       }
34   }
```

Listing 18.1   A timer class that controls the visibility of a game object

18.4.1 The Constructor

The constructor of the GlitterField class has several parameters. Here is the header of
the constructor:

```
public GlitterField(Texture2D target, int density, int width, int height, int xoffset = 0,
                    int layer = 0, string id = "")
        : base(layer, id)
{ // initialize the glitter field object
}
```

The first parameter is the target of the glitter field, which is of type Texture2D. We are going to use this object to determine where we can place our glitters in the rectangle (we will talk more about that later on). The second parameter, density, indicates how many glitters can be visible at the same time. Then, we have the width and height parameters that indicate the size of the rectangle. We also pass along a parameter called xoffset. We will deal with that one later on as well. Finally, we have the layer and id parameters, which are passed on to the base constructor.

Inside the constructor, we store most of these parameters in member variables, so we can access them later:

```
this.glitter = JewelJam.AssetManager.GetSprite("spr_glitter");
this.target = target;
this.xoffset = xoffset;
this.width = width;
this.height = height;
```

18.4.2 Adding Glitters

A glitter field is a rectangle containing multiple glitters, depending on the desired density. Therefore, we are going to need a list to maintain where these glitters should be drawn. This is done in the member variable positions, which is of type List<Vector2>, and it is initialized in the constructor:

```
positions = new List<Vector2>();
```

We are going to fill this list with a number of randomly generated positions. For that, we use a **for**-instruction, and we call the method CreateRandomPosition, which we will discuss later in more detail:

```
for (int i = 0; i < density; i++)
    positions.Add(this.CreateRandomPosition());
```

For drawing the glitters, we need more than just a position. We want to add a nice visual effect that lets the glitters appear and disappear smoothly. We will achieve that by drawing the glitters at a first increasing and then decreasing scale. So, this means we also need to maintain the current scale for each of the glitters that we are drawing. We do this in another list of **float** variables called scales, which is also initialized in the constructor:

```
scales = new List<float>();
```

Every time we add a new position to the positions list, we also add a scale of 0 to the scales list. So the final **for**-instruction becomes

```
for (int i = 0; i < density; i++)
{
    positions.Add(this.CreateRandomPosition());
    scales.Add(0f);
}
```

18.4.3 Accessing Pixel Color Data

Suppose that we want to add glitters to a jewel. If you take a look at the sprite containing the jewels, there are two issues:

- there is no sprite that represents a single jewel;
- there is a lot of transparent space around the jewels.

The first issue means that if we pass along the 'spr_jewels.png' sprite as the target, we need a way to indicate which part of the sprite we should use as a target. This is done using the xoffset variable. Although this is not an ideal design, for this particular game this is sufficient. The second issue is that the jewels sprite contains a lot of transparent space, and we do not want to draw glitters on that part of the sprite, only on the part that represents the jewel. So, we need a way to find out what color the target sprite is at a certain (pixel) position. That way, we can only select random positions that fall on the actual sprite, and not on the transparent background.

Retrieving the color of a pixel in a sprite is done with the GetData method from the Texture2D sprite. This method can retrieve color data from a sprite for a rectangle that indicates for which part of the sprite we want to retrieve color data. So the first step is to create a rectangle located at a certain position in the sprite. We define this rectangle with a width and height of 1 since we only need a single pixel:

```
Rectangle sourceRectangle = new Rectangle(randomx + xoffset, randomy, 1, 1);
```

Later on, we will see how to generate the randomx and randomy values. We add the xoffset to the x value so that we select the desired part of the sprite. Then, we create an array of Color objects in which we will store the retrieved colors:

```
Color[] retrievedColor = new Color[1];
```

Finally, we call the GetData method, which fills the array of Color objects with the 2D sprite data:

```
target.GetData<Color>(0, sourceRectangle, retrievedColor, 0, 1);
```

The first parameter (which we do not use in our game) defines on which level of detail we want to retrieve the data. Sometimes, a sprite can consist of multiple images, each at different resolutions so that when the image is further away, we can draw the simpler version to save computation time. Since we do not use that here, we set that parameter to 0. The second parameter indicates from which part of the image we want to retrieve color data. The third parameter is the array of colors that we want to fill with that data. Then, we can indicate at which pixel index we start collecting the data. Since we want the first (and only) pixel, we set this value to 0. The final parameter indicates from how many pixels we want to get the data, in our case: 1.

Now that we have called this method, we can access the Color object of the single pixel by calling retrievedColor[0]. We can then use that object to check if the pixel is fully transparent. We do that by accessing the *alpha channel value* which indicates transparency. In the Color type, this is done using the A property. The alpha channel value ranges from 0 (fully transparent) to 255 (fully opaque). See the following example:

```
if (retrievedColor[0].A == 255)
    // the pixel is fully opaque
```

Now we can start writing the code for the CreateRandomPosition method using this knowledge. Creating a random position within the rectangle is easy:

```
Vector2 randomPos = new Vector2(JewelJam.Random.Next(width),
                                JewelJam.Random.Next(height));
```

We can then check if this position falls on a part of the sprite that is opaque, as follows:

```
Rectangle sourceRectangle = new Rectangle((int)randomPos.X + xoffset,
                                          (int)randomPos.Y, 1, 1);
Color[] retrievedColor = new Color[1];
target.GetData<Color>(0, sourceRectangle, retrievedColor, 0, 1);
if (retrievedColor[0].A == 255)
    // we're done!
```

If the position is not fully opaque, we generate a new random position and check that, and so on, and so on, until we find a valid position. Although this is not entirely safe, we use a **while**-instruction to keep generating random positions until we find one that is on a fully opaque pixel:

```
Vector2 randomPos = Vector2.Zero;
while (true)
{
    randomPos = new Vector2(JewelJam.Random.Next(width),
                            JewelJam.Random.Next(height));
```

```
if (target == null)
    // we're done
Rectangle sourceRectangle = new Rectangle((int)randomPos.X + xoffset,
                                  (int)randomPos.Y, 1, 1);
Color[] retrievedColor = new Color[1];
target.GetData<Color>(0, sourceRectangle, retrievedColor, 0, 1);
if (retrievedColor[0].A == 255)
    // we're done
}
```

The condition of this **while**-instruction is **true**, meaning that the instruction will never stop, unless we do something within the body of the **while**-instruction to stop it. There are two cases when we have to stop the **while**-instruction. The first one is that the target sprite is **null**, meaning that we do not have a target sprite to check. In that case, we assume that any random glitter position in the rectangle is fine. The second reason can be that we found a random position that is on a fully opaque pixel in the target sprite. Both cases are indicated using comments in the above example. So how can we force the **while**-instruction to stop? One way would be to use the **return**-instruction, for example as follows:

```
if (target == null)
    return randomPos;
```

The **return**-instruction ends the execution of a method (including a **while**-instruction such as this one) and returns a value to the caller of the method. A second way of stopping the **while**-instruction is by using the **break** keyword:

```
if (target == null)
    break;
```

The **break** keyword stops the execution of the closest enclosing loop instruction (**for** or **while**) in which it appears. In the example above, this is the **while**-loop inside the createRandomPosition method. Once that loop is stopped, the program continues on the line after that instruction. The only thing that remains to be done then is returning the randomly generated position:

```
return randomPos;
```

18.4.4 Updating the Glitter Field

In the constructor, we set the scale for each of the glitters to 0. The result is that when these glitters are drawn, they will not be visible to the player. In the Update method, we are going to increase and decrease this scale again until it returns to zero.

When that happens, we generate another random position for that glitter so that it appears elsewhere. We do not want to start increasing the scale of each separate glitter at the same time, but we want the glitters to show up randomly. So, inside the Update method, we iterate through all the glitter positions and scales in the list and depending on the value of a random variable, we start increasing their scale:

```
for (int i = 0; i < scales.Count; i++)
{
    if (scales[i] == 0 && JewelJam.Random.NextDouble() < 0.001)
        scales[i] += 0.05f;
}
```

We only start increasing the scale if it is zero and a random number value is smaller than 0.001. This makes sure that not all scales are immediately increases. Once a scale is not zero anymore, we simply increase it:

```
else if (scales[i] != 0)
{
    scales[i] += 0.05f;
    // more code here
}
```

However, we cannot infinitely increase the scale, we want to start decreasing it again. But how do we know if we should increase or decrease the scale? We do not know in the Update method if we are in the increasing part of the slope or in the decreasing part. We can use a small trick here. We let the scale run from 0 to 2 instead of 0 to 1, and in the Draw method we will calculate the real scale from that value (0 to 1 means increasing, and 1 to 2 means decreasing scale). In the Update method we add an **if**-instruction to deal with the situation when the scale is larger than its maximum value (2):

```
if (scales[i] >= 2.0f)
{
    scales[i] = 0f;
    positions[i] = this.CreateRandomPosition();
}
```

When that happens, we reset the scale to zero, and we generate a new random position for a new glitter.

18.4.5 Drawing the Glitter Field

Inside the Draw method of the glitter field, we have to draw all the glitters on the screen at the desired scale. We want to draw these glitters with their origin at the center, because otherwise the scaling animation would not give the desired result. So, we calculate this center once in the beginning of the method call:

```
Vector2 glitterCenter = new Vector2(glitter.Width, glitter.Height) / 2;
```

Then, we add a **for**-instruction that traverses all the scales and positions of the glitters to be drawn. What we still need to do here, is calculate the real scale value based on the scale value that was stored in the array in the Update method. If that value is between 0 and 1, we do not have to do anything (scale is increasing). If the value is between 1 and 2, we need to convert that value into a decreasing scale. This is done using the following instructions:

```
float scale = scales[i];
if (scales[i] > 1)
    scale = 2 − scales[i];
```

The only thing left to do now is to draw the glitter at the desired position, with the desired scale, using the SpriteBatch.Draw method:

```
spriteBatch.Draw(glitter, this.GlobalPosition + positions[i], null,
                Color.White, 0f, glitterCenter, scale, SpriteEffects.None, 0);
```

For the complete GlitterField class, have a look at the JewelJam7 program in the solution belonging to this chapter.

18.4.6 Adding Glitters to Game Objects

Now that we have made the generic GlitterField class, we can make a few simple extensions to our game objects to add glitters to them. We want to do this with taste, and not blind the player with glitters. So, we will add some glitters to each of the jewels in the playing field, as well as the moving jewel cart. First, let us have a look at how to extend the Jewel class to add glitters to it. The first step is adding a new member variable to the class that contains a reference to the glitter field:

```
protected GlitterField glitters;
```

In the constructor, we give this glitter field a value. We also make sure that its parent is set to the Jewel object. That way, if the jewel is moved in the playing field, the glitters move along with it:

```
glitters = new GlitterField(this.Sprite, 2, sprite.Height, sprite.Height,
                            variation ∗ sprite.Height);
glitters.Parent = this;
```

You can also see that we calculate the x offset using the variation member variable. That way, the glitter field knows on which jewel the glitters are drawn. In the Update method of the Jewel class, we then have to make sure that the glitter field is updated as well:

```
glitters.Update(gameTime);
```

Fig. 18.1 Selecting a
different build configuration

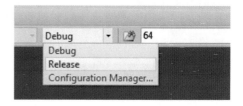

And the same goes for the Draw method. Here we add an extra instruction (*after* having drawn the jewel!) to draw the glitter field. For the complete Jewel class, see the JewelJam7 example.

Adding glitters to the jewel cart is done in a similar fashion. The only difference is that we do not provide a target texture in this case. The reason is that the jewel cart sprite contains partly other colored pixels that are not jewels (such as the cart and the light beams). Therefore, using the transparency to determine if we can add a glitter is not really a consistent method. As a result, we allow glitters to appear everywhere on the top part of the cart by passing **null** as a parameter for the target sprite:

```
glitters = new GlitterField(null, 40, 435, 75);
glitters.Position = new Vector2(275, 475);
glitters.Parent = this;
```

Furthermore, we choose a size and position for the glitter field to match the top part of the cart as closely as possible. For the complete JewelCart class, see the JewelJam7 example.

Debug and release—Just like any piece of software, the compiler that we use to build an executable has many different options. For example, a compiler can try to optimize your code during the compilation phase. Other options are related to the kind of code table used for representing characters, what kind of application we are building, location of assets and other required files, and so on. A complete collection of these settings is called a *configuration*. When you create a new project, two configurations are created automatically for you: a debug and a release configuration (see Fig. 18.1). The debug configuration does not use any code optimization, and adds additional code to your executable, so that when you run the program and encounter a bug or the program crashes, it is easier to find out what happened. When you are running the debug configuration, the development environment also allows you to put *break points* in your code, where the program will automatically pause the execution. This can be very useful if you want to find out what the values of member variables or method parameters are while the game is running.

Because of all these extras that are added to the code, in combination with the lack of code optimization, the resulting application will not be that efficient. The debug configuration is, therefore, mainly useful for the developers. When you actually want to release your game to the public, you should use the release configuration to build the game. In this configuration, the compiler tries to optimize the code in order to make it more efficient. Also, there is no debugging information in the executable, resulting in a smaller file. In the Visual Studio development environment, you can choose which configuration you want to build by selecting it in the menu. If you want, you can even design your own configurations with different compiler settings. A common configuration you might want to add is *optimized debug*. This configuration performs all the code optimizations but still contains debugging information. This way, you can check whether the optimizations that the compiler performs have somehow introduced new bugs.

Once you are sure that the release version of your game works as intended. You can publish your game by building an installer. By right-clicking on the project and selecting 'Publish', you can create an installer for your game.

18.5 Adding Music and Sound Effects

Just like in the Painter game, we would like to add music and sound effects to the game to make it more attractive. Since we now made this nice AssetManager class, let us extend it with some functionality to play music and sound effects. We are going to do this similar to the way that we deal with sprites in that class. First, we add a PlaySound method that plays a sound effect:

```
public void PlaySound(string assetName)
{
    SoundEffect snd = contentManager.Load<SoundEffect>(assetName);
    snd.Play();
}
```

So, let us declare two Dictionary member variables, one for music, and one for sound effects:

```
protected Dictionary<string, SoundEffect> sounds;
protected Dictionary<string, Song> music;
```

The PlayMusic method has an additional parameter that indicates if the music should be repeated or not. The method is then given as follows:

```
public void PlayMusic(string assetName, bool repeat = true)
{
    MediaPlayer.IsRepeating = repeat;
    MediaPlayer.Play(contentManager.Load<Song>(assetName));
}
```

Now we can simply add sound effects and music wherever we like. When the game is started, we start playing the background music in the JewelJam class, as follows:

```
assetManager.PlayMusic("snd_music");
```

And when we get a valid combination of jewels (single, double or triple), we play different sound effects (see the JewelGrid class):

```
if (nrCombis == 1)
    JewelJam.AssetManager.PlaySound("snd_combi");
else if (nrCombis == 2)
{
    score.Score += 50;
    VisibilityTimer doubleTimer = GameWorld.Find("doubleTimer") as VisibilityTimer;
    doubleTimer.startTimer();
    JewelJam.AssetManager.PlaySound("snd_double");
}
else if (nrCombis == 3)
{
    score.Score += 100;
    VisibilityTimer tripleTimer = GameWorld.Find("tripleTimer") as VisibilityTimer;
    tripleTimer.startTimer();
    JewelJam.AssetManager.PlaySound("snd_triple");
}
```

Finally, we play a sound when the game is over (see the JewelJamGameWorld class):

```
if (this.GameOver && !gameover.Visible)
{
    gameover.Visible = true;
    JewelJam.AssetManager.PlaySound("snd_gameover");
}
```

This completes the Jewel Jam game. You can play the game by running the JewelJam7 example project belonging to this chapter. Happy jewel hunting!

Leaderboards—Why do games contain leaderboards or highscore lists? The early games did not have them. The reason was that there was no semi-permanent storage available in the game consoles. So nothing could be remembered between playing sessions. That was also the reason there were no save games, which in turn had an important effect on the game mechanics: a player always had to start again from the beginning, even if he/she was an experienced player.

Once storage became available, designers started to introduce leaderboards. Being better than somebody else always gives a feeling of satisfaction and it adds an important goal for the player. But this only makes sense if there are multiple people playing the game on the same device. If you are the sole player, the only thing you can do is try to beat yourself. Fortunately, nowadays computers and game consoles are connected to the Internet. As a result we can store leaderboards online and you can compete with the whole world.

But this adds an additional problem. A goal is only interesting when it is reachable. Being the best player among a couple of millions is unreachable for most people. So, worldwide leaderboards can actually reduce the satisfaction. To remedy this, games now often introduce sub-leaderboards. For example, you get a leaderboard of the players that is restricted to your own country or to the scores reached this week. Also you can see how you rank amidst your friends.

Carefully designing the scoring system of your game and the way such scores are shown in leaderboards can make a crucial difference in the satisfaction it gives to your players.

18.6 What You Have Learned

In this chapter, you have learned:

- how to build a timer using the GameTime type;
- how to access pixel color information in a Texture2D object;
- how to play sound effects and music using the extended asset manager.

Part IV
Making Your Games Appealing

Fig. IV.1 A screenshot of the game Penguin Pairs

In this part of the book, we are going to develop the game Penguin Pairs (see Fig. IV.1 for a screenshot of the game). We will introduce a few new techniques for programming games, such as sprite sheets, better game state management, file I/O, and more.

The game Penguin Pairs is a puzzle game, in which the goal is to make pairs of penguins of the same color. Penguins can move by clicking on them and selecting the direction in which the penguin should move. A penguin moves until it is stopped by another character in the game (this can be a penguin, a seal, a shark, or an iceberg), or it will drop from the playing field, in which case the penguin falls into the water and is eaten by hungry sharks. Throughout the different levels of the game, we will introduce new gameplay elements to keep the game exciting. For example: there is a special penguin that can match with any penguin, penguins can be stuck in a hole meaning they can't move anymore, and sharks can be placed on the board that eat penguins.

You can run the final version of this game by opening the solution belonging to Chap. 24. Press F5 and you can immediately start playing.

Chapter 19
Sprite Sheets

19.1 Introduction

In this chapter, we will start building the first elements of the Penguin Pairs game. This game is quite a bit more complicated than the previous games. You can already see this by looking at the number of game assets that this game uses. Just like we did in the Jewel Jam game, we are going to use images containing several different sprites. This is actually a technique used in many games. In the Jewel Jam game, we used this to store a strip of jewels in a single sprite. However, using strips is not always a good idea. Especially when an image contains many different sprites in a strip, the strip may become too long for the graphics hardware to handle. This can be solved by storing sprites in a *sheet* instead, consisting of multiple rows and columns. For an example of such a sprite sheet, see Fig. 19.1.

19.2 Overview of the Example Project

In order to test the loading and displaying of a sheet of sprites, we have created a simple example project called PenguinPairs1. In this example project, we are going to show a background, and then draw a sprite from the spritesheet on top of the background. Using the left and right arrows keys, you can then select which sprite from the sheet should be shown.

To get started more easily, we copy a few classes from the previous game. First, we are going to need the GameObject class and the GameObjectList class. We are also going to need the AssetManager class for loading the sprites, and the InputHelper class for dealing with input. We will then write a new SpriteGameObject class, which will have the capability for reading sheets of sprites.

The PenguinPairs class inherits from the Game class, and we do all our initialization (creating a graphics device and a sprite batch, and more) in there. We add a member variable gameWorld of type GameObjectList. This variable is initialized in the

A. Egges et al., *Learning C# by Programming Games*,
DOI 10.1007/978-3-642-36580-5_19, © Springer-Verlag Berlin Heidelberg 2013

Fig. 19.1 An example of a
sheet of sprites (four columns
and two rows)

LoadContent method, and we add the background sprite to it:

```
gameWorld = new GameObjectList();
gameWorld.Add(new SpriteGameObject("Sprites/spr_background_levelselect"));
```

We also add the penguin sprite to the game world, and position it somewhere in the middle of the screen:

```
SpriteGameObject penguin = new SpriteGameObject("Sprites/spr_penguin@4x2", 1,
                                                "penguin");
penguin.Position = new Vector2(500, 420);
gameWorld.Add(penguin);
```

19.3 Loading a Sprite Sheet

In the Jewel Jam game, a SpriteGameObject instance keeps a reference to the sprite, which is represented by an object of type Texture2D. In order to deal with sprite sheets, we are going to create a new class called SpriteSheet that we will use instead of a Texture2D object directly. We will add specific functionality to this class that allows us to maintain the number of rows and columns in the sheet and that can select a different element of the sheet to be drawn.

In the previous section, you've probably seen that the name of the penguin sprite ('spr_penguin@4x2') is quite peculiar. The reason is that we are going to add a nice trick to the SpriteSheet class that allows us to specify in the *file name* what the dimensions of the sprite sheet are. In this case, the penguin sprite has four columns and two rows. The SpriteSheet constructor then analyzes the name of the sprite and determines the dimensions accordingly. There are three different possibilities:

- the image is a single sprite: in that case, no definition is provided at the end of the filename, an example is the sprite 'spr_wall.png';
- the image is a strip of sprites: in that case, we provide a single integer number behind the '@' sign, an example is the sprite 'spr_field@2.png';
- the image is a sheet of sprites: both dimensions (columns times rows) are provided in the filename, for example in 'spr_penguin@4x2.png'.

We are going to use the Split method from the **string** class to find out which possibility we are dealing with. But before we do that, we need to declare a few member variables for storing the sheet dimensions and the part of the sprite sheet that is currently selected. These are all the member variables in the SpriteSheet class:

```
protected Texture2D sprite;
protected int sheetIndex;
protected int sheetColumns;
protected int sheetRows;
protected bool mirror;
```

In the constructor, we initially assign the value 1 to the sheetColumns and sheetRows variables. The sheet index is passed along as a parameter and has 0 as the default value (in other words, the first element in the sheet). We also retrieve the sprite using the asset manager:

```
sprite = PenguinPairs.AssetManager.GetSprite(assetname);
this.sheetIndex = sheetIndex;
this.sheetColumns = 1;
this.sheetRows = 1;
```

Now we can use the **string**.Split method to find out if we need to modify the column and row sizes. The Split method splits a string into substrings and we can pass along one or more characters that are used as delimiters. Here we split the string using the '@' sign as a delimiter:

```
string[] assetSplit = assetname.Split('@');
```

As you can see, the result of calling the Split method on a string is an array of **string** objects. If the delimiter character does not appear in the string, the number of elements in the assetSplit variable will be 1 (the original string). So, if the length of the assetSplit array is greater than 1, we know that the file name contains information about the dimensions of the sheet. What we also know in that case, is that the *last element* of the array contains that information. We can easily handle this in an **if** instruction:

```
if (assetSplit.Length <= 1)
    return; // we're done
string sheetNrData = assetSplit[assetSplit.Length − 1];
// deal with the sheet dimension data
```

As you can see, we store that last element in a new local variable which now contains the string describing the sheet dimensions. We use the Split method one more time, to extract the actual dimensions from that string:

```
string[] colrow = sheetNrData.Split('x');
```

Again, there are two possibilities here. The colrow array contains either one or two elements. In both cases, we have to convert the first string element in the array to an **int** and store it in the sheetColumns variable:

```
this.sheetColumns = int.Parse(colrow[0]);
```

In case the length is two, we also need to parse the second string element, and store it in the sheetRows variable:

```
if (colrow.Length == 2)
    this.sheetRows = int.Parse(colrow[1]);
```

Yet another possibility is that the array contains more than two elements. We do not handle that situation in the constructor (meaning that in that case, we only store the number of columns). In the SpriteGameObject class, we now replace the Texture2D member variable by a variable of type SpriteSheet:

```
protected SpriteSheet sprite;
```

And we create an instance of the sprite sheet in the constructor (only if a non-empty asset name was passed along):

```
if (assetname != "")
    sprite = new SpriteSheet(assetname, sheetIndex);
else
    sprite = null;
```

19.4 Managing the Sprite Sheet

We have already seen in the Jewel Jam game how to deal with a strip of sprites. We had to change the Draw method to draw only part of the sprite. Also, we changed the Width property to take the strip length into account. Here, we are going to add more or less the same functionality to the SpriteSheet class, except that we need to do it for two dimensions instead of one. The first thing that we need to do is to add a Width and Height property to the class that take into account the column and row numbers of the sprite sheet:

```
public int Width
{
    get
    {
        return sprite.Width / sheetColumns;
    }
}

public int Height
{
    get
    {
        return sprite.Height / sheetRows;
    }
}
```

Also, we will add a property that computes the number of elements in the sheet, which is defined as the number of columns times the number of rows:

```
public int NumberSheetElements
{
    get { return this.sheetColumns * this.sheetRows; }
}
```

Yet another property is used for retrieving and setting the currently selected element in the sheet. The selected element should be within the bounds of the possible element indices. We check this inside the **set** part of the property:

```
public int SheetIndex
{
    get
    {
        return this.sheetIndex;
    }
    set
    {
        if (value < NumberSheetElements && value >= 0)
            this.sheetIndex = value;
    }
}
```

Furthermore, we add a property Mirror to control whether the sprite should be drawn mirrored or not, and we add a property Center that calculates the center of the sprite. The next step is being able to draw the correct element in the sprite. This is done in the Draw method of the SpriteSheet class. As a first step, we need to convert the sheetIndex value to column and row indices in the sheet. We calculate the column index as follows:

```
int columnIndex = sheetIndex % sheetColumns;
```

Basically, you can see the sheet index as a value that passes through all the elements in the sheet from left to right, top to bottom. So by applying the modulus operator on the sheet index, we 'throw away' the rows coming before the row that the element is in which leaves us with the column index. Similarly, we calculate the row index by dividing the sheet index by the number of columns:

```
int rowIndex = sheetIndex / sheetColumns;
```

Now we can construct the rectangle that indicates the part of the sprite that should be drawn, using the Width and Height properties:

```
Rectangle spritePart = new Rectangle(columnIndex * this.Width,
                    rowIndex * this.Height, this.Width, this.Height);
```

The next step is to determine if the sprite should be mirrored or not. We can indicate if a sprite should be mirrored by setting a *sprite effect*, as follows:

```
SpriteEffects spriteEffects = SpriteEffects.None;
if (mirror)
    spriteEffects = SpriteEffects.FlipHorizontally;
```

Finally, we draw the sprite part on the screen, as follows:

```
spriteBatch.Draw(sprite, position, spritePart, Color.White,
                 0.0f, origin, 1.0f, spriteEffects, 0.0f);
```

The SpriteGameObject class now becomes rather straightforward. Its main task is to make sure the sprite is properly drawn on the screen. This is done in the Draw method as follows:

```
public override void Draw(GameTime gameTime, SpriteBatch spriteBatch)
{
    if (!visible || sprite == null)
        return;
    sprite.Draw(spriteBatch, this.GlobalPosition, origin);
}
```

For the complete SpriteGameObject class, see the PenguinPairs1 example belonging to this chapter.

19.5 Finalizing the Example

In the PenguinPairs1 example, we draw a background and a penguin on the screen. In order to test our new SpriteGameObject class, we will modify the currently selected sheet index by pressing the left and right arrow buttons. This is done easily in the PenguinPairs class:

```
SpriteGameObject penguin = gameWorld.Find("penguin") as SpriteGameObject;
if (inputHelper.KeyPressed(Keys.Left))
    penguin.Sprite.SheetIndex--;
else if (inputHelper.KeyPressed(Keys.Right))
    penguin.Sprite.SheetIndex++;
```

By the way, because we handle all the sprite sheet aspects inside the SpriteSheet class, it is now completely straightforward to draw the penguin exactly in the middle of the screen, as follows:

```
penguin.Position = new Vector2(screen.X — penguin.Width,
                               screen.Y — penguin.Height) / 2;
```

This will work for any sprite sheet of any dimension!

19.6 What You Have Learned

In this chapter, you have learned:

- how to use the Split method to analyze strings;
- how to handle sprite sheets in games.

Chapter 20
Menus and Settings

20.1 Introduction

In the Jewel Jam game, we have already seen a few basic examples of adding GUI elements to your game such as a button or a frame. In this chapter, we are going to add a few more GUI elements, such as an on/off button and a slider button. Secondly, we will show how you can read and store game settings, such as music volume or whether hints are allowed or not.

20.2 Setting up the Menu

As an example, we will show how to define a basic 'options' menu containing two controls: one for switching hints on or off, and one for controlling the volume of the music. First, we need to draw the elements surrounding these controls. We first add a background to the menu. Second, we add a text label to the menu to describe the 'hints' control. We are going to use the TextGameObject class taken from the Jewel Jam game for that. We define the text that should be drawn, and we place it at the appropriate position:

```
TextGameObject onofftext = new TextGameObject("Fonts/MenuFont", 1);
onofftext.Text = "Hints";
onofftext.Position = new Vector2(150, 340);
onofftext.Color = Color.DarkBlue;
gameWorld.Add(onofftext);
```

Similarly, we add a text label for the music volume controller. For the complete code, see the PenguinPairs2 example belonging to this chapter.

Fig. 20.1 The sprite strip
used for the on/off button

20.3 Adding an on/off Button

The next step is adding an on/off button for being able to show a hint or not during game play. How the value of the on/off button is used is something that we will look into later on in this chapter. Just like we did for the Button class in the Jewel Jam game, we are going to make a special class for on/off buttons, which we will (surprisingly) call OnOffButton. The class is a subclass of SpriteGameObject and it will expect a *sprite strip* containing two sprites: one for the 'off' state and one for the 'on' state (see Fig. 20.1).

An important part of the button is that we need to be able to read and set whether it is on or off. Since the button is based on a sprite strip of length two, we can define the button to be in the 'off' state if the sheet index is zero, and in the 'on' state if the sheet index equals one. We can then add a boolean property that gets and sets this value (you can see the code for this property in Listing 20.1).

Finally, we need to handle mouse clicks on the button to toggle its on or off state. Similar to what we did in the Button class, we check in the HandleInput method if the left mouse button was pressed and if the mouse position is within the bounding box of the button. If that is the case, we modify the sheet index. If the sheet index is zero, it should become one, and vice versa. We can achieve this effect with the following instruction:

```
sprite.SheetIndex = 1 − sprite.SheetIndex;
```

For the complete class, see Listing 20.1.

In the PenguinPairs class, we add an OnOffButton instance to the game world, at the desired position:

```
onOffButton = new OnOffButton("Sprites/spr_button_offon@2");
onOffButton.Position = new Vector2(650, 340);
gameWorld.Add(onOffButton);
```

20.4 Adding a Slider Button

A second kind of GUI control we would like to add is a slider. This slider will be used to control the volume of the background music in the game. The slider will consist of two sprites: a back sprite that represents the bar, and a front sprite that represents the actual slider. Therefore, the Slider class will inherit from GameObjectList. Because the back sprite has a border, we need to take that into account when we move or draw the slider. Therefore, we also define left and right margins that define

```
 1   using Microsoft.Xna.Framework;
 2
 3   class OnOffButton : SpriteGameObject
 4   {
 5       public OnOffButton(string imageAsset, int layer = 0, string id = "")
 6           : base(imageAsset, layer, id, 0)
 7       {
 8       }
 9
10       public override void HandleInput(InputHelper inputHelper)
11       {
12           if (inputHelper.MouseLeftButtonPressed() &&
13               BoundingBox.Contains((int)inputHelper.MousePosition.X,
14                                    (int)inputHelper.MousePosition.Y))
15               sprite.SheetIndex = 1 − sprite.SheetIndex;
16       }
17
18       public bool On
19       {
20           get
21           {
22               return sprite.SheetIndex == 1;
23           }
24           set
25           {
26               if (value)
27                   sprite.SheetIndex = 1;
28               else
29                   sprite.SheetIndex = 0;
30           }
31       }
32   }
```

Listing 20.1 The class for representing an on/off button

the border width on the left and right side of the back sprite. Furthermore, we position the slider slightly lower than the back sprite to account for the top border. The complete constructor is then given as follows:

```
public Slider(string sliderback, string sliderfront, int layer = 0, string id = "")
    : base(layer, id)
{
    leftmargin = 5;
    rightmargin = 7;

    back = new SpriteGameObject(sliderback, 0);
```

```
this.Add(back);

front = new SpriteGameObject(sliderfront, 1);
front.Position = new Vector2(leftmargin, 8);
this.Add(front);

dragging = false;
}
```

As you can see, we also set a boolean variable dragging to **false**. We will need this variable to keep track of when the player is dragging the slider so that we update the slider position when needed, even when the mouse pointer is not within the boundaries of the back sprite.

The next step is adding a property Value that allows us to retrieve and set the value of the slider. We want a value of 0 to indicate that the slider is fully moved to the left, and a value of 1 to indicate the fully right position of the slider. We can calculate the current value by looking at the position of the front sprite, and seeing how much it is moved to the right. Therefore, the following line of code calculates the slider value from the slider position:

```
return (front.Position.X − back.Position.X − leftmargin) /
       (back.Width − leftmargin − rightmargin − front.Width);
```

In the upper part of the fraction, we calculate how far to the right the front sprite has been moved. We calculate this locally to the back position plus the left margin. We then divide this by the total length that the slider can move. This **return**-instruction forms the **get** part of the Value property. For the **set** part of the property, we need to convert a value between zero and one to the front slider x position. This amounts to rewriting the above formula such that the front x position is the unknown, which is then calculated as follows:

```
float newxpos = value * (back.Width − leftmargin − rightmargin − front.Width)
                + back.Position.X + leftmargin;
```

All that remains to be done now is to create the new front position vector with the correct x position:

```
front.Position = new Vector2(newxpos, front.Position.Y);
```

So, now that we have a way to set and get the slider value, we still need to deal with the mouse input to drag the slider to a new position. This is done by overriding the HandleInput method. If the left mouse button is down, we have to check if we are dragging the slider. This is the case if the mouse position is within the bounding box of the back sprite, *or if we were already dragging*. This latter condition allows us to continue dragging the slider when the mouse moves outside of the back sprite bounding box. If so, we calculate the new x position of the slider bar. Ideally we would like the slider bar centered at the mouse *x* position, so we calculate the new *x* position of the front sprite as follows:

```
inputHelper.MousePosition.X − back.GlobalPosition.X − front.Width / 2
```

However, we also want to make sure that the slider bar stays within the boundaries of the back sprite. Therefore, we use the MathHelper.Clamp method to clamp the value between the minimal *x* value (which is back.Position.X + leftmargin) and the maximal *x* value (which is back.Position.X + back.Width − front.Width − rightmargin). Finally, since we are currently dragging, we set the value of the dragging member variable to **true**. As soon as the left mouse button is released, we arrive at the alternative part of the **if**-instruction, which sets the value of the dragging variable to **false**. This completes the Slider class. For the complete code, see the PenguinPairs2 example project belonging to this chapter.

Inside the PenguinPairs class, we then add a slider to the game world:

```
musicVolumeSlider = new Slider("Sprites/spr_slider_bar", "Sprites/spr_slider_button", 1);
musicVolumeSlider.Position = new Vector2(650, 500);
gameWorld.Add(musicVolumeSlider);
```

We can then use the Value property in that class to set the slider bar to match the current volume of the background music with a single line of code:

```
musicVolumeSlider.Value = MediaPlayer.Volume;
```

Finally, in the Update method of the PenguinPairs class, we retrieve the current value of the slider, and use that to update the volume of the background music:

```
MediaPlayer.Volume = musicVolumeSlider.Value;
```

Beautiful menu screens—Most games contain some menu screens. With these screens, the player can set options, choose a level, watch achievements or pause a game. Creating all of these additional screens can be a lot of work that does not really contribute to the actual game play. So developers tend to put less work into them. But that is a very wrong decision.

An artist once said: "Your game is as good as its worst screen". If one of the menu screens has poor quality the player will get the feeling that the game is unfinished and that the developer did not put enough effort into it. So make sure that all your menu screens look beautiful and are very easy to use and navigate. Think carefully about what you put in these screens. You might be tempted to create an option out of everything: the difficulty of the game, the music to play, the color of the background, etc. But remember that you are the person that should create the game, not the player. You or your artist should determine what gives the most interesting gameplay and what gives the most compelling visual style, not the user.

Try to avoid options as much as possible. For example, should a player really set the difficulty? Why not adapt the difficulty automatically by monitoring the player's progress? And do you need a level selection screen? Why not simply remember where the player was the last time and immediately continue there? Keep your interface as simple as possible!

20.5 Reading and Storing Game Settings

Having the slider control the volume of the background music was not very complicated. The MediaPlayer.Volume property is static, so we do not need an actual instance to access it. But now suppose that we want the on/off button to control whether the player can press a button to view a hint or not. Where should we store this option information? Normally, we would probably add a boolean member variable to a class somewhere in our game that indicates if hints are shown or not. But where should we add this variable? And how can we be sure that we can access it everywhere? Another example would be a control for modifying sound effect volume. Sound effects will be used throughout the game in many different classes, so we should be able to access the desired volume from almost anywhere. Clearly, what we need is a generic way for dealing with such kinds of settings in a game, together with a design that allows us to access this information everywhere in the code.

In order to allow for a variety of settings to be stored and retrieved, let us define a class GameSettingsManager, which contains a number of static member variables and methods. For simplicity, let us assume that each setting consists of a key (the identifier of the setting) and a value. For both the keys and the values, we will use the **string** type. And the logical collection structure for storing such key-value pairs is a dictionary. We add a member variable to the class to store this dictionary in:

protected Dictionary<**string, string**> stringSettings;

In the constructor of the GameSettingsManager class, we initialize the dictionary:

```
public GameSettingsManager()
{
    stringSettings = new Dictionary<string, string>();
}
```

Just like we did in the Jewel Jam game for the random number generator and the variable containing the screen dimensions, we will add a static member variable pointing to the game settings manager, together with a static property for accessing it:

```
1   using System.Collections.Generic;
2
3   class GameSettingsManager
4   {
5       protected Dictionary<string, string> stringSettings;
6
7       public GameSettingsManager()
8       {
9           stringSettings = new Dictionary<string, string>();
10      }
11
12      public void SetValue(string key, string value)
13      {
14          stringSettings[key] = value;
15      }
16
17      public string GetValue(string key)
18      {
19          if (stringSettings.ContainsKey(key))
20              return stringSettings[key];
21          else
22              return "";
23      }
24  }
```

Listing 20.2 A basic class for handling game settings

```
protected static GameSettingsManager gameSettingsManager;
...
public static GameSettingsManager GameSettingsManager
{
    get { return gameSettingsManager; }
}
```

We now add two methods to the manager for storing (SetValue) and for accessing (GetValue) settings. The implementation of these methods is rather straightforward, see Listing 20.2 for the complete class.

Updating the hint setting depending on the state of the on/off button is now very easy. We simply add these lines of code to the Update method of the PenguinPairs class:

```
if (onOffButton.On)
    GameSettingsManager.SetValue("hints", "on");
else
    GameSettingsManager.SetValue("hints", "off");
```

Settings of different types—The current version of GameSettingsManager only allows for storing and retrieving settings of type **string**. This may not always be desirable. Of course, basic values such as booleans, integers or double values could be stored as strings and then converted into different types using the Parse method, but that takes a lot of extra computation time. Also, sometimes we might want to use a more complicated type to store a setting. For example, you could imagine that one would like to store network access information (IP address, server login, password, and so on) in a single structure. We kept our example relatively basic, but there are several ways to solve this. One way would be to add several dictionaries to the GameSettingsManager class, one for each basic type. We could then write specific methods to retrieve and store settings of that type. You could even define these methods as *generics* so that they work in a fashion similar to Content.Load<>. Another way of solving it would be to make a single dictionary that retrieves values of a user-defined type ValueType. Specific settings data structures could then be implemented as a subclass of ValueType. Yet another solution would be to implement a kind of tree structure where you can add any basic type as an end node (this would be very similar to defining an XML structure). That way, you do not need user-defined types, but you provide a way to the user to define more complicated settings structures. As you can see, there are different solutions to this problem, and you can choose the one that best fits your particular needs.

20.6 What You Have Learned

In this chapter, you have learned:

- how to define different GUI elements and display them in a menu;
- how to read and store game settings using a static game settings manager.

Chapter 21
Game State Management

21.1 Introduction

Normally, you do not immediately start playing when a game application starts. For example, in the Jewel Jam game, we first saw a title screen before playing. More complicated games will have menus for options, menus for selecting different levels, screens to display the high score after finishing a level, a menu to select different characters and attributes, and so on. In the Jewel Jam game, adding a title screen was not that difficult, because the title screen itself had very little interaction. However, when we look at the example in the previous chapter, you can see that already building a screen with a few options and controls can result in quite a lot of code. And you can imagine that when we add more of these menus and screens to the game, that it is going to be a pain to manage which objects belong to which screen and when they should be drawn or updated. Generally, these different menus and screens are called *game states*. In some programs, these are called *scenes*, and the object responsible for managing the scenes is the *director*. In some cases, a distinction is made between game modes and game states. In that case, things like menus, the main playing screen, and so on are game modes, whereas 'level finished' or 'game over' are game states.

In this book, we will follow a simplified paradigm and call everything game states. In order to deal with these different game states, we are going to need a *manager*. In this chapter, we will develop the main classes needed for such a structure, and show how you can use it to display different menus and switch between them, while keeping the code cleanly separated.

21.2 Basics of Managing Game States

When we want to deal properly with game states, we need to make sure of the following:

A. Egges et al., *Learning C# by Programming Games*,
DOI 10.1007/978-3-642-36580-5_21, © Springer-Verlag Berlin Heidelberg 2013

- Game states should be run completely independently. In other words, we do not want to have to deal with the options menu screen or the game over screen while we are in the game playing state.
- There should be an easy way to define game states, find game states and switch between them. That way, when the player presses the 'options' button in the title screen, we can easily switch to the option menu state.

We are going to follow the procedure where each game state has its own input handling, update, and draw part, just like we did with game objects. It would be nice, though, if we can somehow ensure a bit of consistency within our class design. We could define a generic GameState class that has the same method headers for handling input, updating and drawing as the GameObject class, but that is perhaps not ideal, because apart from these method headers, we do not know anything else about the particular game state. Another way to do this would be to let the game states inherit from the GameObject class. However, this is not a good solution either, since game states are not really game objects. For one, they do not need a position or a velocity. As we have discussed early on in this book, we should use object-oriented design in such a way that subclasses are *a special kind of* the superclass they inherit from.

21.2.1 A Generic Game Loop Object Interface

There is another way to ensure that the method headers are the same for objects that follow the game loop principle: using an *interface*. In this interface, we then specify which methods should be implemented by the class that is based on the interface. Since we want an interface for any objects that partake in the game loop, let us call this interface IGameLoopObject (we prefix the interface with an 'I' character to separate it from regular class names). The IGameLoopObject interface contains four methods, three of which are the main game loop methods (HandleInput, Update and Draw), and a Reset method. The complete interface is given in Listing 21.1. As you will probably notice, we do not put the **virtual** keyword in front of methods in the interface. We only use **virtual** and **override** when we are dealing with *inheritance*. An interface simply specifies which methods should be defined in a class and what their parameters and return value looks like.

Now that we have this interface, the first thing we do is make sure that all the game objects also follow this interface. This was already (sort of) achieved in the GameObject class, but we can now let the GameObject class implement this interface as well, by defining the class as follows:

```
class GameObject : IGameLoopObject
{
    // member variables, methods, and properties
}
```

```
 1    using Microsoft.Xna.Framework;
 2    using Microsoft.Xna.Framework.Graphics;
 3
 4    interface IGameLoopObject
 5    {
 6        void HandleInput(InputHelper inputHelper);
 7
 8        void Update(GameTime gameTime);
 9
10        void Draw(GameTime gameTime, SpriteBatch spriteBatch);
11
12        void Reset();
13    }
```

Listing 21.1 The interface that specifies the methods implemented by objects that partake in the game loop

21.2.2 The GameStateManager Class

Now we can start building our game state manager class. Just like the asset manager, we add an instance of this class as a static member variable to the PenguinPairs class, together with a static property so that we can easily retrieve it:

protected static GameStateManager gameStateManager;

public static GameStateManager GameStateManager
{
    get { **return** gameStateManager; }
}

In the GameStateManager class, we want to keep track of all the different game states. We also want to be able to *find* game states so that we can switch between them at will. Therefore, we will store the different game states in a member variable that is of type Dictionary:

protected Dictionary<**string**, IGameLoopObject> gameStates;

The key type of this dictionary is **string**, meaning that we can find game states by using string identifiers. The value type is IGameLoopObject. So, any object that implements the game loop methods can serve as a game state. Next to this dictionary of game states, we also keep track of the current game state:

protected IGameLoopObject currentGameState;

Inside the constructor, we initially assign **null** to the current game state, since no game state can be selected yet. We then add a few methods and properties to add and retrieve game states based on their string identifier. Since these methods are quite straightforward, we will not discuss the details here, but you can have a look at the code by opening the PenguinPairs3 program in the solution belonging to this chapter.

The main method used for switching between game states is the SwitchTo method. This method takes a string as a parameter and switches to the corresponding game state. This is the complete method:

```
public void SwitchTo(string name)
{
    if (gameStates.ContainsKey(name))
        currentGameState = gameStates[name];
}
```

Inside this method, we check if the provided key exists. If it does, we set the current game state to the state associated with that key.

As you can see, it is relatively easy to check if a dictionary contains a key or not. What if we wanted to check if a dictionary contains a certain *value*? In that case, we have to do a search ourselves using the **foreach**-instruction. The kind of object that **foreach** provides while traversing a dictionary is a KeyValuePair<>. This type contains the properties Key and Value to access the key and value in the pair. Once we find the current game state, we are done. Suppose that we are looking for the name of the state currentGameState. This piece of code returns the key associated with that game state:

```
foreach (KeyValuePair<string, IGameLoopObject> pair in gameStates)
{
    if (pair.Value == currentGameState)
        return pair.Key;
}
return "";
```

Going back to our game example, we still have to handle the different game loop methods. This is actually relatively simple. If a game state is currently selected, we simply call the game loop methods on the game state. For example, the HandleInput method is given as follows:

```
public void HandleInput(InputHelper inputHelper)
{
    if (currentGameState != null)
        currentGameState.HandleInput(inputHelper);
}
```

We follow a similar procedure for the other game loop methods.

21.3 Adding States and Switching Between Them

Now that we have our game state manager, we can start adding different states to it. A very basic game state is the title menu state. In the PenguinPairs3 example, we added a class TitleMenuState to the project that represents this state. Since this state contains a couple of different game objects, we let it inherit from the GameObjectList class. In the constructor of this class, we add the game objects that are required for this state: a background, and three buttons. We reuse the Button class that we developed earlier for the Jewel Jam game.

Because we need to do something when a button is pressed, we have to override the HandleInput method. In that method, we check for each of the buttons if they are pressed, and if so, we switch to another state. For instance, if the player presses the 'play game' button, we need to switch to the level menu:

```
if (playButton.Pressed)
    PenguinPairs.GameStateManager.SwitchTo("levelMenu");
```

We add similar alternatives for the other two buttons. Now our title menu state is basically done (for the complete class, see Listing 21.2). In the PenguinPairs class, the only thing we need to do is make an instance of TitleMenuState and add it to the game state manager. We also do this for all the other states that are in the game. After that we set the current state to be the title menu, so that the player sees the title menu when the game starts:

```
gameStateManager.AddGameState("titleMenu", new TitleMenuState());
gameStateManager.AddGameState("optionsMenu", new OptionsMenuState());
gameStateManager.AddGameState("levelMenu", new LevelMenuState());
gameStateManager.AddGameState("helpState", new HelpState());
gameStateManager.SwitchTo("titleMenu");
```

The help and option menu states are done in a similar fashion. In the constructor of the class, we add our game objects to the game world, and we override the HandleInput method to switch between different states. For example, both the help and option menu state contain a 'back' button that returns us to the title screen:

```
public override void HandleInput(InputHelper inputHelper)
{
    base.HandleInput(inputHelper);
    if (backButton.Pressed)
        PenguinPairs.GameStateManager.SwitchTo("titleMenu");
}
```

21.4 The Level Menu State

A slightly more complicated game state is the level menu. We want the player to be able to select a level from a grid of level buttons. Although we will not implement

```
1    using Microsoft.Xna.Framework;
2
3    class TitleMenuState : GameObjectList
4    {
5        protected Button playButton, optionButton, helpButton;
6
7        public TitleMenuState()
8        {
9            // load the title screen
10           SpriteGameObject title = new SpriteGameObject("Sprites/spr_titlescreen",
11                                                          0, "background");
12           this.Add(title);
13
14           // add a play button
15           playButton = new Button("Sprites/spr_button_play", 1);
16           playButton.Position = new Vector2(415, 540);
17           this.Add(playButton);
18
19           // add an options button
20           optionButton = new Button("Sprites/spr_button_options", 1);
21           optionButton.Position = new Vector2(415, 650);
22           this.Add(optionButton);
23
24           // add a help button
25           helpButton = new Button("Sprites/spr_button_help", 1);
26           helpButton.Position = new Vector2(415, 760);
27           this.Add(helpButton);
28       }
29
30       public override void HandleInput(InputHelper inputHelper)
31       {
32           base.HandleInput(inputHelper);
33           if (playButton.Pressed)
34               PenguinPairs.GameStateManager.SwitchTo("levelMenu");
35           else if (optionButton.Pressed)
36               PenguinPairs.GameStateManager.SwitchTo("optionsMenu");
37           else if (helpButton.Pressed)
38               PenguinPairs.GameStateManager.SwitchTo("helpState");
39       }
40   }
```

Listing 21.2 The class representing the title menu state, consisting of a background, a 'play game' button, an 'options' button, and a 'help button'

that yet, we want to be able to display three different states with these levels buttons, because a level can be locked, unlocked but not yet solved by the player, and solved. For each of these different situations we will use a different sprite for displaying the button. However, in the PenguinPairs3 example, we will simply show the 'locked' status for each level.

So before we can create the LevelMenuState class, we will add a class called LevelButton. This class inherits from GameObjectList. For convenience, we will also store the level index (which is between one and twelve in this example) in a LevelButton object. The constructor of the LevelButton class is then given as follows:

```
public LevelButton(int levelIndex, int layer = 0, string id = "")
    : base(layer, id)
{
    this.levelIndex = levelIndex;
    spr_lock = new SpriteGameObject("Sprites/spr_lock");
    this.Add(spr_lock);
}
```

In the HandleInput method, we check if the button has been pressed by checking if the mouse position is within the bounding box of the sprite we added to the list and the player has pressed the left mouse button:

```
pressed = inputHelper.MouseLeftButtonPressed() &&
            spr_lock.BoundingBox.Contains((int)inputHelper.MousePosition.X,
                            (int)inputHelper.MousePosition.Y);
```

Next to that, we also add Width and Height properties that we will need when we place the level buttons on the screen.

Now that we have a basic LevelButton class, we can add these level buttons in the LevelMenuState class. In this example, we will add twelve level buttons to the menu, using a for-instruction. Depending on the value of the counter variable (i), we calculate the row and column that the button belongs to. This information, together with the width and the height of a level button, can help us to calculate the final position of each level button:

```
for (int i = 0; i < 12; i++)
{
    int row = i / 5;
    int column = i % 5;
    LevelButton level = new LevelButton(1);
    level.Position = new Vector2(column * (level.Width + 30),
                            row * (level.Height + 5))
                + new Vector2(155, 230);
    this.Add(level);
}
```

We also add a property called LevelSelected to the LevelMenuState class. This property only has a **get** part, and it goes through all the LevelButton instances and returns the level index belonging to the first button that was pressed. If the player did not press any button, the property returns minus one. In order to do that, we use a casting trick. We walk through the list of game objects and cast every one of them to a LevelButton instance using **as**. If the **as** operator returns **null**, we ignore the object. Otherwise, we check if the level button was pressed and if so, we return its level index. The whole property is given as follows:

```
public int LevelSelected
{
    get
    {
        foreach (GameObject obj in this.Objects)
        {
            LevelButton levelButton = obj as LevelButton;
            if (levelButton != null && levelButton.Pressed)
                return levelButton.LevelIndex;
        }
        return −1;
    }
}
```

We can then use this property in the HandleInput method:

```
if (LevelSelected != −1)
{
    // start the level
}
```

As you can see, adding different states to a game and switching between them is not very hard, as long as you think about the design of the software beforehand. By thinking beforehand about which classes are needed and how the functionality of your game should be split up between them, you can save yourself a lot of time later on. In the next chapter, we are going to further extend this example by reading the levels and their status from a text file.

21.5 What You Have Learned

In this chapter, you have learned:

- how to define different game states using a game state manager;
- how to switch between game states depending on the player's actions.

Chapter 22
Loading Levels from Files

22.1 Introduction

Many games consist of different levels. Especially in casual games such as puzzles and maze games, the game may have several hundreds of levels. With the programming tools that we have seen thus far, we could add different levels to our game by, for example, writing a generic Level class, and then defining hundreds of subclasses, where each class defines what the particular level looks like. This approach has a few disadvantages. The most important disadvantage is that we are mixing the *game logic* (gameplay, win condition, and so on), with the *game content*. This means that every time we wanted to add another level to the game, we would need to write a new class, which would lead to a lot of classes that need to be compiled. A much better approach would be to store the different levels in a text file, and then read the information from this text file to create the levels. This way, we can define a Level class that loads its content and settings from a file. Then, if we want to add another level to our game, we do not have to change the source code but we can edit the text file. This has the advantage that developers do not need to be involved with creating the levels anymore. We can simply give the program to an artist who can develop the levels by editing the text file, while we can focus on developing the game itself. In this chapter, we will see how we can load levels from a text file using the C# file I/O classes.

22.2 Structure of a Level

Let us first look at what kind of things can be inside a level. First, there will be some kind of background image. Let us assume that this background is fixed when we load the level, so there is no need to store any information about that in the text file.

Inside the level, there will be penguins, seals, sharks, icebergs, background blocks that penguins can move on, and a few more things. We want to store all of this information in a text file. One possibility would be to store for every object

A. Egges et al., *Learning C# by Programming Games*,   297
DOI 10.1007/978-3-642-36580-5_22, © Springer-Verlag Berlin Heidelberg 2013

its position and type, but that would not make the text file very clear. Another possibility is to divide the level up in small blocks, also called *tiles*. Every block has a certain type (this could be a penguin, a white tile, an empty tile, a penguin, and so on). A tile can then be represented by a character, and we can store the structure of the level in a text file like in the following example:

```
#.......#
#...r...#
#.......#
#.     .#
#.     .#
#.     .#
#.......#
#...r...#
#.......#
```

In this level definition, a number of different blocks are defined. An iceberg tile is defined by the '#' sign, a penguin by an 'r' character, a normal tile by a '.' character and an empty tile by a space character. Now we can write a method that reads this information from the text file, creates the tiles and stores them somewhere (probably in a GameObjectGrid instance). This means that we will need different types of tiles: a normal tile on which a penguin can stand, a transparent background tile, and a wall (iceberg) tile against which a penguin can collide.

22.3 The Tile Class

To get things started, let us first write a basic Tile class. This class is going to be a subclass of the SpriteGameObject class. The complete class can be found in Listing 22.1. For now, we do not yet consider items in the level such as penguins, icebergs, seals, or sharks. We only look at background (transparent) tiles, normal tiles, and wall tiles. We introduce an enumerated type TileType to represent these different varieties of tiles:

enum TileType { Normal, Background, Wall };

In the Tile class, we then declare a member variable type to store the type of tile that an instance represents:

protected TileType type;

In order to accommodate for transparent tiles, we override the Draw method in the Tile class to only draw the sprite if the tile is not a background tile:

```
if (type == TileType.Background)
    return;
base.Draw(gameTime, spriteBatch);
```

```
1   using Microsoft.Xna.Framework;
2   using Microsoft.Xna.Framework.Graphics;
3
4   enum TileType { Normal, Background, Wall };
5
6   class Tile : SpriteGameObject
7   {
8       protected TileType type;
9
10      public Tile(string assetname, int layer = 0, string id = "", int stripIndex = 0)
11          : base(assetname, layer, id, stripIndex)
12      {
13          type = TileType.Normal;
14      }
15
16      public override void Draw(GameTime gameTime, SpriteBatch spriteBatch)
17      {
18          if (type == TileType.Background)
19              return;
20          base.Draw(gameTime, spriteBatch);
21      }
22
23      public TileType TileType
24      {
25          get { return type; }
26          set { type = value; }
27      }
28  }
```

Listing 22.1   The Tile class

Furthermore, we add a property to the Tile class to access the current tile type. When we load the level, we will create a tile for each character, and store it in a grid structure such as GameObjectGrid.

22.4 Other Level Information

Next to the tiles in the level, we need to store a few other things as well in the level description text file:

- the title of the level
- the description of the level
- the number of pairs to be made
- the width and the height of the level
- the location and direction of the hint arrow

So, a complete level in the text file looks something like this:

```
Splash!
Don't let the penguins fall in the water!
1
9 9
4 2 2
#.......#
#...r...#
#.......#
#.     .#
#.     .#
#.     .#
#.......#
#...r...#
#.......#
```

For every level, we add such a definition to the text file. The example provided with the book contains 12 levels. When we read the text file, the first line in the file is the number 12, so that we know how many levels we have to read. The question is: how do we get the information that is in the file into our program?

22.5 File Reading in C#

22.5.1 Reading a Text File

Just like other game assets such as sprites or sounds, text files are also placed in the content project. In this example, you can see that the level files are placed in a sub folder called *Levels*. You can drag and drop other text files in this folder if you wish to create more levels. However, Visual Studio does not know what a text file is supposed to be. The default behavior of Visual Studio is to try to compile this text file. This is not what we want. After all: the text file does not contain any C# code. You can change these settings by right-clicking on the text file that you added and select 'Properties'. A property panel should appear (see Fig. 22.1). Make sure that the option 'Build Action' is set to 'None'. If you select any other build action, the compiler will try to execute that action, which will most probably fail, resulting in an error.

C# knows a number of standard classes for dealing with input and output (also ab-breviated as I/O). A number of commonly used I/O-classes together with subclasses are given in Fig. 22.2. Most of these classes are part of the System.IO namespace, but some of them are in separate namespaces for networking, XML, cryptography or compression.

Fig. 22.1 The property panel
of the file 'levels.txt'

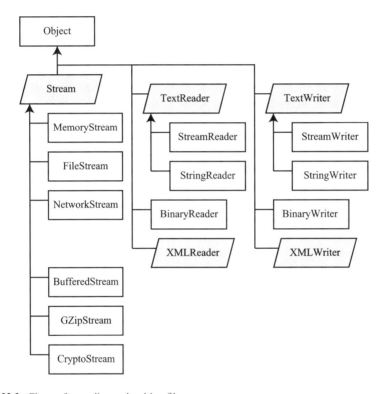

Fig. 22.2 Classes for reading and writing files

22.5.2 Streams Versus Text Readers and Writers

The main difference between the classes in the diagram is that some of them are
Stream subclasses, whereas others are subclasses of a *reader* or *writer* class.

- In a Stream the separate bytes of a file are read or written. A *reader* or *writer* class
  deals with larger units: characters and strings in a TextWriter, integers, doubles and
  other basic types in a BinaryWriter and coherent parts of an XML document in the
  XMLWriter.

- A Stream allows you to both read and write from the same file, as well as overwrite parts of the file. A reader or writer only allows you to read or write, respectively.

22.5.3 Reader

A *reader* class allows reading bigger units than bytes. For example, a TextReader can read text (so: strings consisting of characters). It contains among others the following methods:

int Read(); // reads a char or returns −1 if the end of the file was reached
string ReadLine(); // reads the next line
string ReadToEnd(); // reads the rest of the file

A BinaryReader can read the basic types in their binary coding. An **int** or a **float** always takes 4 bytes, a **long** or a **double** always 8 bytes. This class has (among others) the following methods:

byte ReadByte();
short ReadInt16();
int ReadInt32();
long ReadInt64();
uint ReadUInt32();
double ReadDouble();

Readers are *not* streams! Although some of them have a method Read or ReadByte, these are other methods than the methods carrying the same name in Stream, with other results. Some of the readers (such as BinaryReader) allow you to provide a Stream as a parameter in the constructor. For every reading operation the binary reader will use the underlying stream to read the actual bytes. However, not all readers use an underlying stream, some of them have an underlying string from which they get the data.

22.5.4 Text Reader

It is not allowed to make instances directly of the class TextReader because it is an *abstract class* (more about that later on). If you want to use a kind of text reader, you should use one of its subclasses. You can choose between two subclasses: a StreamReader is a text reader that uses an underlying stream, a StringReader is a text reader that uses an underlying string. In practice, you will probably use the StreamReader most of the times. This is also the class that we use in the example. The naming of the different classes is slightly confusing:

- a BinaryReader reads binary things from an underlying stream

- an XMLReader reads XML things from an underlying stream
- a TextReader reads text things from an underlying something
- a StreamReader reads text things from an underlying stream
- a StringReader reads text things from an underlying string

The confusing thing is that the name of the reader sometimes indicates *what* is being read, and sometimes *from where* it is reading data.

22.5.5 Stream Reader

The most common way to read a file is by using a StreamReader object. This is a TextReader using an underlying stream, meaning that if you want to use this kind of reader, you first need to have a Stream. There are many different kinds of streams, but again the most common one is the FileStream. Using the FileStream in combination with a StreamReader is illustrated by the following lines of code:

```
FileStream s = new FileStream("test.txt", FileMode.Open);
StreamReader r = new StreamReader(s);
string t = r.ReadToEnd();
```

Because of the highly common combination of the StreamReader with the FileStream, the StreamReader class has a constructor that takes a file name as parameter and that creates the FileStream object itself. A FileMode parameter is no longer necessary in this case, because we always want to open an existing file when reading. So, what remains is the following code:

```
StreamReader r = new StreamReader("test.txt");
string t = r.ReadToEnd();
```

By the way, there is an even shorter way to read all the text from a file, because the File class has a static method ReadAllText that creates the StreamReader and calls ReadToEnd. This results in the following (single line of) code:

```
string t = File.ReadAllText("test.txt");
```

The libraries available in C# have many of these shortcuts, but sometimes you may want to do something slightly different from what the shortcut dictates. In that case, you need to take the long approach and you need to know how everything works behind the scenes.

22.5.6 Abstract Classes

We mentioned earlier on that TextReader is an abstract class. The Stream, TextWriter, XmlReader and XmlWriter classes are also abstract. This means that it is not allowed to make an actual instance of that class. You can only inherit from it. Abstract classes can be useful when you want to design a class that serves as the basis of other classes. You could also use an interface for that, but in an abstract class, you can already define a few methods that can be useful to the classes that inherit from the abstract class. For example, in the Stream class, the Read method is already defined using the yet to be implemented ReadByte method.

You can even write your own abstract classes if you want to. An abstract class is exactly the same as a regular class, instead that it has the keyword **abstract** in front of the class. Furthermore, abstract classes can also have abstract methods. Abstract classes are useful if you want to define what methods a subclass should implement (similar to an interface), but, as opposed to an interface, abstract classes may already define methods and properties. For example, the GameObject class could be a good candidate for an abstract class, since we probably will not make an actual instance of it, but we use it as a basic class to define the interface and behavior of subclasses. Have a look at the following example:

```
abstract class GameObject
{
    protected Vector2 position;

    public GameObject()
    {
        this.position = Vector2.Zero;
    }

    public Vector2 Position
    {
        get { return position; }
        set { position = value; }
    }

    public abstract void Draw(GameTime gameTime, SpriteBatch spriteBatch);
}
```

The abstract GameObject class has a few methods and properties that are implemented (the constructor method and the Position property). The Draw method is abstract, meaning that it is not implemented, but *it has to be implemented by any subclass* that inherits from the GameObject class. Since GameObject is an abstract class and not an interface, we can define member variables such as position, or properties/methods such as Position and the GameObject constructor method.

The TextReader class is also a good example of an abstract class: we do not want to make an instance of it, but we use it as a basic implementation structure for the subclasses.

22.6 Reading the Levels from the Text File

22.6.1 The *loadLevels* Method

In the previous chapter, we have seen how to add different game states to a game and how to switch between them. We are going to add a new game state in this chapter, the *playing* game state. This game state is then responsible for loading and displaying the levels. We added a method called LoadLevels to this class which creates a StreamReader instance to read the file. The first step is to read the first line in the file, which contains the number of levels to be loaded. What we will then do is create for each level an instance of a class that we added to the project called Level, and *we pass the StreamReader instance as a parameter to the constructor*. Inside the Level constructor, we will then read the relevant lines from the text file to create the Level object. Once we are done, we close the file reader. The complete LoadLevels method is given as follows:

```
public void LoadLevels(string path)
{
    StreamReader fileReader = new StreamReader(path);
    string line = fileReader.ReadLine();
    int nrLevels = int.Parse(line);
    for (int currLevel = 1; currLevel <= nrLevels; currLevel++)
    {
        levels.Add(new Level(currLevel, fileReader));
    }
    fileReader.Close();
}
```

22.6.2 Creating the Level Object

Inside the Level constructor, we then create the different game objects belonging to each level. First, we add a background image to the game world, then we read the first few lines of information from the level text file, using the stream reader that was passed as a parameter:

```
string levelTitle = reader.ReadLine();
string levelHelp = reader.ReadLine();
int nrpairs = int.Parse(reader.ReadLine());
```

Then, we read the width and height of the level. In order to extract the **int** values from the line that we read, we use the Split method:

```
string[] stringlist = reader.ReadLine().Split();
int width = int.Parse(stringlist[0]);
int height = int.Parse(stringlist[1]);
```

We then create a GameObjectList instance that will contain the playing field, just like we did in the Jewel Jam game. We position this playing field in such a way that it is nicely centered on the screen:

```
GameObjectList playingField = new GameObjectList(1, "playingField");
playingField.Position = new Vector2((PenguinPairs.Resolution.X − width * 73) / 2, 100);
this.Add(playingField);
```

The next step is to read the hint information and add it to the level. For now, we will not yet add the hint arrow to the playing field, but we will already load it. After loading the *x* and *y* position and the direction of the arrow (top, left, down or right), we create a SpriteGameObject instance representing the arrow. All four directions of the arrow are stored in a sprite strip of length 4, and with the hint direction index that we read from the file, we select the sprite strip index that should be used. Finally, we position the hint arrow using the width and height of one tile in the playing field:

```
stringlist = reader.ReadLine().Split();
int hintx = int.Parse(stringlist[0]) − 1;
int hinty = int.Parse(stringlist[1]) − 1;
int hintdirection = int.Parse(stringlist[2]);
SpriteGameObject hint = new SpriteGameObject("Sprites/spr_arrow_hint@4", 2,
                                             "hint", hintdirection);
hint.Position = new Vector2(hintx, hinty) * new Vector2(73, 72);
playingField.Add(hint);
```

Now we need to read the actual tile information from the text file. We will reuse the GameObjectGrid class to represent a grid of tiles. Reading this grid from the text file can be done using a nested **for**-instruction. Have a look at the following lines of code:

```
GameObjectGrid tilefield = new GameObjectGrid(height, width, 1, "tilefield");
tilefield.ObjectHeight = 72;
tilefield.ObjectWidth = 73;
for (int row = 0; row < height; row++)
{
    string currRow = reader.ReadLine();
    for (int col = 0; col < currRow.Length; col++)
    {
        // handle the tile 'currRow[col]' here
    }
}
```

As you can see, we first create a GameObjectGrid instance, we set the width and height of a cell within that grid to a given size, and then we start reading the lines containing the tile information. Now, depending on the character we get from the expression currRow[col], we need to create different kinds of game objects, and add them to the grid. We could use an **if**-instruction for that:

```
if (currRow[col] == '.')
      // create an empty tile
else if (currRow[col] == ' ')
      // create a background tile
else if (currRow[col] == 'r')
      // create a penguin tile
//... and so on
```

But there is another option that allows us to write this down in a slightly cleaner way. With the **if**-instruction, we have to write and re-write a similar condition. C# offers a special kind of instruction for that: **switch**.

22.6.3 The *switch-Instruction: Handling Alternatives*

The **switch**-instruction allows us to specify alternatives, and the instructions that should be executed for each alternative. For example, the above **if**-instruction with multiple alternatives can be rewritten as a **switch**-instruction as follows:

```
switch(currRow[col])
{
      case '.': // create an empty tile
                  break;
      case ' ': // create a background tile
                  break;
      case 'r': // create a penguin tile
                  break;
}
```

The **switch**-instruction has a few handy properties that make it very useful to handle different alternatives. Have a look at the following code example:

```
if (x==1) one();
else if (x==2) { two(); alsoTwo(); }
else if (x==3 || x==4) threeOrFour();
else more();
```

We can rewrite this with a **switch**-instruction as follows:

```
switch(x)
{
    case 1: one();
            break;
    case 2: two();
            alsoTwo();
            break;
    case 3:
    case 4: threeOrFour();
            break;
    default: more();
            break;
}
```

When a **switch**-instruction is executed, the expression between the parentheses is calculated. Then, the instructions after the word **case** and the particular value, are executed. If there is no case that corresponds to the value, then the instructions after the **default** keyword are executed. The values behind the different cases need to be constant values (numbers, characters, or strings between double quotes, or variables declared as constant).

22.6.4 The break-Instruction

If we do not watch out, the **switch**-instruction not only executes the instruction behind the relevant case, but also the instructions behind the other cases. This is prevented by placing the special **break**-instruction after each case. The **break**-instruction basically means: "stop executing the **switch**-, **while**-, or **for**-instruction that we are currently in". If we did not place any **break**-instruction in the example above, then in the case that x == 2, the methods two and alsoTwo would be called, but also the methods threeOrFour and more().

   In some cases, this behavior could be useful, so that, in a sense, the different cases flow through each other. In languages related to C# such as C, C++ and Java, this is indeed possible. However, it also leads to many errors, because if a programmer forgot to place a **break**-instruction somewhere, this would lead to very strange behavior. C# broke with this tradition, and cases always have to be separated by a **break**-instruction, with one exception. You are allowed to write multiple **case** labels in front of a group of instructions, like we did in the example with the cases 3 and 4. The syntax of the **switch**-instruction is a part of the *instruction* syntax diagram. This is the part of that diagram belonging to the **switch**-instruction:

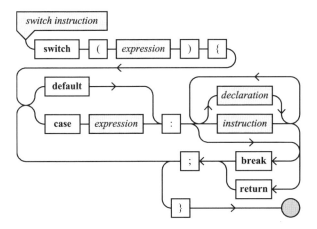

22.6.5 Loading Different Kinds of Tiles

We can use the **switch**-instruction to load all the different tiles and game objects. For each character, we need to perform a different task. For example, when the character '.' is read, we need to create a normal tile. The following instructions do that:

```
t = new Tile("Sprites/spr_field@2", 0, "", (row+col) % 2);
tilefield.Add(t, col, row);
break;
```

The sprite used for the tile is a strip consisting of two different sprites. By switching the sheet index using the formula (row + col) % 2, we get the alternating checkerboard pattern as can be seen when you run the example project belonging to this chapter.

Another example is adding a background (transparent) sprite:

```
t = new Tile("Sprites/spr_wall");
t.TileTypo = TileType.Background;
tilefield.Add(t, col, row);
break;
```

Although the background sprite is invisible, we still load a sprite belonging to this tile. Why is that? The reason is that the Tile class inherits from the SpriteGameObject class, which requires a sprite. Of course, another option would be to modify the SpriteGameObject class so that it can deal with a sprite that is **null**. However, in this case, we chose to follow the simple solution of just providing a sprite, even if the player will never see it.

When we have to place a penguin, actually two things need to be done:

- we need to place a normal tile
- we need to place a penguin

Since penguins need to move around on the playing board and we need to interact with them, we will create a class Animal to represent an animal such as a penguin or a seal. In order to keep track of which animals are in the game, we maintain a list as a member variable of the Level class:

```
protected List<Animal> animals;
```

Inside the **switch** instruction, we then create a normal tile and a penguin, as follows:

```
t = new Tile("Sprites/spr_field@2", 0, "", (row + col) % 2);
tilefield.Add(t, col, row);
string assetname = "Sprites/spr_penguin@8";
if (char.IsUpper(currRow[col]))
    assetname = "Sprites/spr_penguin_boxed@8";
Animal a = new Animal(assetname, 2, "", currRow[col]);
a.Position = t.Position;
a.InitialPosition = t.Position;
playingField.Add(a);
animals.Add(a);
break;
```

As you can see, we are doing a couple of other things as well. For instance, we make a difference between normal animals, and boxed animals (e.g., animals that cannot move). We make this distinction by using either uppercase or lowercase characters. The **char** type has a method called IsUpper that checks if a character is uppercase. We use that method in the condition of an **if**-instruction to determine the name of the asset that should be used. After creating the Animal object, we set its position to the position of the tile we created, so that it is placed correctly. We also set a property called InitialPosition to that same value. We do this so that if the player gets stuck and presses the 'retry' button, we know what the original position is of each animal in the level.

If you look at the Animal constructor, you see that we pass the character along as a parameter. We do this so that inside the constructor we can decide which element of the strip should be selected. Furthermore, we can check the character to find out if we are dealing with a boxed animal or not. The boxed status is stored in a boolean member variable of the Animal class:

```
boxed = char.IsUpper(color);
```

We are using the IndexOf method of the **string** type in the constructor to determine which sheet index we should use, depending on the character that was passed along as a parameter:

```
string animals = "brgyopmx";
sprite.SheetIndex = animals.IndexOf(char.ToLower(color));
```

We convert the character to lowercase so that the instruction works for both normal and boxed penguins. To complete the Animal class, we add a few convenient methods to check if we are dealing with a special case such as a multicolored penguin, an empty box, or a seal. For the complete Animal class, see the example project belonging to this chapter.

Finally, we also have sharks in the Penguin Pairs game. Sharks are relatively simple animals and they cannot be controlled by the player (very much like in real life!). Therefore, we will not use the Animal class for them, but we will simply use SpriteGameObject, which contains everything we need. We follow a similar procedure as with the penguins. We create a tile and a shark, and store the sharks in a List so that we can easily find them later on:

```
t = new Tile("Sprites/spr_field@2", 0, "", (row + col) % 2);
tilefield.Add(t, col, row);
SpriteGameObject s = new SpriteGameObject("Sprites/spr_shark", 2, "");
s.Position = t.Position;
playingField.Add(s);
sharks.Add(s);
break;
```

> **Automatic copying of assets**—You may have noticed that when a game is compiled, it copies all the assets to a folder local to the application file. For example, if you compile the PenguinPairs4 program in release mode, the contents are copied to the folder bin/x86/Release/Content. These are the contents that are really used when you run the game, and not the contents in the content project. So, watch out that if you want to modify for example a text file, you modify the right version of that file.

22.7 Completing the Level Class

Now that we have finished loading the tiles, we still have to add a few more game objects to complete the Level class. The first thing we will do is add a 'quit' button, so that players can quit the level and return to the level menu:

```
quitButton = new Button("Sprites/spr_button_quit", 1);
quitButton.Position = new Vector2(1058, 20);
this.Add(quitButton);
```

We also add a method to the class for checking if the player has pressed the 'quit' button:

```
public bool PlayerQuit
{
    get { return quitButton.Pressed; }
}
```

Inside the PlayingState, we then call the game loop methods on the currently running level, and if the player has pressed the 'quit' button, we reset the level, and return to the level menu, as can be seen in the HandleInput method of the PlayerState class:

```
public virtual void HandleInput(InputHelper inputHelper)
{
    CurrentLevel.HandleInput(inputHelper);
    if (CurrentLevel.PlayerQuit)
    {
        CurrentLevel.Reset();
        PenguinPairs.GameStateManager.SwitchTo("levelMenu");
    }
}
```

Finally, for each level, we maintain whether the level is locked or not and whether the player already solved the level. We need two boolean member variables for that, and we add two properties to the Level class to access them.

22.8 Maintaining the Player's Progress

One more nice thing that is now possible with file I/O is that we can keep track of the player's progress, and we can remember it for the next time the player wants to play the game. To do that, we created a text file 'levels_status.txt' which contains for each level both the locked and solved status. This file has the following contents:

```
false,false
true,false
true,false
true,false
true,false
true,false
true,false
true,false
true,false
true,false
true,false
true,false
```

In total, there are 12 lines, each one corresponding to a level. The first boolean indicates whether the level is locked or not, and the second boolean indicates whether

the player solved the level or not. As you can see, this contents represents the state
where the player starts the game for the first time. In other words: all levels but the
first one are locked, and none of the levels are solved.

We can load this status information after we have loaded all the levels, and update all the Level objects. For that, we added a method LoadLevelsStatus method and
added it to the PlayingState class. In this method, we again create an instance of
the StreamReader class, and we read the lines from the text file. We use the Split
method from the **string** type to split the lines into separate strings, and we then use
bool.Parse to convert these strings to boolean values. We then pass along these values to the Locked and Solved properties of the different levels. The complete method
is given as follows:

```
public void LoadLevelsStatus(string path)
{
    StreamReader fileReader = new StreamReader(path);
    for (int i = 0; i < levels.Count; i++)
    {
        string line = fileReader.ReadLine();
        string[] elems = line.Split(',');
        if (elems.Length == 2)
        {
            levels[i].Locked = bool.Parse(elems[0]);
            levels[i].Solved = bool.Parse(elems[1]);
        }
    }
    fileReader.Close();
}
```

In a similar way, we can create a method WriteLevelsStatus that uses a StreamWriter to
write the current status of all the levels to a file. Here is the complete method:

```
public void WriteLevelsStatus(string path)
{
    StreamWriter fileWriter = new StreamWriter(path, false);
    for (int i = 0; i < levels.Count; i++)
    {
        string line = levels[i].Locked.ToString() + "," + levels[i].Solved.ToString();
        fileWriter.WriteLine(line);
    }
    fileWriter.Close();
}
```

In the WriteLevelsStatus method, we go the other way round. We create the writer
object, then we create the strings representing the status for each level, which are
then written to the file. We pass a boolean value as a parameter to the StreamWriter
constructor to indicate that we do not want to *append* something to the file, but that
we want to *overwrite* the file with new contents. After writing the level status to the

file, we close it. Do not forget to always close file readers and writers when you are finished reading or writing, or you may not be able to open another file afterwards!

We now have completed the example belonging to this chapter. When you run the example, you can see that all the levels are loaded. If you want to see all the levels, you need to change the content of the 'levels_status.txt' file.

The curse of save games—Most games contain a mechanism that allows saving of the player's progress. This is normally used in three ways: to continue playing later, to return to a previous save point when you fail later on in the game, or to exploit alternative strategies or story-lines. Even though this all sounds very reasonable, it also introduces lots of problems and when you design a game you carefully have to consider when (and how) to allow the player to save and load the game state.

For example, in older first person shooters, all enemies were at fixed locations in the game world. A common strategy among players became to save a game, then just run into a room to see where the enemies were (which led to instant death), then loading the save game and, with the information about the location of the enemies, carefully clean out the room. This made the game a lot easier to play, but it was definitely not the intention of the creators. This can partially be remedied by making it difficult to save a game or to load a saved game.

Other games only allow saves at particular save points. Some even make reaching a save point part of the challenge. But this can lead to frustration because the player may have to replay sections of the game over and over again because there is just one very difficult spot. The most interesting games are the ones where you never have to return to save points because you never really fail, but this is extremely difficult to design.

So think carefully about your saving mechanism. When will you allow saves? How many different saves do you allow? How does the saving work? How do you load a saved game? Does it cost something to save or load a game? All these decisions will influence the gameplay and the player satisfaction.

22.9 What You Have Learned

In this chapter, you have learned:

- how to read from and write to text files;
- how to create a tile-based game world;
- how to retrieve and store level status using a file.

Chapter 23
Pairing the Penguins

23.1 Introduction

In this chapter, we will program the main gameplay for the Penguin Pairs game. We will discuss how to move penguins around on the board, and what to do when a penguin collides with another game object such as a shark or another penguin.

23.2 Penguin Selection

Before we can move penguins around, we need to be able to *select* a penguin. When we click on an animal such as a penguin or a seal, four arrows should appear that allow us to control in which direction the animal should move. In order to display these arrows and handle the input, we will add a class called AnimalSelector that will deal with this. Since the animal selector contains four arrows, it will inherit from the GameObjectList class. Furthermore, we want to achieve a nice visual effect that when the player moves the mouse over one of the arrows, it becomes darker. We can achieve this effect by adding a class Arrow that contains two sprites: one for the 'regular' arrow, and one for the arrow image when we hover over it. Furthermore, the Arrow class should be able to show an arrow in any of the four possible directions.

23.2.1 The Arrow Class

Although we could have a single arrow image and rotate it depending on the desired direction, we have chosen to keep things simple by having an image that contains the arrow pointing in all four directions (see Fig. 23.1). Therefore, when we load the sprite, the *sheet index* indicates which arrow we should show. For the hover status, we load another sprite containing the same arrow images, in the same order, but

A. Egges et al., *Learning C# by Programming Games*,
DOI 10.1007/978-3-642-36580-5_23, © Springer-Verlag Berlin Heidelberg 2013

Fig. 23.1 The sprite
containing the four arrows,
each in a different direction

then darker. Since the Arrow class stores multiple sprites, it also inherits from the
GameObjectList class. In the constructor, we load the two arrow images. We set the
visibility of the hover sprite as well as the 'pressed' status to false:

```
arrow_normal = new SpriteGameObject(assetname_normal, 0, id, sheetIndex);
arrow_hover = new SpriteGameObject(assetname_hover, 1, id, sheetIndex);
this.Add(arrow_normal);
this.Add(arrow_hover);
arrow_hover.Visible = false;
pressed = false;
```

The sheet index which is passed as a parameter to the Arrow constructor is passed
along to the actual sprites, so that the correct arrow direction is selected.

Inside the HandleInput method, we check if the hover sprite should be visible by
calculating if the mouse position is inside the bounding box of the arrow sprite. The
arrow is marked as 'pressed' if the hover sprite is visible and the left mouse button
has been clicked:

```
arrow_hover.Visible = arrow_normal.BoundingBox.Contains(
                      (int)inputHelper.MousePosition.X,
                      (int)inputHelper.MousePosition.Y);
pressed = inputHelper.MouseLeftButtonPressed() && arrow_hover.Visible;
```

Finally, we add a few convenient properties to the Arrow class, so that we can check
what the width and height of the object is, and whether it has been pressed.

23.2.2 The Animal Selector

The animal selector uses the Arrow class to display four arrows when the player clicks
on an animal (see Fig. 23.2). These four arrows are stored as member variables in
the AnimalSelector class. Furthermore, since the selector controls a particular animal,
we have to keep track of which one it controls. Therefore, we also store a member
variable containing a reference to the target animal:

```
protected Arrow arrowright, arrowup, arrowleft, arrowdown;
protected Animal selectedAnimal;
```

In the constructor method, we then create the four Arrow objects, and position them
appropriately (for the full code, see the PenguinPairs5 project belonging to this chap-

Fig. 23.2 When the player
clicks on a penguin, four
arrows are shown to choose
the direction in which the
penguin should move

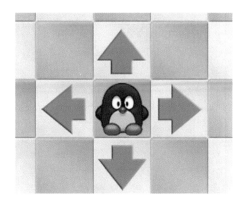

ter). In the HandleInput method, we first check if the selector is visible. If not, it does
not need to handle input:

```
if (!visible)
    return;
```

We then check if one of the arrows was pressed, and if so, we calculate the desired
penguin velocity:

```
Vector2 animalVelocity = Vector2.Zero;
if (arrowdown.Pressed)
    animalVelocity.Y = 1;
else if (arrowup.Pressed)
    animalVelocity.Y = −1;
else if (arrowleft.Pressed)
    animalVelocity.X = −1;
else if (arrowright.Pressed)
    animalVelocity.X = 1;
animalVelocity *= 300;
```

If the player clicked the left mouse button (does not matter where), we set the state
of the animal selector to invisible again:

```
if (inputHelper.MouseLeftButtonPressed())
    this.Visible = false;
```

Finally, if the velocity we calculated is not zero, and there is a target penguin, we
update its velocity:

```
if (selectedAnimal != null && animalVelocity != Vector2.Zero)
    selectedAnimal.Velocity = animalVelocity;
```

Inside the HandleInput method in the Animal class, we have to handle clicking on
an animal. However, there are some situations where we do not have to handle this:

- the animal is in a hole in the ice;
- the animal is not visible;
- or, the animal is already moving.

In all of these cases, we do not do anything and we return from the method:

```
if (!this.Visible || this.boxed || this.velocity != Vector2.Zero)
    return;
```

If we did not click on the animal (in other words: the mouse left button was not pressed or the mouse position is outside of the bounding box of the animal), we can also return from the method, so the complete **if**-instruction then becomes

```
if (!this.Visible || this.boxed || this.velocity != Vector2.Zero ||
    !inputHelper.MouseLeftButtonPressed() ||
    !BoundingBox.Contains((int)inputHelper.MousePosition.X,
                          (int)inputHelper.MousePosition.Y))
    return;
```

If we did click on the animal, we need to make the selector visible, set its position, and assign the animal as the target animal of the selector. This is covered in the following instructions:

```
AnimalSelector selector = GameWorld.Find("animalselector") as AnimalSelector;
selector.Position = this.Position;
selector.Visible = true;
selector.SelectedAnimal = this;
```

Now we can select animals at will and tell them to move in a particular direction. What we need to do now is handle the interaction between the animal, the playing field, and other game objects.

23.3 Input Handling Order

The order in which we draw objects on the screen is important. For example, if we draw the penguins before we draw the background image, the player will never see the penguins. Until now, we did not really pay attention to the order in which the HandleInput and Update methods are called. For instance, in the GameObjectList class, this is how we call the HandleInput method on all the child objects:

```
foreach (GameObject obj in gameObjects)
    obj.HandleInput(inputHelper);
```

In most cases, this approach works just fine. But in the case of the Penguin Pairs game, we may get weird behavior. Suppose that two penguins are next to each other

Fig. 23.3 What happens
when we click on the left
arrow?

on the playing field and we click on one of the penguins. Then four arrows appear. Because the two penguins are next to each other, one of the arrows is drawn over the other penguin (see Fig. 23.3). So, if we click on that arrow, what happens? Does the selected penguin move to the left, or do we select the other penguin?

The outcome of this question depends on the order in which input is handled for each game object. If the penguin handles the input before the penguin selector, then the penguin selector will move to the other penguin. If the selector's HandleInput method is called first, then the selected penguin will move to the left. Generally, when we develop programs, we want to be in control of the behavior of the program. This means that we have to choose in which order we want to handle the input and make sure that it always happens that way. In this case, the desired behavior is that the selected penguin moves to the left. And as a general rule, we would like *objects that are drawn on top to handle input first*. In other words, we need to call the HandleInput method on the objects in the list in reverse order as that they are drawn. This can easily be done with the following **for**-instruction:

```
for (int i = gameObjects.Count − 1; i >= 0; i−−)
    gameObjects[i].HandleInput(inputHelper);
```

As a result, objects that are drawn on top will now handle input first.

23.4 Updating Animals

Interaction between animals and other game objects is done in the Update method of the Animal class. The main reason for doing that in the Animal class is because then each animal handles its own interaction. If we add multiple animals to the game (as we are doing here), we will not have to change anything in the code that handles the interaction. As a first step, we do not have to update the animal if it is not visible, or if its velocity is zero. Therefore, the first instructions in the Update method are:

```
base.Update(gameTime);
if (!this.Visible || velocity == Vector2.Zero)
     return;
```

As you can see, we first call the Update method of the base class. Since the SpriteGameObject class does not override the Update method, this will call the Update method of the GameObject class, which will update the position of the object by adding the velocity multiplied by the elapsed game time. Now, we have to check if we collide with another game object. Because of the check we do at the start of the Update method, we only do this for animals that are both visible and moving.

If the animal is moving, we need to know what tile it is currently moving into. Then we can check what kind of tile it is, and if there are other game objects located at that tile. For this, we will add a method called GetCurrentBlock to the Animal class. How can we calculate the tile we are moving into? When a penguin is moving to the left, we could calculate the x index of the tile as follows:

```
int x = (int)position.X / tilefield.CellWidth;
```

Because of the cast to **int**, we will end up at the tile that the left position of the sprite is in. However, this does not work correctly when we fall off the left end of the playing field. When we move out of the playing field, we will get an x value of zero, whereas we would like to have an x value of -1 (the non-existent tile to the left of the playing field). The reason that this happens is that the cast to **int** *truncates* the **float** value. So, if the outcome of position.X / tilefield.ObjectWidth equals $-0.999f$, we would end up with zero and not with minus one. Fortunately, the Math class has a method called Floor that does exactly what we want. We use this method to create an object of type Point that contains the x- and y-indices of the tile we are currently in:

```
Point p = new Point((int)Math.Floor(position.X / tilefield.CellWidth),
            (int)Math.Floor(position.Y / tilefield.CellHeight));
```

However, this only finds the correct tile when we are moving *left or down*. When we are moving to the right, for example, we want to calculate the tile that the *rightmost pixel* of the penguin sprite moves into. Therefore, if the x velocity is positive, we add one to the x index so that we get the tile to the right-hand side of the animal, and similar for when the y velocity is positive:

```
if (velocity.X > 0)
     p.X++;
if (velocity.Y > 0)
     p.Y++;
```

We can now use the GetCurrentBlock method to calculate what tile we are currently moving into, and we can check what kind of tile it is. For that, we will add a few more convenient methods to the Animal class. One useful method is checking if a given *x* and *y* coordinate is outside of the tilefield. For that, we add a method IsOutsideField to the Animal class. This method is rather straightforward:

```
public bool IsOutsideField(Point p)
{
    GameObjectGrid tilefield = GameWorld.Find("tilefield") as GameObjectGrid;
    return (p.X < 0 || p.X >= tilefield.Columns || p.Y < 0 || p.Y >= tilefield.Rows);
}
```

This method is used in another method, GetTileType, that retrieves the type of the tile for a given point *p*. The first thing we check in this method is if the point is outside of the tilefield. If that is the case, we return a 'background' tile type:

```
if (IsOutsideField(p))
    return TileType.Background;
```

In all other cases, we can retrieve the tile type by getting the Tile object from the tile field, and accessing its TileType property:

```
GameObjectGrid tilefield = GameWorld.Find("tilefield") as GameObjectGrid;
Tile t = tilefield.Objects[p.X, p.Y] as Tile;
return t.TileType;
```

Now we can go back to the Update method and check if we have fallen off of the tile field. If so, we set the animal visibility to **false**, and its velocity to zero, to ensure that the animal does not keep moving indefinitely while it is invisible:

```
Point target = GetCurrentBlock();
if (this.GetTileType(target) == TileType.Background)
{
    this.Visible = false;
    velocity = Vector2.Zero;
    return;
}
```

Another possibility is that we ran into a wall tile. If that is the case, we have to stop moving:

```
else if (this.GetTileType(target) == TileType.Wall) // we ran into a wall
{
    this.StopMoving();
    return;
}
```

Stopping moving is not as easy as it sounds. We could simply set the animal velocity to zero, but then the animal would be partly in another tile. What we want to do is

to place the animal at the tile *it just moved out from*. We added a method called
StopMoving that accomplishes exactly that. In that method, we first have to calculate
what the position of the old tile is. We can do that by starting from the x and y
coordinates of the tile that we are currently moving into. These are passed along as
a parameter. If for example the penguin's velocity is the vector $(5, 0)$ (moving to the
right), we need to subtract one from the x coordinate to get the x coordinate of the
tile we are moving out of. If the penguin's velocity is $(0, -5)$ (moving up), then we
need to *add* one to the y coordinate to get the y coordinate of the tile we are moving
out of. We can achieve this by *normalizing the velocity vector* and the subtracting it
from the x and y coordinates. This works because normalizing a vector results in a
vector of length one (unit length). Since we only move in either the x or y direction,
we will end up with a vector $(1, 0)$ in the first example, and $(0, -1)$ in the second
example. Therefore, the position of the old tile is then calculated as follows:

```
GameObjectGrid tilefield = GameWorld.Find("tilefield") as GameObjectGrid;
velocity.Normalize();
Vector2 oldBlock = new Vector2(GetCurrentBlock().X, GetCurrentBlock().Y) − velocity;
```

Calculating the actual position of the penguin is then done as follows:

```
position = oldBlock ∗ new Vector2(tilefield.CellWidth, tilefield.CellHeight);
```

And finally, we set the animal velocity to zero, so that it stays in its new position:

```
velocity = Vector2.Zero;
```

23.5 Dealing with Meeting Other Game Objects

What we still need to do is check if we collide with another game object, such as
another penguin or a shark. There are a few special types of animals:

- multicolored penguins;
- empty boxes;
- seals.

We will add a few methods to the Animal class that determine if we are dealing with
these special cases. For example, we are dealing with a seal if the sheet index equals
seven, and it is not boxed:

```
public bool IsSeal()
{
    return this.sprite.SheetIndex == 7 && !this.boxed;
}
```

We are dealing with an empty box if the sheet index is 7 and it is boxed:

```
public bool IsEmptyBox()
{
    return this.sprite.SheetIndex == 7 && this.boxed;
}
```

Finally, we are dealing with a multicolored penguin if the sheet index is 6 and we are not boxed:

```
public bool IsMultiColoredPenguin()
{
    return this.sprite.SheetIndex == 6 && !this.boxed;
}
```

First, we will check if there is a shark at the tile we are moving into. For that, we retrieve the level and we use the FindSharkAtPosition method from the Level class to find out if there is a shark:

```
Level level = Root as Level;
GameObject s = level.FindSharkAtPosition(target);
if (s != null && s.Visible)
{
    // handle the shark interaction
}
```

If we encounter a shark, we are eaten and the shark leaves the playing field with a belly full of penguin. In the game, this means that the penguin will stop moving (forever) and both the shark and the penguin will become invisible (insert Jaws music score here). The following lines of code achieve this:

```
s.Visible = false;
this.Visible = false;
this.stopMoving(x, y);
```

The next thing to check is if there is another penguin or a seal. For that we use the FindAnimalAtPosition method from the Level class. We retrieve the animal as follows:

```
Animal a = level.FindAnimalAtPosition(target);
```

If the method returns null, or the animal is not visible, we do not have to do anything and we can return from the method:

```
if (a == null || !a.Visible)
    return;
```

The first case we will solve is if we are colliding with an empty box. If that is the case, we move the animal inside the box by setting the sheet index of the box to the sheet index of this animal, and we make this animal invisible:

```
if (a.IsEmptyBox())
{
    this.Visible = false;
    a.sprite.SheetIndex = this.sprite.SheetIndex;
}
```

If the sheet index of animal a is the same as the sheet index of this animal, or either one of the penguins is multicolored, and the animal is not a seal, we have a valid pair of penguins and we make both penguins invisible:

```
else if ((a.sprite.SheetIndex == sprite.SheetIndex || this.IsMultiColoredPenguin()
        || a.IsMultiColoredPenguin()) && !a.IsSeal())
{
    a.Visible = false;
    this.Visible = false;
}
```

We also have to display an extra pair in the top left of the screen, but we will deal with that in the next section.

Finally, in all other cases, we simply stop moving:

```
else
    this.StopMoving();
```

23.6 Maintaining the Number of Pairs

In order to maintain the number of pairs and draw it nicely on the screen, we will add another class called PairList to the game. In the Level class, we add an instance of this class to the game world, and position it near the top left of the screen:

```
PairList pairList = new PairList(nrpairs, 1, "pairList");
pairList.Position = new Vector2(20, 15);
this.Add(pairList);
```

The PairList class inherits from the SpriteGameObject class. It consists of a frame, and on top of it we draw a number of sprites indicating the number of required pairs. Since we want to indicate the color of the pair that was made, we store these pairs in an array of **int** values, which is a member variable of the PairList class:

```
protected int [] pairs;
```

The reason that we use an array of **int** values is that we can define per pair which color it is, and how many pairs we need in total. In the member variable pairSprite we store the sprite representing a pair. The image we use for that sprite is a sprite strip,

Fig. 23.4   The sprite containing all the possible pair images

and the colored pairs are ordered in the same way as the penguins (see Fig. 23.4). The rightmost image in the strip (sheet index equals seven) is the image we want to display if the pair still needs to be made. So if the pairs array would contain the values {0, 0, 2, 7, 7} then it would mean that the player made two pairs of blue penguins, one pair of green penguins, and that the player would need to make two more pairs in order to finish the level.

We pass along a parameter, nrPairs, to the constructor of the PairList class, so that we know how large the array should be. We then fill the array so that each element is set to the empty slot (sheet index equals seven):

```
pairs = new int[nrPairs];
for (int i = 0; i< pairs.Length; i++)
    pairs[i] = 7;
```

We also add a method AddPair to the class, which will find the first occurrence of the value seven in the array and replace it with the index that was passed along as a parameter:

```
public void AddPair(int index)
{
    int i = 0;
    while (i < pairs.Length && pairs[i] != 7)
        i++;
    if (i < pairs.Length)
        pairs[i] = index;
}
```

In this example, we used a **while**-instruction to increment the i variable until we find an empty spot.

Now we will add a useful property to check whether we have completed the level. The level is completed if the list of pairs no longer contains any value of seven (meaning that all empty spots have been replaced by a pair):

```
public bool Completed
{
    get
    {
        for (int i = 0; i < pairs.Length; i++)
            if (pairs[i] == 7)
                return false;
        return true;
    }
}
```

Finally, we need to draw the pairs on the screen, in the Draw method. Here, we use a **for**-instruction to traverse all the indices in the pair list. For each index, we draw the right sprite at the appropriate position. Note that we use the same sprite and simply draw it multiple times, with different sheet indices:

```
public override void Draw(GameTime gameTime, SpriteBatch spriteBatch)
{
    base.Draw(gameTime, spriteBatch);
    if (!visible)
        return;
    for (int i=0; i<pairs.Length; i++)
    {
        pairSprite.Position = new Vector2(110 + i * sprite.Height, 8);
        pairSprite.Sprite.SheetIndex = pairs[i];
        pairSprite.Draw(gameTime, spriteBatch);
    }
}
```

The call to the base Draw method ensures that the background frame is drawn first.

Now that we have the PairList class, we can create an instance of it in the Level class and add it to the game world:

```
PairList pairList = new PairList(nrpairs, 1, "pairList");
pairList.Position = new Vector2(20, 15);
this.Add(pairList);
```

And inside the Animal class, we add a pair to the list with the following two lines of code:

```
PairList pairList = GameWorld.Find("pairList") as PairList;
pairList.AddPair(sprite.SheetIndex);
```

For the complete example, see the PenguinPairs5 program in the solution belonging to this chapter. In the next chapter, we will add the final touches to the Penguin Pairs game, and we will show you a better way to reuse code among different projects.

23.7 What You Have Learned

In this chapter, you have learned:

- how to program a game object selector;
- how to model interactions between different kinds of game objects;
- how to maintain and draw the number of pairs made by the player.

Chapter 24
Finishing the Game

24.1 Introduction

In this chapter, we will finalize the Penguin Pairs game. As a first step, we will reorganize our code a bit so that parts of it are more easily usable by other programs. Then, we will finish the game by extending the user interface and adding sound effects and music.

24.2 Separating Code into Different Libraries

Until now, we have developed three different games in this book. These games are quite different: we made a shooting game, a pattern-recognition game, and a more complicated puzzle game consisting of different levels. Even though the types of these games are quite different, there are a lot of similarities as well. For example, all three games have some concept of a basic game object, and both the Jewel Jam game and the Penguin Pairs game use a grid as a basis for their playing field. Also, the concept of a hierarchy of game objects that are drawn on several layers is something that is used in different games. All in all, we keep going back to using similar classes among different games. In fact, we even copied classes from the Jewel Jam game, and used them as is in the Penguin Pairs game.

As we have already discussed a couple of times in this book, copying around code is a bad thing. Making copies of code means that bugs can be copied as well, and if we make any changes or improvements, we would have to do it everywhere we copied that code. So how can we avoid copying code between *different projects*? For that, we can use a *library*. A library is basically a separate project in a solution that contains code that is useful for several other projects. When a project wants to use a library, we have to put a *reference* to that library in our project, just like we have to do with a content project.

A. Egges et al., *Learning C# by Programming Games*,
DOI 10.1007/978-3-642-36580-5_24, © Springer-Verlag Berlin Heidelberg 2013

24.2.1 Creating and Filling a Library

Creating a library in Visual Studio is easy. The XNA Game Studio provides a project type called 'Windows Game Library'. When you select that template and you choose a suitable name, a library project will be added to the solution. Then, you can add a reference to that library in the project by right clicking on 'References' in the solution explorer and selecting 'Add Reference'. If you do not want to create a new library, but you want to use an already existing one, right click on the solution in the solution explorer and select Add → Existing Project.... Then, you can browse to the location of the already existing library project you want to add to the solution.

Now you can add classes to the library and these classes will be accessible to any project that has a reference to that library. We created a library called GameManagement, which contains all the basic classes that we have developed throughout the book. Most of these classes should look familiar to you since they are copied directly from the previous version of the Penguin Pairs game. As a result, the PenguinPairs6 program now only contains the classes that are specific to the Penguin Pairs game. Generic classes that can be used by any other game, such as SpriteGameObject, or InputHelper are now located in the GameManagement library. As a result, we will not have to copy the classes anymore between different projects, we simply add a reference to the library and we are done.

24.2.2 Public or Private Classes

Just like methods can be public, protected or private, so can classes as a whole. Until now, we always started our class definitions as follows:

```
class GameObject : IGameLoopObject
{
    // member variables, methods, properties
}
```

Defining a class like this means that the class is defined as *internal*. This means that the class can only be accessed by other code in the same assembly, but not from another assembly. As a result, if we would have defined the GameObject class like that in the GameManagement library, we could only use it in that library, and not outside of it. If we want to be able to access the class in the PenguinPairs6 project, we need to make that class **public**. We can do this by placing the **public** keyword in front of the class definition, as follows:

```
public class GameObject : IGameLoopObject
{
    // member variables, methods, properties
}
```

If you take a look in the GameManagement library, you will see that all the classes are public. As a result, they can be used in other projects.

> **Classes internal to the library**—What is the use of having classes that can only be used within a library and not outside it? The main reason that this is important is that it allows software developers to make a distinction between the functionality that should be available to the outside users and the functionality that is used inside the library. Suppose that we were to develop a library for dealing with collisions. You could imagine that the library exposes a number of classes to represent basic geometry used for collision checking, but that the low-level math-related classes for calculating if objects collide are not visible to the user of the library. The downside is that the user does not have access to all the low-level functionality. The upside is that the library documentation and design looks much cleaner, so it is probably easier to learn how to use the library. It is not always clear which classes should be internal and which classes should be external. Try to be consistent though, and for each class you develop for a library, think beforehand if the class is for internal or for external use (or both).

24.2.3 A Convenient GameEnvironment Class

While developing the different games, we have slowly extended the Game subclass we used to incorporate more useful objects and methods. There is an input helper, a game settings manager, a sprite batch, an asset manager, a method for going to full screen mode, and much more. In order to allow for quicker game development, we added a class called GameEnvironment that already contains all of these things. If we want to create a new game, we simply have to make a subclass of GameEnvironment, add our game states, and we are done. You can see this effect in Listing 24.1: a small class definition, containing only the things specific to the Penguin Pairs game.

You can actually see that we are reusing all of these classes in the final game developed in this book, Tick Tick. If you open the solution belonging to the final chapter in this book, you will see that the Tick Tick game project has a reference to the GameManagement library as well. As a result, all of the features we developed in earlier chapters of this book are instantly available to the game!

```
 1  using Microsoft.Xna.Framework;
 2  using Microsoft.Xna.Framework.Media;
 3
 4  class PenguinPairs : GameEnvironment
 5  {
 6      static void Main()
 7      {
 8          PenguinPairs game = new PenguinPairs();
 9          game.Run();
10      }
11
12      public PenguinPairs()
13      {
14          Content.RootDirectory = "Content";
15          this.IsMouseVisible = true;
16          GameSettingsManager.SetValue("hints", "on");
17      }
18
19      protected override void LoadContent()
20      {
21          base.LoadContent();
22          screen = new Point(1200, 900);
23          this.SetFullScreen(false);
24
25          // add the game states
26          gameStateManager.AddGameState("playingState", new PlayingState(Content));
27          gameStateManager.AddGameState("titleMenu", new TitleMenuState());
28          gameStateManager.AddGameState("optionsMenu", new OptionsMenuState());
29          gameStateManager.AddGameState("levelMenu", new LevelMenuState());
30          gameStateManager.AddGameState("helpState", new HelpState());
31          gameStateManager.AddGameState("levelFinishedState",
32                                        new LevelFinishedState());
33          gameStateManager.SwitchTo("titleMenu");
34
35          // play background music
36          AssetManager.PlayMusic("Sounds/snd_music");
37      }
38  }
```

Listing 24.1 The final version of the PenguinPairs class, now a subclass of GameEnvironment

24.3 Finishing the User Interface

24.3.1 Showing Hints

Now that we have reorganized our code, there are still a couple of features we would like to add to the Penguin Pairs game. As a first step, we want to be able to show a hint when the user clicks on a button. The hint consists of an orange arrow that is visible for a second. When we loaded the level, we read the hint position and direction from the file:

```
stringlist = reader.ReadLine().Split();
int hintx = int.Parse(stringlist[0]) − 1;
int hinty = int.Parse(stringlist[1]) − 1;
int hintdirection = int.Parse(stringlist[2]);
```

We then create a SpriteGameObject instance to load the arrow, select the correct sheet index, and position it appropriately before we add it to the game world.

```
SpriteGameObject hint = new SpriteGameObject("Sprites/spr_arrow_hint@4", 2,
                                             "hint", hintdirection);
hint.Position = new Vector2(hintx, hinty) ∗ new Vector2(73, 72);
playingField.Add(hint);
```

In order to temporarily display the arrow, we reuse the VisibilityTimer class from the Jewel Jam game. We create an instance of this class, and add it to the game world as well:

```
VisibilityTimer hintVisible = new VisibilityTimer(hint, 0, "hintVisible");
playingField.Add(hintVisible);
```

We also add a button that the player can click to display the hint on the screen:

```
hintButton = new Button("Sprites/spr_button_hint", 1, "hintButton");
hintButton.Position = new Vector2(916,20);
this.Add(hintButton);
```

Finally, we extend the HandleInput method to deal with the hint button being pressed:

```
if (hintButton.Pressed && hintButton.Visible)
{
    VisibilityTimer hintVisible = this.Find("hintVisible") as VisibilityTimer;
    hintVisible.StartVisible();
}
```

Why do we check if the hint button is visible? The reason for that is that in some cases, the hint button is no longer visible:

- After the player makes the first move, the hint button should disappear, and the retry button should appear.
- If the player chose to switch off hints in the options menu, the hint button should never be visible.

For the first case, we need to keep track of when then player makes his/her first move. We add an extra member variable firstMoveMade to the Level class, as well as a method FirstMoveMade to set it to **true**. When we give an animal a velocity, this is done in the AnimalSelector class. Once the player has clicked on an arrow and the animal is moving, we call the FirstMoveMade method:

```
Level l = GameWorld as Level;
l.FirstMoveMade();
```

Secondly, we have to handle the 'hints' setting from the game settings manager. We do this in the Update method of the Level class. We simply check what the value of the 'hints' setting is in the game settings manager, and update the button visibility state accordingly:

```
hintButton.Visible = GameSettingsManager.getValue("hints") == "on" && !firstMoveMade;
retryButton.Visible = !hintButton.Visible;
```

As you can see from these two lines of code, the hint button is only visible if the 'hints' value is equal to 'on' and the player has not yet made a first move. The retry button visibility status is always the opposite of the hint button's visibility status. So if the hint button is visible, the retry button is not, and vice versa.

24.3.2 Resetting the Level

After a player moves a couple of penguins around, it happens that the level cannot be solved anymore. Instead of having to quit and restart the game, let us give the player a means to *reset* a level to its initial state.

Because of the proper implementation of the Reset method everywhere throughout the game object classes, resetting a level to its initial state is now fairly easy. We have to call the Reset method on all the game objects, and then we have to deal with resetting things in the Level class itself. The only thing we need to do there is set the firstMoveMade variable to **false**, so that the player can view a hint again:

```
public override void Reset()
{
    base.Reset();
    firstMoveMade = false;
}
```

24.3.3 Moving to the Next Level

When the player finishes a level (hurray!), we would like to display an encouraging overlay. When the player clicks, the next level is shown. Since we created this nice GameStateManager class, let us profit from it by adding another state: LevelFinishedState. The only thing that this state does is display the overlay and react to a player clicking. Since the overlay is displayed on top of the level, we still need to do something with the playing state. Therefore, we store it in a member variable. Next to that, we load an overlay, position it in the center of the screen, and add it to the game world. For the complete constructor, see Listing 24.2.

We want to display the overlay on top of the playing state, but we do not want the playing state to be able to process input anymore (otherwise, the player could still move penguins around). Therefore, we only call the Update and Draw methods, and not the HandleInput method, on the playingState object.

In the HandleInput method of LevelFinishedState, we check if the player has pressed the space bar, or the left mouse button. If so, we set the current state to be the playing state, and we call the NextLevel method on it (see Listing 24.2).

How does the NextLevel method work? As a first step, it resets the current level so that if the player wants to play the level again he/she can do so. Then, there are two possibilities. The first possibility is that the player finished the last level. In that case, we go back to the level menu by setting the current state to "level-Menu". In all other cases, we increment the current level index, and we unlock the next level for the player. Finally, since we changed the level status, we write it to a file so that the next time the player starts the game, the game remembers which levels the player has solved. The complete NextLevel method looks like this:

```
public void NextLevel()
{
    CurrentLevel.Reset();

    if (currentLevelIndex >= levels.Count − 1)
        GameEnvironment.GameStateManager.SwitchTo("levelMenu");
    else
    {
        currentLevelIndex++;
        levels[currentLevelIndex].Locked = false;
    }
    WriteLevelsStatus(Content.RootDirectory + "/Levels/levels_status.txt");
}
```

The only thing we still need to do is make sure that the game goes to the 'level finished' state when the player has won. We can do this in the Update method of the playing state, by using the PlayerWon property from the Level class:

```
if (CurrentLevel.PlayerWon)
{
    CurrentLevel.Solved = true;
    GameEnvironment.GameStateManager.SwitchTo("levelFinishedState");
}
```

```
 1  using Microsoft.Xna.Framework;
 2  using Microsoft.Xna.Framework.Graphics;
 3  using Microsoft.Xna.Framework.Input;
 4
 5  class LevelFinishedState : GameObjectList
 6  {
 7      protected IGameLoopObject playingState;
 8
 9      public LevelFinishedState()
10      {
11          playingState =
12              GameEnvironment.GameStateManager.GetGameState("playingState");
13
14          SpriteGameObject overlay =
15              new SpriteGameObject("Sprites/spr_level_finished", 1, "you_win");
16          overlay.Position = new Vector2(GameEnvironment.Screen.X,
17                                          GameEnvironment.Screen.Y) / 2
18                                  − overlay.Center;
19          this.Add(overlay);
20      }
21
22      public override void HandleInput(InputHelper inputHelper)
23      {
24          if (!inputHelper.KeyPressed(Keys.Space) &&
25              !inputHelper.MouseLeftButtonPressed())
26              return;
27          GameEnvironment.GameStateManager.SwitchTo("playingState");
28          (playingState as PlayingState).NextLevel();
29      }
30
31      public override void Draw(GameTime gameTime, SpriteBatch spriteBatch)
32      {
33          playingState.Draw(gameTime, spriteBatch);
34          base.Draw(gameTime, spriteBatch);
35      }
36  }
```

Listing 24.2 The state that the game is in when the player has finished a level. This state shows the playing state with an overlay on top of it

If the player has finished the level, we set the 'solved' status of the level to **true**, and we change the current game state to the 'level finished' state.

Tutorials—As you have probably noticed, the first few levels of the Penguin Pairs game also serve as a tutorial that explains how the game should be played. When you create a game, players have to learn how to play it. If you do not tell the players what the challenges and goals are and how to control the game they will probably get frustrated and stop playing.

Some games provide extensive help files with long texts explaining the story and the controls. Players no longer want to read such documents or screens. They want to jump right into the game. You have to educate the player while playing.

You can create a few specific tutorial levels where the player can practice the controls without drastically affecting the progress of the game itself. This approach is popular with casual gamers as an introduction to your game. Seasoned gamers prefer to immediately dive into the action. Be careful not to explain everything in the tutorial levels. Only explain the basic controls. Explain more advanced controls during the game as they are required, for example by simple pop-up messages, or in a visible spot in a HUD.

It works best when the tutorials naturally integrate into the game story. For example, the game character might start running around in his safe home town, learning the basic movement controls. Next he/she practices fighting together with a few friends. And after that the player goes into the woods trying to shoot some birds with his bow. This will provide all the practice needed for the fights later in the game.

You should really make sure that tutorial levels actually work and that the players remember the controls, even if they put the game away for a couple of days. Because otherwise, they may never come back to the game.

24.3.4 Music and Sounds

To finish the game, we should add sounds and music at the right spots. As you may remember, one of the options in the options menu was changing the background volume. We did that using the following line of code:

```
MediaPlayer.Volume = musicVolumeSlider.Value;
```

In the PenguinPairs class, we start playing the music, using the methods available in the AssetManager class:

```
AssetManager.PlayMusic("Sounds/snd_music");
```

Similarly, we simply use our AssetManager class to play sound effects at appropriate moments, just like we did in the JewelJam game. For example, whenever a pair of penguins is made, we play a sound effect (see the Update method in the Penguin class:

```
GameEnvironment.AssetManager.PlaySound("Sounds/snd_pair");
```

If you look at the PenguinPairs6 example project belonging to this chapter, you can see how the complete game works, and of course you can also play it.

Working in teams—The first generation of games was created by programmers. They did all the work. They designed the game mechanics, they created the art (which consisted of just a few pixels anyway) and they programmed the game in an Assembler language. All the work focused on the programming. The game mechanics were often adapted to what could be programmed efficiently.

But when more memory became available this slowly changed. Creating fancy looking objects with a limited number of pixels and a limited number of colors became an art form and such pixel artists started to play an important role in developing games. Realize that in the early days there were no drawing programs (no computer was powerful enough for that). Pixelated characters were designed on graph paper and then turned into hexadecimal numbers to be put into the game code.

With the increase of computer power and storage media like the CD, the art started to play an increasingly important role and the artists developed with it. 3D graphics and animations became common, leading to new specialists that could also use the new tools and technologies developed to support such work. Nowadays the artists make up the majority of the game production teams.

At some stage also the design of the game became a separate job. Game mechanics were tuned to the interests of user groups and were more and more based on principles from psychology and educational sciences. This required a separate expertise. Stories started to play a crucial role, leading to the inclusion of writers. And the teams were extended with producers, sound engineers, composers, and many other types of people. Nowadays, teams for top games can consist of hundreds of people. But realize, without the programmers, nothing would work.

24.4 Some Final Notes

In this part, we have created a game that is quite a bit more complicated than the previous example game Jewel Jam. You have probably noticed that the number of different classes has started to become quite big, and we are relying more and more on a certain design of the game software. For example, we have chosen to organize game objects in a tree structure, and we have designed a class for handling game states. On a more basic level, we assume that game objects themselves are responsible for handling their input, updating themselves and drawing themselves on the screen. You may not agree with some (or all) of these design choices. Perhaps, after reading the book until now, you have formed your own ideas about how game software should be designed. That is a good thing. The design that we propose in this book is not the only way to do things. Designs can always be evaluated and improved, or even thrown away completely to be replaced by something entirely different. So, do not hesitate to look critically at the design we propose and try out other designs yourself. By trying out different approaches to solve a problem, you will better understand that problem and become a better software developer as a result.

24.5 What You Have Learned

In this chapter, you have learned:

- how to create a separate library with classes that are used by another project;
- the difference between public and internal classes;
- how to reset a level to its initial state and how to handle going to the next level.

Part V
Animation and Complexity

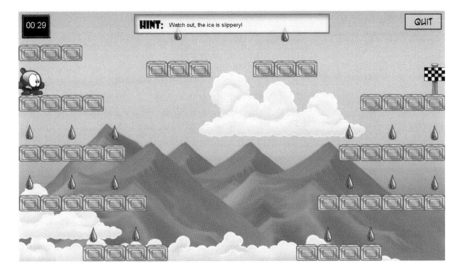

Fig. V.1 A screenshot of the game Tick Tick

We have shown how to build several different types of games in the previous chapters of this book. In this final part, we're going to build a platform game with animated characters, physics and different levels (see Fig. V.1). The name of the game is Tick Tick, and the story revolves around a slightly stressed out bomb that is going to explode within 30 seconds. This means that each level in the game should be finished within 30 seconds. A level is finished if the player collects all the refreshing water drops and reaches the finish panel in time.

We will put a number of basic elements in this platform game that are found in many other games as well:

- it should be possible to play different levels;
- these levels should be loaded from a text file so that they can be changed without having to change the source code;
- the game should support animated characters, both for the player and the enemies;
- the player should control the actions of the player character that has a capability to run or jump;
- there should be some basic physics in this game to manage falling, colliding with objects, jumping on platforms, and so on.

That is quite a long list! Fortunately, we can reuse many of the classes that we have already developed in the previous chapters in this book. In the following chapters, we will look into all these items on the list. If you want to play the complete version of the Tick Tick game, open the solution belonging to Chap. 30 and press F5.

Chapter 25
Creating the Main Game Structure

25.1 Introduction

In this chapter, we will layout the framework that we will use for the Tick Tick game. Because of all the work we already did for the previous games, we can rely on a lot of pre-existing classes. In fact, we will build the game upon the GameManagement library that we developed and used in the PenguinPairs game. This means that we already have a basic design for handling game states and settings, a hierarchy of game objects and more. We are going to extend the GameManagement library later on by adding classes related to animated game objects. You can already see these classes in the library, but we will discuss these classes in the next chapter.

25.2 Overview of the Game Structure

We will be following a very similar structure as for the Penguin Pairs game. There will be a title screen that allows us to go to either the level selection menu, or a help page. To keep things simple, we will not implement an options page, even though adding it would be very straight forward since we can simply use the same approach as we did in Penguin Pairs. Since this menu structure is so similar, we will not discuss it here. If you want, you can have a look at the code by opening the TickTick1 project in the solution belonging to this chapter.

The PlayingState class maintains the current level, and deals with loading and saving level status (solved/locked), just like the Penguin Pairs game. There is a minor difference in the way that we load levels from files, as we will discuss next.

25.3 The Structure of a Level

Let us first look at what kind of things can be inside a level in Tick Tick. First, there will be some kind of background image. For now, we will display a simple background sprite, there is no need to store any information about that in the text file.

There are also different kinds of blocks that the player can jump on, there will be water drops, enemies, the start position of the player, and the end position that the player has to reach. As in the Penguin Pairs game, we will store level information in a text file. To do things slightly differently here, let us store one level in one text file, instead of all levels in a single text file. There is no real disadvantage to either approach.

We will define a level using tiles, where each tile has a certain type (wall, background, and so on). We then represent each tile type with a character in the text file. Next to the actual tiles, we also store a hint together with the level definition. Here you can see the definition of the first level:

```
....................
..................X..
..........#########
....................
WWW....WWWW.........
---....####.........
....................
WWW.................
###.........WWWWW...
............#####...
....WWW.............
....###.............
....................
.1........W.W.W.W.W.
###################
Pick up all the water drops and reach the exit in time.
```

In this level definition, a number of different tiles and objects are defined. A 'wall' tile is defined by the '#' sign, a water drop by a 'W' character, the start position of the player by the '1' character, and the end position of the player by the 'X' character. If there is no tile at the specific position, we use the '.' character. For the platform game, we need different types of tiles: a 'wall' tile on which the player can stand or collide with, and a 'background' tile that indicates that there is no block on that position. We also want to define a *platform tile*. This tile has the property that you can stand on it like a wall tile, but if you are standing under this tile, you can jump through it. This kind of tile is used in many classic platform games, and it would be a pity not to include it here! In the level file, platform tiles are represented by a '-' character.

25.4 Water Drops

The goal of each level is to collect all the water drops. Each water drop is represented by an instance of the WaterDrop class. This class is a SpriteGameObject subclass, but we want to add a little behavior to it: the water drop should bounce up and down. We can do this in the Update method. First, we will compute a *bounce offset* that we can add to the current position of the water drop. In order to calculate this offset, we use a sine function, and depending on the *x*-position of the water drop, we change the phase, so that not all drops move up or down at the same time. We store the offset in a member variable called bounce:

```
double t = gameTime.TotalGameTime.TotalSeconds * 3.0f + position.X;
bounce = (float)Math.Sin(t) * 0.2f;
```

Finally, we add the bounce value to the *y*-position:

```
position.Y += bounce;
```

In the next chapter, we are going to add more game objects, such as the player and a variety of enemies. But let us first have a look at how we define the tiles in a platform game such as Tick Tick.

25.5 The Tile Class

The Tile class is very similar to the one we used in Penguin Pairs, but it has a few differences. First, we define the different tile types as an enumerated type:

```
enum TileType
{
    Background,
    Normal,
    Platform
}
```

In the Tile class, we then declare a member variable type to store the type of tile that an instance represents:

```
protected TileType type;
```

Next to these basic tile types, we also have ice tiles and hot tiles. In the level file, an ice tile is represented by the '*' character (or the '@' character if it is a platform tile), and a hot tile is represented by the '^' character (or the '+' character for the platform version). We add two boolean member variables to the Tile class with their associated properties to be able to represent these different kinds of tiles. Now, let us have a look at the Level class.

25.6 Setting up the Level Class

Given everything that we want to do, the Level class is likely going to be quite large. Inside that class, we have to load the tiles from a text file, deal with different game states such as the player dying or completing the level, and other aspects of the general game loop. All of these things belong to the Level class, so splitting them in different classes just to increase readability does not make sense. On the other hand: placing all this code in a single source file will lead to a less readable class definition. For these kinds of cases, C# provides so-called *partial classes*. Partial classes allow us to spread the definition of a class over different source files. In this example, we have done that for the Level class, which is spread over three different source files: Level.cs, LevelGameLoop.cs, and LevelLoading.cs, where the latter file contains the code for loading the level from a file. The Level.cs file for now only contains the constructor, but we will add other generic things such as properties to this file. The LevelGameLoop contains the game loop methods of the Level class.

If you look inside the Level.cs file, you see that the keyword **partial** is written in front of the class definition. This indicates that we are dealing with a partial definition of the class, and that other partial definitions might be located in different source files. If you open the LevelGameLoop.cs and LevelLoading.cs files, you will see the same keyword being used there as well. The **partial** keyword does nothing besides allowing the code to be spread over different source files. The compiler will combine all these source files into a single Level class when it compiles the files.

25.7 Creating the Level Object

In the constructor of the Level class, we are going to do a couple of things:

- create the background sprite game object;
- add a 'quit' button;
- load the tiles from a text file.

For loading the tiles from the text file, we are going to use an approach similar to the one we used in Penguin Pairs, except that one text file contains one level. Retrieving the data from the file is done in the Level class by calling the LoadTiles method. Depending on the level index, a different file is loaded. In order to read the tiles from the text file, we create a StreamReader:

```
StreamReader fileReader = new StreamReader(path);
```

Now as a first step, we are going to read all the lines of text from the file and store them in a list. For this, we use a **while**-instruction to continue reading while there are lines available:

```
List<string> textlines = new List<string>();
string line = fileReader.ReadLine();
int width = line.Length;
while (line != null)
```

```
{
    textlines.Add(line);
    line = fileReader.ReadLine();
}
```

As you can see, the first time we read a line, we also store the number of characters in that line, so that we know how many columns our game object grid should have. Once we have read all the lines, we create the GameObjectGrid with the right number of columns (width) and number of rows, which is the same as the number of lines in the textlines list (textlines.Count − 1):

```
GameObjectGrid tiles = new GameObjectGrid(textlines.Count − 1, width, 1, "tiles");
this.Add(tiles);
```

We also set the width and height of each cell in the grid, so that the game object grid knows where to draw the tiles on the screen:

```
tiles.CellWidth = 72;
tiles.CellHeight = 55;
```

Then, we create the Tile objects and add them to the GameObjectGrid object.

```
for (int x = 0; x < width; ++x)
    for (int y = 0; y < textlines.Count; ++y)
    {
        Tile t = LoadTile(textlines[y][x], x, y);
        tiles.Add(t, x, y);
    }
```

The nested **for**-loop examines all the characters that we read from a file. Just like we did in Penguin Pairs, we use a method called LoadTile, which creates a Tile object for us, given a character and the *x* and *y* positions of the tile in the grid.

Inside the LoadTile method, we want to load a different tile according to the character that was passed as a parameter. For each type of tile, we add a method to the Level class that creates that particular kind of tile. For example, the LoadWaterTile loads a background tile with a water drop on top of it.

All of the methods in the LevelLoading.cs file are **private**. This means that only methods inside the Level class can access these methods. Why did we do this? The reason is that we want to be sure that a level is only loaded when needed. Users of the Level class do not have to call LoadTiles or LoadWaterTile explicitly. If they did (by accident hopefully), then the Level object might contain invalid information afterwards. It might contain a different level than what the designer had in mind, or perhaps some information related to the level, such as the number of water drops gathered or the time left to finish the game, might no longer be up to date. By making these methods **private**, we are sure that a level can only be loaded from a file within the Level class itself.

What we did not yet address in our file reading methods, is what to do if something goes wrong. For example, what happens when one of the lines in the text file has a different length? And what if the file cannot be found? These are things that are impossible for the compiler to detect beforehand, so this will not generate a compiler error. There is a way of dealing with these issues by using *exceptions*.

25.8 Exceptions

25.8.1 Dealing with Errors

When you call a method, it is possible that due to some unforeseen circumstances, the method cannot be executed. For example, the player of your game has the excellent idea to disable the network adapter during the setup of an on-line game. Or: because of a virus, some files that you expected to be there are suddenly missing. There are several ways of dealing with this. One way is to do nothing and let the program crash. This is a very cheap solution for the game developer (initially at least …), but it does not result in a very robust game which will in turn surely affect sales negatively. A very common way of dealing with these kinds of errors is by handling *exceptions*. An exception is *thrown* by a method, and the caller of the method will have to deal with it.

An example of a method that throws an exception is the static method Parse that is available in types such as **int** and **double**. This method throws an exception if the **string** to be parsed contains something else than numbers (or a minus sign and in the case of **double**.Parse, a decimal point or the E character).

25.8.2 The try-catch Instruction

You could try to avoid exceptions by checking beforehand if all the conditions are satisfied. In the case of **int**.Parse, this means checking if the string consists only of numbers/signs. However, you would be doing double the work, since this is also checked in **int**.Parse. Better is to react to the exception. This is done using the **try-catch**-instruction. The method call that may throw an exception is put inside the body of a **try**-instruction. In the case that there is an exception, the program continues in the body of the **catch**-part. If there is no exception, then the **catch**-body is not executed. For example:

```
try
{
    n = int.Parse(s);
}
```

```
catch (Exception e)
{
    spriteBatch.DrawString(s + "is not a number", Vector2.Zero, Color.Red);
}
```

In the **catch**-part the exception is 'caught'. Behind the word **catch**, there is some kind of parameter. Through this parameter it is possible to find out what exactly went wrong. In the case of Parse, there are not a lot of options, but the parameter has to be declared in any case, even if we do not use it.

In the body of the **try**-instruction, multiple instructions may be placed. But as soon as an exception occurs, the execution is halted and the body of the **catch** is executed. The remaining instructions after the **try** may therefore assume that there was no exception if they are executed.

Watch out that the bodies of the **try** and the **catch** part need to be between braces, even if there is only a single instruction in the body. This is a bit illogical, given that the braces may be omitted in for example the **if** or **while** instructions.

The Exception type, of which we declared a variable after the **catch**, is a class with all kinds of subclasses: FormatException, OverflowException, DivideByZeroException, and so on. Each subclass differs in the kind of details that may be obtained from them through accessing the properties. Instead of using these subclasses, you could simply use the Exception type between the parentheses after the **catch** keyword as we did in the example code. However, this will catch an exception of *any* type, and you will not know what kind of exception it is. Therefore, always catch exceptions by using the subclasses, unless you have a good reason not to.

It is allowed to place multiple **catch** parts with one **try**-instruction. You can give each of these **catch** parts a different exception type. When an exception occurs, the first **catch** with a corresponding exception type is selected. For example:

```
try
{
    n = int.Parse(s);
}
catch (FormatException e)
{
    spriteBatch.DrawString(s + "is not a number", Vector2.Zero, Color.Red);
}
catch (OverflowException e)
{
    spriteBatch.DrawString(s + "is too big", Vector2.Zero, Color.Red);
}
```

After the **catch** part, it is possible to place a **finally** part, which is executed no matter whether an exception of a certain kind is caught or not. For example:

```
try
{
    n = int.Parse(s);
}
```

```
catch (FormatException e)
{
    spriteBatch.DrawString(s + "is not a number", Vector2.Zero, Color.Red);
}
catch (OverflowException e)
{
    spriteBatch.DrawString(s + "is too big", Vector2.Zero, Color.Red);
}
finally
{
    spriteBatch.DrawString("Program finished", Vector2.Zero, Color.White);
}
```

25.8.3 Throwing Your Own Exceptions

You can make your own code more robust by checking if some conditions hold, and throwing an exception if they do not. For example, if we are loading a level from a file and we notice that not all the lines in the file have the same length, we can throw an exception:

```
if (line.Length != width)
    throw new FormatException("The length of the lines is different.");
```

Somewhere else in the program this exception can then be caught and dealt with (for example, by showing the player a message that the level file is corrupted). By using exceptions in your game, and properly handling them, your game will become more robust. If you plan to deploy your game commercially, it is crucial that you deal with possible exceptions in your program, so that your game can stand up to the abuse of the player, as well as deal with any unforeseen circumstances. Both the **try-catch**-instruction as well as the **throw**-instruction as part of the *instruction* syntax diagram:

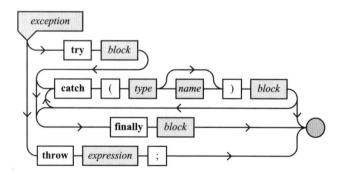

25.9 What You Have Learned

In this chapter, you have learned:

- how to create a partial class;
- how to deal with exceptions;
- how to setup the general structure of the Tick Tick game.

Chapter 26
Animation

26.1 Introduction

In this chapter, we are going to show you how to add *animations* to your game. In the games we have developed until now, game objects could move around on the screen, but adding something like a running character to your game is slightly more challenging. In this chapter, we will write a program that contains a character walking on the bottom of the screen. The character can walk from the left to the right and vice versa, based on which arrow key (left or right) the player is pressing.

26.2 What Is Animation?

Before we are going to look into how to program a character walking around on the screen, we first have to think about what animation actually is. To grasp this, we have to go back to the 1930s, when several animation studios (among which Walt Disney) produced the first cartoons in black and white. Cartoons are actually a very fast sequence of still images, also called *frames*. A television draws these frames at a very high rate, about 25 times per second. By varying the image that we draw each time, our brain interprets this as motion. This special 'feature' of the human brain is very useful, especially when we want to program games that need to contain moving or animated objects. We have also used this feature in the previous games we developed in this book. Every time the Draw method is called, we draw a new 'frame' on the screen. By drawing sprites on different positions every time, we get the impression that the sprites actually move. However, this is not really what is happening. In fact, we are simply drawing the sprite at different positions many times per second, which makes the player think that the sprite is moving. In a very similar fashion, we can also draw a walking or running character. We do not only move the sprite, we also draw a slightly different sprite every time. By drawing a sequence of sprites that all represent a part of a walking motion, we can create the illusion that a character is walking on the screen. An example of such a sequence of sprites is given in Fig. 26.1.

A. Egges et al., *Learning C# by Programming Games*,   351
DOI 10.1007/978-3-642-36580-5_26, © Springer-Verlag Berlin Heidelberg 2013

Fig. 26.1 A sequence of images representing a walking motion

Why use animations?—There are different reasons for putting animations in your games. When you create 3D games, animation is normally necessary to enhance realism, but for 2D games this is not always the case. Still, animations can considerably enrich a game.

Animation brings objects to life. But it does not have to be complicated to do this. The simple animation of a character closing and opening eyes already results in a strong feeling that the character is alive. Animated characters are also easier to relate to. If you look at a game like Cut The Ropes, the main character is simply sitting in a corner. But from time to time the character makes some funny moves to show you it is there and wants you to bring it food. This creates a very effective motivation for the player to continue playing the game.

Animations also help to draw the attention of the player to a certain object, task, or event. For example, having a small animation in a button makes it clearer for the player that she/he has to press the button. And a bouncing waterdrop or a rotating star indicates more clearly that this object should be collected or avoided. Animations can also be used to provide feedback. When a button is actually moving down when you press it with the mouse it is immediately clear that the button press was successful.

However, creating animations is a lot of work. So think carefully beforehand where animations are needed and where they can be avoided, to save time and money.

26.3 The Animation Class

For animated characters, we usually design one sprite for each type of movement. The example in Fig. 26.1 is the sprite for animating a running character. During the development of the Penguin Pairs game, we already designed the SpriteSheet class that represents a strip or a sheet of images. Therefore, we are going to use that class as a base class for a new class, Animation. The *sheet index* of the Animation object will then indicate which *frame* we are currently drawing. When we create an animation, we need to store some additional information. For example, we would like to indicate how long each frame should be shown on the screen. We store this value in a member variable called frameTime:

protected float frameTime;

Furthermore, we would like to be able to *loop* our animation, meaning that once we reach the last frame, the first frame should be shown again afterwards. Looping an animation is very useful. In the case of a walking character, we only have to draw one walk cycle and then loop the animation to get a continuous walking motion. Not all animations should be looped though. For example, a dying animation should not be looped (that would be very cruel to the character). So we want to *choose* if an animation should be looped or not. For that, we declare a **bool** variable:

```
protected bool isLooping;
```

In the constructor of the Animation class, we assign values to each of these member variables:

```
public Animation(string assetname, bool isLooping, float frametime = 0.1f)
            : base(assetname, 0, "")
{
    this.frameTime = frametime;
    this.isLooping = isLooping;
}
```

We added a few convenient properties to the Animation class to access the different member variables, as well as a few properties and methods related to playing an animation. Furthermore, there is one additional member variable; time. This variable is used to maintain how long we still need to show the current frame, as we will explain later on.

26.4 Playing an Animation

The Animation class provides us with a few useful methods and properties for dealing with animated sprites. Now, we still need to be able to play an animation. What does 'playing' mean exactly? It means that we have to determine which frame should be shown depending on the time that has passed, as well as drawing that frame on the screen. Calculating which frame should be drawn is something we do in the Update method of the Animation class. Since each frame in the animation corresponds to a certain sheet index, we simply have to calculate which sheet index corresponds to the current frame. The Draw method that is inherited from SpriteSheet does not have to be modified.

In order to start playing the animation, we have to reset the values of the member variables. We add a method called Play that does this:

```
public void Play()
{
    this.sheetIndex = 0;
    this.time = 0.0f;
}
```

As you can see, we set the animation to initially show the first frame, and we initialize the time variable to zero (more about that later).

26.4.1 Updating the Animation that Is Currently Playing

In the Update method, we have to calculate which frame should be drawn. But that means that we need to know how much time has passed since the last frame was drawn. If we were to increment the frame index in every call to the Update method, the animation would be played way too fast. So, we will save the time that has passed since the last frame was drawn inside the member variable time. We have to update this variable in the beginning of the Update method:

```
time += (float)gameTime.ElapsedGameTime.TotalSeconds;
```

We are using the property ElapsedGameTime here, which indicates how much time has passed since the last time Update was called. This property gives us an object of type TimeSpan which in turn has a property called TotalSeconds that expresses the elapsed time, in seconds, as a **double**.

Now we can calculate the index of the frame that should be shown. For this, we will use a **while**-instruction:

```
while (time > frameTime)
{
    time −= frameTime;
    if (isLooping)
        sheetIndex = (sheetIndex + 1) % this.NumberSheetElements;
    else
        sheetIndex = Math.Min(sheetIndex + 1, this.NumberSheetElements − 1);
}
```

What happens here exactly? The **while**-instruction continues as long as the time variable contains a value larger than frameTime. Inside the **while**-instruction, we subtract the frame time from the time variable. Suppose that the time that each frame is displayed is set to 1 second. Now we enter the Update method and we add the elapsed time to the time member variable. Suppose that this variable now contains the value 1.02, meaning that the frame we are currently showing has been shown for 1.02 seconds. This means that we should show the next frame instead. We do this by incrementing the index of the frame we are currently showing. We then update the time variable and subtract the frame time (1 second), so that the new value of time becomes 0.02. We have put this code inside a **while**-instruction, so that we are sure that we always show the right frame, even if the time passed since the last update was multiple times the frame time. For example, if the new value of time was 3.4, then we would need to move three frames ahead and subtract the frame time three times from the time variable. The **while**-instruction takes care of that.

Instead of simply incrementing the current frame index, we do something slightly more complicated to allow for looping behavior. For this, we use the modulo operation on the sheet_index variable. As soon as the sheet index is larger or equal to **this**.NumberSheetElements, the modulo operation resets the value of sheet_index to zero by returning zero as the remainder of the division. The result is that the animation is looping. If we do not want to have looping behavior (this is the **else** part of the **if**-instruction), then we calculate the new frame index by simply incrementing it. In order to avoid that we try to draw a frame outside of the sprite image, we use the Math.Min method to ensure that the new frame index never is higher than **this**.NumberSheetElements − 1.

26.4.2 Mirroring Sprites

Simply using the sprite shown in Fig. 26.1 allows us to animate a character walking to the right. In order to animate a character walking to the left, we could use another sprite. However, there is an easier way to accomplish this: by using sprite effects. The SpriteEffects enumerated type allows specifying whether a sprite should be flipped horizontally or vertically. A horizontal flip does exactly what we need in this case: flip the image around the standing axis, resulting in a sprite animation consistent with walking in the opposite direction. Mirroring sprites can be useful for any kind of sprite, so inside the SpriteSheet class, we add a member variable mirror, which indicates if the sprite should be mirrored or not. We use this variable to determine the desired sprite effect in the Draw method of the class:

```
SpriteEffects spriteEffects = SpriteEffects.None;
if (mirror)
    spriteEffects = SpriteEffects.FlipHorizontally;
spriteBatch.Draw(sprite, position, spritePart, Color.White,
    0.0f, origin, 1.0f, spriteEffects, 0.0f);
```

26.5 An Animated Game Object

The Animation class provides the ground work for playing animations. In this section, we will introduce a new kind of game object: the *animated* game object, which makes use of this class. An animated game object may contain a number of different animations, so we can have a character that can perform different (animated) actions such as walking, running, jumping, and more. Each action is represented by an animation. Depending on the player input, we change the animation that is currently playing. We will define a class called AnimatedGameObject which is a subclass of SpriteGameObject.

In order to store the different animations, we will use a Dictionary object. This way, we can easily select another animation by looking through the dictionary and choosing the appropriate animation based on an ID. The dictionary is declared as a member variable in the AnimatedGameObject class.

```
protected Dictionary<string,Animation> animations;
```

We also add two methods to the class: LoadAnimation and PlayAnimation. The first method creates an Animation object and adds it to the dictionary:

```
Animation anim = new Animation(assetname, looping, frametime);
animations[id] = anim;
```

The AnimatedGameObject class is a subclass of SpriteGameObject. That means that when this object is drawn on the screen, it will try to draw the sprite sheet that the member variable sprite points to. However, note that the AnimatedGameObject class has the following constructor:

```
public AnimatedGameObject(Int layer = 0, string id = "")
    : base("", layer, id)
{
    animations = new Dictionary<string, Animation>();
}
```

Because we pass along the empty string to the base constructor, the sprite variable will contain the value **null**. What we need to do is assign the currently running animation to the sprite member variable, so that this animation is then drawn on the screen. We can easily do this, since the Animation class is a subclass of SpriteSheet, which is also the type of the sprite member variable. We do this in the PlayAnimation method.

In that method, we first check if the animation we want to play is already playing. If that is the case, we do not have to do anything else and we can return from the method:

```
if (sprite == animations[id])
    return;
```

Next, we check if we should copy the current mirror information, so that the newly assigned animation will have the same mirrored state:

```
if (sprite != null)
    animations[id].Mirror = sprite.Mirror;
```

Then, we call the Play method on the animation, so that the animation is initialized and reset to the first frame:

```
animations[id].Play();
```

Now that the preparatory work is done, we assign the current animation to the sprite member variable:

```
sprite = animations[id];
```

Finally, we also change the origin of the animated game object. If we want to draw animated characters moving on the floor, then it would be much more useful to use a point on the *bottom* of the character sprite as its origin. Also, as we will see later on, this is useful for collision checking. For these reasons, we are going to define the origin of the animated game object as the point in the middle of the bottom of the sprite element:

```
origin = new Vector2(sprite.Width / 2, sprite.Height);
```

Finally, the Update method of the AnimatedGameObject class calls the Update method on the currently selected animation. For the complete AnimatedGameObject class, see Listing 26.1.

26.6 The Player Class

In order to use the AnimatedGameObject class introduced in the previous section, we inherit from it. Since the player will control the animated character, let us define a Player class that is a subclass of the AnimatedGameObject class. Within this class, we load the animations belonging to the player, and handle the input from the player. The full Player class is shown in Listing 26.2. In the constructor of the Player class, we load the animations that are needed for this character. In this example, we want the character to walk or stand still. So, we load two animations and add them to the dictionary by calling the LoadAnimation method. We want both of these animations to loop, so we set the looping parameter to **true**:

```
this.LoadAnimation("Sprites/Player/spr_idle", "idle", true);
this.LoadAnimation("Sprites/Player/spr_run@13", "run", true);
```

Now we need to handle the input of the player in this class. When the player presses the left or right arrow key, the velocity of the character should change. We do this in the HandleInput method using an **if**-instruction (see Listing 26.2).

In the Update method, we select which animation to play based on the velocity. If the velocity is zero, we play the idle animation, otherwise we play the 'run' animation:

```
if (velocity.X == 0)
    this.PlayAnimation("idle");
else
    this.PlayAnimation("run");
```

```
 1   using System.Collections.Generic;
 2   using Microsoft.Xna.Framework;
 3
 4   public class AnimatedGameObject : SpriteGameObject
 5   {
 6       protected Dictionary<string,Animation> animations;
 7
 8       public AnimatedGameObject(int layer = 0, string id = "")
 9           : base("", layer, id)
10       {
11           animations = new Dictionary<string, Animation>();
12       }
13
14       public void LoadAnimation(string assetname, string id, bool looping,
15                                 float frametime = 0.1f)
16       {
17           Animation anim = new Animation(assetname, looping, frametime);
18           animations[id] = anim;
19       }
20
21       public void PlayAnimation(string id)
22       {
23           if (sprite == animations[id])
24               return;
25           if (sprite != null)
26               animations[id].Mirror = sprite.Mirror;
27           animations[id].Play();
28           sprite = animations[id];
29           origin = new Vector2(sprite.Width / 2, sprite.Height);
30       }
31
32       public override void Update(GameTime gameTime)
33       {
34           if (sprite == null)
35               return;
36           Current.Update(gameTime);
37           base.Update(gameTime);
38       }
39
40       public Animation Current
41       {
42           get { return sprite as Animation; }
43       }
44   }
```

Listing 26.1 A class that represents an animated game object

```
1    using Microsoft.Xna.Framework;
2    using Microsoft.Xna.Framework.Input;
3
4    class Player : AnimatedGameObject
5    {
6        public Player() : base(0, "player")
7        {
8            this.LoadAnimation("Sprites/Player/spr_idle", "idle", true);
9            this.LoadAnimation("Sprites/Player/spr_run@13", "run", true);
10       }
11
12       public override void HandleInput(InputHelper inputHelper)
13       {
14           velocity.X = 0.0f;
15           if (inputHelper.IsKeyDown(Keys.Left))
16               velocity.X = −400;
17           else if (inputHelper.IsKeyDown(Keys.Right))
18               velocity.X = 400;
19       }
20
21       public override void Update(GameTime gameTime)
22       {
23           if (velocity.X == 0)
24               this.PlayAnimation("idle");
25           else
26               this.PlayAnimation("run");
27           Mirror = velocity.X < 0;
28           base.Update(gameTime);
29       }
30   }
```

Listing 26.2 A class for the player character

If the player character is walking in the left direction (e.g., the velocity is negative), we have to mirror the animation. We can write this down neatly in a single instruction using some boolean logic:

Mirror = velocity.X < 0;

The right-hand side of this instruction yields **true** if the character is walking in the left direction, and **false** if the character walks in the right direction. The value of this expression is set to the Mirror property, which leads exactly to the behavior that we want. Finally, we call the Update method in the base class, to make sure that the animation game object version of the Update method is called as well.

In order to test our animation class, we create a single AnimationState instance, which we add to the game state manager:

```
gameStateManager.AddGameState("animationState", new AnimationState());
gameStateManager.SwitchTo("animationState");
```

Inside the AnimationState class, we create a Player instance, set it at the desired position and add it to the game world:

```
Player player = new Player();
player.Position = new Vector2(50, 600);
this.Add(player);
```

If you execute this program, you will see an animated character that you can control with the left and right arrow keys.

26.7 What You Have Learned

In this chapter, you have learned:

- how to create and control an animation;
- how to build an animated game object consisting of multiple animations.

Chapter 27
Game Physics

27.1 Introduction

In the previous chapters, we have seen how to create an animated character. We have also shown how you can load levels from files and how to build a tile-based game world. One of the most important aspects is still missing: defining *how the character interacts with the game world*. We can make a character move from left to right, but if we simply place the character in the level, he/she will only be able to walk on the bottom of the screen. This is not enough. We want the character to be able to jump on top of wall tiles, we want the character to fall down if he/she moves off a wall tile, and we do not want the character to fall off the edge of the screen. For these things, we need to implement a basic physics system. Since it is the character interacting with the world, we are going to implement this physics inside the Player class. There are two aspects of dealing with physics: one is giving the character the ability to jump or fall, the other is handling collisions between the character and other game objects, and responding to these collisions.

27.2 Locking the Character in the Game World

The first thing that we are going to do, is lock the character in the game world. In the examples in Chap. 26 the character could walk out of the screen without any problem. We can solve this by placing a virtual pile of 'wall' type tiles to the left and to the right of the screen. We then assume that our collision detection mechanism (which we have not written yet) will ensure that the character cannot walk through these walls. We only want to block the character walking out of the left or the right of the screen. The character should be able to jump out of sight on the top of the screen. Also the character should be able to fall off the game world through a hole in the ground (and die, obviously).

In order to build this virtual pile of 'wall' tiles on the left and right side of the screen, we have to add some behavior to the grid of tiles. We do not want to modify

A. Egges et al., *Learning C# by Programming Games*,
DOI 10.1007/978-3-642-36580-5_27, © Springer-Verlag Berlin Heidelberg 2013

the GameObjectGrid class. This behavior has nothing to do with the grid of game objects, but it is particular to our platform game. Therefore, we will define a new class called TileField that *inherits from* the GameObjectGrid class. We add a single method to that class called GetTileType, which returns the type of the tile, given its x and y position in the grid. The nice thing about this method is that we allow these indices to fall *outside* of the valid indices in the grid. For example, it would be perfectly fine to ask for the tile type of the tile at position $(-2, 500)$. By using an **if**-instruction in this method, we check if the x index is out of range. If so, we return a normal (wall) tile type:

```
if (x < 0 || x >= Columns)
    return TileType.Normal;
```

If the y index is out of range, we return a 'background' tile type, so that the character can jump through the top of the screen, or fall into a hole:

```
if (y < 0 || y >= Rows)
    return TileType.Background;
```

If both of the **if** instructions' conditions are **false**, this means that the type of an actual tile in the grid is requested, so we retrieve that tile and return its tile type:

```
Tile current = this.Objects[x, y] as Tile;
return current.TileType;
```

The complete class can be found in Listing 27.1.

27.3 Setting the Player at the Right Position

When we load the level tiles from the text file, we use the character '1' to indicate on which tile the player is starting. Based on the location of that tile, we have to create the Player object and set it at the right position. For this, we add a method LoadStartTile to the Level class in the LevelLoading.cs file. In this method, we first retrieve the tile field, and then we calculate the starting position of the player. Since the origin of the player is the *bottom-center* point of the sprite, we can calculate this position as follows:

```
TileField tiles = this.Find("tiles") as TileField;
Vector2 startPosition = new Vector2(((float)x + 0.5f) * tiles.CellWidth,
                                    (y + 1) * tiles.CellHeight);
```

Note that we use the width and height of the tiles and multiply them with the x and y indices of where the player should be located. We multiply with x + 0.5f so that the player is placed in the middle of the tile position and we multiply with y + 1 to place the player on the bottom of the tile. We can then create the Player object and add it to the game world.

```
1   class TileField : GameObjectGrid
2   {
3       public TileField(int rows, int columns, int layer = 0, string id = "")
4           : base(rows, columns, layer, id)
5       {
6       }
7
8       public TileType GetTileType(int x, int y)
9       {
10          if (x < 0 || x >= Columns)
11              return TileType.Normal;
12          if (y < 0 || y >= Rows)
13              return TileType.Background;
14          Tile current = this.Objects[x, y] as Tile;
15          return current.TileType;
16      }
17  }
```

Listing 27.1 The TileField class

```
Player player = new Player(startPosition);
this.Add(player);
```

Finally, we still need to make an actual tile here that can be stored in the grid, since each character should represent a tile. In this case, we can simply create a background tile, which is placed where the player is standing:

```
return new Tile();
```

27.4 Jumping . . .

We have already seen how we can walk to the left or to the right. How can we deal with jumping and falling? By pressing either the arrow up key or the space bar, the character should jump. Jumping basically means that the character will have a *negative* y-velocity. This can be easily done inside the HandleInput method of the Player class:

```
if (inputHelper.KeyPressed(Keys.Space) || inputHelper.KeyPressed(Keys.Up))
    Jump();
```

The Jump method is given as follows:

```
public void Jump(float speed = 1100)
{
    velocity.Y = −speed;
}
```

So, the effect of calling the Jump method without providing any parameter value is that the *y* velocity is set to a value of −1100. This is a sort of randomly chosen number. By choosing a bigger number, the character can jump higher. A lower number means that our character has to go to the gym more often, or quit smoking. We chose this value, so that the character can jump high enough to reach the tiles, but not too high so that the game becomes too easy (then the character could just jump to the end of the level).

There is a minor problem with this approach: we always allow the player to jump, no matter what the current situation of the character is. So, if the player is currently jumping or falling down a cliff, we allow the player to jump his/her way back to safety. This is not really what we want. We want the player only to jump when he/she is standing on the ground. This is something that we can detect by looking at collisions between the player and wall or platform tiles (which are the only tiles that the player can stand on). Let us assume, for now, that our yet to be written collision detection algorithm will take care of this, and it will keep track of whether the player is on the ground or not by using a member variable:

protected bool isOnTheGround;

If this member variable is **true**, we know that the player is standing on the ground. We can now change our initial **if**-instruction so that it only allows a player to jump from the ground and not from the air:

```
if ((inputHelper.KeyPressed(Keys.Space) || inputHelper.KeyPressed(Keys.Up))
    && isOnTheGround)
    Jump();
```

27.5 … and Falling

The only place where we are currently changing the *y* velocity is in the HandleInput method, when the player wants to jump. Since the *y* velocity will indefinitely keep the value of −1100, the character will simply move up in the air, outside of the screen, out of the planet's atmosphere into outer space. Since we are not making a game about bombs in space, we will have to do something about this. What we forgot to add to the game world is *gravity*.

We follow a very simple approach to simulate the effect of gravity on the character's velocity. We simply add a small value to the velocity in the *y* direction in each update step:

velocity.Y += 55;

What happens is that if the character has a negative velocity, this velocity slowly becomes smaller until it reaches zero, and then starts to increase again. The effect is that the character jumps to a certain height, and then starts falling down again, just like in the real world. However, the collision detection mechanism now becomes even more important. If there is no collision detection, the character would simply start falling down at the start of the game!

27.6   Collision Detection

Detecting collisions between game objects is a very important part of simulating interacting game worlds. Collision detection is used for many different things in games: detecting if you walk over a power up, detecting if you collide with a projectile, detecting collisions between the character and walls or floors, and so on. Given this very common occurrence, it is almost strange that we did not have the need for collision detection in our previous games. Or wait, didn't we? Look at this code from the Update method in the PaintCan class from the Painter game:

```
Vector2 distanceVector = ((Painter.GameWorld.Ball.Position
                            + Painter.GameWorld.Ball.Center)
                        − (position + Center));
if (Math.Abs(distanceVector.X) < Center.X && Math.Abs(distanceVector.Y) < Center.Y)
{
    Color = Painter.GameWorld.Ball.Color;
    Painter.GameWorld.Ball.Reset();
}
```

What we are doing, here, is in fact detecting a collision between the ball and the paint can (though be it in a very rudimentary fashion). We take the positions of the center of each object, and see if their distance is smaller than a certain value. If so, we say they collide and we change the color of the canister. If you look at this case more closely, you can see that we are representing our game objects by basic shapes such as *circles* and we check if they collide with each other by verifying that the distance between the centers is smaller than the sum of the radii of the circles.

So here you see a first, simple example of doing collision checking in games. Of course, this is not a very precise way of checking collisions. The ball might be approximated by the shape of a circle, the paint can does not look like a circle at all. As a result, in some cases a collision will be detected when there is none, and sometimes a collision will not be detected when the sprites are actually colliding. Still, many games use *simplified shapes* to represent the objects when they do collision detection. Circles are a good candidate to use as a simplified shape for collision detection. Rectangles are also widely used. Because these shapes bind the object within, they are also called *bounding circles* and bounding boxes. The Tick Tick game

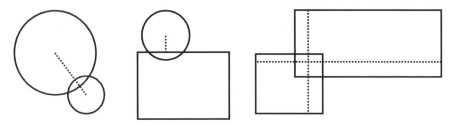

Fig. 27.1 Different types of collision: circle–circle, circle–rectangle, and rectangle–rectangle

uses *axis-aligned* bounding boxes, meaning that we do not consider boxes whose sides are not parallel to the *x*- and *y*-axes.

Unfortunately, just doing collision detection using these bounding boxes is not always precise enough. Especially when game objects are close to each other their bounding shapes may intersect (and thus trigger a collision), but the actual objects do not. Especially in the case when the game objects are animated, their shape changes over time. Now you could make the bounding shape bigger so that the object fits in it under all circumstances but that would lead to even more false collision triggers.

A solution for this is to check for collisions on a per-pixel basis. So basically, you could write an algorithm that walks over the non-transparent pixels in the sprite (using a nested **for**-instruction), and checking if one or more of these pixels collide with one of the pixels in another sprite (again, by walking through them using a nested **for**-instruction). Fortunately, we will not have to perform this rather expensive task very often. It only has to be done when two bounding shapes intersect. And then we only have to do it for the parts of the shapes that actually intersect.

When we use circles and rectangles for detecting collisions, we need to handle three different cases (see also Fig. 27.1):

- a circle intersects with another circle
- a circle intersects with a rectangle
- a rectangle intersects with another rectangle

The first case is the simplest one. The only thing we need to do is to check if the distance between the two centers is smaller than the sum of the radii. We have already seen an example of how to do that.

For the case where a circle intersects a rectangle, we can use the following approach:

- locate the point on the rectangle that lies closest to the circle center
- calculate the distance between this point and the center of the circle
- if this distance is smaller than the radius of the circle, there is a collision

Let us assume we want to find out if an object of type Rectangle intersects with a circle, represented by an object of type Vector2 and a radius. We can find the point closest to the circle center by using MathHelper.Clamp in a smart way. Take a look at the following code:

```
Vector2 closestPoint = Vector2.Zero;
closestPoint.X = MathHelper.Clamp(circleCenter.X, rectangle.Left, rectangle.Right);
closestPoint.Y = MathHelper.Clamp(circleCenter.Y, rectangle.Top, rectangle.Bottom);
```

We find the closest point by clamping the x and y values of the center between the rectangle edges. If the circle center is inside the rectangle, this method also works, since the clamping will have no effect in that case, and the closest point will be the same as the circle center.

The next step is calculating the distance between the closest point and the circle center:

```
Vector2 distance = closestPoint − circleCenter
```

If this distance is smaller than the radius, we have a collision:

```
if (distance.Length() < circleRadius)
    collision!
```

The final case is checking if two rectangles collide. We need to know the following about both rectangles in order to calculate this:

- lowest x value of the rectangle (rectangle.Left)
- lowest y value of the rectangle (rectangle.Top)
- greatest x value of the rectangle (rectangle.Right)
- greatest y value of the rectangle (rectangle.Bottom)

Let us say we want to know if rectangle A collides with rectangle B. In that case, we have to check for the following conditions:

- A.Left (A's lowest x value) $<=$ B.Right (B's greatest x value)
- A.Right (A's greatest x value) $>=$ B.Left (B's lowest x value)
- A.Top (A's lowest y value) $<=$ B.Bottom (B's greatest y value)
- A.Bottom (A's greatest y value) $>=$ B.Top (B's lowest y value)

If all these conditions are met, then rectangles A and B have collided. Why these particular conditions? Let us look at the first condition to see what happens if it is not true. Suppose that A.Left > B.Right instead. In that case, rectangle A will lie completely to the right of rectangle B, so they cannot collide. If the second condition is not true (e.g. A.Right < B.Left) then rectangle A lies completely to the left of B, which means that they do not collide either. Check for yourself the other two conditions as well. In summary, what these conditions actually say, is that if rectangle A lies neither completely to the left, right, top, or bottom of B, then the two rectangles collide.

In C#, writing down the code for checking collisions between rectangles is easy. If you feel like you want some extra coding exercise, try and implement this for yourself. The Rectangle class already has a method Intersects that does this work for us:

```
if (A.Intersects(B))
    perform per-pixel collision detection here
```

27.7 Retrieving Bounding Boxes

In order to handle collision efficiently in our game, we are going to extend the
SpriteGameObject class with a property BoundingBox that returns the bounding box of
the sprite:

```
public override Rectangle BoundingBox
{
    get
    {
        int left = (int)(GlobalPosition.X − origin.X);
        int top = (int)(GlobalPosition.Y − origin.Y);
        return new Rectangle(left, top, Width, Height);
    }
}
```

As you can see, we take into account the origin of the sprite in order to calculate the
correct position of the box. Also, note that the bounding box position is expressed
using *global positions*. When doing collision detection, we want to know where the
objects are in the world, we do not care about their local positions in some hierarchy
of game objects.

27.8 Per-pixel Collision Detection

Next to the BoundingBox property, we have added a method CollidesWith to the
SpriteGameObject class that deals with the collision detection. Next to checking if
the bounding boxes intersect, this method performs a per-pixel collision detection.
The first step in this method is to determine if we need to do any collision detection at all. If either of the two objects is invisible, or if their bounding boxes do not
intersect, we return from the method:

```
if (!this.Visible || !obj.Visible || !BoundingBox.Intersects(obj.BoundingBox))
    return false;
```

The next step is calculating the overlapping part of the two bounding boxes. Since
this is a useful thing to calculate when dealing with collision detection in general,
we are going to create a new class Collision that contains a number of static methods that are useful for collision detection, very similar to how MathHelper functions.

Fig. 27.2 Calculating the
overlap rectangle using the
minimal and maximal *x* and
y coordinates

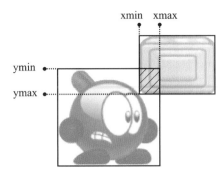

The Intersection method takes two bounding boxes and returns another rectangle that
represents the overlap of the two boxes.

In order to calculate this overlap rectangle, we need to know what the minimal
and maximal *x* and *y* coordinates are of the rectangle (see Fig. 27.2). Using a few
useful properties from the Rectangle class in combination with the Min and Max methods of the Math class, we can calculate these values quite easily:

```
int xmin = (int)MathHelper.Max(rect1.Left, rect2.Left);
int xmax = (int)MathHelper.Min(rect1.Right, rect2.Right);
int ymin = (int)MathHelper.Max(rect1.Top, rect2.Top);
int ymax = (int)MathHelper.Min(rect1.Bottom, rect2.Bottom);
```

Now we can calculate the position and size of the overlap rectangle, and return it
from the method:

```
return new Rectangle(xmin, ymin, xmax − xmin, ymax − ymin);
```

Inside the CollidesWith method in SpriteGameObject, we store the overlap rectangle by
calling the Intersection method from the Collision class:

```
Rectangle b = Collision.Intersection(BoundingBox, obj.BoundingBox);
```

In order to check for collision within the overlap rectangle, we use a nested **for**-
instruction to walk over all the pixels in the rectangle:

```
for (int x = 0; x < b.Width; x++)
    for (int y = 0; y < b.Height; y++)
        check if the pixels at position (x, y) are both not transparent
```

Inside the nested loop, we have to calculate what the local pixel coordinates are in
the current sprite, as well as the sprite that was passed as a parameter. Again, we
need to calculate these local coordinates using global positions, and we need to take
the origin into account:

```
int thisx = b.X − (int)(GlobalPosition.X − origin.X) + x;
int thisy = b.Y − (int)(GlobalPosition.Y − origin.Y) + y;
int objx = b.X − (int)(obj.GlobalPosition.X − obj.origin.X) + x;
int objy = b.Y − (int)(obj.GlobalPosition.Y − obj.origin.Y) + y;
```

Finally, we check if both pixels are not transparent at these local positions. If that is
the case, we have a collision:

```
if (sprite.GetPixelColor(thisx, thisy).A != 0
    && obj.sprite.GetPixelColor(objx, objy).A != 0)
    return true;
```

Here you can see that we reuse the GetPixelColor method that we developed in the
Jewel Jam game. Now that our basic collision detection methods are implemented,
we can simply check if two game objects collide by calling the CollidesWith method:

```
if (this.CollidesWith(enemy))
    ouch...
```

27.9 Handling Collisions Between the Character and the Tiles

In the Tick Tick game, we need to detect collisions between the character and the tiles.
We will do this in a method called HandleCollisions, which we call from the Update
method in the Player class. The idea behind this is that we do all the calculations for
jumping, falling and running first (we did this in the previous sections). If there is a
collision between the character and the tile, we correct the position of the character
so that it no longer collides. Inside the HandleCollisions method, we walk through the
grid of tiles, and we check if there is a collision between the bounding box of the
character and the bounding box of the tile we are currently examining.

We do not need to check all the tiles in the grid, only those close to the current
location of the player. We can calculate the closest tile to the position of the player
as follows:

```
TileField tiles = GameWorld.Find("tiles") as TileField;
int x_floor = (int)position.X / tiles.CellWidth;
int y_floor = (int)position.Y / tiles.CellHeight;
```

Now we can use a nested **for**-instruction to look at the tiles surrounding the player.
In order to account for fast jumping and falling, we will take more tiles into account in the y direction. Inside the nested **for**-instruction, we will then check if the
player is colliding with the tile. However, we only need to do that if the tile is *not* a
background tile. The code to do all that is given as follows:

```
for (int y = y_floor − 2; y <= y_floor + 1; ++y)
    for (int x = x_floor − 1; x <= x_floor + 1; ++x)
    {
        TileType tileType = tiles.GetTileType(x, y);
        if (tileType == TileType.Background)
            continue;
        Rectangle tileBounds = new Rectangle(x * tiles.CellWidth, y * tiles.CellHeight,
                                            tiles.CellWidth, tiles.CellHeight);
        if (!tileBounds.Intersects(BoundingBox))
            continue;
        handle the collision

    }
```

As you can see, we do not directly access the Tile objects. The reason for this is that sometimes, the x or y index can be negative because the character is near the edge of the screen. Here we see the advantage of using the GetTileType method we added to the TileField class. We do not care here if we are really dealing with a tile or not, as long as we know its type and bounding box, we can do our job.

Inside the nested **for**-instruction, you also see a new keyword: **continue**. This keyword can be used in **for**- or **while**- instructions to stop executing the current iteration of the loop and continue to the next one. In this case, if the tile type is of type 'background', the rest of the instructions will not be executed anymore, and we continue to increment x and start a new iteration to check the next tile. The result is that only tiles that are not of type background are considered.

This code will not always work correctly though. Especially when the character is standing on a tile, rounding errors when calculating the bounding box could lead to the algorithm thinking that the character is not yet standing on the ground. The character's velocity will then be increased and it might fall through the tile because of it. In order to compensate for any rounding errors, we increase the height of the bounding box by 1:

```
Rectangle boundingBox = this.BoundingBox;
boundingBox.Height += 1;
if (!tileBounds.Intersects(boundingBox))
    continue;
handle the collision
```

Again, if the bounding box does not intersect the current tile, we can stop this loop and continue to the next tile. Another thing that we need to do is take advantage of the per-pixel collision detection between the player and the tile. Therefore, we retrieve the tile we are currently examining:

```
Tile currentTile = tiles.Get(x, y) as Tile;
```

Now we extend the **if**-instruction above to use the CollidesWith method. If the current tile is not **null** and it does not collide with the character, or if the current tile is **null**, we do not have to handle the collision, except when we intersect with the slightly enlarged bounding box:

```
if (((currentTile != null && !currentTile.CollidesWith(this)) || currentTile == null)
    && !tileBounds.Intersects(boundingBox))
    continue;
```

27.10 Dealing with the Collision

Now that we can detect collisions between the character and the tiles in the world, we have to determine what to do when a collision happens. There are a couple of possibilities. We could let the game crash (not good if you want to sell your game to many people), we could warn the user that he/she should not collide with objects in the game (results in a lot of pop-up messages), or we could automatically correct the position of the player if he/she collides with an object.

In order to correct the position of the player, we need to know how 'bad' the collision was. For example, if the player walked into a wall on the right, we have to know how far we have to move the player character to the left again to undo the collision. You could also call this the *intersection depth*. We extend the Collision class that we introduced earlier with a method called CalculateIntersectionDepth. This method takes two Rectangle objects as parameters. In our example, the parameters we give to this method are the bounding box of the player and the bounding box of the tile that we are colliding with.

The intersection depth can be calculated by first determining the minimum allowed distance between the centers of the rectangle such that there is no collision between the two rectangles:

```
Vector2 minDistance = new Vector2(rectA.Width + rectB.Width,
                                  rectA.Height + rectB.Height) / 2;
```

Then, we calculate the *real* distance between the two rectangle centers:

```
Vector2 centerA = new Vector2(rectA.Center.X, rectA.Center.Y);
Vector2 centerB = new Vector2(rectB.Center.X, rectB.Center.Y);
Vector2 distance = centerA − centerB;
```

Now we can calculate the difference between the minimum allowed distance and the actual difference, to get the intersection depth. If we look at the actual distance between the two centers, there are two possibilities for both dimensions (x and y): the distance is either negative or positive. If for example the x distance is negative, this means that rectangle B is placed to the right of rectangle A (because then centerB.X > centerA.X). If rectangle A represents the player, this means we have to move the player to the left to correct this intersection. Therefore, we will return the x intersection depth as a *negative* value, which can be calculated as −minDistance.X − distance.X. Why? Because there is a collision, the distance between the two rectangles is smaller than minDistance. And because distance is negative, the expression −minDistance.X − distance.X gives the difference between the two as a *negative* value. If distance was positive, then the expression minDistance.X − distance.X gives the *positive* difference between the two. The same reasoning holds for the *y* distance. We can then calculate the depth as follows:

```
Vector2 depth = Vector2.Zero;
if (distance.X > 0)
    depth.X = minDistance.X − distance.X;
else
    depth.X = −minDistance.X − distance.X;
if (distance.Y > 0)
    depth.Y = minDistance.Y − distance.Y;
else
    depth.Y = −minDistance.Y − distance.Y;
```

Finally, we return the depth vector as the final result of this method.

```
return depth;
```

When we know that the character collides with the tile, we calculate the intersection depth using the method that we just added to the Collision class:

```
Vector2 depth = Collision.CalculateIntersectionDepth(boundingBox, tileBounds);
```

Now that we have calculated the intersection depth, there are two ways to solve this collision: move the character in the *x*-direction, or move the character in the *y*-direction. Generally, we want to move the character the least possible distance to avoid unnatural motions or displacements. So, if the *x* depth is smaller than the *y* depth, we will move the character in the *x* direction, otherwise in the *y* direction. We can check this with an **if**-instruction. When comparing the two depth dimensions, we have to take into account that they might be negative. We solve this by comparing the absolute values:

```
if (Math.Abs(depth.X) < Math.Abs(depth.Y))
{
    move character in the x direction
}
```

Do we always want to move the player if there is a collision with a tile? Well, that depends on the tile type. Remember that the enumerated type TileType is used to represent three possible tile types: TileType.Background, TileType.Normal, and TileType.Platform. If the tile that we are colliding with is a *background* tile, we definitely do not want to move the player. Also, in the case of moving in the *x*-direction, we want the player to be able to *pass through* platform tiles. Therefore, the only case where we want to move the player to correct the collision is when she/he is colliding with a *wall* tile (TileType.Normal). In that case, we move the player by adding the *x* depth value to the player position:

```
if (tileType == TileType.Normal)
    position.X += depth.X;
```

If we want to correct the player position in the *y*-direction, things become slightly more complicated. Since we are dealing with movement in the *y*-direction, this is also a good place to determine whether the player is on the ground or not. In the beginning of the HandleCollisions method, we set the isOnTheGround member variable to **false**. So, our starting point is to assume that we are *not* on the ground. In *some* cases, we are on the ground, and we have to set the variable to **true**. How can we check if we are on the ground or not? If we are not on the ground, we must be falling. You can verify this unmistakable truth by jumping off a high building and asking yourself that question (do not actually do this). If we are falling, then our *previous* *y*-position will be smaller than our current position. In order to have access to the previous *y*-position, we store it in a member variable at the end of each call to the handleCollisions method:

```
previousYPosition = position.Y;
```

Now it is very easy to determine if we are on the ground. If the previous *y*-position was smaller than the top of the tile that we are colliding with, and the tile is *not* a background tile, then we were falling down and we have now reached a tile. If so, we set the isOnTheGround variable to **true** and the *y*-velocity to zero:

```
if (previousYPosition <= tileBounds.Top && tileType != TileType.Background)
{
    isOnTheGround = true;
    velocity.Y = 0;
}
```

Now we still have to correct the player position in some cases. If we are colliding with a wall tile, we always want to correct the player position. If we are colliding with a platform tile, we only want to correct the player position if we are standing on top of this tile. The latter is only **true** if the isOnTheGround variable is set to **true**. Therefore, we can write all of this down in the following **if**-instruction:

```
if (tileType == TileType.Normal || isOnTheGround)
    position.Y += depth.Y + 1;
```

Note that for correcting the position, we need to add one extra pixel in order to compensate for the extra pixel we added to the bounding box height.

Finally, we have to round the final player position after we handled the collision so that the player sprite ends up neatly on an exact position. If we do not do rounding, an oscillating effect can occur where the player is bouncing up and down very fast (causing a severe headache). For rounding the position value, we use the Math.Floor method. The result of this method is not a **float**, so we have to cast the result to a **float** since this is what the Vector2 constructor expects:

```
position = new Vector2((float)Math.Floor(position.X), (float)Math.Floor(position.Y));
```

27.11 What You Have Learned

In this chapter, you have learned:

- how to constrain a character within the environment;
- how to simulate jumping and falling;
- how to deal with collisions in games.

Chapter 28
Intelligent Enemies

28.1 Introduction

As a next step in developing our game, let us introduce some peril to the player by adding dangerous enemies. If the player touches an enemy, the player dies. The enemies are generally not controlled by the player (that would make it too easy). Therefore, we need to define some kind of smart (or stupid) behavior. We do not want these enemies to be too smart either: the player should be able to complete the level. After all, that is the goal of playing a game: winning it. What is nice is that we can build different types of enemies that exhibit different types of behavior. As a result, the player will have different gameplay options, and has to develop different strategies to complete the level.

Defining the behavior of an enemy can lead to some very complex code, with many different states, reasoning, path planning and much more. We will show a few different types of enemies in this chapter: a rocket, a sneezing turtle (seriously), sparky, and a couple of different patrolling enemies. In this chapter, we will not yet deal with how the player should *interact* with the enemies. We will only define their basic behavior.

28.2 The Rocket

One of the most basic enemies is the rocket. A rocket flies from one side of the screen to the other side, then reappears after some time has passed. If the player comes in contact with the rocket, the player dies. Inside the level description, we indicate with the 'r' and 'R' characters that a rocket enemy should be placed inside a level. For example, see this level description:

A. Egges et al., *Learning C# by Programming Games*,
DOI 10.1007/978-3-642-36580-5_28, © Springer-Verlag Berlin Heidelberg 2013

```
. . . . . . . . . . . . . . . . . . .
r..W...........X....
...--..W.......--...
....W.--........W..R
...--...........--...
r..W......W....W....
...--....--....--...
....W..........W...
...--........W.--...
r..W.........--.W....
...--...........--...
....W..........W..R
...--...........--...
.1.................
######..####..######
Many, many, many, many, many rockets...
```

An 'r' character means that the rocket should fly from left to right, an 'R' character means that it should fly from right to left.

28.2.1 Creating and Resetting the Rocket

We are going to create a Rocket class that represents this particular kind of enemy. We will inherit from the AnimatedGameObject class, since the rocket will be animated. In the constructor, we initialize the Rocket object. We need to load the rocket animation and play it, and then we need to check if the animation should be mirrored. Since the animation has the rocket moving to the right, we need to mirror it if the rocket moves to the left. We also store the starting position of the rocket, so we can place it back at that position when it moves out of the screen. This is the complete constructor:

```
public Rocket(bool moveToLeft, Vector2 startPosition)
{
    this.LoadAnimation("Sprites/Rocket/spr_rocket@3", "default", false, 0.5f);
    this.PlayAnimation("default");
    this.Mirror = moveToLeft;
    this.startPosition = startPosition;
    Reset();
}
```

The last instruction in the constructor is a call to the Reset method. In this method, we set the current position of the rocket to the starting position, we set the Visible property to **false** (so the rocket is initially invisible), and we set its velocity to zero. We also use the random number generator to calculate a random time (in seconds) after which the rocket should appear and start moving. We store this time in a member variable called spawnTime. The reason we put these instructions in a separate Reset method is that we are going to call this method later on as well after the rocket has flown out of the screen.

28.2.2 Programming the Rocket Behavior

The behavior of the rocket is (as usual) encoded in the Update method. Basically, there are two main types of behavior that a rocket exhibits. Either the rocket is visible and moving from one end of the screen to the other end, or the rocket is invisible and waiting to appear. We can determine in which of the two states we are by looking at the value of the spawnTime variable. If this variable contains a value larger than zero, the rocket is waiting to be spawned. If the value is smaller than or equal to zero, the rocket will be visible and moving from one end of the screen to the other.

Let us first look at the first case. If the rocket is waiting to be spawned, we simply subtract the time that was elapsed since the last Update call from the spawn time:

```
if (spawnTime > 0)
{
    spawnTime −= gameTime.ElapsedGameTime.TotalSeconds;
    return;
}
```

The second case is slightly more complicated. In the second case, we are moving from one end of the screen to the other. So, we set our visibility status to **true**, we calculate our velocity depending on the direction we are moving in, and we update our position:

```
this.Visible = true;
this.velocity.X = 600;
if (Mirror)
    this.velocity.X *= −1f;
```

Finally, we have to check if the rocket has flown outside of the screen. If that is the case, the rocket is reset. We check if the rocket is outside of the screen using bounding boxes. If the bounding box enclosing the screen does not intersect the rocket bounding box, we know that the rocket is outside of the screen, and we reset it:

```
Rectangle screenBox = new Rectangle(0, 0, GameEnvironment.Screen.X,
                                    GameEnvironment.Screen.Y);
if (!screenBox.Intersects(this.BoundingBox))
    this.Reset();
```

This completes the Rocket class, except for the interaction with the player, which is something we will look at in more detail in the following chapter. For the complete class, see Listing 28.1.

```
1    using Microsoft.Xna.Framework;
2
3    class Rocket : AnimatedGameObject
4    {
5        protected double spawnTime;
6        protected Vector2 startPosition;
7
8        public Rocket(bool moveToLeft, Vector2 startPosition)
9        {
10           this.LoadAnimation("Sprites/Rocket/spr_rocket@3", "default", false, 0.5f);
11           this.PlayAnimation("default");
12           this.Mirror = moveToLeft;
13           this.startPosition = startPosition;
14           Reset();
15       }
16
17       public override void Reset()
18       {
19           this.Visible = false;
20           this.position = startPosition;
21           this.velocity = Vector2.Zero;
22           this.spawnTime = GameEnvironment.Random.NextDouble() * 5;
23       }
24
25       public override void Update(GameTime gameTime)
26       {
27           base.Update(gameTime);
28           if (spawnTime > 0)
29           {
30               spawnTime -= gameTime.ElapsedGameTime.TotalSeconds;
31               return;
32           }
33           this.Visible = true;
34           this.velocity.X = 600;
35           if (Mirror)
36               this.velocity.X *= -1f;
37           // check if we are outside the screen
38           Rectangle screenBox = new Rectangle(0, 0, GameEnvironment.Screen.X,
39                                               GameEnvironment.Screen.Y);
40           if (!screenBox.Intersects(this.BoundingBox))
41               this.Reset();
42       }
43   }
```

Listing 28.1 A class that represents a moving rocket

28.3 A Patrolling Enemy

The rocket is a type of enemy that basically has no intelligent behavior. It flies from left to right or vice versa until it flies out of the screen, and then it resets itself. We can also add enemies that are slightly smarter, such as a *patrolling* enemy. Let us setup a few different types of patrolling enemies that we can add to our game.

28.3.1 The Basic PatrollingEnemy Class

The PatrollingEnemy class is quite similar to the Rocket class. We want the patrolling enemy to be animated, so it will inherit from the AnimatedGameObject class. Second, we need to define the *behavior* of the enemy inside the overridden Update method. The basic behavior of the patrolling enemy is that it walks from left to right and back again. If the enemy character reaches a gap, or a wall tile, the enemy will stop walking, wait for some time, and turn around again. We can then place enemies on arbitrary positions in the level. For the player, we have defined some rudimentary physics like falling and jumping. We will not do that for the Enemy class, since the enemies we will define for this game will only walk from the left to the right and back again.

In the constructor of the PatrollingEnemy class, we load the main animation for the patrolling enemy character (which is an angry-looking flame). Initially, we set a positive velocity so that the enemy character starts walking to the right. Also, we initialize another member variable called waitTime that will maintain how long the enemy has been waiting on one of the edges of the platform that it is walking on.

```
waitTime = 0.0f;
velocity.X = 120;
this.LoadAnimation("Sprites/Flame/spr_flame@9", "default", true);
this.PlayAnimation("default");
```

Inside the Update method, we have to distinguish between two cases: the enemy is walking or waiting. We can distinguish between these to states by looking at the waitTime variable. If this variable contains a positive value, the enemy is apparently waiting. If the variable contains a value of zero or smaller, the enemy is walking. When the enemy is waiting, we do not have to do much. Just like we did in the Rocket class, we subtract the elapsed game time from the waitTime variable. If the wait time has reached zero, we have to turn around the character. Here is the code that handles this:

```
if (waitTime > 0)
{
    waitTime −= (float)gameTime.ElapsedGameTime.TotalSeconds;
    if (waitTime <= 0.0f)
        TurnAround();
}
```

The TurnAround method simply inverts the velocity and mirrors the animation:

```
public void TurnAround()
{
    Mirror = !Mirror;
    this.velocity.X = 120;
    if (Mirror)
        this.velocity.X = −this.velocity.X;
}
```

If the enemy is currently not waiting but walking, we need to find out if we have reached the edge of the platform that we are walking on. We have reached an edge in two cases: either there is a gap, so we cannot move any further, or there is a wall tile that is blocking our way. We will use the bounding box of the enemy to find this information. If the enemy is walking to the left, we check if the leftmost x-value has reached a wall tile, or the border of the platform. If the enemy is walking to the right, we check the rightmost x-value. We can calculate this x-value as follows:

```
TileField tiles = GameWorld.Find("tiles") as TileField;
float posX = this.BoundingBox.Left;
if (!Mirror)
    posX = this.BoundingBox.Right;
```

Now, we calculate in which tile this x-value falls. We can do that by dividing the x-value by the width of a tile. In order to make sure that we always get the correct (lower bound) tile index, we use the Math.Floor method:

```
int tileX = (int)Math.Floor(posX / tiles.CellWidth);
```

In a similar way, we can also calculate the y-index of the tile that we are currently standing on:

```
int tileY = (int)Math.Floor(position.Y / tiles.CellHeight);
```

Note that because we use the *bottom* of the sprite to represent the position of the enemy, the y-index we get is the one of the tile *below* the enemy. Now, we have to check if we have reached a wall tile, or the border of the platform. If the tile at the calculated indices is a background tile, then we have reached the border of the platform and we have to stop walking. If the tile at indices (tileX, tileY−1) (e.g., the tile right next to the enemy) is a wall tile, we also have to stop walking. In order to stop walking, we assign a positive value to the wait time and we set the x velocity to zero:

```
if (tiles.GetTileType(tileX, tileY − 1) == TileType.Normal ||
    tiles.GetTileType(tileX, tileY) == TileType.Background)
{
```

```
1   using System;
2   using Microsoft.Xna.Framework;
3
4   class UnpredictableEnemy : PatrollingEnemy
5   {
6       public override void Update(GameTime gameTime)
7       {
8           if (waitTime <= 0 && GameEnvironment.Random.NextDouble() < 0.01)
9           {
10              TurnAround();
11              velocity.X = Math.Sign(velocity.X) *
12                              (float)GameEnvironment.Random.NextDouble() * 5.0f;
13          }
14          base.Update(gameTime);
15      }
16  }
17  }
```

Listing 28.2   An enemy that randomly changes direction while walking

```
waitTime = 0.5f;
velocity.X = 0.0f;
}
```

28.3.2 Different Types of Enemies

We can make the patrolling enemy slightly more interesting by introducing a few varieties. Here we can use the power of inheritance to write a few subclasses of the PatrollingEnemy class to define different enemy behavior.

For example, we can think of an enemy that is a bit more unpredictable by letting it change direction once in a while. At that point, we can also change the walking speed of the enemy to some random value. We do this by defining a class UnpredictableEnemy that inherits from the Enemy class. So, by default, it exhibits the same behavior as a regular enemy. What we will do is override the Update method and add a few lines of code that randomly change the direction that the enemy is walking in, as well as its velocity. In Listing 28.2, you can find the complete UnpredictableEnemy class.

As you can see, we use an **if**-instruction to check if a randomly generated number falls below a certain value. As a result, in a few cases the condition will yield **true**. Inside the body of the **if**-instruction, we first turn around the enemy, and then we calculate a new x velocity. Note that we multiply the randomly generated velocity with the sign of the old velocity value. This is to ensure that the new velocity is set

```
 1   using System;
 2   using Microsoft.Xna.Framework;
 3
 4   class PlayerFollowingEnemy : PatrollingEnemy
 5   {
 6       public override void Update(GameTime gameTime)
 7       {
 8           GameObjectList gameWorld = Root as GameObjectList;
 9           Player player = gameWorld.Find("player") as Player;
10           float direction = player.Position.X − position.X;
11           if (Math.Sign(direction) != Math.Sign(velocity.X) && player.Velocity.X != 0.0f
12               && velocity.X != 0.0f)
13               TurnAround();
14           base.Update(gameTime);
15       }
16   }
```

Listing 28.3   An enemy that follows the player when the player is moving

in the right direction. Finally, we call the Update method of the base class, so that
the right animation is selected, collisions with the player are dealt with, and so on.

Another variety that we can think of is an enemy that follows the player instead
of simply walking from the left to the right and back again. Here also, we inherit
from the PatrollingEnemy class. Listing 28.3 shows the class PlayerFollowingEnemy that
defines an enemy following the player if the player is moving around. This is done
by checking if the enemy is currently walking in the direction where the player is
standing (only taking the x-direction into account). If not, the enemy turns around.
We have placed a limitation on the enemy's intelligence by only doing that if the
player is not moving in the x direction (in other words: the player's x velocity is
zero). You should never make your enemies too smart. Enemies are there to be
beaten by the player so that the player can win the game. Playing a game where the
enemies are too smart or unbeatable is not a lot of fun, unless you like dying over
and over again!

28.4 Other Types of Enemies

Yet another enemy we would like to add to the game is a sneezing turtle. Why a
turtle, you might ask. And why a sneezing one? Well, we do not really have the
answer to that question. But the idea behind this enemy is that it has both a negative
and a positive side. On the negative side, the turtle grows spikes when it sneezes, so
you should not touch it. But if the turtle is not sneezing, you can use the turtle to
jump higher. Since we will not deal with interaction just yet, we will only add the
animated turtle for now. The turtle can be used for jumping during 5 seconds, then

it sneezes and grows spikes for 5 seconds, after which it returns to the previous state again for 5 seconds, and so on.

The enemy is represented by the Turtle class, which is setup in a similar fashion to the previous enemies. A turtle has two states: it has spikes, or not. In this case, we maintain two member variables to maintain in which state we are and how much time has passed in that state: the idleTime variable maintains how much time is left in the 'idle' state, and the sneezeTime variable maintains how much time is left in the 'sneezing' (dangerous) state. Again, in the Update method we handle the transition between the two phases, in a similar fashion to the rocket and the patrolling enemies. We will not go into detail here, since the code is so similar. If you want to have a look at the complete code, check out the TickTick3 program in the solution belonging to this chapter.

Sparky is the final enemy type that we will add to the game. Just like the other enemies, Sparky also has two states. Sparky is a very dangerous electricity-loving enemy. Sparky hangs quietly in the air, until he receives a bolt of energy. When that happens, he falls down. While Sparky is hanging in the air, he is not dangerous, but as soon as he falls, do not touch him! Have a look at the Sparky class to see what the code looks like.

> **Enemy software architecture**—As you can see, all these different types of enemies look different and behave different, but they generally have a very common class design. You could probably design a better way to define these enemies by using a couple of generic classes that allow one to define states and transitions between them. There could be conditions attached to each transition, such as that a certain amount of time must have passed or that an animation should be finished playing. We call such a structure a *finite state machine* It is a very common technique using in artificial intelligent systems. If you are up to the challenge, try to write a finite state machine library, and redefine the existing enemies to use it!

28.5 Loading the Different Types of Enemies

Now that we have defined different varieties of enemies, the only thing left to do is load them from the level definition file. We have designed the sprites for each of these different enemies, which we identify using characters. We store these enemy characters in a GameObjectList object, which we create in the Level class constructor:

```
this.Add(new GameObjectList(2, "enemies"));
```

Depending on the character that we read when loading the level, we call a different method for loading the enemy, by adding a few cases to the **switch** instruction in the Level class:

```
case 'T':
    return LoadTurtleTile(x, y);
case 'R':
    return LoadRocketTile(x, y, true);
case 'r':
    return LoadRocketTile(x, y, false);
case 'S':
    return LoadSparkyTile(x, y);
case 'A':
case 'B':
case 'C':
    return LoadFlameTile(x, y, tileType);}
```

Loading an enemy is rather straightforward. We simply create an instance of the enemy we would like to add, set its position, and add it to the enemies list of game objects. For example, here is the method for loading a turtle enemy:

```
private Tile LoadTurtleTile(int x, int y)
{
    GameObjectList enemies = this.Find("enemies") as GameObjectList;
    TileField tiles = this.Find("tiles") as TileField;
    Turtle enemy = new Turtle();
    enemy.Position = new Vector2(((float)x + 0.5f) * tiles.CellWidth,
                                 (y + 1) * tiles.CellHeight + 25.0f);
    enemies.Add(enemy);
    return new Tile();
}
```

We now have defined a few different kinds of enemies, with varying intelligence and capabilities. It is up to you to define enemies that are smarter, more deviant, or even more stupid, depending on the needs of your game. We did not apply any physics to the enemies. However, once you start building smarter enemies that for example can also jump or fall, you are going to need physics just like we implemented for the player. As an exercise, try to think how you can make these enemies smarter, without having to rely on physics. Can you let them move faster when the player is nearby? Or perhaps you can create an enemy that launches particles toward the player? The possibilities are endless, so try these things out for yourself!

28.6 What You Have Learned

In this chapter, you have learned:

• how to define different kinds of enemies;
• how to use inheritance to create variety in behavior of enemies.

Chapter 29
Adding Player Interaction

29.1 Introduction

In this chapter, we will add more interaction between the player and the objects in the level. Currently, the player can walk around, and there is a basic physics system that allows the player to jump, collide with wall tiles, or fall out of the screen. First, we will look at a very simple kind of interaction: collecting the water drops. Then, we will show how to create the behavior that allows the player to slide over ice. Finally, we will deal with the part of the program that deals with the various player–enemy interactions in the game.

29.2 Collecting Water Drops

The first thing we are going to add is the possibility for the player to collect the water drops. A player collects a water drop if the bomb character collides with that drop. In that case, we make the drop invisible. The place where we will do this is in the WaterDrop class. The reason for this is clear: like before, each game object is responsible for its own behavior. If we handle these collisions in the WaterDrop class, each water drop checks if it collides with the player. We write this code in the Update method. The first step is retrieving the player:

```
Player player = GameWorld.Find("player") as Player;
```

If the water drop is currently visible, we check if the water drop collides with the player using the CollidesWith method. If so, we set the visibility status of the drop to **false**. Furthermore, we also play a sound to let the player know that the water drop has been collected:

```
if (this.visible && this.CollidesWith(player))
{
```

```
this.visible = false;
GameEnvironment.AssetManager.PlaySound("Sounds/snd_watercollected");
}
```

The **this**.visible expression in the condition of the **if** instruction is very important. If we left that out, the 'water collected' sound would be played every time there was a collision, even after the drop has been made invisible, and this is not what we want. Later on, we can check if the level is completed by checking the visibility of each water drop. If all water drops are invisible, then we know that the player has collected all of them.

29.3 Ice Blocks

Another type of interaction that we would like to add to the game is special behavior when the player is walking over ice. When the player moves over ice, we want the character to continue sliding, and not stop moving when the player release the arrow key. This means we have to do two things:

- extend the HandleInput method to deal with moving over ice;
- calculate whether the player is standing on ice or not.

We will keep track of whether the player is standing on ice or not in a member variable walkingOnIce in the Player class. Let us assume for now that this variable is updated somewhere else, and let us first have a look at extending the HandleInput method. The first thing we want to do is increase the walking speed when the player is walking on ice. We can do that as follows:

```
float walkingSpeed = 400;
if (walkingOnIce)
    walkingSpeed *= 1.5f;
```

Then, we handle the actual player input. If the player is pressing the left or right arrow key, we set the appropriate *x* velocity:

```
if (inputHelper.IsKeyDown(Keys.Left))
    velocity.X = −walkingSpeed;
else if (inputHelper.IsKeyDown(Keys.Right))
    velocity.X = walkingSpeed;
```

We then add another alternative to this **if** instruction that sets the *x* velocity to zero. We could simply do this:

```
else
    velocity.X = 0f;
```

The result of which would be that as soon as the player releases the left or right arrow key, the *x* velocity would become zero. However, there are two situations in which case we do not want this to happen, namely if the player is not on the ground, or if the player is moving on ice. Therefore, we will only set the *x* velocity to zero if the player is not walking on ice, and the player is standing on the ground:

```
else if (!walkingOnIce && isOnTheGround)
    velocity.X = 0.0f;
```

The only thing we still need to do is find out whether the player is walking on ice or not, and update the walkingOnIce member variable accordingly. We already look at the tiles surrounding the player in the HandleCollisions method, so if we extend that method to also check if the player is walking on ice, we only need to add a few lines of code.

In the beginning of this method, we assume that we are not walking on ice:

```
walkingOnIce = false;
```

We can only walk on ice, if we are on the ground. We check if we are on the ground in the following **if** instruction:

```
if (previousYPosition <= tileBounds.Top && tileType != TileType.Background)
{
    isOnTheGround = true;
    velocity.Y = 0;
}
```

In order to check if the tile we are standing on is an ice tile, we have to retrieve the tile from the tile field and check its Ice property. We can simply access this tile through the currentTile variable that contains the current tile. Finally we update the walkingOnIce variable. We use a logical or operator, so that if the player is only partly on an ice tile, the variable will also be set to **true**:

```
if (currentTilo != null)
    walkingOnIce = walkingOnIce || currentTile.Ice;
```

We only perform this instruction if the currentTile variable does not point to **null**. The reason we use the logical or to calculate whether we are walking on ice is to take all surrounding tiles into account. The effect is that the character will keep on moving until he/she is not standing on an ice tile anymore (not even partly).

29.4 Enemies Colliding with the Player

The final kind of interaction that we would like to add is collisions with enemies. In many cases, when the player collides with an enemy, it causes the player's untimely demise. In some cases, we have to do something special (such as jumping extra high when jumping on the turtle). On the player side, we have to load an extra animation for the player dying. Because we do not want to handle input of the player anymore once he/she has died, we need to update the current alive status of the player. We do this by a member variable isAlive that we set to **true** in the constructor of the Player class. Inside the HandleInput method, we first check if the player is still alive. If not, we do not handle any input by returning from the method:

```
if (!isAlive)
    return;
```

Furthermore, we will add a method called Die to let the player die. There are two ways the player can die: by falling in a hole out of the game screen, or by colliding with an enemy. Therefore, we pass a boolean parameter to the Die method to indicate if the player died by falling or by colliding with an enemy.

In the Die method, we do a couple of things. First, we check if the player was already dead. If so, we return from the method without doing anything (after all, you can only die once). We first set the isAlive variable to **false**. Then, we set the velocity in the x direction to zero, to stop the player from moving to the left or the right. We do not reset the y-velocity, so that the player keeps on falling: gravity does not cease to exist when you die. Then, we determine which sound to play upon dying. If the player falls to death, the sound produced is quite different from dying by an enemy's hand (do not try this for real, just take our word for it). If the player dies because of a collision with an enemy, we give the player an upward velocity as well. Finally, we play the 'die' animation. The complete method is given as follows:

```
public void Die(bool falling)
{
    if (!isAlive)
        return;
    isAlive = false;
    velocity.X = 0.0f;
    if (falling)
        GameEnvironment.AssetManager.PlaySound("Sounds/snd_player_fall");
    else
    {
        velocity.Y = -900;
        GameEnvironment.AssetManager.PlaySound("Sounds/snd_player_die");
    }
    this.PlayAnimation("die");
}
```

We can check in the Update method if the player is falling to death by calculating if the player's y-position falls outside of the screen. If this is the case, we call the Die method:

```
TileField tiles = GameWorld.Find("tiles") as TileField;
if (BoundingBox.Top >= tiles.Rows * tiles.CellHeight)
    this.Die(true);
```

In the beginning of the Update method, we call the **base**.Update method to ensure that the animation is updated. Then, we do the physics and collisions (which still needs to be done, even if the player is dead). Then, we check if the player is alive. If not, we are done, and we return from the method.

Now that the player can die in various gruesome ways, we have to extend the enemy classes to deal with the collisions. In the Rocket class, we added a method called CheckPlayerCollision, which we call in the rocket's Update method. Inside the CheckPlayerCollision method, we simply check if the player collides with the rocket. If that is the case, we call the Die method on the player object. The complete method is given as follows:

```
public void CheckPlayerCollision()
{
    Player player = GameWorld.Find("player") as Player;
    if (this.CollidesWith(player))
        player.Die(false);
}
```

In the case of the patrolling enemy, we do exactly the same. We add the same method to that class, and call it from the Update method. The version in the Sparky class is slightly different. The player should only die if Sparky is currently being electrocuted. Therefore, we slightly change the method, as follows:

```
Player player = GameWorld.Find("player") as Player;
if (this.CollidesWith(player) && idleTime <= 0.0f)
    player.Die(false);
```

Finally, the turtle enemy adds even more behavior. As a first step, we check if the turtle collides with the player. If that is not the case, we simply return from the CheckPlayerCollision method since we are done:

```
Player player = GameWorld.Find("player") as Player;
if (!this.CollidesWith(player))
    return;
```

If there is a collision, there are two possibilities. The first one is that the turtle is currently sneezing. In that case the player dies:

```
if (sneezeTime > 0)
    player.Die(false);
```

The second case is that the turtle is in waiting mode, and the player is jumping on the turtle. In that case the player should make an extra high jump. An easy way to check if the player is jumping on the turtle is by looking at the *y* velocity. We assume that if that velocity is positive the player is jumping on the turtle. In that case, we call the Jump method to make the player jump extra high:

```
else if (idleTime > 0 && player.Velocity.Y > 0)
    player.Jump(1500);
```

This completes the main interaction programming. In the next chapter, we will finish this game by adding some mountains and moving clouds in the background. We will also manage the transitions between the levels.

29.5 What You Have Learned

In this chapter, you have learned:

- how to program various kinds of player interaction, between water drops and enemies;
- how to program ice tile behavior;
- how to let the player die in certain situations.

Chapter 30
Finishing the Game

30.1 Introduction

In this chapter, we will finish the Tick Tick game. First, we will add a timer such that the player has a limited amount of time to complete each level. Then, we will add a few mountains and clouds to the background to make the game visually more interesting. Finally, we will discuss progressing through the levels by adding two extra game states: the 'game over' state, and the 'level finished' state.

30.2 Adding a Timer

The first thing we will look at is adding a *timer* to the game. We do not want the timer to take up too much screen space, so we opt for a text-version of the timer. Therefore, the TimerGameObject class inherits from the TextGameObject class. We want to be able to pause the timer (for example, when the level is finished), so we add a boolean variable running that we can get and set through a property Running. Furthermore, we store the time that is still left in a TimeSpan object. This class is not only useful for representing a timespan, but it also includes convenient methods for converting the time span into a string and more. We override the Reset method to initialize the object. We want to give the player 30 seconds to finish each level. We use the static method FromMinutes in the TimeSpan class to create a TimeSpan instance for us:

```
public override void Reset()
{
    base.Reset();
    this.timeLeft = TimeSpan.FromMinutes(0.5);
    this.running = true;
}
```

For convenience, we also add a property GameOver that indicates if the timer has reached zero. We will use this property later on to handle the event that the player does not finish the level in time:

A. Egges et al., *Learning C# by Programming Games*,   393
DOI 10.1007/978-3-642-36580-5_30, © Springer-Verlag Berlin Heidelberg 2013

```
public bool GameOver
{
    get { return (timeLeft.Ticks <= 0); }
}
```

Now, the only thing we still need to do is implement the Update method to program the timer behavior. As a first step, we only update the timer if it is running. So if the timer is not running, we return from the method:

```
if (!running)
    return;
```

Then, as usual we subtract the elapsed game time from the current remaining time:

```
timeLeft −= gameTime.ElapsedGameTime;
```

Now, we create the text that we want to print on the screen. For that, we can use the formatting methods of the DateTime class. We also set the color of the text to yellow, so that it better fits the design of the game:

```
DateTime timeleft = new DateTime(timeLeft.Ticks);
this.Text = timeleft.ToString("mm:ss");
this.color = Color.Yellow;
```

As you can see, the DateTime class has a special ToString method, which takes a formatting string as a parameter. In this case, we allow two digits for the minutes and two digits for the seconds, separated by a colon.

Finally, we want to warn the player if he/she does not have a lot of time left to finish the level. We do this by alternating between a red and a yellow color when printing the text on the screen. This we can do using an **if**-instruction and smartly using the modulus operator.

```
if (timeLeft.TotalSeconds <= 10 && (int)timeLeft.TotalSeconds % 2 == 0)
    this.color = Color.Red;
```

30.2.1 Making the Timer Go Faster or Slower

Depending on the kind of tile the player is walking on, the time should go faster or slower. Walking on a hot tile will increase the speed at which time passes, walking on an ice tile will decrease it. In order to allow for a timer running at different speeds, we introduce a *multiplier* value in the TimerGameObject class. We gain access to this multiplier using a property:

```
public double Multiplier
{
    get {return multiplier; }
    set { multiplier = value; }
}
```

Unfortunately, TimeSpan objects cannot be multiplied directly with **double** values. Therefore, we first calculate the total number of seconds passed times the multiplier value:

```
double totalSeconds = gameTime.ElapsedGameTime.TotalSeconds ∗ multiplier;
```

Then, we convert this value into a TimeSpan object, and we subtract it from the total time left:

```
timeLeft −= TimeSpan.FromSeconds(totalSeconds);
```

Now that we can change the speed at which the time passes, we can do this depending on the kind of tile that the player is walking on. We already maintain a variable walkingOnIce, which indicates whether we are walking on an ice tile. In order to handle hot tiles as well, we define another variable walkingOnHot, in which we will maintain if we are walking on a hot tile or not. In order to determine the value of this variable, we follow the exact same approach as we did for the walkingOnIce variable. In the HandleCollisions method, we initially set this variable to **false**:

```
walkingOnHot = false;
```

Then, we add one line of code to update the value of the variable depending on the current tile we are standing on:

```
walkingOnHot = walkingOnHot || currentTile.Hot;
```

For the complete code, see the Player class belonging to the TickTick5 example.

Using the walkingOnIce and walkingOnHot variables, we can now update the timer multiplier. We do this in the Update method of the player:

```
TimerGameObject timer = GameWorld.Find("timer") as TimerGameObject;
if (walkingOnHot)
    timer.Multiplier = 2;
else if (walkingOnIce)
    timer.Multiplier = 0.5;
else
    timer.Multiplier = 1;
```

Adapting to the skills of the player—Changing the speed of the timer can make a level much easier or harder. You could extend the game so that in some cases the timer would stop, or move back a few seconds if the player picks up a special item. You could even make the level progression adaptive, so that if the player dies too often, the maximum time of 30 seconds per level is increased. However, you should watch out with this. If helping the player is done in a too obvious way, the player will realize it and adapt his/her strategy to it (in other words, the player starts playing worse in order to make the levels easier). Also, the player might feel he/she is not treated seriously. A better way in this case to deal with adapting the maximum time per level is by allowing the player to (partly) transfer time left over from previous levels to the current level. That way, difficult levels can be made easier, but the player has to do something for it.

30.2.2 *When the Timer Reaches Zero...*

When the player does not finish the level on time, the bomb explodes, and the game is over. We added a boolean member variable to the Player class that indicates if the player has exploded. We then add a method called Explode to the class that sets the explosion in motion. This is the complete method:

```
public void Explode()
{
    if (!isAlive || finished)
        return;
    isAlive = false;
    exploded = true;
    velocity = Vector2.Zero;
    position.Y += 15;
    this.PlayAnimation("explode");
}
```

First off, we cannot explode if we were not alive in the first place, or if we finished the level. In either of those cases, we simply return from the method. Then, we set the alive status to **false** and the exploded status to **true**. We set the velocity to zero (explosions do not move). We slightly increase the *y* position to better align the explosion animation to the character position, and finally, we play the 'explode' animation. This animation is stored in a sprite sheet and consists of 25 frames of an explosion animation.

Since gravity also no longer affects an exploded character, we only do the gravity physics if the player is not exploded:

if (!exploded)
    velocity.Y += 55;

In the Update method of the Level class, we then check if the timer has reached zero, and if so, we call the Explode method.

if (timer.GameOver)
    player.Explode();

30.3 Drawing Mountains and Clouds

In order to make the level background a bit more interesting, let us add mountains and clouds to it. We do this in the Level constructor. First, let us have a look at how to add a few mountains. For that, we use a **for**-instruction. In the body of that instruction, we create a sprite game object, give it a position and add it to the backgrounds list. This is the complete **for**-instruction:

```
for (int i = 0; i < 5; i++)
{
    SpriteGameObject mountain=new SpriteGameObject("Backgrounds/spr_mountain_" +
                            (GameEnvironment.Random.Next(2) + 1), 1);
    mountain.Position = new Vector2((float)GameEnvironment.Random.NextDouble() *
                        GameEnvironment.Screen.X − mountain.Width / 2,
                        GameEnvironment.Screen.Y − mountain.Height);
    backgrounds.Add(mountain);
}
```

The first step is to create the sprite game object. Since we have two different mountain sprites, we randomly select one of them using the random number generator. Then, we calculate the position of the mountain. The x position is chosen randomly, and we use a fixed y position so that the mountain is at the appropriate height (we do not want mountains hanging in the sky). Finally, the mountain object is added to the backgrounds list.

For clouds, we will do something slightly more complicated. We want the clouds to move from left to right or vice versa, and if a cloud disappears from the screen, we want a new one to appear. In order to do this, we added a Clouds class, which takes care of this. We create an instance of this class in the Level constructor, and assign it a layer value of two, so that the clouds are drawn in front of the mountains:

```
Clouds clouds = new Clouds(2);
backgrounds.Add(clouds);
```

Since the Clouds class contains a number of moving clouds, it is a subclass of the GameObjectList class. Inside the constructor, we use a **for**-instruction to create a number of clouds and add them to the list. Each cloud is given a random position and a random *x* velocity. Then, we add an Update method to the Clouds class, in which we check if a cloud has exited the screen. Since we need to do this for each cloud game object, we do this using a **foreach**-instruction that traverses all the game objects in the list. If a cloud has exited the screen, we create a new cloud object with a random position and velocity. A cloud can exit the screen either on the left side or on the right side. If a cloud is positioned outside of the screen on the *left*, and its *x* velocity is *negative*, we know it has exited the screen. If the cloud is positioned outside of the screen on the *right* side, and its velocity is *positive*, we also know it has exited the screen. We can capture these two situations for a cloud c in the following **if**-instruction:

```
if ((c.Velocity.X < 0 && c.Position.X + c.Width < 0) ||
    (c.Velocity.X > 0 && c.Position.X > GameEnvironment.Screen.X))
    // remove this cloud and add a new one
```

Removing the cloud is easy:

```
this.Remove(c);
```

Then, we create a new cloud game object:

```
SpriteGameObject cloud = new SpriteGameObject("Backgrounds/spr_cloud_"
                            + (GameEnvironment.Random.Next(5) + 1));
```

We assign an *x* velocity to this cloud, which can be either positive or negative. The *y* velocity of the cloud is always zero, so that the cloud only moves horizontally:

```
cloud.Velocity = new Vector2((float)(
                    (GameEnvironment.Random.NextDouble() * 2) − 1) * 20, 0);
```

Then, we calculate a random cloud height by multiplying the *y* screen resolution with a random number between zero and one. From that number, we subtract half of the cloud height to make sure that we never generate a cloud that is drawn fully below the screen:

```
float cloudHeight = (float)GameEnvironment.Random.NextDouble() *
                    GameEnvironment.Screen.Y − cloud.Height / 2;
```

We position the cloud either at the left border or the right border of the screen, depending on the direction in which the cloud is moving:

```
if (cloud.Velocity.X < 0)
    cloud.Position = new Vector2(GameEnvironment.Screen.X, cloudHeight);
else
    cloud.Position = new Vector2(−cloud.Width, cloudHeight);
```

Now we add the new cloud to the list:

this.Add(cloud);

Let us look at the complete code one more time:

```
foreach (GameObject obj in gameObjects)
{
    SpriteGameObject c = obj as SpriteGameObject;
    if (/* c is outside of the screen */)
    {
        this.Remove(c);
        SpriteGameObject cloud = new SpriteGameObject(...);
        // calculate cloud position and velocity
        // ...
        this.Add(cloud);
    }
}
```

If you look closely at the code inside the loop, you see that we are removing and adding objects to a list while we are traversing it with a **foreach**-instruction. If we ran the program like this, we would get a System.InvalidOperationException at some point. We are allowed to modify the list (adding or removing elements) inside a **foreach**-instruction, but we can no longer continue traversing the list afterwards, since the list has changed. Therefore, we need to *break* out of the loop using either a **break** or a **return** call. As a result, there is a chance that, if two clouds move out of the screen, one of the two is still outside of the screen after this **foreach**-instruction. However, in this case it is not a problem, since that cloud will be taken care of in the next iteration of the game loop.

30.4 Finalizing the Level Progression

To complete the game, we still need to add the game states for dealing with the event that the player has lost, or that the player has won a level. We approach this in a fashion similar to how we handled it in the Penguin Pairs game, except that here we have an explicit 'game over' game state, next to the 'level finished' game state. These states are coded in a fairly straightforward way, similar to how we did it in previous games. You can find the complete code in the GameOverState and LevelFinished state classes in the TickTick5 example belonging to this chapter.

For determining if the player has finished a level, we add a property Completed to the Level class that checks for two things:

- has the player collected all the water drops?
- has the player reached the end sign?

Both of these things are fairly easy to check. For checking if the player reached the end sign, we can see if their bounding boxes are intersecting. Checking if the player has collected all the water drops can be done by verifying that all water drops are invisible. This is the complete property:

```
public bool Completed
{
    get
    {
        SpriteGameObject exitObj = this.Find("exit") as SpriteGameObject;
        Player player = this.Find("player") as Player;
        if (!exitObj.CollidesWith(player))
            return false;
        GameObjectList waterdrops = this.Find("waterdrops") as GameObjectList;
        foreach (GameObject d in waterdrops.Objects)
            if (d.Visible)
                return false;
        return true;
    }
}
```

Inside the Update method of the Level class, we then check if the level was completed. If so, we call the LevelFinished method in the Player class, which plays the 'celebration' animation:

```
if (this.Completed && timer.Running)
{
    player.LevelFinished();
    timer.Running = false;
}
```

Inside the PlayingState class, we then deal with switching to other states depending on the state of the level. These lines of code in the Update method are responsible for that:

```
public virtual void Update(GameTime gameTime)
{
    CurrentLevel.Update(gameTime);
    if (CurrentLevel.GameOver)
        GameEnvironment.GameStateManager.SwitchTo("gameOverState");
    else if (CurrentLevel.Completed)
    {
        CurrentLevel.Solved = true;
        GameEnvironment.GameStateManager.SwitchTo("levelFinishedState");
    }
}
```

The code for dealing with transitions between levels is fairly straightforward and is almost a copy of the code used in the Penguin Pairs game. And that means that we have now completely shown you how to build a platform game with commonly occurring elements such as collecting items, avoiding enemies, game physics, going from one level to another, and so on. So does it end here? Well, that depends on you. In order to make Tick Tick a game that is commercially viable, a lot of work still has to be done. You probably want to define more of everything: more levels, more enemies, more different items to pickup, more challenges, more sounds. You may also want to introduce a few things that we did not address in this book: playing with other players over a network, side scrolling, maintaining a high score, playing in-game movies between levels, and you can probably think of a couple of other things that are interesting to add. Use the Tick Tick game as a starting point for your own game. With the techniques that we have provided you with in this book, you should be able to do this on your own now. Your only limit is your own creativity!

Publishing games—Now that you are programming your own games, you might have started to think about how to get your games published. Maybe you want to publish games just for the achievement, but maybe you also want to make some money with it. Fortunately, nowadays getting games published is very easy. For mobile devices there are app stores to which you can submit your games. And you can of course make your games available on your own website.

The challenge lies in making your game visible. On iOS or Android more than 100 new games appear every day. Most of them are played just by a few people. And if you create your own website for the game, how are you going to get any visitors?

First of all, you need to produce a quality game. Do not think you can do everything yourself. If you are a good programmer it does not mean you are also a good artist. And, unfortunately for you, initially it is often the visuals that determine whether a person is going to try your game. It is a good idea to form a team with an artist and maybe also with a game designer and an audio expert.

Do not be over-ambitious. You are not going to create the next Halo! Set reasonable goals. Start with small, but excellent games. Do not trust your own judgment. Talk to others about your game and let them play prototypes to make sure players actually like your game.

Get yourself connected. Be active in social networks, start your own blog, post on forums, and so on. You are going to be an Indie developer so check out websites like http://www.indiegames.com/ to learn what other Indies are doing. Be active in game jams, like the Global Game Jam (http://www.globalgamejam.org/) to meet other developers.

When your game is nearing completion, make a marketing plan. Post about your game wherever you can, make a press kit, create a video, send information to blogs and other websites, and so on. People will only play your game when they hear about it. So you would better make a lot of noise.

30.5 What You Have Learned

In this chapter, you have learned:

- how to add a timer to a level;
- how to create animated backgrounds consisting of mountains and clouds.

Appendix A
Exercises and Challenges

A.1 Exercises and Challenges for Part I

Exercises

1. *Programming paradigms*
   Indicate whether the following statements are true or not (and explain why):
   (a) All imperative languages are object-oriented.
   (b) There are object-oriented languages that are not procedural.
   (c) Procedural languages have to be compiled.
   (d) Declarative languages cannot run on the same processor are imperative languages, since that processor can execute an assignment instruction, which doesn't exist in declarative languages.

2. *The compiler as a program*
   A compiler itself is also a program.
   (a) Can the compiler itself be written in a higher programming language?
   (b) And if so, can that language be the same as the language that the compiler compiles?
   (c) If so, can the compiler compile itself?

3. *Names*
   In mathematics and physics, it is quite common to use fixed variable and constant names. Which ones? Is this useful?

4. *Classes and types*
   Name five standard classes, and for three of those, also name a method that belongs to it. Also name three types that are not classes.

5. *Comments*
   What are the two ways to write comments in a C# program?

A. Egges et al., *Learning C# by Programming Games*, 403
DOI 10.1007/978-3-642-36580-5, © Springer-Verlag Berlin Heidelberg 2013

6. *Concepts*

Provide short definitions of the concepts 'instruction', 'variable', 'method', and 'object'. Which two relations does the concept 'class' have with these concepts?

7. *Declaration, instruction, expression*

What's the difference between a declaration, an instruction and an expression?

8. *Statement versus instruction*

Many programming books use the word 'statement' to indicate an instruction in a programming language. Why do you think we avoid that word in this book?

9. *Changing names*

Look at the class DiscoWorld that we discussed in Chap. 4. What do we have to change if we wanted to change the name of this class into Hello? What is not necessary to change, but is logical to change anyway?

10. *Syntactical categories*

Indicate for each of the following program fragments to which syntactical category it belongs: (M)ethod call, (D)eclaration, (E)xpression, (I)nstruction, and (A)ssignment. There may be 0, 1, or 2 correct answers for each.

int x;	**int** 23;	(y+1)*x	**new** Color(0,0,0)
(**int**)x	23	(x+y)(x−1)	**new** Color black;
int(x)	23x0	x+1=y+1;	Color blue;
int x	x=23;	x=y+1;	GraphicsDevice.Clear(Color.White);
int x, **double** y;	"x=23;"	spriteBatch.Begin();	Content.RootDirectory = "Content";
int x, y;	x23	Math.Sqrt(23)	Color.CornflowerBlue
"/"	0x23	"\\"	Color.CornflowerBlue.ToString()
"\"	23%x	(x%23)	game.Run()
"//"	x/*23*/	""	23=x;

11. *Relation between syntactical categories*

Have another look at the five syntactical categories mentioned in the previous exercise, but now add a sixth one: C(onstant).

(a) Which of the combinations of 2 categories are possible? For example: M+D is possible if there exists a program fragment that is both a method call and a declaration.

(b) Which of the six categories are always together with which others?

(c) Which of the six categories always ends with a semicolon? Which sometimes? Which never?

12. *Variable assignment*
Consider the following two variable declarations and assignments:

```
int x, y;
x = 40;
y = 12;
```

Indicate for each of the following groups of instructions what the values of x and y are when these instructions are executed after the above declarations and instructions.

y = x+1;	x = y;	x = y+1;	x = x+y;	y = x/3;	y = 2/3*x;	y = x%6;
x = y+1;	y = x;	y = x−1;	y = x−y;	x = y*3;	x = 2*x/3;	x = x/6;
			x = x−y;			

In one of the cases, the values of x and y are swapped. Does this work for all possible values of x and y? If so, why is that? If not, in what cases does it fail?

13. *Multiplying and dividing*
Is there a difference between the following three instructions?

```
position = 300 − 3*time / 2;
position = 300 − 3/2 * time;
position = 300 − time/2 * 3;
```

14. *Hours, minutes, seconds*
Suppose that the integer variable time contains a (possibly large) number of seconds. Write down a number of instructions that assign a value to the variables hours, minutes and seconds corresponding to their meaning, where the values of minutes and seconds should be smaller than 60. Secondly, write the instruction that performs the reverse operation. So, given the variables hours, minutes, and seconds, calculate the value that the variable time should contain.

15. *The game loop*
Which actions does the game loop consist of? Which actions are executed only once, and which actions are executed multiple times? What is the use of these different actions?

16. *Updating and drawing*
We could put all the code from the Update method in the Draw method, and leave out the Update method altogether. Why is it still useful to have different methods?

Challenges

1. *Changing colors*
   In this challenge, we're going to modify the DiscoWorld example explained in
   Chap. 4.
   (a) Change the program so that the color changes from black to blue instead of
       from black to red.
   (b) Now modify the program so that the color changes from black to purple.
       Can you also modify the program so that the color changes from *purple to
       black*?

2. *Drawing sprites in different locations*
   As a basis for this challenge, we use the SpriteDrawing example explained in
   Chap. 4.
   (a) Modify the program so that three balloons are drawn: one in the top right
       corner of the screen, one in the bottom left corner of the screen, and one in
       the middle of the screen. (Hint: use the Width and Height properties part of the
       Texture2D class.)
   (b) Find a few nice sprites on the Internet (confetti, clowns, candy, or any other
       party-related things) and draw them on the screen at different positions.
       Search for appropriate background music and play it when the application
       starts.

3. *Flying balloons*
   This challenge uses the FlyingSprites example (also from Chap. 4) as a basis.
   (a) Modify the program so that the balloon flies from the top to the bottom of
       the screen.
   (b) Now modify the program so that the balloon flies in circles around the point
       that indicates the center of the screen. Use the Sin or Cos methods that are
       available in the Math class. Define a constant that contains the speed at which
       the balloon turns around the center point. Also define a constant that con-
       tains the distance from the balloon to the center point (e.g. the radius of the
       circle).
   (c) Change the program so that the balloon flies in circles around a point moving
       from the left to the right.
   (d) Change the program so that a second balloon also turns in circles around
       that point, but in the opposite direction, and with a bigger radius. Feel free
       to try a couple of other things as well such as: a balloon that flies in a circle
       around another flying balloon, or use another Math method to change the
       position of the balloon. Don't go too crazy on this or you'll end up with a
       headache!
   (e) Finally, add a few flying objects (you could for example use the 'spr_ball_xx'
       sprites for that) that bounce off the edges of the screen, by using the Sign
       method in the Math class.

A.2 Exercises and Challenges for Part II

Exercises

1. *Keywords*
   (a) What does the word **void** mean, and when do we need this keyword?
   (b) What does the word **int** mean, and when do we need this keyword?
   (c) What does the word **return** mean in a C# instruction, and when do we need it?
   (d) What does the word **this** mean in a C# instruction, and when do we need it? In what kind of method can we not use this word?

2. *Type conversions*
   Suppose that the following declarations have been made:

   ```
   int x;
   string s;
   double d;
   ```

   Expand the following assignments with the necessary type conversions (assuming that the string indeed represents a number):

   ```
   x = d;
   x = s;
   s = x;
   s = d;
   d = x;
   d = s;
   ```

3. *Methods with a result*
   (a) Write a method RemainderAfterDivision with two parameters x and y, which returns the value of x%y, *without* using the % operator.
   (b) Write a method Circumference that gives as a result the circumference of a rectangle, whose width and height are given as parameters.
   (c) Write a method Diagonal that gives as a result the length of the diagonal of a rectangle, whose width and height are given as parameters.
   (d) Write a method ThreeTimes, that returns three concatenated copies of a string passed as a parameter. So, ThreeTimes("hurray!") should result in the string "hurray!hurray!hurray!".
   (e) Write a method SixtyTimes. that returns sixty concatenated copies of a string passed as a parameter. Try to limit the number of instructions in that method.
   (f) Write a method ManyTimes. that returns a number of concatenated copies of a string passed as a parameter, where that number is also passed as a parameter (you may assume that this number is 0 or larger). So, ManyTimes("what?", 4) should result in "what?what?what?what?".

4. *Cuneiform*

   (a) Write a method Stripes with a number as a parameter (you may assume that this parameter is 0 or larger). The method should give as a result a string with as many vertical dashes as the parameter indicates. For example, the call **this**.Stripes(5) results in "|||||".

   (b) Write a method Cuneiform with a number as a parameter. You may assume that this parameter will always be 1 or bigger. The method should give as a result a string containing the number in a cuneiform notation. In that notation, every number is represented by vertical dashes and the digits are separated by a horizontal dash. Horizontal dashes are also placed at the beginning and at the end of the string. Here are a few examples:

   - **this**.Cuneiform(25) results in "−||−|||||−"
   - **this**.Cuneiform(12345) results in "−|−||−|||−||||−|||||−"
   - **this**.Cuneiform(7) results in "−|||||||−"
   - **this**.Cuneiform(203) results in "−||−−|||−"

   Hint: deal with the last digit first and then repeat for the rest of the digits.

5. *Sequences*

   (a) Write a method Total with a number n as a parameter that returns the total of the numbers from 0 until n as a result. If n has a value smaller than or equal to 0, the method should return 0.

   (b) The factorial of a natural number is the result of the multiplication of all the numbers smaller than that number. For example, the factorial of 3 equals $1 \times 2 \times 3 = 6$. Write a method Factorial which calculates the factorial of its parameter. You may assume that the parameter always is larger than or equal to 1.

   (c) Write a method Power that has two parameters: a number x and an exponent n. The result should be x^n, so x is multiplied n times with itself. You may assume that n is a positive integer. The method should also work if n equals 0, and if x isn't an integer number.
   Hint: use a variable for calculating the result, and don't forget to give that variable an initial value!
   (Note: many programming languages have the power operator ^. C# doesn't have this operator, although there is a method Math.Pow. You are not allowed to use that method here otherwise this exercise would be too easy :)).

   (d) We can approximate the hyperbolic cosine of a real number x as follows:

   $$1 + \frac{x^2}{2!} + \frac{x^4}{4!} + \frac{x^6}{6!} + \frac{x^8}{8!} + \frac{x^{10}}{10!} + \cdots$$

   In this case, the notation 6! means factorial of 6. Write a method Coshyp that calculates this approximation by summing 20 of these terms and returning that value as a result.

6. *Prime numbers*
   (a) Write a method Even which indicates whether a number passed as a parameter is an even number. Determine what the best type is for the parameter and the return value.
   (b) Write a method MultipleOfThree that indicates whether its parameter is a multiple of three.
   (c) Write a method MultipleOf with two parameters x and y, that determines if x is a multiple of y.
   (d) Write a method Divisible with two parameters x and y that determines if x is divisible by y (so x/y should have no remainder).
   (e) Write a method SmallestDivider that determines the smallest integer number ≥ 2 by which the parameter can be divided.
   Hint: try the dividers one by one, and stop as soon as you found one.
   (f) Write a method that determines if a number is a prime number. This means that it is only divisible by 1 and by itself.

7. *Drawing the memory*
   Given are the following class definitions:

```
class One
{
    int x;
    public One()
    {
        x = 0;
    }
    public void SetX(int a)
    {
        x = a;
    }
}

class Two
{
    int x;
    One o;

    public Two(One b, int c)
    {
        o = b;
        x = c+1;
    }
    public One GetO()
    {
        return o;
    }
}
```

```
class Three : One
{
    Two p, q;
    public Three()
    {
        p = new Two(new One(), 1);
        p.GetO().SetX(7);
        q = new Two(p.GetO(), 2);
        q.GetO().SetX(8);
        p = new Two(this, 3);
        p.GetO().SetX(9);
    }
}
```

Make a drawing of what the memory looks like after executing:

```
Three t = new Three();
```

Just like the examples in this book, make a clear distinction between the name and the value of the variables: the name should be next to the boxes, and the value in it. Object-references should start with a clear dot inside the box of the reference variable, and point to the border of the object.

8. *Classes and inheritance*
   Given are the following class definitions:

```
class A
{
    public float var1;
    protected int var2;
    private bool var3;

    public float Var1
    {
        get { return var1; }
    }
    public int Var2
    {
        get { return var2; }
        set { if (value > 0) var2 = value; }
    }

    public void MethodInA()
    {
        ...
    }
}
```

```
class B : A
{
    public int var4;
    private int var5;

    public void MethodInB()
    {
        ...
    }
}
```

(a) Indicate if the following expressions are allowed in MethodInA:

this.var1	this.var2	this.var3
this.var4	this.Var2	base.var1

(b) Indicate if the following expressions are allowed in MethodInB:

this.var1	this.var2	this.var3
this.var5	this.Var2	base.var1
base.var2	base.var3	base.Var2

9. *Type checking*

   Are the types of expressions checked during the compilation phase, or when the program is running? There is a exception to this rule. In which case is this? And why is that exception necessary?

Challenges

1. *More flying balloons*

   This challenge uses the Balloon2 program from Chap. 5 as a basis.
   (a) Modify the program so that the balloon follows the mouse pointer, but with a delay. Hint: add a balloon velocity vector to the program, and change the velocity depending on the distance of the balloon to the mouse pointer.
   (b) Modify the program so that the balloon cannot fly outside of the screen. Take into account the width and height of the sprite.
   (c) Change the program so that the balloon flies in circles around a point moving from the left to the right.
   (d) Add a few flying balloons (in any direction you like) that bounce off the edges of the screen. Use the **if**-instruction to reverse their velocities.

2. *Extending the Painter game*

   This challenge uses the Painter game as a basis.

(a) Extend the game, so that there is a generic 'wind' parameter that varies throughout playing the game. When there is more wind, the paint cans and balloon rotate and move more heavily. If you define this 'wind' parameter as a vector, it can also be used to indicate the direction of the wind. The direction and strength of the wind then influences how the balloons move, but also how fast the ball moves.

(b) Make a two-player version of the game, where each player controls his/her own cannon (think of a good input mechanism for each player). You could make it a symmetrical game in that the players collaborate to give the paint cans the right color, and the player that colors the most paint can correctly wins the game. You could also make it an *asymmetrical* game, where the goal of one player is to correctly paint as many cans as possible, and the other player's goal is to obstruct the first player as much as possible.

A.3 Exercises and Challenges for Part III

Exercises

1. *Arrays*
    (a) Write a method CountZeros which has an array of integers as a parameter. The result of the method is the number of zeros in the array.
    (b) Write a method Add which has two integer arrays as parameters. You may assume that the length of each array is the same. The method adds the values in the two arrays and returns as a result another integer array. For example, given is an array array1 = {0, 3, 8, −4} and an array array2 = {10, 2, −8, 8}. The result of the method call add(array1, array2) will be another array {10, 5, 0, 4}.
    (c) Write a method FirstPosition which has two parameters: a **string** and a **char**. The method returns the first position of the character in the string. If the character doesn't occur in the string, the method should return −1. For example:

    ```
    int result = this.FirstPosition("arjan", 'a'); // returns 0
    result = this.FirstPosition("jeroen", 'a'); // return −1
    result = this.FirstPosition("mark", 'a'); // returns 1
    ```

2. **string** *methods*
    (a) The **string** class contains the method ToUpper that returns a version of the string containing only capital letters. You can call this method as follows:

    ```
    h = s.ToUpper();
    ```

    If you had to write the class **string** yourself, how would you implement this method (using other methods in the **string** class?

(b) Another method in the **string** class is the Replace method. This method returns a new string in which each character that corresponds to the character given as the first parameter is replaced by the character given as the second parameter. For example:

```
"Good morning".replace('o','u') // returns "Guud murning"
"A+2+#?".replace('+','9') // returns "A929#?"
```

Implement the Replace method (using other methods of the **string** class where necessary).

(c) Now let's have a look at the method EndsWith, which returns whether a string ends with the string passed as a parameter. For example:

```
"Allyourbasearebelongtous".endsWith("belongtous") // returns true
```

Implement the EndsWith method. You may use existing methods in the **string** class, except for the Substring and IndexOf methods.

3. *Highway*

Have a look at the program below. The program should draw a line of cars on the highway, as can be seen from the screenshot below. Every third car is a truck, and every second truck is a combination with a trailer.

```
public class Highway : Game
{
    public SpriteBatch spriteBatch;
    public Texture2D wheel, car, truck, connection, trailer;

    static void Main()
    {
        Highway game = new Highway();
        game.Run();
    }

    public Highway()
    {
        graphics = new GraphicsDeviceManager(this);
        graphics.PreferredBackBufferWidth = 1800;
        graphics.PreferredBackBufferHeight = 80;
        Content.RootDirectory = "Content";
        // TODO: missing part of the constructor
    }
```

```
    protected override void LoadContent()
    {
        spriteBatch = new SpriteBatch(this.GraphicsDevice);
        wheel = Content.Load<Texture2D>("wheel");
        car = Content.Load<Texture2D>("car");
        truck = Content.Load<Texture2D>("truck");
        connection = Content.Load<Texture2D>("connection");
        trailer = Content.Load<Texture2D>("trailer");
    }

    protected override void Draw(GameTime gameTime)
    {
        GraphicsDevice.Clear(Color.Grey);
        spriteBatch.Begin();
        for (int t = 0; t < road.Length; t++)
            road[t].Draw(this, t*120, 60);
        spriteBatch.End();
    }
}

class MotorizedVehicle
{
    public void Draw(Game g, int x, int y)
    {
    }
}

class Car : MotorizedVehicle
{
    public void Draw(Game g, int x, int y)
    {
        g.spriteBatch.Draw(g.car, new Vector2(x, y − 30), Color.Blue);
        g.spriteBatch.Draw(g.wheel, new Vector2(x + 5, y − 10), Color.Red);
        g.spriteBatch.Draw(g.wheel, new Vector2(x + 25, y − 10), Color.Red);
    }
}

class Truck : MotorizedVehicle
{
    public void Draw(Game g, int x, int y)
    {
        g.spriteBatch.Draw(g.truck, new Vector2(x, y − 45), Color.Green);
        g.spriteBatch.Draw(g.wheel, new Vector2(x + 5, y − 10), Color.Red);
        g.spriteBatch.Draw(g.wheel, new Vector2(x + 20, y − 10), Color.Red);
        g.spriteBatch.Draw(g.wheel, new Vector2(x + 55, y − 10), Color.Red);
    }
}
```

```
class Combination : Truck
{
    public void Draw(Game g, int x, int y)
    {
        // the truck
        g.spriteBatch.Draw(g.truck, new Vector2(x, y − 45), Color.Green);
        g.spriteBatch.Draw(g.wheel, new Vector2(x + 5, y − 10), Color.Red);
        g.spriteBatch.Draw(g.wheel, new Vector2(x + 20, y − 10), Color.Red);
        g.spriteBatch.Draw(g.wheel, new Vector2(x + 55, y − 10), Color.Red);
        // the trailer
        g.spriteBatch.Draw(g.connection, new Vector2(x − 5, y − 10), Color.Black);
        g.spriteBatch.Draw(g.trailer, new Vector2(x − 45, y − 45), Color.Green);
        g.spriteBatch.Draw(g.wheel, new Vector2(x − 40, y − 10), Color.Red);
        g.spriteBatch.Draw(g.wheel, new Vector2(x − 20, y − 10), Color.Red);
    }
}
```

(a) One declaration is still missing. Write down this declaration and indicate where it should be placed in the program.

(b) Write down the missing part of the Highway constructor.

(c) Because the program still contains an error, nothing is drawn on the screen. What error is this, and how can it be corrected?

(d) The programmer has duplicated quite some code with copy and paste. Why is that not a good idea?

(e) How could this code copying have been avoided?

(f) We would like to continue improving the object-oriented approach of this program, so that also the 'wheel' and 'trailer' concepts are modeled with classes. How can that be done properly? Make sure that code duplication is avoided as much as possible, and that a loose trailer can never end up on the highway because of a programming error. You don't have to completely implement this, just indicate which extra classes are needed, how they are related to their subclasses and which declarations are needed in new or existing classes.

4. *Searching and sorting*

(a) Write a method Largest which has as a parameter an array of doubles that gives as a result the *largest value* that occurs in the array.

(b) Write another method IndexLargest which has as a result the index in the array of the largest value. If there are more than one largest values in the array, the method should return the index of the first one.

(c) Write a method HowManySmallest which has as a parameter an array of doubles. The method should return how often the smallest value of the array occurs in it. For example, if the array contains the values 9, 12, 9, 7, 12, 7, 8, 25, 7, then the result of the method call will be 3 because the smallest value (7) occurs three times in the array.

(d) Write a special version of the IndexLargest method which doesn't look through the entire array, but only the first n elements, where n is passed as a parameter to the method.

(e) Write a method Sort, which has as a parameter an array of doubles. The return value type is **void**. After the method is called, the elements in the array should be sorted in increasing order.
Hint: first find the index of the largest value in the array (using the IndexLargest method). Then, swap this value with the value at the last index. After doing that, the largest value is already and the end of the array where it belongs. Then, find the largest value in the rest of the array and swap that value with the penultimate value in the array. And so on, until the entire array has been sorted.

(f) Write a method which has as parameters an array of integers and one single integer that returns as a result the index at which the single integer occurs first in the array. If the integer doesn't occur anywhere in the array, the method should return -1.

(g) (*more difficult*) If you know that the array is sorted, it is possible to search in a smarter way: look at the middle element in the array if it contains the value that you're looking for. If so, great! If not, you'll know if the element you're looking for is in the left part or in the right part of the array. This way, looking through the array becomes very efficient because at each iteration the part of the array you have to search through becomes half as big. Write this improved search method. Use two integers to keep track of the boundaries of the piece of array that you're searching in.

Challenges

1. *Weather control*
   In this challenge, we will extend the Snowflakes program from Chap. 12.
   (a) Extend the program by allowing for more or less snowflakes depending on user input (up arrow means more snow, down arrow means less snow). Set a maximum number of snowflakes (for example 1000). Make sure that the program is robust (never more than 1000 snowflakes, and no crash when you reach 0 snowflakes).
   (b) Extend the program so that there is varying wind. You can implement 'wind' by not letting the snowflakes fall down straight but according to an angle. Vary the angle with which the flakes fall down over time using random numbers. Try to find a range of random values and a rate of change that looks realistic.

2. *More jewels*
   This challenge is an extension of the Jewel Jam game.

(a) Extend the game so that sometimes all the colors of the jewels change. This can be something controlled by the player (if he/she is stuck), or it can be done randomly.

(b) When a valid combination of three jewels has been found, add a nice 'disappearing' effect for the jewels, such as making them smaller and smaller, or flying them outside of the screen in random directions.

(c) Add a feature where there is an extra restriction in some cases, such as only combinations allowed of the same color, or some jewels are not allowed in any combination.

3. *Tic-tac-toe*

Another nice example of a grid-based game is Tic-tac-toe. In this challenge, we'll go step-by-step through the important parts of building that game.

(a) Start by looking up some nice sprites that you can use for this game. In any case, you are going to need a sprite for the cross and a sprite for the circle. Once you've found these sprites, start by making a first version which only displays circles or crosses on a 3 × 3 grid on the screen. Here, you can reuse some of the classes that we built for the Jewel Jam game.

(b) Next, add player input to the game. When the player clicks in the screen, a cross should appear at that position in the grid. Make sure that you only add a cross to the grid if the position in the grid is free. In the first version, you can make it a two-player game, where each player takes a turn after the other by clicking somewhere. Therefore, you should keep track of whose turn it is, so that you can add the right element (cross or circle) to the grid.

(c) Now, you need to write the code that handles whether three symbols of the same type are in a row, column or diagonal. You can do this by using a couple of **for**-instructions that check each of the possible combinations.

(d) Finally, handle the different game states: indicate on the screen whose turn it is, show an overlay if the game has been finished, and add a restart option.

(e) (*difficult*) As a nice extension, you could program a single player mode, where the player has to play against the computer. The question is: how do you program the part where the computer decides what to do? A very well-known common way of implementing computer behavior in such games is by using the *Minimax* algorithm. The basic idea behind this algorithm is to represent all the possible ways that the game can be played as a tree, and then search through that tree to find an optimal path. The nodes in each tree represent a choice that is made by the player or by the computer, and the edges determine the sequence in which these choices are made.

In the case of tic-tac-toe, you can imagine the tree as follows. After starting the game, the first player has 9 possible locations to choose from. So from the root node there will be nine outgoing edges. After that, the second player can choose between the remaining 8 locations. So from each of the 9 nodes, there will be 8 outgoing edges. From each of these 8 sub nodes, there will be 7 outgoing edges, and so on, and so on. This will result in a huge tree containing all the possible outcomes of the game. For each path in this tree, you can see immediately who has won (player 1 or player 2). So what you can do then, is to assign a cost or a reward value to each of the edges, for example +10 for an edge that helps leading to your victory, −10 for an edge that leads to your opponent's victory, and 0 for an edge that leads to a draw. Then, after the real player has made a choice, the computer can walk through the tree and find the path that minimizes the loss for the worst case (maximum loss) scenario (which also explains the name of the algorithm).

The Minimax algorithm is a classic AI algorithm that is used in many games where the computer has to make a choice between a number of alternatives and where there are discrete turns with a predetermined outcome. Many board games are suitable for this, such as chess, checkers, and so on. This algorithm is not always useful, since it means that you have to (partly) construct the tree of possible decisions and their outcomes, which can get quite complicated depending on the type of game. For example in chess, the number of different states is estimated at 10^{43} and the number of different nodes in the game tree at 10^{120}!

A.4 Exercises and Challenges for Part IV

Exercises

1. *Lists*

   The List<**string**> class contains (among others) methods that have the following headers:

   public void Reverse()
   public int LastIndexOf(**string** item)
   public bool Contains(**string** item)

   Suppose that you are the author of the List class and these methods have not yet been implemented. Implement these three methods. You may not use existing methods carrying the same name, or other varieties of these methods with these names, because we assume that these methods are not there yet. Apart from these methods, you may use any other method in the List class, as well as your own methods.

2. *Collections*

   Write a method RemoveDuplicates which receives as a parameter a List of **int** values. The method removes all of the duplicates of the numbers in the list that is provided as a parameter. For example, the list containing the numbers 0, 1, 3, 2, 1, 5, 2 becomes 0, 1, 3, 2, 5. Watch out: the return type of this method should be **void**!

3. *Classes and interfaces*

One of the following three combined declarations and assignments is correct. Which one is that, and why are the other two not correct?

```
List<int> a = new IList<int>(); // version 1
IList<int> b = new List<int>(); // version 2
IList<int> c = new IList<int>(); // version 3
```

Describe a situation in which the correct version of the above lines of code has an advantage over the also correct declaration and assignment:

```
List<int> d = new List<int>(); // version 4
```

4. *List and **foreach***

Provided is the following class:

```
class Counter
{
    int val = 0;
    public Counter(int v)
    { val = v;
    }
    public void Increment()
    {
        val++;
    }
}
```

and the following instructions in a class that uses the Counter class:

```
List<Counter> list = new List<Counter>();
for (int i=0; i<25; i++)
    list.Add(new Counter(i));
```

(a) Write a method Increment, which gets an IList<Counter> object as a parameter and which increments all the counters (using the Increment method in the Counter class). Provide a version that uses the **foreach** instruction, as well as a version that uses a **for** or a **while** instruction.

(b) Suppose that instead of passing a List<Counter> object, we would like to pass an object of type OwnList<Counter>, where the OwnList class is our own version of a list, which implements the IList interface. What do we need to change in the Increment method we wrote in the previous question so that we can use this method with our own list class?

5. *Strings*

The **string** class contains (among others) methods that have the following headers:

```
public string Substring(int startIndex, int length);
public string Substring(int startIndex);
public int IndexOf(char c)
```

Suppose that you are the author of the **string** class and these methods have not yet been implemented. Implement these three methods. You may not use any existing methods carrying the same name, or other varieties of these methods with these names, because we assume that these methods are not there yet. Apart from these methods, you may use any other method in the **string** class, as well as your own methods.

6. *Classes and inheritance*
   Consider the following two classes:

```
class A {
    public void Method1() { Console.WriteLine("A::Method1"); }
    public virtual void Method2() { Console.WriteLine("A::Method2"); }
}
class B : A {
    public void Method1() { Console.WriteLine("B::Method1"); }
    public override void Method2() { Console.WriteLine("B::Method2"); }
}
```

What is the output of the following series of instructions?

```
A x = new A();
A y = new B();
B z = new B();
x.Method1();
x.Method2();
y.Method1();
y.Method2();
z.Method1();
z.Method2();
```

7. *Sidescrolling*
   Consider the following class:

```
class Scrolling : Game
{ GraphicsDeviceManager graphics;
    SpriteBatch spriteBatch;
    Texture2D background;
    Vector2 position;

    public Scrolling()
    { graphics = new GraphicsDeviceManager(this);
```

```
            Content.RootDirectory = "Content";
            position = Vector2.Zero;
    }

    protected override void LoadContent()
    { spriteBatch = new SpriteBatch(GraphicsDevice);
            background = Content.Load<Texture2D>("background");
    }

    protected override void Draw(GameTime gameTime)
    { GraphicsDevice.Clear(Color.White);
            spriteBatch.Begin();
            spriteBatch.Draw(this.background, this.position, Color.White);
            spriteBatch.End();
    }
}
```

The background sprite has the same height as the screen, but it is a lot wider. As a result, we can only draw a part of the sprite. The goal of this exercise is to implement side scrolling. We do this by using the mouse position. If the mouse is positioned left to the screen, the background moves to the right. If the mouse is positioned right to the screen, the background moves to the left. Write the Update method that results in this behavior.

8. *Decorator streams*
   The Stream class has (among others) the following methods:

```
int ReadByte(); // returns the next byte, or −1 if there is no more byte
int Read(byte[] goal, int n); /* reads a maximum of n bytes and puts them in goal,
                               and returns the number of bytes read. */
```

In many cases it is more efficient to read an entire block with the Read method. On the other hand, it's easier to read a separate byte whenever you need it.
The class BufferedStream can help out here. The constructor method of these class has a Stream object as a parameter. When the ReadByte method is called on an object of type BufferedStream, it uses the Stream object it manages to read 1000 bytes. It then returns the first one it read, the rest is saved temporarily in an array (in other words, a buffer). The next time the ReadByte method is called, the byte can be retrieved from the array and we don't have to access the underlying file. Only when there are no more bytes left in the array, a new block of 1000 bytes is read.
Implement the BufferedReader class, containing a constructor method and the ReadByte method.

Challenges

1. *Penguin Pairs*

   In this challenge, we will extend the Penguin Pairs game.

   (a) Currently, the level menu consists of a single page displaying a maximum of fifteen levels. Extend the game such that multiple pages of levels are allowed. Add two buttons to the level menu screen to be able to navigate through the different pages.

   (b) Extend the game so that it also contains polar bears that can be moved by the player. Whenever a penguin collides with a polar bear, the penguin is so scared that it immediately starts moving away from the bear. Design a few different levels around this concept.

   (c) Add a 'hole' object to the game. Whenever the penguin goes in the hole, it appears from another hole elsewhere in the level and continues moving in the same direction. Think of a smart way to represent this in the text file. Especially, how do you represent the connections between the holes? Create a couple of levels that use holes.

   (d) Add a 'curve in the ice' item to the game that changes the direction of the penguin if it moves over it. For example, if a penguin is moving up through a curve object, and the curve is of the type 'turn left', the penguin will change direction so that it continues moving to the left. Add a few more levels to the game that use this item.

   (e) Introduce a conveyor belt, which moves the penguin a fixed number of steps in a certain direction. The penguin resumes in the original direction after it.

A.5 Exercises and Challenges for Part V

Exercises

1. *Text files and collections*

   Write a (console) application with the following specification. The program is started from the command line and the user specifies two filenames. The program reads the file corresponding to the first filename. Then it writes a text file with as a name the second filename. The output file will contain the text of the first file, but every word should be placed on a separate line. Also, the words will be ordered alphabetically (or actually: according to the Unicode order). Each word should be written to the file only once.

   We consider every group of characters without a space between them as a word. You may assume that there is exactly one space between each word in the input file.

   If the user provides too few or too many filenames, or there is an error during reading or writing, the program reports this to the user.

For example, if the input file contains the following two lines:

```
this IS an *%#$ example
of an input text file!
```

then the output should contain the following nine lines:

```
*%#$
IS
an
example
file!
input
of
text
this
```

In case this is too complicated, you can simplify the question as follows: use fixed file names instead of names specified by the user; leave out the sorting and the duplicate word removal; do not process the words, but the lines of the text; leave out reporting the error.

2. *Abstract classes and interfaces*
   What is the difference between an abstract class and an interface? Give an example of a situation in which you would use an abstract class. Give another example of a situation in which you would use an interface.

3. *Tetris blocks*
   Suppose that you are working on creating a Tetris game. In that game, a tetris block is represented by a two-dimensional array of boolean values. The first dimension indicates the column, the second dimension indicates the row. For example, here are two different tetris blocks:

```
true   true   false          false true    false false
false true   true           false true    false false
false false false          false true    false false
                                    false true    false false
```

(a) Write a method HorizontalMirror which receives as a parameter a two dimensional array of booleans. The goal of the method is that the values of the array are mirrored horizontally. After calling the method, the two blocks given as an example above will appear as follows:

```
false true   true           false false true    false
true   true   false          false false true    false
false false false          false false true    false
                                    false false true    false
```

For example, you could use this method as follows:

```
bool[,] tetrisblock = ...
this.Print(tetrisblock);
this.HorizontalMirror(tetrisblock);
this.Print(tetrisblock)
```

(b) Also implement the Print method. This method writes the contents of a two-dimensional boolean array to the console, in the way it is done in the examples given in this exercise.

4. *Abstract classes*
   Given are the following classes:

```
abstract class A
{
    public abstract void Method1();
    public void Method2()
    {
        return;
    }
}
class B : A
{
    public override void Method1()
    {
        return;
    }

    public void Method3(A a)
    {
        a.Method1();
    }
}
```

Indicate for each of the following instructions whether or not it is allowed:

```
A obj;
obj = new A();
obj = new B();
obj.Method1();
obj.Method2();
obj.Method3(obj);
B otherObject = (B)(new A());
A yetAnotherObject = (A)obj;
obj.Method3(otherObject);
A[] list;
list = new A[10];
list[0] = new A();
list[1] = new B();
List<A> otherList = new List<A>();
```

Challenges

1. *Adding side scrolling to Tick Tick*

   If you look at the background sky image, you see that it is quite a bit larger than the actual screen size. One of the reasons for this is that we can use the sky image as a moving background for side scrolling. The goal of this challenge is to add side scrolling capabilities to the Tick Tick game.

   (a) The first thing you will have to do is extend the game environment framework so that you can define a *camera*. Using a virtual camera, we can specify which part of the game world we're seeing. What happens when we're side scrolling is that we move around this camera so that different parts of the world are seen. Add a Camera class to the GameManagement library that decides which part of the world we're currently seeing. In order to test your camera, try to run the program with a few different values for the camera position. Make sure that the camera works correctly in full-screen mode as well.

   (b) The next step is extending the TickTick... game so that we can read levels of any number of dimensions. Extend the game so that this works without problems.

   (c) Finally, we want to move the camera around based on the character position. There are a few different possibilities. Either you can always try to have the character in the middle of the screen, or you can move the camera when the character crosses a certain boundary, for example, past two-thirds of the visible screen. Add the automatically moving camera behavior to the game. Make sure that it is robust, and that the player never sees beyond the edges of the defined game world. For example: if the character falls out or jumps above the screen, the camera shouldn't move along with it.

   (d) Parallax scrolling is a way to create the illusion that there is a three dimensional world. You can achieve this effect by having several layers of mountains. The further away a layer of mountains is, the slower it will move when the viewport is moving. Add parallax scrolling to the game by introducing three different layers of mountains, each moving at a different speed. Of course, you don't have to use only mountains. If you find nice other sprites that could serve as a parallax layer, go right ahead.

   (e) Since our levels are now much bigger, extend the game so that for each level, you can define how much time the player has in the text file. Create a few different levels that use this ability.

2. *Other additions to Tick Tick*

   (a) Extend the Rocket class so that when the player jumps on the rocket, the rocket dies.

   (b) Add shooting behavior to the player. For example, the bomb could throw smaller bombs which would kill an enemy if it collides with the bomb.

   (c) Add a health indicator for the player. Every time the player touches an enemy, or if the player falls down from more than three tiles high, the health is reduced with a certain amount. If the health reaches zero, the player dies. Add health packs to the game, so that the player can restore part of his/her health again.

(d) Add an item to the game that shields the player for a while so that her/his health is reduced less or not at all.

(e) Try to make some of the enemies smarter. For example, can you add behavior to the flames so that they can jump from one platform to another? Or can you make the rockets smarter so that they sometimes follow the player?

(f) Introduce a new type of tile: the moving tile. This is not an easy extension, because you have to make sure that if the player stands on the tile, he/she moves along with it. Also, you have to take into account that multiple moving tiles might appear next to each other to form a single moving platform. When a moving platform collides with another moving platform or a wall tile, it turns around and starts moving in the other direction.

(g) Add hidden levels to the game. By going to a particular place in the level, you can enter a hidden level. Think of a good class design where these hidden levels fit in. Of course, hidden levels should also be read from a file, just like the normal levels.

(h) Add a type of object to the game that results in the player walking much faster or slower for a while.

(i) Games often contain extras that don't really add anything to the gameplay, but that make the game a lot more fun. An example of such an extra is that a character says something ridiculous when you click on it. Even more fun is if the character says something different every time. Extend the game such that when you click on the player, the character says something funny. Write a class that allows to select a random sound and play it, so that there is more variety. You can use existing sound fragments, but of course you can also go crazy and record sounds yourself with a microphone.

Appendix B
Syntax Diagrams

B.1 Introduction

In this appendix, we list a number of syntax diagrams that show how to create the most important C# constructs that are introduced in this book. Note that this is by no means a *complete* grammar of the C# language. It simply serves as an aid in constructing syntactically correct C# programs.

B.2 Compilation Unit

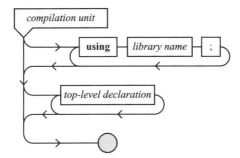

B.3 Top-Level Declaration

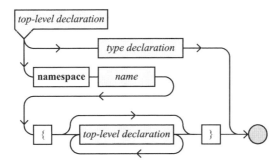

A. Egges et al., *Learning C# by Programming Games*,
DOI 10.1007/978-3-642-36580-5, © Springer-Verlag Berlin Heidelberg 2013

B.4 Type Declaration

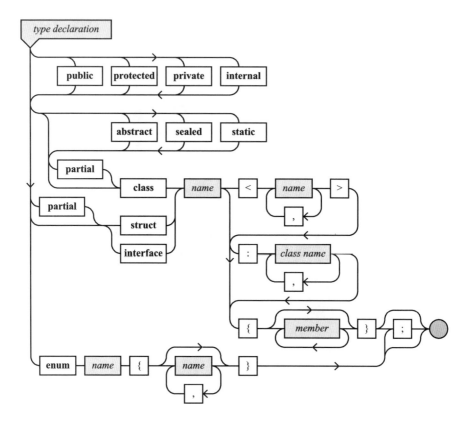

B.5 Parameters

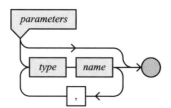

B.6 Member

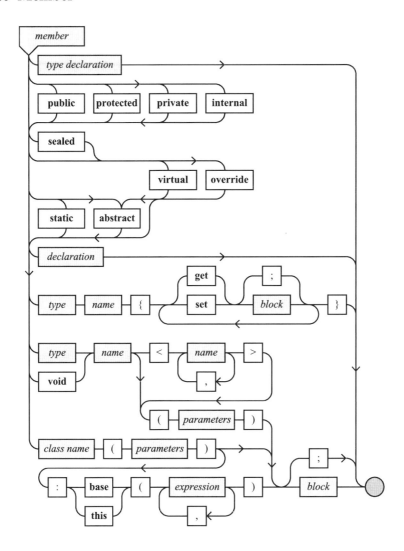

B.7 Block

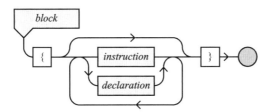

B.8 Declaration

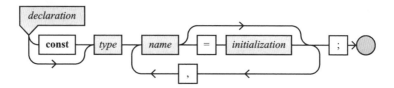

B.9 Initialization

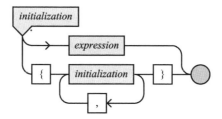

B.10 Type

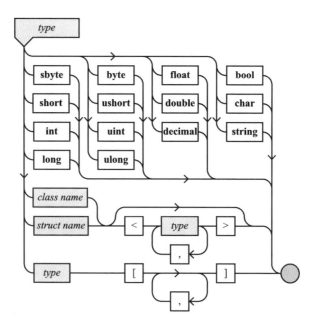

B.11   Instruction

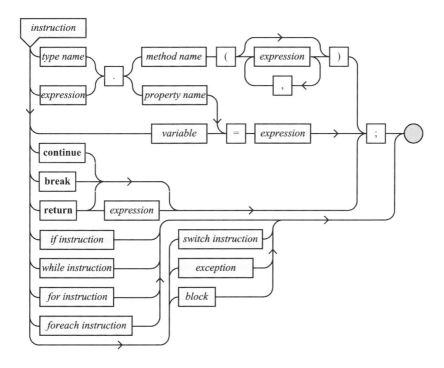

B.11.1   If-Instruction

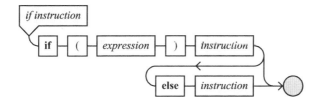

B.11.2   While-Instruction

B.11.3 For-Instruction

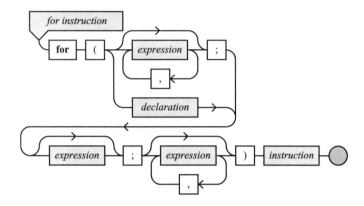

B.11.4 Foreach-Instruction

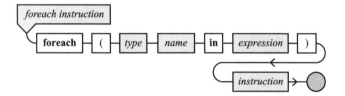

B.11.5 Switch-Instruction

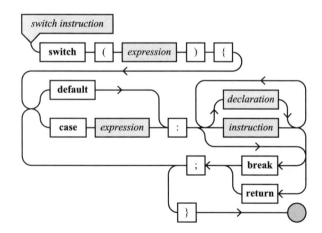

B.11.6 Try-Catch-Instruction

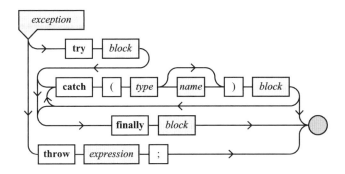

B.12 Expression

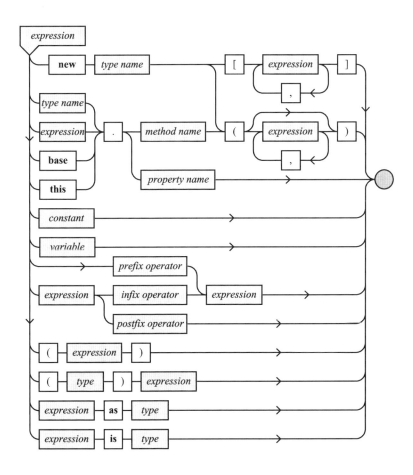

B.13 Constant

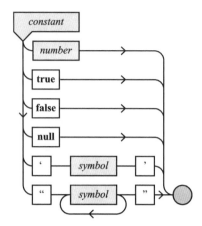

B.14 Symbol

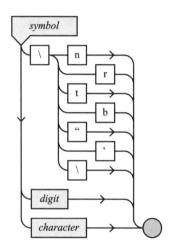

B.15 Number

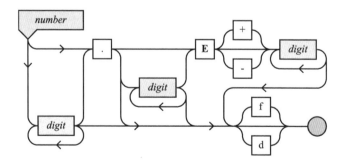

Further Reading

Ernest Adams. *Fundamentals of Game Design*. New Riders, second edition, 2010. ISBN 978-0321643377.

Paul J. Deitel and Harvey M. Deitel. *C# 2010 for Programmers*. Pearson Education, fourth edition, 2011. ISBN 978-0132618205.

Barbara Doyle. *C# Programming: From Problem Analysis to Program Design*. Cengage Learning, third edition, 2010. ISBN 978-0538453028.

Rob Miles. *Microsoft XNA Game Studio 4.0: Learn Programming Now!* Microsoft Press, second edition, 2011. ISBN 978-0735651579.

Tom Miller and Dean Johnson. *XNA Game Studio 4.0 Programming: Developing for Windows Phone 7 and Xbox 360*. Pearson Education, 2011. ISBN 978-0672333453.

Joel Murach. *Murach's C# 2010*. Mike Murach & Associates, 2010. ISBN 978-1890774592.

Benjamin Nitschke. *Professional XNA Programming: Building Games for Xbox 360 and Windows with XNA Game Studio 2.0*. Wiley Publishing, 2008. ISBN 0470261285.

Jeannie Novak. *Game Development Essentials: An Introduction*. Cengage Learning, third edition, 2012. ISBN 978-1111307653.

Nick Randolph, David Gardner, Michael Minutillo, and Chris Anderson. *Professional Visual Studio 2010*. Wiley Publishing, 2010. ISBN 978-0470548653.

Aaron Reed. *Learning XNA 4.0: Game Development for the PC, Xbox 360, and Windows Phone 7*. O'Reilly Media, 2011. ISBN 978-1449394622.

Scott Rogers. *Level Up!: The Guide to Great Video Game Design*. Wiley Publishing, 2010. ISBN 978-0470688670.

Daniel Schuller. *C# Game Programming: For Serious Game Creation*. Cengage Learning, 2011. ISBN 978-1435455566.

A. Egges et al., *Learning C# by Programming Games*,
DOI 10.1007/978-3-642-36580-5, © Springer-Verlag Berlin Heidelberg 2013

Jon Skeet. *C# in Depth*. Manning Publications, second edition, 2011. ISBN 978-1935182474.

Rod Stephens. *Stephens' C# Programming with Visual Studio 2010 24-Hour Trainer*. Wiley Publishing, 2010. ISBN 978-0470596906.

Glossary

abstract class   class containing abstract methods, intended as base class for subclasses but not for creating instances, 303

abstract method   method without body that must be redefined in a subclass, 304

animation   rapid display of a sequence of images to create an illusion of movement, 351

app   program that can be run on a smartphone, 32

applet   program that can be run inside a web browser, 32

application   program that can be run, 31

array   (object containing a) numbered row of values of the same type, 190

asset   resource used for developing a game, such as a sprite or a sound effect, 55

assignment   instruction to change the value of a variable, 44

base class   class that a class inherits from, 152

bit   unit of memory in which two different values can be stored, 48

bitmap   description of a picture consisting small colored dots called pixels (the word is imprecise, as with a bit only a black-or-white pixel can be designated; an alternative is "pixmap"), 261

block   group of instructions and declarations that can be treated as a single instruction, 88

bool   (type of a) logical value, i.e. either false or true, 84

bounding box   two-dimensional box that encompasses an object, 365

bounding circle   circle that encompasses an object, 365

branch   conditional execution of an instruction, e.g. in an **if** or a **switch** instruction (named after the bifurcation that occurs in a diagram showing the flow of execution), 82

byte   (type of a) value which is an integer number in the range $-128\ldots127$; or: unit of memory in which 256 different values can be stored, 48

cast   forcing an expression to have a different, though related type (a more restricted numeric type, or a subclass), 49

char   type of a) value that represents an Unicode character, 175

child class   see subclass, 153

class   group of declarations, methods, and properties, that serves as the type of an object, 33

code   program text, 19

collision   intersection between bounding volumes, 365

compiler   program that checks and translates a program from source code to executable code, 18

condition   expression that yields either **true** or **false**, 82

constructor method   method, having the same name as its class, that is automatically called upon creation of a new instance, 104

declaration   program fragment that introduces a name for a class, method, variable etc., 44

derived class   see subclass, 153

double   (type of a) floating-point value in double precision, 47

enum   type of values belonging to an explicitly enumerated set, 81

exception   abnormal event that may occur during program execution, that can be thrown when it occurs, and be caught to handle it, 346

executable code   the program in its form as translated by the compiler, 23

expression   program fragment that has a value, 45

false   the one of the two bool values denoting falsehood, 84

float   (type of a) value which is a number containing a floating point, 48

game   program that gives its user a playful experience, 32

game engine   collection of classes for governing commonly used structures and tasks in games, 22

game loop   fundamental loop in a game that repeatedly calls the Update and Draw methods, 28

game state   description of objects in the game at a particular in time; examples of game states are a level finished state or a game over state, 249

implementation   class that complies to the methods specified in an interface; or: program that fulfills its specification, 25

infix operator   operator that is written between two expressions (e.g., arithmetical, comparison, or logical), 46

inherit   have access to members that were defined in a base class, 152

inheritance   the fact that a subclass implicitly also declares the members of its base class, allowing to reuse code without copying it, 152

initialization	assigning the initial value to a variable, 44
instance of a class	object having the class as type, 73
instruction	program fragment that changes memory in some way, 12
int	(type of a) value which is an integer number, 44
interface	group of method headers that specifies the methods that are needed in classes implementing it; or: the way a program interacts with a user, 186
interpreter	program that checks a program from source code and executes it, 18
iteration	repeated execution of an instruction, e.g. in a **while**, **for** or **foreach** instruction; or: one of the steps in an iteration, 142
iterator	(type of a) value that can keep track of an iteration, 194
level	part of a game progression that stands on its own, 297
library	pre-defined classes that can be used in a program, 35
local declaration	declaration of a variable that can only be used in the block that it is declared in, 158
loop	repeated execution of an instruction, e.g. in a **while**, **for** or **foreach** (named after the cycle that occurs in a diagram showing the flow of execution), 142
member	variable, method, or property belonging to an object, 76
member variable	variable belonging to an object, 76
method	group of instructions, with a name, that can manipulate an object, 14
method call	instruction to execute the instructions in the body of the method, 36
namespace	group of classes that can refer to each other without explicitly qualifying the library that they come from, 34
null	the value of a reference when it is not referring to a particular object, 122
object	group of variables, having a class as its type, 71
operator	symbol that combines (one or) two expressions, 46
override a method	redefine a method in a subclass, 157
parameter	declaration in the header of a method that specifies the type of values that need to be passed when the method is called; or: expression that evaluates to the value that is passed in the method call, 36
parent class	see base class, 152
partial class	class of which the members are declared in more than one top-level declaration, 343
pixel	picture element, a single dot in a picture described by a bitmap, 261
polymorphism	the ability to process objects differently depending on their class type, 166
postfix operator	operator that is written after an expression (e.g., increment, or decrement), 46

prefix operator	operator that is written before an expression (e.g., minus, not, increment, or decrement), 46
private declaration	declaration of a member that can be used only from the class that it is declared in, 158
property	value related to an object that you can get and/or set, 39
protected declaration	declaration of a member that can be used only from the class that it is declared in and its subclasses, 158
public declaration	declaration of a member that can be used from within all other classes, 158
qualify	specify the library that a class comes from, 35
recursion	defining a method or property in terms of itself, 235
reference	value with class type that refers to the actual instance of the class, 120
return value	value that a method delivers after its execution, 97
rgb	description of a color by its red, green, and blue components, 52
scope	part of the program in which a declared name can be used, 53
sealed method	overridden virtual method that cannot be redefined again in subclasses, 166
semantics	rules that describe the meaning of programs in a language, 33
serious game	game that can be used for training of professionals, 179
source code	the text of the program as written by the programmer, i.e. before compilation, 19
sprite	a two-dimensional image that is integrated into a larger scene, 55
static method	group of instructions with a name that does not manipulate a particular object, 72
static variable	member variable that is shared by all instances of the class, 117
string	(type of a) value that represents a text, 176
struct	type of objects that are accessed directly, i.e. without references, 123
subclass	a class that inherits from another class, 153
super class	see base class, 152
syntax	rules that describe the form of programs in a language, 33
tile	basic element of a two-dimensional level definition, 297
true	the one of the two bool values denoting truth, 84
variable	memory location with a name, 44
vector	object denoting a point in two- or three-dimensional space, 59
virtual method	method that can be redefined in a subclass, 158
void	placeholder for the return type of a method that does not return a value, 99

Index